Introductory Readings for COGNITIVE PSYCHOLOGY

SECOND EDITION

Introductory Readings for

COGNITIVE PSYCHOLOGY

SECOND EDITION

Edited, Selected, and with Introductions by

Richard P. Honeck
University of Cincinnati

The Dushkin Publishing Group, Inc.

For Jon, scholar, athlete, traveler, and ecologist

Manufactured in the United States of America

Second Edition, First Printing

Library of Congress Cataloging-in-Publication Data

Main entry under title:
    Introductory readings in cognitive psychology / edited, selected, and with introductions by Richard P. Honeck.—2nd ed.
        Includes bibliographical references and index.
        1. Cognitive psychology. I. Honeck, Richard P., *comp.*
            BF201.I57   1994   153—dc20
            ISBN: 1–56134–296–3   93–21581

 Printed on Recycled Paper

The Dushkin Publishing Group, Inc.
Sluice Dock, Guilford, CT 06437

Preface

Introductory Readings for Cognitive Psychology, Second Edition, is specifically designed for the student who is taking a first course in cognitive psychology. It can be used in conjunction with a textbook or on its own. Students in more advanced courses in cognitive psychology and related disciplines may also find this collection useful.

My motivation for developing this collection of readings grew out of a sense of frustration with textbooks in cognitive psychology. A few are well written, but many texts leave a great deal to be desired because the excitement and in-depth analysis that are present in original materials generally get filtered out of standard textbooks. Students can find it difficult to relate to texts that treat abstract topics in a colorless fashion. Moreover, texts rarely give students any idea of the methodological and theoretical struggles of researchers in this area. These readings capture the excitement and flow of cognitive psychology, and it is my view that students will benefit from being directly exposed to the pursuits and passions of cognitive psychologists, the questions they grapple with, and the inner workings of their research.

This book is composed of 31 short, accessible readings—mostly journal articles and a couple of book excerpts. All the journal articles have been reprinted in their entirety. In selecting articles for *Introductory Readings for Cognitive Psychology, Second Edition,* I attempted to keep students' concerns uppermost in my mind. One precondition for an article's inclusion was that it had to be written by an expert. Once that was established, I then used the following questions to guide my work:

- Is the article appropriate to the knowledge level of students taking a first course in cognitive psychology?
- Is it well written, interesting, not too long, and not a rehash of material inevitably covered in depth in textbooks?
- Is it informative about methodological problems?

Wide coverage of topics was another goal, as was the inclusion of a large section on practical applications. Finally, except for the paper by A. M. Turing and the one by Paul Rozin, Susan Poritsky, and Raina Sotsky, "classic" readings were purposely avoided, both because they tend to be written for the professional audience only and because they are treated in the textbooks. Of necessity, some topics were left out, but given their vast number, that was inevitable. Eight new articles are included in this second edition. The omitted articles were replaced for reasons of length, informational density, and conceptual level. Both the instructor and the student should find the new articles more to their liking.

The arrangement of the selections in *Introductory Readings for Cognitive Psychology, Second Edition*, follows a sequence typical of textbooks in cognitive psychology—foundations, memory, thought, language, and applications. Each part opens with an introduction that reviews why cognitive psychologists study the area addressed by the articles and previews each of the articles in the section. There is also an introduction to the volume that addresses the question, What is cognitive psychology?

A word to the instructor   An *Instructor's Manual With Test Questions* is available through the publisher. It contains a synopsis of each selection, suggestions for generating in-class discussions of the selections, and multiple-choice and essay questions.

Acknowledgements   For the first edition, several people helped put this collection together. Michael J. Firment and Tammy J. S. Case helped edit the first edition. Dan Berch, William Dember, and Joel Warm at the University of Cincinnati made interesting and useful suggestions. Virginia A. Diehl of Western Illinois University and David E. Irwin of Michigan State University were generous with their advice. Mimi Egan, program manager for The Dushkin Publishing Group, was, from the beginning to end, efficient and encouraging in her handling of the project. And Shirley Doxsey typed a reference section for one of the articles. To all of these people, a hearty thanks.

For the second edition, I once again acknowledge the friendly and efficient assistance of Mimi Egan, as well as that of David Dean, who handled administrative details, and David Brackley, copy editor. My thanks as well to students and instructors who made helpful comments on the first edition.

Finally, it is my hope that *Introductory Readings for Cognitive Psychology, Second Edition*, will stimulate students' interests, help them to see the relevance of the study of cognition to their everyday lives, and encourage them to explore further the general area of cognitive psychology.

R. P. H.

Contents

Part ❖ One

FOUNDATIONS OF COGNITIVE PSYCHOLOGY   1

Part ❖ Two

MEMORY AND MENTAL REPRESENTATION 43

Part ❖ Three

THOUGHT: CATEGORIZATION, EXPERTISE, AND METAKNOWLEDGE

Part ❖ Four

LANGUAGE 187

Part ❖ Five

About the Editor

RICHARD P. HONECK is a professor of psychology and serves on the graduate faculty of the Department of Psychology at the University of Cincinnati in Cincinnati, Ohio, where he has taught courses in cognitive psychology, statistics, psycholinguistics, and the history and systems of psychology. He is a member of the Psychonomic Society, the Southern Society for Philosophy and Psychology, and Sigma Xi, and he also serves on the editorial board of *Metaphor and Symbolic Activity*. His research interests focus on cognition and psycholinguistics, and he has contributed numerous articles on these areas to such journals as *Poetics* and the *Journal of Psycholinguistic Research*. He received a B.S. in psychology from the University of Wisconsin–Milwaukee in 1962 and an M.S. and a Ph.D from the University of Wisconsin–Madison in 1966 and 1969, respectively.

AUTHORS

JOANNE ALEXANDER was affiliated with the Department of Psychology at the University of Michigan in Ann Arbor, Michigan, when she coauthored the *Memory & Cognition* paper that is featured in this volume.

BENJAMIN ALGAZE is the assistant director of clinical training at North Miami Community Mental Health Center and an independent psychologist with Affiliates for Evaluation and Therapy, Inc., in Miami, Florida. He has also taught psychology at Florida International University.

ALAN BADDELEY is the director of the Medical Research Council's Applied Psychology Unit in Cambridge, England. His research interests focus on memory in general and on the measurement of everyday memory, both in normal subjects and in patients with memory problems following brain damage. This approach is reflected in his publications *Working Memory* (Oxford University Press, 1986) and *Human Memory: Theory and Practice* (Allyn & Bacon, 1990).

BERYL LIEFF BENDERLY is a prizewinning journalist and author whose articles appear regularly in national magazines. Her publications include *Dancing Without Music: Deafness in America* (Doubleday, 1980) and *The Myth of Two Minds: What Gender Means and Doesn't Mean* (Doubleday, 1987).

TAMMY J. S. CASE teaches occasionally at the University of Cincinnati in Cincinnati, Ohio. She has also served as a teaching assistant in the Department of Psychology at the University of Cincinnati and as an intern at the Institute for Policy Research.

CRAIG J. CHAMBERLIN is a professor in the Department of Kinesiology and Physical Education at the University College of the Fraser Valley in Abbotsford, British Columbia, Canada. He has also taught in the School of Kinesiology and Physical Education at the University of Northern Colorado.

The late **WILLIAM G. CHASE** was a professor in the Department of Psychology at Carnegie-Mellon University in Pittsburgh, Pennsylvania.

DEAN DELIS is a staff psychologist at the San Diego Veterans Administration Medical Center and an associate professor of psychiatry in the School of Medicine at the University of California, San Diego. He is the author of *Passion Paradox* (Bantam Books, 1990).

GEORG DEUTSCH is an associate professor of research in neurology and the director of the Cerebral Blood Flow Laboratory at the University of Alabama in Birmingham. His main research interests concern brain/behavior relationships as studied by functional neuroimaging in normal subjects during different cognitive tasks and mental states. He also conducts clinical research on normal aging, Alzheimer's disease, and vascular disease with emphasis on cerebral blood flow and metabolism.

K. ANDERS ERICSSON is an associate professor of psychology at the University of Colorado in Greeley, Colorado. The research reported in the *Science* paper that appears in this volume was completed when he worked as research associate at Carnegie-Mellon University. He is the coauthor, with Herbert A. Simon, of *Protocol Analysis: Verbal Reports as Data* (MIT Press, 1984).

The late **STEVE FALOON** was a professor in the Department of Psychology at Carnegie-Mellon University in Pittsburgh, Pennsylvania.

MICHAEL FIRMENT is a professor in the Department of Psychology at Kennesaw State College in Kennesaw, Georgia. Prior to teaching, he worked extensively in programming and systems analysis at both the University of Cincinnati Computer Center and the Hoxworth Blood Center in Cincinnati.

RONALD P. FISHER is a professor of psychology at Florida International University in Miami, Florida, and a consulting editor for the journal *Memory & Cognition*. His research interests are in applying theories of cognition to eyewitness testimony and investigative interviewing. He has conducted training workshops on improving interviewing techniques to enhance eyewitness recollection in police departments in the United States and Israel.

JOHN H. FLAVELL is a professor in the Department of Psychology at Stanford University in Stanford, California. His research interests focus on cognitive development, and he is a coauthor, with Patricia Miller and Scott Miller, of *Cognitive Development* (Prentice Hall, 1993).

JOHN FLEER is a civil trial attorney and a partner in the law firm Bjork, Fleer, Lawrence, and Harris in Oakland, California. He received a Ph.D. in clinical psychology from the University of Wyoming in 1977 and a J.D. from the University of California, Berkeley, in 1981. His research interests lie in the field of mental health and the law.

PAUL W. FOOS is a professor of psychology and the chairperson of the Department of Psychology at the University of North Carolina at Charlotte. His research interests focus on cognitive processes in older adults and in students preparing for examinations.

R. EDWARD GEISELMAN is a professor in the Department of Psychology at the University of California, Los Angeles.

SUSAN A. GELMAN is an associate professor of psychology at the University of Michigan in Ann Arbor, Michigan. The 1990 recipient of the Boyd McCandless Award from the American Psychological Association, her research interests include language acquisition, conceptual development, and the interrelations of thought and language.

DIANE F. HALPERN is a professor of psychology at California State University, San Bernardino. She is interested in applying the principles of cognitive psychology to the teaching, thinking, and learning processes. She has received numerous awards, most notably the Outstanding Professor Award for the California State University (systemwide) and the Silver Medal Award from the Council for the Advancement and Support of Education.

DIANNE HORGAN is an assistant professor of educational psychology in the Department of Education at Memphis State University in Memphis, Tennessee. Prior to her work at Memphis State, she was a professor of psychology at Indiana University, at Illinois State University, and at Northern Illinois University.

JOHN JONIDES is a professor of psychology and an associate dean for research in the College of Literature, Science, and the Arts at the University of Michigan in Ann Arbor, Michigan. His current research interests focus on reasoning, memory, and perception.

MARY KISTER KAISER is the Principal Scientist of the Rotorcraft Human Factors Research Branch at NASA Ames Research Center at Mount View, California. She received a Ph.D. in psychology from the University of Virginia, and she was a postdoctoral research scholar at the University of Michigan.

GEORGE KALLAS is a professor in the Department of Psychology at Florida International University in Miami, Florida.

HOWARD H. KENDLER was a project director at the Office of Naval Research, a consultant to the U.S. Department of Defense, and a consultant to *Encyclopaedia Britannica* prior to becoming a professor of psychology at the University of California, Santa Barbara. His publications include *Historical Foundations of Modern Psychology* (Dorsey Press, 1986).

NANCY H. KERR is a professor of psychology at Oglethorpe University in Atlanta, Georgia. She is a member of the American Psychological Society, the Psychonomic Society, and the European Sleep Research Society.

WILLIAM RAFT KUNST-WILSON, now known as William Raft Wilson, taught at the University of Michigan, the University of Texas, and the William Marsh Rice University before becoming the executive vice president for Vyvx, Inc., a holding company for communications and telecommunications businesses.

GEORGE LAKOFF is a professor in the Department of Linguistics at the University of California, Berkeley. He is the coauthor, with Mark Turner, of *More Than Cool Reason: A Field Guide to Poetic Metaphor* (University of Chicago Press, 1989) and the author of *Women, Fire, and Dangerous Things* (University of Chicago Press, 1990).

JUDITH H. LANGLOIS is a professor of psychology at the University of Texas at Austin. Her research interests focus on developmental psychology.

ELIZABETH F. LOFTUS is a professor in the Department of Psychology at the University of Washington in Seattle, Washington. She is the coauthor, with Geoffrey R. Loftus, of *Essence of Statistics* (Random House, 1988) and the author of *Witness for the Defense* (St. Martin's Press, 1991).

GEOFFREY R. LOFTUS is a professor in the Department of Psychology at the University of Washington in Seattle, Washington, where he has been teaching since 1972. He is the author of more than 70 articles and 4 books on issues in experimental psychology, and his research is supported through 1999 by an NIMH grant and an associated MERIT award.

RICHARD E. MAYER is a professor of psychology at the University of California, Santa Barbara, where he has been teaching and conducting research since 1975. His research interests focus on mathematical and scientific thinking, learning from text and pictures, and learning computer programming languages. He has served as editor of *Educational Psychologist* and coeditor of *Instructional Science*.

GEORGE A. MILLER is the James S. McDonnell Distinguished University Professor of Psychology, Emeritus, at Princeton University in Princeton, New Jersey, and the program director of Princeton's McDonnell-Pew Program in Cognitive Neuroscience. He has also taught at Harvard University, the Massachusetts Institute of Technology, and the Rockefeller University. In 1990, he received the American Psychological Foundation's Award for Life Achievement in Psychological Science.

NATIONAL RESEARCH COUNCIL is the principal operating agency of the National Academy of Sciences and the National Academy of Engineering. Part of the National Research Council's function is to stimulate research in the mathematical, physical, and biological sciences in order to increase knowledge in those disciplines and to find ways to use this knowledge for the public welfare.

ULRIC NEISSER taught at Brandeis University, the University of Pennsylvania, and Cornell University before moving to Emory University in Atlanta, Georgia, where he has been the Robert W. Woodruff Professor of Psychology since 1983. A member of the National Academy of Sciences, Neisser is best known for three books on cognition: *Cognitive Psychology* (W. H. Freeman, 1967), *Cognition and Reality: Principles and Implications of Cognitive Psychology* (W. H. Freeman, 1976), and *Memory Observed: Remembering in Natural Contexts* (W. H. Freeman, 1982), which introduced the ecological approach to the study of memory.

SUSAN PORITSKY was affiliated with the Department of Psychology at the University of Pennsylvania in Philadelphia when she co-authored the *Science* paper that is featured in this volume.

LORI A. ROGGMAN, a developmental psychologist, is an assistant professor at Utah State University in Logan, Utah. She received a Ph.D. at the University of Texas at Austin.

PAUL ROZIN is a professor in the Department of Psychology at the University of Pennsylvania in Philadelphia, Pennsylvania, and the editor of the scientific journal *Appetite*. His interest in how animals select foods of nutritional value (specific hungers) led to his work on the problem of special types of learning and on the evolution of intelligence.

DAVID J. SCHNEIDER is a professor in and the chairperson of the Department of Psychology at the William Marsh Rice University in Houston, Texas. He has also taught at Amherst College, Brandeis University, Stanford University, Indiana University, and the University of Texas at San Antonio. He is the author of *Person Perception* (McGraw-Hill, 1979).

ROGER N. SHEPARD is a professor in the Department of Psychology at Stanford University in Stanford, California. For his work in cognitive science, he has been elected to the National Academy of Sciences and to the American Academy of Sciences and has received the American Psychological Association's Distinguished Scientific Contribution Award.

VIRGINIA SLAUGHTER was affiliated with the Department of Psychology at Swarthmore College in Swarthmore, Pennsylvania, when she coauthored the *Perception & Psychophysics* paper that is featured in this volume.

MATTHEW D. SMITH is a professor in the College of Education, Area of Health and Human Performance Studies, at the University of Alabama in Tuscaloosa, Alabama.

RAINA SOTSKY was affiliated with the Department of Psychology at the University of Pennsylvania in Philadelphia when she coauthored the *Science* paper that is featured in this volume.

SALLY P. SPRINGER is the executive assistant to the chancellor at the University of California, Davis. She received a Ph.D. in psychology from Stanford University, and she is the coauthor, with Georg Deutsch, of *Left Brain/Right Brain*, now in its third edition.

CHRISTINE M. TEMPLE is affiliated with the Developmental Neuropsychology Unit at the University of Essex in Wivenhoe Park, Colchester, England.

A. M. TURING (1912–1954) was a British mathematician, logician, and pioneering computer scientist. He created the Turing machine, a blueprint for the modern digital computer, revealing both its nature and logical limitations almost a decade before any such machine was constructed. He studied the relationship between the abstract world of mathematics and the mechanical world of engineering, and he believed that the computer could be programmed to imitate and thereby explain human intelligence.

M. MITCHELL WALDROP received his Ph.D. in theoretical physics from the University of Wisconsin in 1975. Currently writing for *Science* magazine, he has spent 15 years as a science writer for national news magazines, specializing in physics, chemistry, astronomy, space, geoscience, global change, computers, cognitive science, science policy, and complexity theory.

HANS WALLACH is a professor emeritus and a research psychologist associated with Swarthmore College in Swarthmore, Pennsylvania. He has received the American Psychological Association's Distinguished Scientific Contribution Award and the Society of Experimental Psychologists' Howard Crosby Warren Medal. He has been a member of the National Academy of Sciences since 1986.

DANIEL M. WEGNER is a professor of psychology at the University of Virginia in Charlottesville. He is the author of *White Bears and Other Unwanted Thoughts* (Viking Penguin, 1989) and the coeditor, with James W. Pennebaker, of *Handbook of Mental Control* (Prentice Hall, 1993).

R. B. ZAJONC is a professor of psychology in the Department of Psychology at the University of Michigan in Ann Arbor, Michigan, and the director of the University of Michigan's Institute for Social Research.

MATTHEW ZEIDENBERG was a graduate student in computer science at the University of Wisconsin when he published the *Byte* paper that is featured in this volume. He is the author of *Neural Networks in Artifical Intelligence* (Prentice Hall, 1990).

What Is Cognitive Psychology?

Cognitive psychology is generally acknowledged to be a part of cognitive science, which is an interdisciplinary enterprise that focuses on phenomena, issues, and theories concerned with the acquisition and use of knowledge. Cognitive science therefore includes some aspects of computer science, philosophy, linguistics, anthropology, sociology, and, of course, psychology.

But what *is* cognitive psychology? It is the study of perception, learning, memory, reasoning, problem solving, decision-making, and the like. This definition of cognitive psychology is certainly serviceable enough; however, it does gloss over questions about whether or not a particular set of assumptions, methods, and theories—a paradigm—characterizes the field. It is probably fair to say that, at this point in time, no such paradigm exists. Cognitive psychology can be thought of more as an undulating mass rather than as a fixed target. Nevertheless, cognitive psychologists typically ask certain kinds of questions, such as the following general ones:

- What happens to an environmental stimulus when it is first received by the senses?
- Does knowledge affect perception of a stimulus?
- What is memory? Are there different memory systems?
- What form does memory/knowledge take?
- What facilitates or hinders remembering?
- How is language understood?
- How do people reason?
- How do people recognize patterns and categorize things?
- What factors influence problem solving?
- Are cognition and emotion separable systems?
- What happens when people read?
- Are people aware of what their minds do?

Even though there are no overarching, all-encompassing theories in cognitive psychology, there are many specific theories about a restricted range of phenomena—for example, short-term memory, categorization, syllogistic reasoning, and the like. There are "mini-theories" about particular phenomena—for example, there are theories about the "belief bias effect," which explain how people's judgments about the validity of a logical argument are influenced by their beliefs about the content of the argument. There are also mini-theories to explain why recall is generally different than recognition, how people discover analogies between things, why people tend to overlook misspellings of the word *the*, why pictures tend to be remembered better than words, how mental images are constructed, what makes for an expert in physics, what young infants tend to notice, and so on. If anything, this set of mini-theories, the phenomena they address, the methods used to study the phenomena, and the assumptions brought to bear are what characterize the field.

STILL, THE MINI-THEORY PHENOMENON IS UNSET-tling. One would hope for a more coherent, organized picture of the field. To some extent this organization is provided by a particular point of view, the *information-processing view*. This is the predominant view among cognitive psychologists and the one that is almost exclusively represented in *Introductory Readings for Cognitive Psychology*. The central assumption of this view is that people recode information received from their environment; that is, the senses take in stimuli and change them in various ways. A simple example is that the letter *A* is processed not simply as a physical mark on a page but as having a certain sound associated with it, as the first letter of the alphabet, as the kind of grade someone might want to receive on a test, as a best friend's middle initial, and so on. In other words, recoding involves changing the stimulus, often with the result that the physical stimulus is imbued with some sort of symbolic significance. The information "in" the stimulus is not "in" the recoded form but is simply an initiating event. In this sense, the information-processing view forces the conclusion that the mind is different from the environment, shaped and constrained by it, but not a pale reflection of it. Needless to say, this view comports with—indeed, is aided and abetted by—the computer revolution. Just as is the case with computers, humans are seen as systematically taking in, operating on, and outputting information by means of complex structures (e.g., long-term memory, short-term memory) and processes (e.g., putting auditory events into a phonetic form, holding the form for a short time, and then matching it with information in long-term memory). The mind is seen as a fancy symbol-manipulating device and, as such, can be imitated (simulated) by a computer program. The ultimate form of this argument is that there is nothing special about the human mind—its activity is, in principle, capable of being made explicit, and therefore its activity can be simulated.

WHILE THE INFORMATION-PROCESSING VIEW CUR-rently prevails in cognitive psychology, it is not the only view. There are at least two other, less widely held positions. The first, the *ecological view*, contrasts sharply with the information-processing view. The ecological view, which is built on the writings of psychologist James J. Gibson, holds that much of perception, and therefore much of cognition, occurs in a direct way. That is, perception is caused by information in the stimulus. Of course, perceptual systems have been "tuned" by millions of years of evolution to pick up certain information in the stimulus. The important implication is that perception is not due to mediating factors—expectations, schemas, motives, mind sets, and the like. To use current jargon, there are no "top-down" components to perception in the ecological view. The organism's knowledge does not somehow meet the stimulus halfway and jointly produce a perception. The stimulus dictates the perception. Thus, perception is "bottom-up." This axiom obviously contradicts the central axiom of the information-processing view, the recoding axiom. For the ecological psychologist, the environment is mirrored in the mind; indeed, the mind is simply part of the environment. And things that go on in the mind are perception-like. Some psychologists who take this view maintain that memory is "in the stimulus." Organisms learn, but learning is generally seen as an "education of attention," such that successively finer discriminations of stimulus features are made. The ecological view is a radical view, one that most cognitivists either reject or feel uncomfortable with. Nevertheless, research within this framework has generated a host of findings about perception, and its advocates are a viable and vocal part of the community of cognitive psychologists.

ANOTHER MINORITY, BUT FAST-GROWING, POSITION is represented by *connectionism*, also sometimes called the *parallel distributed processing view.* Connectionism is essentially a modern, formally sophisticated form of associationism. As such, it is quite complicated, and here we will only provide a simple overview. A basic assumption of this view is that behavior is a product of the strength of connections between input and output elements. Such connections constitute the knowledge that an individual has. Connectionism acknowledges that even simple behaviors are due to simultaneous (parallel) processing in a number of elements or units. From a neurophysiological perspective, such massive parallel processing is a virtual certainty. Thousands or millions of neurons may be responsible for a seemingly simple act. Like the information-processing view, connectionism allows for recoding of the stimulus, but, unlike that view, it is less likely to describe outputs as being due to a series of information-processing stages in which formal rules are applied to inputs. Connectionists see behavior as exhibiting regularities, but these are explained in terms of the correlations between huge numbers of elements. Thus, behavior is some probabilistic function of inputs that have been transformed by "hidden units," whose outputs are combined to yield a final, total output. Much, if not all, of this activity is seen as occurring outside the awareness of the individual. People are aware of symbols, which are brought about by "subsymbolic" connections.

Thus, connectionism is similar to the information-processing view in that it assumes that inputs are successively recoded. But, unlike the information-processing view, it attempts to specify the (presumedly) more continuous, correlational nature of the relationship between inputs and their recoded forms, and it pays more respect to the environment than does the information-processing view. Connectionists have begun to do some exciting work on various topics, including speech recognition, speech recognition of text, and text recognition.

THE INFORMATION-PROCESSING VIEW IS THE MAINstream view—its adherents have defined the problems and phenomena to be studied, and they have generated the bulk of the models and theories. Therefore, the articles presented

in *Introductory Readings for Cognitive Psychology* are largely consistent with this view. However, both the traditional information-processing or "symbolic" view (the mind is a symbol-manipulating device) and the connectionistic view (the mind is a massive connecting device) are represented.

The articles are divided into five sections: foundations, memory, thought, language, and applications. The foundations section attempts to provide a sense of how cognitive psychology came about as well as a taste of the assumptions and research that have flowed from the computer metaphor that underlies much of the information-processing view. I have chosen to emphasize the computer because the impact of the computer is immense in cognitive psychology. Few students realize this until they enter a course on the topic. I therefore felt that it was necessary to deal with this reality from the start.

The section on memory provides a wide-ranging set of articles on our mental lifeblood—our memory system. The section starts with a basic question about the neuroanatomical basis of memory, in particular its representation on one side of the brain or the other. Other articles document the role of long-term memory in improving short-term memory skills, in the generation of images, in facilitating the perceptual process, in affecting the emotionality of minimally processed stimuli, and in autobiographical memory. The final article in the memory section addresses the question of whether information in long-term memory is permanent or subject to blending and distortion.

The section on thought considers a number of different topics. The theme of the section concerns how people develop a deep understanding of the world, including their own minds. People are not at the mercy of the physical features of their environment. Indeed, people develop concepts, categories, hypotheses, views, theories, and world views that enable them not only to survive but also to function effectively in a complex physical and social world. Of course, different people develop different levels and degrees of understanding of things, and several articles concern expertise and the extent of its generalizability. If, for example, you are good at chess, will you also be good at reasoning about social issues? How can your skill at chess be characterized, and are these skills usable in other areas? The section ends with two articles on metaknowledge, or what people think and believe about their own mental processes. One article considers young children's ideas about mind, while the other details how adults attempt to suppress their own unwanted thoughts.

Language, the topic of the next section, is intimately tied to cognition. In fact, there is probably no such thing as language without cognition. And while the converse is not true, there is no question that language has a powerful impact on our private mental and social lives. Moreover, all the great theoretical issues are played out on the stage of language. Questions about innateness, the separateness or modularity of a psychological system, the purposefulness of behavior, reasoning abilities, and so on, have all appealed to language as the primary arbiter. Because of its practical and theoretical salience, then, I have included a section on language, a section that focuses on the innateness, species uniqueness, and influence of language on reasoning and thought in general.

The final section on applications reflects the current emphasis on this topic. Psychologists have "taken to the streets" for several reasons—everyday behavior and thought is a rich source of hypotheses; it is a testing ground for more laboratory-based ideas; it is interesting and deserving of study in its own right; and it satisfies a demand for relevance that comes from many segments of society, including cognitive scientists. It is probably fair to say that no aspect of our lives goes untouched by our cognition, whether it is reading, dreaming, bird watching, listening to music, playing tennis, sex, or our emotions. A psychology that has nothing to say about such things is empty. Thus, I have included a rather long section on applications. However, the reader will find that many of the articles in this section show a nice balance and interaction between practical interest and theoretical relevance.

PART ✦ ONE

FOUNDATIONS
OF
COGNITIVE PSYCHOLOGY

Howard H. Kendler

❖

A. M. Turing

❖

M. Mitchell Waldrop

❖

Matthew Zeidenberg

Foundations of Cognitive Psychology

During much of the first half of this century, the predominant force in academic psychology was *behaviorism*, which promoted the idea that human behavior could best be understood in terms of conditioned responses. The favored topic during this era, the so-called great white rat era, was learning, and various theories of learning were fashioned. Most of these theories made the assumption that learning is a simple matter of strengthening stimulus-response (S-R) bonds. Depending upon the theory, bonds could be strengthened by repetition of the stimulus-response connection or by reinforcement of the response in the presence of the stimulus. Learning was thereby reduced to Pavlovian or operant conditioning, both of which incorporate repetition and reinforcement principles. Even though the theories proposed by various behaviorists differed somewhat on the principle emphasized, all behaviorists agreed on the following basic assumptions: naturally occurring phenomena operate according to mechanistic laws; behavior is a natural phenomenon and so it must operate by such laws as well; mental phenomena, if they exist, are subject to the same laws, but since these phenomena cannot be directly observed and seem to be unreliable and evanescent in any case, they cannot be the primary subject matter of psychology. The dominant belief came to be that psychology must deal only with publicly observable and therefore measurable pieces of behavior. In effect, behaviorism was an attempt to bring into psychology the attitudes and assumptions that seemed to have worked so well in other sciences, especially physiology and physics. Behaviorism was a kind of physics applied to people's movements. Indeed, it was John B. Watson, the founder of behaviorism, who described behavior as "bodies in motion." For the most part, such a view precluded the study of imagery, attention, reasoning, feelings, and anything else associated with cognition. World War II changed all that, and in part the roots of cognitive psychology can be traced to the wartime experiences of psychologists.

ACADEMIC PSYCHOLOGISTS, LIKE OTHER ABLE-BODIED MEN, WERE DRAFTED during World War II, and many found themselves working to solve military problems. Needless to say, these were very practical problems, involving such questions as how to improve marksmanship, how to fly airplanes without crashing them, how to improve men's performance in battle conditions, how to keep morale up, and so on. Answering these questions often required psychologists to look deeply into perceptual processes, decision-making, problem solving, and the delicate interface between people and machines. For example, it became clear that perceptual-motor performance was greatly affected by visual and kinesthetic feedback, rather than by reinforcement. This finding hastened the assimilation of *cybernetic theory* into psychology, since cybernetics is fundamentally concerned with the regulation of systems through feedback.

At the same time as these more practical psychological research projects were going on, a large group was gathering in England to work on the Ultra Project. The goal of this project was to break the intelligence codes used by the Axis powers (Germany, Italy, and Japan). Mathematicians, logicians, engineers, and others set about working on Enigma, the typewriter-like machine that the Germans used to encrypt messages. As part of this effort, the first modern working computer, Colossus, was developed in order to do calculations that were too tedious to be done by hand. The Ultra Project was a success and played a major role in ending the war.

After the war, when many psychologists came back to practice their trade, they were changed people, with new sets of ideas, new questions, and, perhaps most important, a new perspective on humanity. This perspective emphasized the complexity of human behavior, with the corollary that the mind would have to be studied in earnest in order to gain a complete picture of behavior. People were no longer viewed as mere bundles of stimulus-response associations; rather, they were processors of information. The mind was seen as a huge transforming device that takes in information from the environment and radically changes it before outputting it in some behavioral form. And since information was involved, it would have to be described in some way. This issue was addressed by Claude Shannon and Warren Weaver, two electrical engineers, in their *mathematical theory of com-*

munication, which was published in 1949. In this theory, communication was viewed as a process by which information is first encoded, transmitted over some channel, and finally decoded by a receiver (e.g., a radio or a human being). Information itself was defined as a reduction in uncertainty and was measured in terms of binary digits or *bits* (a bit being anything that reduces uncertainty by one-half).

In conclusion, in the aftermath of World War II, cybernetics, information theory, and computers were conceptual forces to be reckoned with in psychology. Together, their impact resulted in a new, information-processing framework, which would eventually come to predominate in psychology. In the late 1950s, the linguist Noam Chomsky published *Syntactic Structures,* and that work, along with several papers by psychologist George A. Miller, challenged and undermined the behavioristic approach to language, particularly with regard to syntax. Chomsky and Miller argued that language is rule-governed and describable in formal (logic-like) terms, and they rejected the idea that language could be understood as an elongated chain of probabilistic connections between words. For many psychologists, their work symbolized the eclipse of behaviorism. At the same time, however, some behaviorists were beginning to admit subjective or "mediating" variables into their theories. Indeed, some neobehaviorists such as psychologists Clark L. Hull and Edward C. Tolman had already done so before the war.

It is against this background of war-related developments, most of them originating outside of academic psychology, that the articles by Howard H. Kendler, A. M. Turing, and M. Mitchell Waldrop can be appreciated. Kendler fills out the historical background just provided. He traces cognitive psychology back to William Wundt in the latter part of the nineteenth century and to several major theorists in the middle part of the twentieth century, including G. A. Miller and J. Bruner. He then describes the impact of human engineering (cybernetics, signal detection theory, man-machine systems), communications engineering (including information theory), Chomsky (his emphasis on biology, rules, the creativeness and the hierarchical nature of language), and computer science. Kendler closes with the thesis that stimulus-response psychology was expanding to include cognition, that writers such as Woodworth had in fact included the organism in the stimulus-response equation. Nevertheless, he goes on, S-R psychology did not yield a full-fledged cognitive psychology. A revolution had to occur, and Kendler traces that revolution to the failure of Hull's theory, to the desire for a less animal-oriented psychology, to the growing belief that the mind cannot be ignored when interpreting human cognition, and to the impact of science historian Thomas Kuhn's views. Kuhn proposed that sciences advance through stages, including one in which the prevailing paradigm is overthrown due to factual anomalies in the paradigm. In psychology, behaviorism was the paradigm that was being overthrown.

COMPUTERS, OR RATHER THE ANALOGIES AND METaphors they have suggested to scientists, have played a major role in shaping modern cognitive psychology. Cognitive scientists have borrowed a number of computer-related concepts—input, sensory register, data base, program, hardware, etc.—and have applied them to human cognition. Even more important, however, many psychologists have adopted the belief that, at a formal/mathematical/logical level, there is no difference between computers and humans. Thus, computers should be capable of thinking just as a human does. But how does one arrive at this conclusion?

This question is addressed in Turing's paper, "Computing Machinery and Intelligence," which was published in 1950. Turing, a mathematician, was a leader in the Ultra Project and played a key role in the development of Colossus. Although Turing's paper did not have a direct impact on cognitive psychology, it did indirectly influence it because a generation of mathematicians, philosophers, and computer scientists passed on its meaning to the new cognitive scientists. Turing couched his answer to the question of whether or not computers

can think in terms of an imitation game, now called the *Turing Test*, in which an interrogator is called upon to guess, based on typewritten replies only, which of two people is a man and which a woman. If a computer were substituted for the man or woman, could the interrogator tell the difference? In general, would the interrogator's task be made easier? Turing felt that if the output of the computer could not be distinguished from that of a human, then the computer could be considered to be thoughtful. Thus, the computer could be credited with having simulated a human mind or at least some aspect of it. Turing stated that in 50 years (2000 A.D.) computers would be able to play the imitation game so well that the interrogator would not be able to distinguish between computer and human being better than 70 percent of the time. Of course, the view that people's minds are "just" machines can be anathema for a number of reasons, which Turing considers in his paper.

The explosion of interest in computers, their uses in psychology, and the problems of computer simulation are all described in Waldrop's paper, "Machinations of Thought." Waldrop describes how the view of computers has changed from that of a fast arithmetic or logic calculator to a sophisticated manipulator of abstract symbols. He points out that while computers are doing increasingly well at various expert tasks—diagnosing disease, finding oil, etc.—they are faring less well at tasks that humans find easy or consider to be common sense. Waldrop also describes some of the work on vision, language, and the use of massive parallel processing systems. But every attempt to mimic human functioning seems to run up against the same sorts of problems, which include the need for vast amounts of information to be programmed in, the importance of background cultural knowledge, the role of context, and inferred information. Waldrop concludes the paper with teasers about the relative consciousness of knowledge, whether or not knowledge is holistic, and issues of self-awareness.

COGNITIVE SCIENCE AND COGNITIVE PSYCHOLOGY have their detractors. As mentioned in the

Introduction to this volume, those who take an ecological (or Gibsonian) view are unhappy with the cognitivist's penchant for inventing mental processes and mental structures as explanatory mechanisms. Some are unhappy with the computer metaphor because in their view humans have special qualities not found in nonbiological mechanisms. Others are simply unhappy with the tendency toward reductionism, the notion that the mind can be reduced to a set of simple elements and their relationships. Still others have criticized cognitive science on the grounds that it pays too much attention to the mind at the expense of the environment, ignores practical problems, and has failed to develop general theories.

The most recent and strongest challenge to mainstream cognitive psychology comes not from outside the area but from within. This challenge, variously known as *connectionism*, *parallel distributed processing*, and *neural network views*, among other names, is presented in Matthew Zeidenberg's article "Modeling the Brain." The basic premise of connectionism is that the brain is a massive connecting device in which billions of neurons are synaptically interconnected and that knowledge is represented in the patterns of interconnection. As presented by Zeidenberg, connectionism attempts to model the brain—and therefore knowledge— by using computer software or hardware in which there are "nodes" that become connected through "experience." The connections are not programmed by a computer programmer but come into existence as the layers of nodes "learn," that is, as the nodes "fire" and "weights" on the connections change. A key aspect of connectionism is that knowledge is represented by the simultaneous activation of certain connection patterns and that the nodes/connections may be distributed over the entire network. Zeidenberg explains how connectionism applies to *competitive learning*, in which certain connection patterns vie with others to be the basis of some piece of knowledge, as well as how connectionism applies to generalization, the semantics of sentences, and schemas. He also describes some of the differences between traditional computer simulation, in which programs are built according to specific rules, and the connectionism approach, in which the "rules" emerge as a result of the network's activity.

1

Howard H. Kendler

Cognitive Psychology

Cognitive psychology was never born; it gradually coalesced. A variety of orientations, within and outside of psychology, merged to produce a new force in the 1950s that achieved a clear identity in 1966 with the publication of Ulric Neisser's *Cognitive Psychology.*

Today cognitive psychology, which seeks to understand how the mind works, represents the most popular orientation in psychology, receiving a level of support among a broad range of psychologists unmatched in its history. Because cognitive psychology represents a mingling of many different ideas, it fails to have the unity of systematic positions that have been dominated by a single spokesman (e.g., Titchenerian structuralism) or by a closely knit group (e.g., Gestalt psychology). Thus, cognitive psychologists do not speak with one voice; although they share a common orientation, they frequently disagree about important methodological and theoretical issues.

HISTORICAL ROOTS

The numerous historical roots of cognitive psychology can be divided into two main classes; those that emerged within psychology and those that originated in other disciplines.

Influences Within the History of Psychology

Several streams of psychological thought contributed to the development of this movement. These contributions include experimental methods for investigating the mind, theoretical interpretations of the mind, and a new field of psychology that became known as *human engineering.*

Experimental Analysis of the Mind.

Although Wundt denied that thinking could be introspectively observed he nevertheless assumed that mental activity could be inferred from both experimental and historical evidence. His complication experiment and the application of mental chronometry to the analysis of reaction time illustrated the logic of inferring mental activity from empirical evidence. Wundt's efforts anticipated the strategy that was to be followed by most contemporary cognitive psychologists.

General Theoretical Notions.

While conceptualizing the mind as a general system, psychologists differed about how it is organized and functions. Wundt and Titchener distinguished between different kinds of mental content (e.g., sensations, feelings). Functionalists, who were concerned with both mental activity and adjustment, stressed the importance of mental operations. Angell (1904) expressed this interest by suggesting that the major task of the functionalist is to discover "the typical *operations* of consciousness under actual life *conditions*." Embedded in Angell's statement is a central concern of modern cognitive psychology—how the mind operates on information in order to solve a problem, whether it be simply the recall of a person's name or the proof of a complex mathematical principle.

In contrast to the functionalists' emphasis on mental acts and their adaptive significance, structural features of the mind were stressed by both Gestalt psychology and Tolman's cognitive behaviorism. The *psychological environment* of Gestalt psychology and Tolman's *cognitive map* were mental constructions designed to represent an organism's environment.

Mental structures and cognitive processes.

Psychologists who anticipated cognitive psychology all seemed to be proposing hypotheses about the workings of the mind. As a result, the distinction between mental structures and mental processes gradually became apparent although it is often subtle and sometimes even confusing. The distinction is analogous to the difference between anatomy and physiology. For example, anatomy describes the structure of the stomach while physiology describes the processes with which that organ digests food. Sir Frederic Bartlett (1886–1969), an English psychologist, introduced this distinction when investigating memory. He rejected the conception of remembering as a reproductive process in which information is passively duplicated in memory. Bartlett (1932) proposed that memory is a reconstructivist process; when hearing a story a person transforms, or more technically, *encodes* the incoming information into a mental structure, a *schema*, that represents the interpretation of the story in line with the listener's preconceptions and attitudes. When recalling the story, the schema is *decoded*, transferred back into the remembered version. In this example the mental structure is the schema and the cognitive processes are encoding and decoding.

Jean Piaget (1896–1980), who was trained as a biologist, became interested in epistemological issues. Instead of treating epistemology as a speculative armchair discipline, Piaget decided to study it scientifically by empirically investigating the development of thought, or what he called *conceptual operations* from infancy through adolescence. In general, Piaget concluded that the growth of intelligence is not a continuous affair in which intellectual functioning gradually improves, but instead occurs in an invariant order of successive stages, each laying the foundation for the next.

Piaget hypothesizes that the structure of the mind undergoes qualitative changes just as a human embryo does during the period of gestation. The human embryo does not simply get larger; its structure changes dramatically. So do schemas, mental representations of objects, and their relations. Piaget's theory, like that of Freud's, was rich in ideas but vague in conception. His impact on modern cognitive psychology was twofold. His formulation stimulated interest in cognitive processes and thereby encouraged research and theorizing in the field of thought and intelligence. At the same time, Piaget's theory, based initially on naturalistic observations, appeared too ambiguous and therefore challenged cognitively oriented psychologists to formulate more precise theories of cognition.

George Miller (born 1920) published an influential paper entitled, *"The magical number seven, plus or minus two: Some limits on our capacity for processing information,"* in 1956. This paper sought to interpret the psychological phenomenon known as the *memory span*, the number of items an individual can recall after just one presentation. By analyzing a variety of findings, Miller concluded the magical number—seven plus or minus two—represented the storage capacity of short-term memory, a finding that was reported in 1871, but subsequently forgotten (Blumenthal, 1977). In other words, Miller suggested that the mind contains a mental structure analogous to a file with several slots with the exact number, depending on the individual, varying from five to nine.

In addition to postulating a memory structure, Miller proposed a process called *chunking*, which refers to the reorganization (encoding) of information to increase the number of items that can be packed into a single slot. For example, the task of remembering the phone number, 961-2834, can be made easier by chunking the number into five slots of information instead of seven; for example, 9-6-1-28-34 instead of 9-6-1-2-8-3-4.

Along with two collaborators, Eugene Galanter and Karl Pribram, Miller published *Plans and the Structure of Behavior* in 1960, which proposed that the *plan* should be substituted for the *stimulus-response (S-R) association* as the basic unit of behavior. A plan, in contrast to an S-R association, is a self-regulating system that uses available information to guide subsequent behavior. A thermostat is an example of a self-regulating system in which a target temperature (70°F) is maintained by the thermostat shutting down the furnace when that temperature is attained and starting the furnace when the temperature falls below that level. In an analogous manner, Miller, Galanter, and Pribram (1960) suggest that information feedback is basic to the execution of a plan. A plan has two functions: to compare the present situation with the desired goal and to activate routines of behavior that reduce the difference between the current situation and the goal state. A

simple plan is illustrated in the task of hammering a nail into wood. The goal state is to have the head of the nail flush with the wood. The discrepancy between the goal state and the initial state when the point of the nail is resting against the wood is successively reduced by hammering the nail into the wood until the goal is achieved.

Another important book that encouraged the development of cognitive psychology was *A Study of Thinking* (1956) by Jerome Bruner (born 1915) and two collaborators, Jacqueline Goodnow and George Austin. They offered a mentalistic interpretation of concept learning that stressed a subject's strategy in marked opposition to the passive associationism that Hull had proposed in his interpretation of concept learning in 1920, and which had, from that time, tended to dominate this research area. Jerome Bruner felt that "the banning of 'mental' concepts from psychology was a fake seeking after the gods of the nineteenth-century physical sciences" (Bruner, 1980). Bruner and Miller helped found *The Center for Cognitive Studies* at Harvard in 1962. Establishing a physical presence as well as an active research program contributed to the launching of cognitive psychology.

Human Engineering.

A new branch of psychology, human engineering, developed in response to the needs of the military during and after World War II. The dominant attitude that prevailed at the beginning of the war was that the design of weapon systems, such as airplanes, submarines, radar, and the like, was a purely physical problem. This view proved to be naive. For example, one war plane that seemed to be perfectly engineered suffered a high rate of landing accidents. The reason was discovered to be due to the close proximity between two levers the pilot had to use for braking and retracting the landing gear. Instead of braking after landing the plane, the pilot, who had to keep his eyes on the runway, sometimes accidentally pulled the lever for retracting the landing gear and landed the plane on its belly. Such accidents could have been avoided had the reactions of the pilot been considered. The controls should have been designed, as psychologists would be quick to point out (Chapanis, Garner, & Morgan, 1949), so as to require entirely different arm movements for braking and retracting the landing gear. When the controls were redesigned accordingly, the source of the dangerous confusion was eliminated, and so were the accidents.

A core concept in human engineering is the *man-machine system* which stresses the principle that humans and machines operate as a single system. Thus, both psychological and engineering knowledge is essential for the effective design of machines. In addition, information processing, the flow of information through a man-machine system, was recognized as a basic variable in human engineering. If the necessary information does not reach the human, as was the case for the pilot who could not distinguish clearly between braking and retracting the landing gear, the man-machine system breaks down.

The radar operated advance warning system in Alaska is another example of a man-machine system. The radar operator's job is to detect any flying object traveling toward the United States. On his radar screen, which is similar to a TV screen, flying objects are seen as *blips,* points of light against a background of less intense light. In reacting to his scope, the radar operator must decide whether the activity observed indicates that a missile or plane is approaching. The task confronting the radar operator was conventionally conceptualized as purely a sensory problem. Did the operator see a blip or not? The analysis of this problem by signal detection theory (Green & Swets, 1966) suggested that nonsensory, as well as sensory processes are involved. When the blip is very faint, the operator is not sure he senses anything. A decision must be made to report or not to report a blip. One factor that will influence the decision is the relative cost of making one of the two mistakes: either not detecting a flying object (a miss) or reporting a blip when one is not there (a false alarm). What are the consequences of each? A miss could lead to disaster. Reporting a false alarm would waste some interceptor missiles. The relative weight

of each error will influence an operator's decision. An operator who establishes a lenient criterion will produce many false alarms. A strict criterion will minimize false alarms but will risk the possibility that an incoming missile or airplane will not be reported and consequently not intercepted.

Signal detection theory provided a mathematical technique to sort out the observer's sensitivity from his decision criterion. In addition, it conceptualized humans as information processors and decision makers, basic constructs in the newly emerging cognitive orientation.

Contributions of Other Disciplines to Cognitive Psychology

A reasonable case can be made that cognitive psychology, or what some prefer to call *cognitive science,* is more a product of engineering, linguistics, and computer science than it is of psychology. These disciplines provided fundamental ideas that molded the development of cognitive psychology, particularly in the research area designated as information processing.

Communications Engineering.

Modern technology demands numerous kinds of communication: telephone, television, radio, and so forth. Can all forms of communication be analyzed within a common framework? Claude Shannon (1948), a mathematician in the employ of Bell Telephone Laboratories thought so, and presented a general theory of communication for inanimate systems such as the telephone that took account of all the changes that occurred within the system from the physical input to the physical output. The basic structure of this general communication system is illustrated in Figure 1. Several psychologists applied Shannon's ideas to human communication, both to the cognitive processes within an individual, and to communication between individuals.

Consider the relevance of Shannon's general communication system to the case of a student

Figure 1 _____

The Basic Structure of Shannon's General Communication System

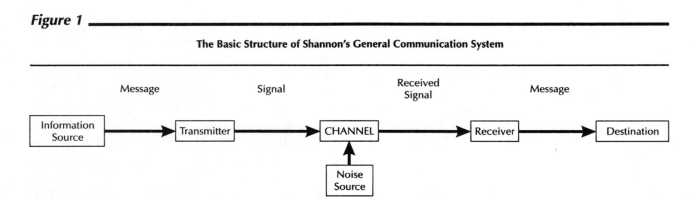

The text describes the operating characteristics of this system.

in a classroom listening to a professor's lecture. The professor is the *source* of the *message* which is *transmitted* by both auditory signals (the lecture) and visual *signals* (diagrams on blackboard) to the auditory and visual *channels*. The signals in a channel can be degraded by *noise*. For example, a neighboring conversation can prevent a student from hearing the professor clearly. The concept of noise in communication theory, however, is not simply limited to interfering sound. Noise refers to all events, outside or within a receiver, that degrade a signal. Just as static reduces the clarity of a radio signal, so do the fantasies of a student degrade the signals emitted by the professor.

The signals *received* by the student are transformed (encoded) into a message that is remembered and later decoded into information that can be utilized during an examination; test performance is determined by the quality of the message at its *destination* (examination). Numerous events throughout the general communication system can influence the quality of that message. For example, the professor's too-rapid lecturing style could overload the auditory channel and prevent the student from encoding the entire message.

Communication engineering had an important influence on the development of cognitive psychology, not because its theory could be simply superimposed on human cognition, but instead because it offered a fruitful analogy for interpreting cognitive processes. Of basic importance was the concept of *information* which, in Shannon's theory, referred to physical changes (e.g., electrical changes in a telephone line) in an inanimate communication system. Shannon offered a mathematically precise interpretation of information that proved extremely useful in designing computers and communication systems but was discovered to be inadequate for representing human knowledge. Nevertheless, the notion that information is a basic component in human cognition was encouraged, and numerous structures and processes were suggested by communication theory which provided direction, as well as hypotheses, for the experimental analysis of the mind. Examples include *encoding, decoding, information processing, communication channels, channel capacity, noise,* and so forth. Finally, communication engineering suggested the idea of a flowchart of the sort that appears in Figure 1. The flowchart is a diagrammatic representation of a sequence of successive events within an integrated system. Cognitive theorists found flowcharts useful for analyzing cognitive activities into their basic components.

Chomsky's Linguistic Theory.

Since the time of Wundt, psychologists have sought to understand language. Skinner (1957) offered an interpretation of verbal behavior that assumed that contingencies of reinforcement govern linguistic actions. Implicit in this assumption are several important corollaries: (1) Verbal behavior is conceptualized in terms of its adaptive characteristics; (2) Human language is continuous with animal behavior; (3) Verbal behavior is primarily learned behavior;

and (4) Theories, particularly mentalistic ones, are not required for understanding human language.

Noam Chomsky played a major role in stimulating the development of cognitive psychology by vigorously opposing all of Skinner's basic assumptions at the time that Skinner reigned as the dominant behaviorist. Chomsky argues that the understanding of language is not to be found in the contingencies of reinforcement but instead in the innate biological structure of human beings. Every child is born with a general notion of a universal syntax that enables her to communicate, in her native language, at an early age in a grammatically appropriate form. Even though the child cannot state the grammatical rules, and at times makes errors, linguistic usage is nevertheless guided by the innate syntactical rules, as demonstrated by the fact that she intuitively distinguishes between a correct sentence like, *Jimmy ate the apple*, and ungrammatical strings of words like, *Ate Jimmy the apple.*

Chomsky also argues that linguistic behavior is a creative enterprise; it cannot be reduced to a simple mechanical chaining conception in which a sentence is formed by each successive word triggering the next one. Two reasons are offered for rejecting this associative chaining hypothesis. One is that an enormous amount of time would be required to learn grammatically correct sentences, much too long for children to be able to speak grammatically. Second, each person is capable of uttering and understanding an *infinite* number of sentences, sentences that are different (e.g., *the unicorn jumped over the satellite*) from those previously uttered or heard. The principle of associative chaining could not possibly explain such novelty. Because of these two criticisms, Chomsky was led to the position that "rules in the head" generated sentences, not an associative network of words.

Chomsky distinguishes between *linguistic performance* and *linguistic competence*, a distinction that bears some similarity to the *learning-performance* distinction of Tolman and Hull. Linguistic performance involves sentences uttered or comprehended. Linguistic competence is the knowledge of language that enables a person to determine whether a sentence is syntactically correct.

A sentence consists of two components: *surface structure* and *deep structure*. Surface structure refers to the syntactical organization of a sentence. *The girl throws the ball* and *The ball is thrown by the girl* have two different phrase structures; the first being a simple active sentence while the second is a simple passive sentence. Both sentences express the common notion that a girl is throwing a ball, but each expresses it with a different surface structure. To account for their shared meaning, Chomsky formulates the construct *deep structure*, the crucial element of his original theory. Deep structure is a theoretical construct that represents a basic syntactical structure within the mind from which a series of sentences such as *The girl throws the ball, The ball is thrown by the girl, Is the ball thrown by the girl?* and so forth are generated into their surface form.

Supporting the distinction between deep structure and surface structure are cases of ambiguous sentences. *The shooting of the hunters was terrible* can mean either that *The hunters were poor marksmen* or *The hunters were targets.* Chomsky concludes that the ambiguity occurs when the same surface structure emerges from different deep structures. Such differences cannot be understood, Chomsky argues, if language is analyzed simply in terms of an associative chaining mechanism.

This brief description of a complicated linguistic theory stresses several of Chomsky's important attitudes and ideas that encouraged the development of cognitive psychology. First, Chomsky's concerns shifted attention away from the functional properties of verbal behavior to the organization of language, which is responsible for its endless novelty and diversity: "The central fact to which any significant theory must address itself is this: a mature speaker can produce a new sentence of his language on the appropriate occasion, and other speakers can understand it immediately, though it is equally new to them" (Chomsky, 1964). Second, Chomsky insisted that a theoretical effort was necessary to explain language, one in which postulating mental structures (e.g., deep structure) and cognitive processes (e.g., transformation of deep structure into surface structure) were demanded. Third, by emphasizing genetic factors, Chomsky alerted psychologists to theoretical distortions resulting from ignoring genetic preprogramming. Fourth, Chomsky's theory conceptualized human language behavior as species-specific, thus encouraging the view that the higher mental processes could only be understood by studying humans. By accepting this position, Chomsky was essentially bucking the Darwinian trend in American psychology which assumed that all forms of human behavior were continuous with the behavior of lower animals.

Computer Science.

Computer science is a loosely organized collection of related disciplines that have emerged from the development of computers. Computers, with which most students are now familiar, are electronic machines capable of accepting, processing, and communicating information. These activities correspond to the three functional units of the typical computer: *input, information processing,* and *output* (Figure 2). The input unit of the computer receives the information, which is then encoded and transferred in its coded state into the information-processing unit, where the information is stored in a simple magnetic code on a disk, tape, or drum. The arithmetic-logic component performs arithmetical and logical operations on the information that is stored in memory. The control component interprets and executes the commands of the *program,* a set of instructions that is stored in memory. The computer will do exactly what it is instructed to do—nothing more, nothing less. To illustrate: at one college campus, a computer was programmed to select partners for blind dates on the basis of students' interests, attitudes, likes, and dislikes. The results were rather successful except for a brother and sister who were paired together. No one had bothered to program the instruction that siblings should not be paired.

The output unit communicates the processed information to the user of the computer in a particular form desired (e.g., printer, cathode ray oscilloscope, etc.). Computers, as you

Figure 2 _____

Schematic Diagram of the Main Functional Units of a Computer

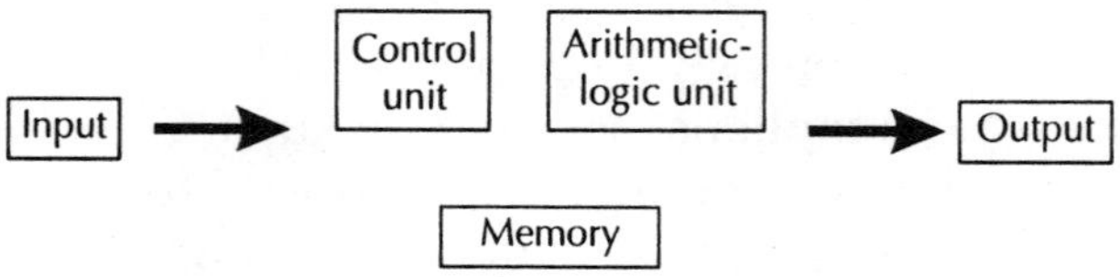

know, can be programmed to furnish immediate information about available seatings for all flights of an airline or to steer a spacecraft to a rendezvous in space. The ability of computers to *behave* intelligently has been referred to as *artificial intelligence,* a term that can be most clearly defined as "the art of creating machines that perform tasks considered to require intelligence when performed by humans" (attributed to Minsky by Kurzweil, 1985). It is important to recognize that this definition of artificial intelligence is neutral as to whether or not a particular example of artificial intelligence simulates human cognition.

While the computer, with its capacity for artificial intelligence, was revolutionizing society, two computer scientists, Alan Newell (born 1927) and Herbert Simon (born 1916), who was awarded a Nobel Prize in economics in 1978, offered an idea that revolutionized psychology, namely, that *computers can be programmed to simulate human thinking.* The justification for this strategy is that the human mind, according to Newell and Simon, can be conceptualized as a symbol manipulating system, and *so can the computer.* Both the mind and the computer are instances of the same kind of system; they both process information. This assumption led to an important research program that was designed to unravel the mysteries of the mind—the principles of human cognition—with the assistance of the digital computer.

THE EMERGENCE OF COGNITIVE PSYCHOLOGY

The historical roots of cognitive psychology all, in some way or another, are related to how the mind is functionally organized and operates. These general ideas were perceived by a large segment of the psychological community in the 1960s as being in direct opposition to the views of radical behaviorism, which had become the preeminent stimulus-response psychology. In fact, radical behaviorism's status had become so dominant that it was frequently, and erroneously, taken to be equivalent to all of behaviorism. The result of this historical error was to ignore evolutionary changes that were occurring in stimulus-response psychology from its early beginnings.

Robert S. Woodworth (1869–1962), who helped establish the Functionalist school at Columbia University, noted that:

> The objections raised to S-R formula [to describe behavior] means that it is too limited. It seems to imply that nothing important occurs between the stimulus and motor response. Or it seems to imply that the sensory stimulus is the only causative factor in the arousal of a response. These limitations can be avoided by the addition of another symbol to stand for the organism (the S-O-R formula). The O inserted between S and R makes explicit the obvious role of the living and active organism in the process; O receives the stimulus and makes the response. This formula suggests that psychologists should not limit their investigations to the input of stimuli and output of motor responses. They should ask how the input of stimuli can possibly give rise to the output; they should observe intervening processes if possible or at least hypothesize them and devise experiments for testing the hypothesis (Woodworth, 1958, p. 31).

This general S-O-R orientation was adopted by many neofunctionalists to investigate a variety of problem-solving phenomena that was later to interest cognitive psychologists. The general approach to these research problems by neofunctionalists and cognitivists differed. Influenced by the antimentalism of behaviorism, neofunctionalists minimized, if not eliminated, any mentalistic processes in their interpretation of thinking while subsequent cognitive psychologists felt no such inhibitions.

Woodworth's S-O-R conception anticipated the efforts of S-R mediational psychologists, who sought to interpret cognitive phenomena by postulating intervening processes between stimulus input and the response output within the general orientation of Hull and Spence. Osgood (1957) offered an elaborate mediational analysis of perception and language while Kuenne (1946) and Kendler and Kendler (1962) emphasized the importance of representation in developmental changes that occur in the discriminative behavior of young children. Spence (1950) acknowledged that different mechanisms were required to explain the cognitive behavior of humans than were needed to interpret animal behavior. In analyzing human cognitive behavior, Spence proposed a flow-chart that anticipated later information-processing conceptions, and that radically departed from his own analysis of the discrimination learning of the rat (Spence, 1936). In his flow diagram, he employed concepts (e.g., sense reception, signification, verbal meaning) that referred to the innate organization of the brain, cognitive expectations, and linguistic meaning. These higher level processes "badly need the attention of all psychologists, cognition, S-R, or whatever else" (Spence, 1950).

Thus, the stimulus-response psychology of Hull and his disciples, which had its roots in the theoretical analysis of animal learning, was gradually expanding to the cognitive process of humans. Why did psychology have to experience a *cognitive revolution* instead of gradual evolutionary development of stimulus-response learning theories to encompass human cognition?

Four interrelated historical forces operated to encourage a cognitive revolution instead of a gradual evolutionary extension of stimulus-response psychology. First, because Hull's general theory fell far short of its stated objectives, little interest was expressed in employing the Hullian framework as a launching pad for the investigation of human cognition. Second, a disenchantment was spreading with the general strategy of basing a theory of human cognition, even partly, on the analysis of animal behavior. Many psychologists perceived human cognition as unique in the animal kingdom and, therefore, any theory of animal behavior was considered irrelevant to the task of understanding cognitive psychology, a position that S-R mediational theorists strongly rejected. Third, and probably of paramount importance, was the emerging intuition that the mind could not be ignored when interpreting human cognition. Even though the idea that the direct examination of consciousness could yield valid theoretical principles was generally rejected, the conception of a psychology free of the mind, as Hull proposed, was considered inadequate to the task of interpreting human cognition. A satisfactory theory demanded a conception of the mind, which in turn required an appropriate descriptive language. The idea that a stimulus-response language, even when enlarged by mediational mechanisms, could describe cognition seemed unrealistic. Stimulus-response language, with its antimentalistic bias, seemed too sterile and restrictive to represent the full richness of human cognition. Cognitively oriented psychologists decided it would be more strategic to start with a new language than to continue with an impoverished stimulus-response idiom. Fourth, the need for a revolution in psychology was encouraged by Thomas Kuhn's *The Structure of Scientific Revolutions* (1962), a book that described the history of physics from the time of Copernicus. Kuhn's major thesis is that scientific progress is not based on the accumulation of individual discoveries and theoretical refinements, but instead results from a repetitive historical cycle that consists of two markedly different enterprises, *normal science* and *revolution*. Normal science refers to the accumulation of knowledge within a widely adopted global orientation known as a *paradigm*, a "strong network of commitments—conceptual, theoretical, instrumental, and methodological, and quasimetaphysical" (Kuhn, 1962), that shapes the kind of research that is conducted and the type of theoretical interpretation that is offered. During this period of normal science, facts are discovered that cannot be easily incorporated into the prevailing paradigm. This initiates the second state of historical development, during which time a prevailing paradigm is overthrown by a new one. *The Structure of Scientific Revolutions* enjoyed instant popularity and its historical conception was perceived to be applicable to psychology. Many psychologists became convinced that a paradigmatic shift from stimulus-response behaviorism to cognitive psychology was demanded. Because Kuhn's historical analysis appeared so compelling, the cognitive revolution was encouraged.

REFERENCES

Angell, J. R. (1904). *Psychology.* New York: Holt, Rinehart & Winston.

Bartlett, F. C. (1932). *Remembering: A study in experimental and social psychology.* Cambridge: Cambridge University Press.

Blumenthal, A. L. (1977). *The process of cognition.* Englewood Cliffs, NJ: Prentice-Hall.

Bruner, J. S. (1980). Jerome S. Bruner. In G. Lindzey (Ed.), *A history of psychology in autobiography.* Vol. 7, San Francisco: W. A. Freeman.

Bruner, J. S., Goodnow, J. J., & Austin, G. A. (1956). *A study of thinking.* New York: John Wiley & Sons.

Chapanis, A., Garner, W. R. & Morgan, C. T. (1949). *Applied experimental psychology.* New York: John Wiley & Sons.

Chomsky, N. (1964) *Current issues in linguistic theory.* The Hague: Mouton.

Green, D. M. & Swets, J. A. (1966). *Signal detection theory and psychophysics.* New York: John Wiley & Sons.

Kendler, H. H. & Kendler, T. S. (1962). Vertical and horizontal processes in problem solving. *Psychological Review, 69,* 1–16.

Kuenne, M. R. (1946). Experimental investigation of the relation of language to transposition behavior in young children. *Journal of Experimental Psychology, 36,* 471–490.

Kuhn, T. S. (1962). *The structure of scientific revolutions.* Chicago: University of Chicago Press.

Miller, G. A., Galanter, E. & Pribram, K. H. (1960). *Plans and the structure of behavior.* New York: Holt, Rinehart & Winston.

Neisser, U. (1966). *Cognitive psychology.* New York: Appleton-Century-Crofts.

Osgood, C. E. (1957). A behavioristic analysis of perception and language as cognitive phenomena. *Contemporary approaches to cognition: A symposium held at the University of Colorado.* Cambridge, MA: Harvard University Press.

Shannon, C. E. (1948). A mathematical theory of communication. *Bell Systems Technical Journal, 27,* 379–423, 623–656.

Skinner, B. F. (1957). *Verbal behavior.* New York: Appleton-Century-Crofts.

Spence, K. W. (1950). Cognitive versus stimulus-response theories of learning. *Psychological Review, 57,* 159–172.

Woodworth, R. S. (1958). *Dynamics of behavior.* New York: Holt, Rinehart & Winston.

2

A. M. Turing

Computing Machinery and Intelligence

THE IMITATION GAME

I propose to consider the question, 'Can machines think?' This should begin with definitions of the meaning of the terms 'machine' and 'think'. The definitions might be framed so as to reflect so far as possible the normal use of the words, but this attitude is dangerous. If the meaning of the words 'machine' and 'think' are to be found by examining how they are commonly used it is difficult to escape the conclusion that the meaning and the answer to the question, 'Can machines think?' is to be sought in a statistical survey such as a Gallup poll. But this is absurd. Instead of attempting such a definition I shall replace the question by another, which is closely related to it and is expressed in relatively unambiguous words.

The new form of the problem can be described in terms of a game which we call the 'imitation game'. It is played with three people, a man (A), a woman (B), and an interrogator (C) who may be of either sex. The interrogator stays in a room apart from the other two. The object of the game for the interrogator is to determine which of the other two is the man and which is the woman. He knows them by labels X and Y, and at the end of the game he says either 'X is A and Y is B' or 'X is B and Y is A'. The interrogator is allowed to put questions to A and B thus:

C: Will X please tell me the length of his or her hair?

Now suppose X is actually A, then A must answer. It is A's object in the game to try and cause C to make the wrong identification. His answer might therefore be

'My hair is shingled, and the longest strands are about nine inches long.'

In order that tones of voice may not help the interrogator the answers should be written, or better still, typewritten. The ideal

From A. M. Turing, "Computing Machinery and Intelligence," *Mind*, vol. 59, no. 236 (October 1950), pp. 433–436, 441–454, and 460. Copyright © 1950 by The Mind Association. Reprinted by permission of Oxford University Press.

arrangement is to have a teleprinter communicating between the two rooms. Alternatively the question and answers can be repeated by an intermediary. The object of the game for the third player (B) is to help the interrogator. The best strategy for her is probably to give truthful answers. She can add such things as 'I am the woman, don't listen to him!' to her answers, but it will avail nothing as the man can make similar remarks.

We now ask the question, 'What will happen when a machine takes the part of A in this game?' Will the interrogator decide wrongly as often when the game is played like this as he does when the game is played between a man and a woman? These questions replace our original, 'Can machines think?'

CRITIQUE OF THE NEW PROBLEM

As well as asking, 'What is the answer to this new form of the question', one may ask, 'Is this new question a worthy one to investigate?' This latter question we investigate without further ado, thereby cutting short an infinite regress.

The new problem has the advantage of drawing a fairly sharp line between the physical and the intellectual capacities of a man. No engineer or chemist claims to be able to produce a material which is indistinguishable from the human skin. It is possible that at some time this might be done, but even supposing this invention available we should feel there was little point in trying to make a 'thinking machine' more human by dressing it up in such artificial flesh. The form in which we have set the problem reflects this fact in the condition which prevents the interrogator from seeing or touching the other competitors, or hearing their voices. Some other advantages of the proposed criterion may be shown up by specimen questions and answers. Thus:

Q: Please write me a sonnet on the subject of the Forth Bridge.
A: Count me out on this one. I never could write poetry.
Q: Add 34957 to 70764
A: (Pause about 30 seconds and then give as answer) 105621.
Q: Do you play chess?

A: Yes.
Q: I have K at my K1, and no other pieces. You have only K at K6 and R at R1. It is your move. What do you play?
A: (After a pause of 15 seconds) R-R8 mate.

The question and answer method seems to be suitable for introducing almost any one of the fields of human endeavor that we wish to include. We do not wish to penalise the machine for its inability to shine in beauty competitions, nor to penalise a man for losing in a race against an aeroplane. The conditions of our game make these disabilities irrelevant. The 'witnesses' can brag, if they consider it advisable, as much as they please about their charms, strength or heroism, but the interrogator cannot demand practical demonstrations.

The game may perhaps be criticised on the ground that the odds are weighted too heavily against the machine. If the man were to try and pretend to be the machine he would clearly make a very poor showing. He would be given away at once by slowness and inaccuracy in arithmetic. May not machines carry out something which ought to be described as thinking but which is very different from what a man does? This objection is a very strong one, but at least we can say that if, nevertheless, a machine can be constructed to play the imitation game satisfactorily, we need not be troubled by this objection.

It might be urged that when playing the 'imitation game' the best strategy for the machine may possibly be something other than imitation of the behaviour of a man. This may be, but I think it is unlikely that there is any great effect of this kind. In any case there is no intention to investigate here the theory of the game, and it will be assumed that the best strategy is to try to provide answers that would naturally be given by a man.

THE MACHINES CONCERNED IN THE GAME

The question which we put [earlier—'Can machines think?'] will not be quite definite until we have specified what we mean by the word 'machine'. It is natural that we should wish to permit every kind of engineering technique to be used in our machines. We also wish to allow the possibility that an engineer or team of engineers may construct a machine which works, but whose manner of operation cannot be satisfactorily described by its constructors because they have applied a method which is largely experimental. Finally, we wish to exclude from the machines men born in the usual manner. It is difficult to frame the definitions so as to satisfy these three conditions. One might for instance insist that the team of engineers should be all of one sex, but this would not really be satisfactory, for it is probably possible to rear a complete individual from a single cell of the skin (say) of a man. To do so would be a feat of biological technique deserving of the very highest praise, but we would not be inclined to regard it as a case of 'constructing a thinking machine'. This prompts us to abandon the requirement that every kind of technique should be permitted. We are the more ready to do so in view of the fact that the present interest in 'thinking machines' has been aroused by a particular kind of machine, usually called an 'electronic computer' or 'digital computer'. Following this suggestion we only permit digital computers to take part in our game. . . .

This special property of digital computers, that they can mimic any discrete state machine, is described by saying that they are *universal* machines. The existence of machines with this property has the important consequence that, considerations of speed apart, it is unnecessary to design various new machines to do various computing processes. They can all be done with one digital computer, suitably programmed for each case. It will be seen that as a consequence of this all digital computers are in a sense equivalent. . . .

CONTRARY VIEWS ON THE MAIN QUESTION

We may now consider the ground to have been cleared and we are ready to proceed to the debate on our question, 'Can machines think?' We cannot altogether abandon the original form of the problem, for opinions will differ as to the appropriateness of the substitution and we must at least listen to what has to be said in this connexion.

It will simplify matters for the reader if I explain first my own beliefs in the matter. Consider first the more accurate form of the question. I believe that in about fifty years' time it will be possible to programme computers, with a storage capacity of about 10^9, to make them play the imitation game so well that an average interrogator will not have more than 70 percent chance of making the right identification after five minutes of questioning. The original question, 'Can machines think?' I believe to be too meaningless to deserve discussion. Nevertheless I believe that at the end of the century the use of words and general educated opinion will have altered so much that one will be able to speak of machines thinking without expecting to be contradicted. I believe further that no useful purpose is served by concealing these beliefs. The popular view that scientists proceed inexorably from well-established fact to well-established fact, never being influenced by any unproved conjecture, is quite mistaken. Provided it is made clear which are proved facts and which are conjectures, no harm can result. Conjectures are of great importance since they suggest useful lines of research.

I now proceed to consider opinions opposed to my own.

(1) The Theological Objection

Thinking is a function of man's immortal soul. God has given an immortal soul to every man and woman, but not to any other animal or to machines. Hence no animal or machine can think.[1]

I am unable to accept any part of this, but will attempt to reply in theological terms. I should find the argument more convincing if animals were classed with men, for there is a greater difference, to my mind, between the typical animate and the inanimate than there is between man and the other animals. The arbitrary character of the orthodox view becomes clearer if we consider how it might appear to be a member of some other religious community. How do Christians regard the Moslem view that women have no souls? But let us leave this point aside and return to the main argument. It appears to me that the argument quoted above implies a serious restriction of the omnipotence of the Almighty. It is admitted that there are certain things that He cannot do such as making one equal to two, but should we not believe that He has freedom to confer a soul on an elephant if He sees fit? We might expect that He would only exercise this power in conjunction with a mutation which provided the elephant with an appropriately improved brain to minister to the needs of this soul. An argument of exactly similar form may be made for the case of machines. It may seem different because it is more difficult to "swallow". But this really only means that we think it would be less likely that He would consider the circumstances suitable for conferring a soul. The circumstances in question are discussed in the rest of this paper. In attempting to construct such machines we should not be irreverently usurping His power of creating souls, any more than we are in the procreation of children: rather we are, in either case, instruments of His will providing mansions for the souls that He creates.

However, this is mere speculation. I am not very impressed with theological arguments whatever they may be used to support. Such arguments have often been found unsatisfactory in the past. In the time of Galileo it was argued that the texts, "And the sun stood still . . . and hasted not to go down about a whole day" (Joshua x. 13) and "He laid the foundations of the earth, that it should not move at any time" (Psalm cv. 5) were an adequate refutation of the Copernican theory. With our present knowledge such an argument appears futile. When that knowledge was not available it made a quite different impression.

(2) The 'Heads in the Sand' Objection

"The consequences of machines thinking would be too dreadful. Let us hope and believe that they cannot do so."

This argument is seldom expressed quite so openly as in the form above. But it affects most of us who think about it at all. We like to believe that Man is in some subtle way superior to the rest of creation. It is best if he can be shown to be *necessarily* superior, for then there is no danger of him losing his commanding position. The popularity of the theological argument is clearly connected with this feeling. It is likely to be quite strong in intellectual people, since they value the power of thinking more highly than others, and are more inclined to base their belief in the superiority of Man on this power.

I do think that this argument is sufficiently substantial to require refutation. Consolation would be more appropriate: perhaps this should be sought in the transmigration of souls.

(3) The Mathematical Objection

There are a number of results of mathematical logic which can be used to show that there are limitations to the powers of discrete-state machines. The best known of these results is known as Gödel's theorem, and shows that in any sufficiently powerful logical system statements can be formulated which can neither be proved nor disproved within the system, unless possibly the system itself is inconsistent. There are other, in some respects similar, results due to *Church, Kleene, Rosser, and Turing.*[2] The latter result is the most convenient to consider, since it refers directly to machines, whereas the others can only be used in a comparatively indirect argument: for instance if Gödel's theorem is to be used we need in addition to have some means of describing logical systems in terms of machines, and machines in terms of logical systems. The result in question refers to a type of machine which is essentially a digital computer with an infinite capacity. It states that there are certain things that such a machine cannot do. If it is rigged up to give answers to questions as in the imitation game, there will be some questions to which it will either give a wrong answer, or fail to give an answer at all however much time is allowed for a reply. There may, of course, be many such questions, and questions which cannot be answered by one machine may be satisfactorily answered by another. We are of course supposing for the present that the questions are of the kind to which an answer 'Yes' or 'No' is appropriate, rather than questions such as 'What do you think of Picasso?' The questions that we know the machines must fail on are of this type, "Consider the machine specified as follows. . . . Will this machine ever answer 'Yes' to any question?" The dots are to be replaced by a description of some machine in a standard form. When the machine described bears a certain comparatively simple relation to the machine which is under interrogation, it can be shown that the answer is either wrong or not forthcoming. This is the mathematical result: it is argued that it proves a disability of machines to which the human intellect is not subject.

The short answer to this argument is that although it is established that there are limitations to the powers of any particular machine, it has only been stated, without any sort of proof, that no such limitations apply to the human intellect. But I do not think this view can be dismissed quite so lightly. Whenever one of these machines is asked the appropriate critical question, and gives a definite answer, we know that this answer must be wrong, and this gives us a certain feeling of superiority. Is this feeling illusory? It is no doubt quite genuine, but I do not think too much importance should be attached to it. We too often give wrong answers to questions ourselves to be justified in being very pleased at such evidence of fallibility on the part of the machines. Further, our superiority can only be felt on such an occasion in relation to the one machine over which we have scored our petty triumph. There would be no question of triumphing simultaneously over *all* machines. In short, then, there might be men cleverer than any given machine, but then again there might be other machines cleverer again, and so on.

Those who hold to the mathematical argument would, I think, mostly be willing to accept the imitation game as a basis for discussion. Those who believe in the two previous objections would probably not be interested in any criteria.

(4) The Argument from Consciousness

This argument is very well expressed in *Professor Jefferson's* Lister Oration for 1949, from which I quote. "Not until a machine can write a sonnet or compose a concerto because of thoughts and emotions felt, and not by the chance fall of symbols, could we agree that machine equals brain—that is, not only write it but know that it had written it. No mechanism could feel (and not merely artificially signal, an easy contrivance) pleasure at its successes, grief when its values fuse, be warmed by flattery, be made miserable by its mistakes, be charmed by sex, be angry or depressed when it cannot get what it wants."

This argument appears to be a denial of the validity of our test. According to the most extreme form of this view the only way by which one could be sure that a machine thinks is to *be* the machine and to feel oneself thinking. One could then describe these feelings to the world, but of course no one would be justified in taking any notice. Likewise according to this view the only way to know what a *man* thinks is to be that particular man. It is in fact the solipsist point of view. It may be the most logical view to hold but it makes communication of ideas difficult. A is liable to believe 'A thinks but B does not' whilst B believes 'B thinks but A does not'. Instead of arguing continually over this point it is usual to have the polite convention that everybody thinks.

I am sure that Professor Jefferson does not wish to adopt the extreme and solipsist point of view. Probably he would be quite willing to accept the imitation game as a test. The game (with player B omitted) is frequently used in practice under the name of *viva voce* to discover whether some one really understands something or has 'learnt it parrot fashion'. Let us listen in to a part of such a *viva voce*:

Interrogator: In the first line of your sonnet which reads 'Shall I compare thee to a summer's day', would not 'a spring day' do as well or better?

Witness: It wouldn't scan.

Interrogator: How about 'a winter's day'? That would scan all right.

Witness: Yes, but nobody wants to be compared to a winter's day.

Interrogator: Would you say Mr. Pickwick reminded you of Christmas?

Witness: In a way.

Interrogator: Yet Christmas is a winter's day, and I do not think Mr. Pickwick would mind the comparison.

Witness: I don't think you're serious. By a winter's day one means a typical winter's day, rather than a special one like Christmas.

And so on. What would Professor Jefferson say if the sonnet-writing machine was able to answer like this in the *viva voce*? I do not know whether he would regard the machine as 'merely artificially signalling' these answers, but if the answers were as satisfactory and sustained as in the above passage I do not think he would describe it as 'an easy contrivance'. This phrase is, I think, intended to cover such devices as the inclusion in the machine of a record of someone reading a sonnet, with appropriate switching to turn it on from time to time.

In short then, I think that most of those who support the argument from consciousness could be persuaded to abandon it rather than be forced into the solipsist position. They will then probably be willing to accept our test.

I do not wish to give the impression that I think there is no mystery about consciousness. There is, for instance, something of a paradox connected with any attempt to localise it. But I do not think these mysteries necessarily need to be solved before we can answer the question with which we are concerned in this paper.

(5) Arguments from Various Disabilities

These arguments take the form, "I grant you that you can make machines do all the things you have mentioned but you will never be able to make one to do X". Numerous features X are suggested in this connexion. I offer a selection:

Be kind, resourceful, beautiful, friendly, have initiative, have a sense of humour, tell right

from wrong, make mistakes, fall in love, enjoy strawberries and cream, make some one fall in love with it, learn from experience, use words properly, be the subject of its own thought, have as much diversity of behaviour as a man, do something really new.

No support is usually offered for these statements. I believe they are mostly founded on the principle of scientific induction. A man has seen thousands of machines in his lifetime. From what he sees of them he draws a number of general conclusions. They are ugly, each is designed for a very limited purpose, when required for a minutely different purpose they are useless, the variety of behaviour of any one of them is very small, etc., etc. Naturally he concludes that these are necessary properties of machines in general. Many of these limitations are associated with the very small storage capacity of most machines. (I am assuming that the idea of storage capacity is extended in some way to cover machines other than discrete-state machines. The exact definition does not matter as no mathematical accuracy is claimed in the present discussion.) A few years ago, when very little had been heard of digital computers, it was possible to elicit much incredulity concerning them, if one mentioned their properties without describing their construction. That was presumably due to a similar application of the principle of scientific induction. These applications of the principle are of course largely unconscious. When a burnt child fears the fire and shows that he fears it by avoiding it, I should say that he was applying scientific induction. (I could of course also describe his behaviour in many other ways.) The works and customs of mankind do not seem to be very suitable material to which to apply scientific induction. A very large part of space-time must be investigated, if reliable results are to be obtained. Otherwise we may (as most English children do) decide that everybody speaks English, and that it is silly to learn French.

There are, however, special remarks to be made about many of the disabilities that have been mentioned. The inability to enjoy strawberries and cream may have struck the reader as frivolous. Possibly a machine might be made to enjoy this delicious dish, but any attempt to make one do so would be idiotic. What is important about this disability is that it contributes to some of the other disabilities, *e.g.* to the difficulty of the same kind of friendliness occurring between man and machine as between white man and white man, or between black man and black man.

The claim that "machines cannot make mistakes" seems a curious one. One is tempted to retort, "Are they any the worse for that?" But let us adopt a more sympathetic attitude, and try to see what is really meant. I think this criticism can be explained in terms of the imitation game. It is claimed that the interrogator could distinguish the machine from the man simply by setting them a number of problems in arithmetic. The machine would be unmasked of its deadly accuracy. The reply to this is simple. The machine (programmed for playing the game) would not attempt to give the *right* answers to the arithmetic problems. It would deliberately introduce mistakes in a manner calculated to confuse the interrogator. A mechanical fault would probably show itself through an unsuitable decision as to what sort of a mistake to make in the arithmetic. Even this interpretation of the criticism is not sufficiently sympathetic. But we cannot afford the space to go into it much further. It seems to me that this criticism depends on a confusion between two kinds of mistakes. We may call them 'errors of functioning' and 'errors of conclusion'. Errors of functioning are due to some mechanical or electrical fault which causes the machine to behave otherwise than it was designed to do. In philosophical discussions one likes to ignore the possibility of such errors; one is therefore discussing 'abstract machines'. These abstract machines are mathematical fictions rather than physical objects. By definition they are incapable of errors of functioning. In this sense we can truly say that 'machines can never make mistakes'. Errors of conclusion can only arise when some meaning is attached to the output signals from the machine. The machine might, for instance, type out mathematical equations, or sentences in English. When a false proposition is typed we say that the machine has committed an error of conclusion.

There is clearly no reason at all for saying that a machine cannot make this kind of mistake. It might do nothing but type out repeatedly 'O = 1'. To take a less perverse example, it might have some method for drawing conclusions by scientific induction. We must expect such a method to lead occasionally to erroneous results.

The claim that a machine cannot be the subject of its own thought can of course only be answered if it can be shown that the machine has *some* thought with *some* subject matter. Nevertheless, 'the subject matter of a machine's operations' does seem to mean something, at least to the people who deal with it. If, for instance, the machine was trying to find a solution of the equation $x^2 - 40x - 11 = 0$ one would be tempted to describe this equation as part of the machine's subject matter at that moment. In this sort of sense a machine undoubtedly can be its own subject matter. It may be used to help in making up its own programmes, or to predict the effect of alterations in its own structure. By observing the results of its own behaviour it can modify its own programmes so as to achieve some purpose more effectively. These are possibilities of the near future, rather than Utopian dreams.

The criticism that a machine cannot have much diversity of behaviour is just a way of saying that it cannot have much storage capacity. Until fairly recently a storage capacity of even a thousand digits was very rare.

The criticisms that we are considering here are often disguised forms of the argument from consciousness. Usually if one maintains that a machine *can* do one of these things, and describes the kind of method that the machine could use, one will not make much of an impression. It is thought that the method (whatever it may be, for it must be mechanical) is really rather base. Compare the parenthesis in Jefferson's statement [above].

(6) Lady Lovelace's Objection

Our most detailed information of Babbage's Analytical Engine comes from a memoir by *Lady Lovelace.* In it she states, "The Analytical

Engine has no pretensions to *originate* anything. It can do *whatever we know how to order it to perform*" (her italics). This statement is quoted by *Hartree* who adds: "This does not imply that it may not be possible to construct electronic equipment which will 'think for itself', or in which, in biological terms, one could set up a conditioned reflex, which would serve as a basis for 'learning'. Whether this is possible in principle or not is a stimulating and exciting question, suggested by some of these recent developments. But it did not seem that the machines constructed or projected at the time had this property".

I am in thorough agreement with Hartree over this. It will be noticed that he does not assert that the machines in question had not got the property, but rather that the evidence available to Lady Lovelace did not encourage her to believe that they had it. It is quite possible that the machines in question had in a sense got this property. For suppose that some discrete-state machine has the property. The Analytical Engine was a universal digital computer, so that, if its storage capacity and speed were adequate, it could by suitable programming be made to mimic the machine in question. Probably this argument did not occur to the Countess or to Babbage. In any case there was no obligation on them to claim all that could be claimed.

A variant of Lady Lovelace's objection states that a machine can 'never do anything really new'. This may be parried for a moment with the saw, 'There is nothing new under the sun'. Who can be certain that 'original work' that he has done was not simply the growth of the seed planted in him by teaching, or the effect of following well-known general principles. A better variant of the objection says that a machine can never 'take us by surprise'. This statement is a more direct challenge and can be met directly. Machines take me by surprise with great frequency. This is largely because I do not do sufficient calculation to decide what to expect them to do, or rather because, although I do a calculation, I do it in a hurried, slipshod fashion, taking risks. Perhaps I say to myself, 'I suppose the voltage here ought to be the same as there: anyway let's assume it is'.

Naturally I am often wrong, and the result is a surprise for me for by the time the experiment is done these assumptions have been forgotten. These admissions lay me open to lectures on the subject of my vicious ways, but do not throw any doubt on my credibility when I testify to the surprises I experience.

I do not expect this reply to silence my critic. He will probably say that such surprises are due to some creative mental act on my part, and reflect no credit on the machine. This leads us back to the argument from consciousness, and far from the idea of surprise. It is a line of argument we must consider closed, but it is perhaps worth remarking that the appreciation of something as surprising requires as much of a 'creative mental act' whether the surprising event originates from a man, a book, a machine, or anything else.

The view that machines cannot give rise to surprises is due, I believe, to a fallacy to which philosophers and mathematicians are particularly subject. This is the assumption that as soon as a fact is presented to a mind all consequences of that fact spring into the mind simultaneously with it. It is a very useful assumption under many circumstances, but one too easily forgets that it is false. A natural consequence of doing so is that one then assumes that there is no virtue in the mere working out of consequences from data and general principles.

(7) Argument from Continuity in the Nervous System

The nervous system is certainly not a discrete-state machine. A small error in the information about the size of a nervous impulse impinging on a neuron, may make a large difference to the size of the outgoing impulse. It may be argued that, this being so, one cannot expect to be able to mimic the behaviour of the nervous system with a discrete-state system.

It is true that the discrete-state machine must be different from a continuous machine. But if we adhere to the conditions of the imitation game, the interrogator will not be able to take any advantage of this difference. The situation can be made clearer if we consider some other simpler continuous machine. A differential analyser will do very well. (A differential analyser is a certain kind of machine not of the discrete-state type used for some kinds of calculation.) Some of these provide their answers in a typed form, and so are suitable for taking part in the game. It would not be possible for a digital computer to predict exactly what answers the differential analyser would give to a problem, but it would be quite capable of giving the right sort of answer. For instance, if asked to give the value of π (actually about 3.1416) it would be reasonable to choose at random between the values 3.12, 3.13, 3.14, 3.15, 3.16 with the probabilities of 0.05, 0.15, 0.55, 0.19, 0.06 (say). Under these circumstances it would be very difficult for the interrogator to distinguish the differential analyser from the digital computer.

(8) The Argument from Informality of Behaviour

It is not possible to produce a set of rules purporting to describe what a man should do in every conceivable set of circumstances. One might for instance have a rule that one is to stop when one sees a red traffic light, and to go if one sees a green one, but what if by some fault both appear together? One may perhaps decide that it is safest to stop. But some further difficulty may well arise from this decision later. To attempt to provide rules of conduct to cover every eventuality, even those arising from traffic lights, appears to be impossible. With all this I agree.

From this it is argued that we cannot be machines. I shall try to reproduce the argument, but I fear I shall hardly do it justice. It seems to run something like this. 'If each man had a definite set of rules of conduct by which he regulated his life he would be no better than a machine. But there are no such rules, so men cannot be machines.' The undistributed middle is glaring. I do not think the argument is ever put quite like this, but I believe this is the argument used nevertheless. There may however be a certain confusion between 'rules of conduct' and 'laws of behaviour' to cloud the issue. By 'rules of conduct' I mean precepts such as 'Stop if you see red lights', on which one can act, and of which one can be conscious. By 'laws of behaviour' I mean laws of nature as applied to a man's body such as 'if you pinch him he will squeak'. If we substitute 'laws of behaviour which regulate his life' for 'laws of conduct by which he regulates his life' in the argument quoted the undistributed middle is no longer insuperable. For we believe that it is not only true that being regulated by laws of behaviour implies being some sort of machine (though not necessarily a discrete-state machine), but that conversely being such a machine implies being regulated by such laws. However, we cannot so easily convince ourselves of the absence of complete laws of behaviour as of complete rules of conduct. The only way we know of for finding such laws is scientific observation, and we certainly know of no circumstances under which we could say, 'We have searched enough. There are no such laws.'

We can demonstrate more forcibly that any such statement would be unjustified. For suppose we could be sure of finding such laws if they existed. Then given a discrete-state machine it should certainly be possible to discover by observation sufficient about it to predict its future behaviour, and this within a reasonable time, say a thousand years. But this does not seem to be the case. I have set up on the Manchester computer a small programme using only 1000 units of storage, whereby the machine supplied with one sixteen figure number replies with another within two seconds. I would defy anyone to learn from these replies sufficient about the programme to be able to predict any replies to untried values.

(9) The Argument from Extra-Sensory Perception

I assume that the reader is familiar with the idea of extra-sensory perception, and the meaning of the four items of it, *viz.* telepathy, clairvoyance, precognition, and psycho-kinesis. These disturbing phenomena seem to deny all our usual scientific ideas. How we should like to discredit them! Unfortunately the statistical evidence, at least for telepathy, is overwhelming. It is very difficult to rearrange one's ideas so as to fit these new facts in. Once one has accepted them it does not seem a very big step to believe in ghosts and bogies. The idea that our bodies move simply according to the known laws of physics, together with some others not yet discovered but somewhat similar, would be one of the first to go.

This argument is to my mind quite a strong one. One can say in reply that many scientific theories seem to remain workable in practice, in spite of clashing with E.S.P.; that in fact one can get along very nicely if one forgets about it. This is rather cold comfort, and one fears that thinking is just the kind of phenomena where E.S.P. may be especially relevant.

A more specific argument based on E.S.P. might run as follows: "Let us play the imitation game, using as witnesses a man who is good as a telepathic receiver, and a digital computer. The interrogator can ask such questions as 'What suit does the card in my right hand belong to?' The man by telepathy or clairvoyance gives the right answer 130 times out of 400 cards. The machine can only guess at random, and perhaps gets 104 right, so the interrogator makes the right identification." There is an interesting possibility which opens here. Suppose the digital computer contains a random number generator. Then it will be natural to use this to decide what answer to give. But then the random number generator will be subject to the psycho-kinetic powers of the interrogator. Perhaps this psycho-kinesis might cause the machine to guess right more often than would be expected on a probability calculation, so that the interrogator might still be unable to make the right identification. On the other hand, he might be able to guess right without any questioning, by clairvoyance. With E.S.P. anything may happen.

If telepathy is admitted it will be necessary to tighten our test up. The situation could be regarded as analogous to that which would occur if the interrogator were talking to himself and one of the competitors was listening with his ear to the wall. To put the competitors into a 'telepathy-proof room' would satisfy all requirements.

NOTES

1. Possibly this view is heretical. St. Thomas Aquinas (*Summa Theologica*, quoted by Bertrand Russell, p. 480) states that God cannot make a man to have no soul. But this may not be a real restriction on His powers, but only a result of the fact that men's souls are immortal, and therefore indestructible.

2. Authors' names in italics refer to the Bibliography.

BIBLIOGRAPHY

Samuel Butler, Erewhon, London, 1865. Chapters 23, 24, 25, *The Book of the Machines*.

Alonzo Church, "An Unsolvable Problem of Elementary Number Theory", *American J. of Math.*, 58 (1936), 345–363.

K. Gödel, "ber formal unentscheidbare Sätze der Principia Mathematica und verwandter Systeme, I", *Monatshefte für Math. und Phys.*, (1931), 173–189.

D. R. Hartree, *Calculating Instruments and Machines*, New York, 1949.

S. C. Kleene, "General Recursive Functions of Natural Numbers", *American J. of Math.*, 57 (1935), 153–173 and 219–244.

G. Jefferson, "The Mind of Mechanical Man". Lister Oration for 1949. *British Medical Journal*, vol. i (1949), 1105–1121.

Countess of Lovelace, 'Translator's notes to an article on Babbage's Analytical Engine', *Scientific Memoirs* (ed. by R. Taylor), vol. 3 (1842), 691–731.

Bertrand Russell, *History of Western Philosophy*, London, 1940.

A. M. Turing, "On Computable Numbers, with an Application to the Entscheidungsproblem", *Proc. London Math. Soc.* (2), 42 (1937), 230–265.

3

M. *Mitchell Waldrop*

Machinations of Thought

After three decades of frustrating work, artificial intelligence is coming of age—moving out of the laboratories and into the marketplace. Expert systems, computer programs that give advice like a human specialist, are pinpointing mineral deposits and diagnosing diseases. Programs are taking shape that can do a pretty fair job of understanding plain English or French. Robotics will soon benefit from computer vision systems able to store a digitized photograph of an object or scene and "recognize" a good bit of what is there.

As the more exuberant enthusiasts see it, we might soon have machines to advise us about our income taxes or the baby's fever; silicon tutors could help a child master the enthralling possibilities of geometry and numbers; trucks might drive themselves through the night and unload themselves at their destination. In short, we could one day have machines to do almost anything that now requires "intelligence" in a human.

Many AI researchers find this kind of talk a little premature. AI has become commercial, they feel, not because of any fundamental breakthroughs but because venture capital is available. They've learned just how far from fulfillment some of the promises really are. "You've got to separate the science from the hype," says John Seely Brown of Xerox Corporation's Palo Alto Research Center.

Besides overselling, those who trumpet the impending triumphs of AI often miss the point. At heart, AI isn't about creating smart computers. The computer is simply a tool, a laboratory for testing out ideas. AI itself is about something much more interesting: intelligence. Mind. The nature of thought. What is it that we *do* up there in our skulls? And how, exactly, do we do it?

Doing AI research is a bit like doing problems in physics or mathematics. First turn a set of abstract speculations about the mind

TOMASO POGGIO: MATHEMATICIAN OF VISION

As a researcher at MIT's Whitaker College for Science, Health, and Technology, Tomaso Poggio is studying how nerve cells respond to the image falling on the retina of the eye. As a member of MIT's Artificial Intelligence Laboratory, he is studying the *mathematics* of vision and how computers might exploit that math to help them "understand" what they see through optical sensors.

"Vision can be defined as 'reverse optics,' " he says. "You start with the two-dimensional image on the retina, and from that you have to reconstruct the 3-D object that caused the image."

The problem is that a 2-D image is very ambiguous. Close one eye and look across the room at a chair. Next, imagine that you're actually looking at the tip of an infinitely long, chair-shaped rod directed straight away from your eye. Now, are you sure that you're not? The image on your retina would be no different.

In fact, says Poggio, we can never be certain. But we must deal with traffic, stairways, and hard line drives to second base. The visual system doesn't have time for theories. It has to recognize what's there right *now*.

So what happens, says Poggio, is that the eye uses a set of tricks to identify objects and figure out what they are: stereo vision. Shading. Color. Surface texture. Changes of the image with motion. What we *expect* to see. None of the tricks are foolproof—sometimes, when the eye guesses wrong, we get optical illusions—but together they can usually get the job done quickly.

During the last several years, Poggio and his colleagues have been able to duplicate most of these tricks, one by one, on a computer. Ultimately their work could lead to much improved vision systems for robots. More recently, Poggio has been working on the idea that all of the visual system's tricks can be described by the same mathematical equations. If so, researchers would gain a powerful tool for understanding the mechanics of vision.

into a computer program (write down the equations); then make the program perform (solve the equations). If it works, then your speculations may have something to do with reality. If not, try again. Since everything, down to the tiniest detail, has to be explained to a computer, this approach does tend to weed out fuzzy ideas.

But it also changes the whole way AI researchers think about the mind. Instead of talking about an abstract, disembodied mentality, they talk about a mind that is mechanistic, finite, operating in real time. "It can be summed up in one word," says Yale University's Roger Schank, a pioneer in natural language programming. "Process. Seeing what the steps are, seeing what the inputs are, and providing algorithms to get from place A to place B."

People started writing AI-like programs in the late 1940s, almost as soon as there were computers to run them on, and by the mid-1950s AI had emerged as a field of research in its own right. Very quickly, pioneers discovered that many of our "higher" mental powers are actually rather easy to mimic on a computer. For example, one of the first true AI programs was Logic Theorist, written in the mid-1950s by Allen Newell and Herbert Simon of Carnegie-Mellon University, together with J. Clifford Shaw of the RAND Corporation. Logic Theorist proved theorems in mathematical logic. One of its proofs, in fact, was more direct than the standard textbook proof of that theorem.

A decade later, AI researchers began to realize just how far they could go in imitating "expert" behavior with just a few rules of thumb and some elementary reasoning power. The inspiration came again from Newell and Simon. In the late 1960s they pointed out that much of human knowledge could be represented rather simply by "if-then" rules. For example, "If it looks like a duck, and walks like a duck, and quacks like a duck, then it probably is a duck." Or, "If it's a tiger, and it looks hungry, and it's headed your way, then run."

While this was obviously limited—we know our friends and our families in a far deeper sense than if-then rules can express—the New-ell-Simon approach did turn out to be ideal for capturing the kind of specialized expertise used, say, by a doctor in diagnosing a disease.

The result was a flowering of the so-called expert systems in the late 1960s through the mid-1970s, largely growing from work done by Edward Feigenbaum and his colleagues at Stanford. Mycin, one of their most important efforts, was able to diagnose infectious diseases just about as well as the human specialists could. A sample rule: "If (i) the infection is meningitis and (ii) organisms were not seen in the stain of the culture and (iii) the type of infection may be bacterial and (iv) the patient has been seriously burned, then there is suggestive evidence that *Pseudomonas aeruginosa* might be one of the organisms causing the infection."

More recently, other laboratories have developed systems such as Internist-1, a diagnostic program for internal medicine; Prospector, an expert system for petroleum geologists; and Puff, which interprets pulmonary tests. The pace of development is picking up: Such useful expert systems are responsible for much of the wave of commercial interest at AI.

But there is a disconcerting fact. Such seemingly sophisticated tasks can often be relatively easy to program, while the ordinary, everyday things we do—walk, read a letter, plan a trip to the grocery store—turn out to be incredibly difficult.

To illustrate, try writing down everything a child has to do to stack up three blocks in a little tower—*everything*, including how she finds the next block, how she moves her hand to it, what position she holds her hand, how she grasps the block, which direction she moves it. . . . And then try to figure out how she knows what to do next.

This sort of thing can lead to misunderstandings about AI, because theorem-proving programs look impressive and block-stackers don't. When an AI researcher shows a layman his proudest accomplishment, a seemingly simpleminded program he has slaved over for years, the reaction is often, "So what?" In the late 1960s and early 1970s, for example, the AI group at MIT really did tackle the block prob-

lem. On command, a simulated robot arm would manipulate simulated blocks on a simulated tabletop. Blocks World was the name for the collection of programs needed. At various times dozens of people worked with it. Graduate students wrote theses about it, some of them milestones in natural language understanding, planning, and computer vision. And in the end, the system could stack and unstack the blocks on request about as well as a human three-year-old. (Among other things, the computer had to be told that when building a tower, don't try to pick up the block on the bottom of the tower and put it on top. . . .)

In fact, the really striking thing about most AI systems is not how smart they are but how limited they are. Commercial expert systems are idiot savants: Mycin knew all about blood diseases, but it had no idea what a patient was, or what a human being is all about. Commercial natural language systems "understand" language in roughly the same sense that the family dog understands "dinner" or "walk." The vision system has not been built that can recognize a human face, nor is there a robot that can set the table for dinner.

We're simply so accustomed to the marvels of everyday thought that we never wonder about it.
—MIT's Marvin Minsky in his essay, "Why People Think Computers Can't"

In part, what makes our everyday, commonsense abilities so extraordinary is the sheer quantity of knowledge involved. A current-generation expert system can handle at most a few thousand rules before the program gets intolerably slow (though more advanced computers may soon speed that up considerably). A chess master, say, seems to use the equivalent of roughly 50,000 rules in his domain of expertise. But all of us know how to put our shoes on in the morning. We know how to cross the street. We know not to pick up the bottom block of the tower. We know millions, perhaps billions of commonsense things. And we can only guess at how many "rules" that corresponds to.

AI researchers learned a long time ago that knowledge is *the* critical element in intelligence, more important even than reasoning ability. Newell, Simon, Shaw, and their col-

---

BRUCE BUCHANAN: MAKING KNOWLEDGE USEFUL

The only way to get a computer to act intelligently is to give it plenty of knowledge about the task at hand, says Stanford's Bruce B. Buchanan.

The problem is that putting the knowledge in the computer is like cramming for an exam. First you teach it a long list of facts, then the special cases, then some rules of thumb, then examples from the real world, then some. . . . It goes on and on. "So one of the critical research problems in AI," says Buchanan, "is finding efficient means of building new knowledge bases."

For more than a decade, Buchanan has been a leader in developing expert systems—programs that distill the experience of a doctor, or a lawyer, or an accountant, so that a computer can give near-human advice. Today he is one of the senior principal investigators of Stanford's Heuristic Programming Project, in which some 70 faculty, researchers, and graduate students are investigating how computers can use and represent knowledge.

Buchanan himself is concentrating on three projects. One project is to teach computers how to learn in a medical setting—specifically, how to extract a general rule about diagnosing jaundice by studying individual patients' case histories. A second is to write programs that can generate hypotheses and test them; the specific application is to determine the structure of proteins from data supplied by nuclear magnetic resonance and other techniques. And the third is to write programs that can evaluate the contents and quality of certain medical research articles, and then derive their own inferences.

"Medicine is a fairly strong focus of what I do," says Buchanan. In fact, much of Stanford's pioneering work in expert systems has been done in collaboration with the medical school. "It's a very good test bed," he says, "and nobody will allow us to cut corners."

---

leagues worked for years to perfect the General Problem Solver, a program that was supposed to reason its way through almost any kind of problem on general principles. It didn't. To think about chess, it turned out that you had to know about chess. To think about physics problems, you had to know about physics problems. As Stanford's Feigenbaum likes to say, "Knowledge is power."

Nowhere is knowledge more critical than in understanding natural language. Language is much more than words. Somewhere beneath the surface structure of human language there lies an enormous body of shared knowledge about the world, an acute sensitivity to nuance and context, an intuitive insight into human goals and beliefs.

Consider: "Will you come to dinner with me this evening?" On one level it is a simple request, but on another level it might symbolize a desperate longing for love.

Or consider the question, "Could you pass the salt?" A robot might reply "Yes," which would be very annoying. Allowing for the occasional smart-aleck, most of us know a request when we hear it. Finally, consider a sentence like "John hit Mary," which instantly brings to mind a whole swirl of ideas about John, about Mary, about their relationship, and about what might happen next—such as "Mary hit John back."

Machines have to know all these things if they are going to "understand" the expectations and intuitive behavior that permeate the lives of human beings. And in fact, much work in AI during the past decade has been devoted to codifying such knowledge and storing it in a form machines can use.

Minsky at MIT devised an approach called frames. On the screen, a frame looks somewhat like a questionnaire, filled in with facts about a single subject or concept. A frame for Snoopy, for example, would include such facts as Breed ("beagle") and Owner ("Charlie Brown"). A frame can also pull in information from other frames, so that Snoopy is a Dog, a Dog is a Mammal, and so on.

That kind of information, however, is little help to a computer trying to understand a sequence of events. So Roger Schank and his colleagues at Yale developed an approach called scripts. A script is a sequence of typical steps in an everyday scenario. A restaurant script, for example, might list: making the reservation, being seated, reading the menu, ordering, and, before departing, leaving a tip. (Of course, the computer must be told that this is a tip for service and not a tout of the winner of the fifth race at the track.) Schank has also made a start at modeling human emotions such as love or ambition, while other researchers are trying to codify our intuitive grasp of physics or psychology.

But common sense is more than lots of knowledge. If that were the whole story, then all we would have to do is build bigger and faster computers, put hordes of graduate students to work typing in more facts and rules, and the machines would get smarter. But it doesn't quite happen that way. Things go on deep in the mind that we don't fully understand, that are different in kind.

It is almost mystical. People talk about intuition, insight, inspiration, gestalt—not because those words explain anything, but because they capture this sense of a spontaneous, holistic part of ourselves forever beyond understanding.

On the other hand, maybe that part of the mind is not magical so much as just . . . hidden. Maybe, for all our sense of being self-aware, we are almost oblivious to what really goes on in our brains.

Certainly that is what psychologists and neuroscientists seem to be telling us. Consider the capabilities involved in strolling down the sidewalk, for example. Leaving aside such things as balance and coordination, you still have to see where you are going, which means you somehow have to make sense out of the ever-changing swirl of motion and color and light and shadow.

To accomplish this, you have at your command roughly 100 million receptor cells—the rods and cones—in the retina of each eye. The retina also contains four other layers of nerve cells; all together the system probably makes the equivalent of 10 billion calculations a second before the image information even gets to the optic nerve. And once the visual data reaches the brain, the cerebral cortex has more than a dozen separate vision centers to process it. In fact, it has been estimated that vision in one form or another involves some 60 percent of the cortex.

Of course, you remain blissfully unaware of all this. You simply glance across the street and think "Oh, there's Sally."

But now consider what *that* involved. Somehow, without your conscious mind being aware of it, you compared the visual image from across the street with all the remembered images of all the millions of people and trees and dogs and ashtrays that you have seen in your life. And once you found the right image, you matched the face with Sally's name; with a whole set of shared experiences; with how you feel about her; with the outrageous thing your boss did that morning that you can't wait to tell her about. And all this is simply there, pouring into your conscious mind before you've even lifted your arm to wave.

Try another example. You beat your brains out against a problem at work and then, "Aha!"—the solution flashes on in neon lights. Now, how did you do that?

Nobody else knows either. But a big part of it—in fact, a big part of human problem solving in general—seems to be that jolt of recognition, that ability to suddenly see things as a whole. Simon and his colleagues at Carnegie-Mellon have shown in a number of experiments that experts rarely use logic and reason to solve problems, say, in physics. Instead, they just seem to look at a problem and say, "Aha! That's a conservation of energy problem," or "Aha! That's an ideal gas law problem." Unlike novices, who painfully step their way through, experts seem to store the appropriate problem-solving sequences so that they are simply there when needed.

AI researchers have only just begun to explore this dynamic, holistic part of the mind. They've built programs that can learn, at least in a limited sense. They've built programs that can "recognize" things or that can reorganize their knowledge. They've even built programs

GEOFFREY HINTON: PARALLEL INTELLIGENCE

Like a busy bank with one teller, even the fastest modern computers still run big programs essentially one step at a time, the way the first computers did in the 1940s. The human brain gets around this bottleneck by putting billions of neurons to work simultaneously. So a lot of people are trying to copy the brain, designing computers that have maybe a million processors working in parallel.

Carnegie-Mellon University's Geoffrey Hinton believes these new machines, besides being faster, will teach us new ways to think about thinking: "The kind of hardware you have available determines the kind of problems you can do well."

For example, "If you're in a jungle and you see a tiger," he says, "you don't just make a visual identification. You recognize a great deal more about tigers, and danger, and running."

Hinton and his colleagues are working on a way of doing this kind of processing. Known as the Boltzmann architecture, it is both a programming concept and a hardware design. It will take input data (say, a jungle scene), combine it with previously stored "memories" (what a tiger looks like), and search for the best-fitting interpretation. It will do that by first jostling the computer's many processors into a random state and then "cooling" them down; the overall structure of the input data and the memories force the processors to "crystallize" around the desired best match (a tiger).

Boltzmann will find this best match, says Hinton, even if the initial data was incomplete. (Say you only got a glimpse of the tiger's tail.) And a single input (the tiger's tail) might find a match within a much richer structure of information (Tiger, Danger, Run . . .), just as it happens with people.

Boltzmann has been tested so far only on ordinary, one-step-at-time computers, and only with very small problems. "Until we know how to do the proper programming," says Hinton, "we wouldn't know what kind of parallel system to build."

that make analogies, which may be a key to the whole thing: After all, people learn by analogy and even come up with creative new ideas by analogy.

None of these programs can perform with anything like the ease at human command. In part, this is because it is almost impossible, by definition, to look into the unconscious part of the mind. So it is hard to know what the programs are supposed to be modeling and how they ought to be constructed. (To get a feel for the problem, try to catch yourself in the act of having an idea. Now figure out where it came from.)

But just as important is the fact that the current generation of computer hardware is simply not up to the task. While signals move much faster through silicon than through nerve cells, almost all modern computers still chug through problems one step at a time. The brain beats them out at things like instantaneous recognition and "Aha!" problem-solving because it has millions or billions of neurons working simultaneously.

In fact, the effort to build computers organized more like the brain is one of the frontiers of AI research. Computers are being designed that will have up to one million processors operating in parallel. AI researchers are devising new ways to program these machines—and it may well be that the exercise will teach us new ways to think about thinking.

My operations might be incessantly baffled, and at last my work be imperfect, yet when I considered the improvement which every day takes place in science and mechanics, I was encouraged to hope my present attempts would at least lay the foundations of future success. Nor could I consider the magnitude and complexity of my plan as any argument of its impracticability. It was with these feelings that I began the creation of a human being.
—Victor Frankenstein

The quest to create and manipulate thinking life is the stuff of legend—and the reports are not reassuring: Frankenstein. Joseph Golem. Faust. Pandora. The Sorcerer's Apprentice. Thus the inevitable question, asked with undertones of fascination and horror: Will a machine ever think? *Really* think?

One possible answer is: Who cares? If a machine can do its job very, very well, what does it matter if it *really* thinks?

Another answer is: No, machines can't think, because thinking and feeling are simply too complicated. Even if we someday come to understand all the laws and principles that govern the mind, that does not mean that we can duplicate it. Understanding astrophysics does not allow us to build a galaxy.

Still another answer is: Yes, machines will think some day—but not as we do. Some people might argue on philosophical grounds that nonhuman thinking cannot possibly be *real* thinking.

But in his book *Mindstorms*, MIT computer scientist Seymour Papert hypothesizes an analogous argument against "artificial flight" in the early days of the 20th century: "This leads us to imagine skeptics who would say, 'You mathematicians deal with idealized fluids— the real atmosphere is vastly more complicated,' or 'You have no reason to suppose that airplanes and birds work the same way—birds have no propellers, airplanes have no feathers.' But the premises of these criticisms are true only in the most superficial sense: the same *principles* (e.g., Bernoulli's law) apply to real as well as ideal fluids, and they apply whether the fluid flows over a feather or an aluminum wing."

But none of this gets at the soul-disturbing essence of the question. If a machine can be made to think, then perhaps *we* are machines.

Most people hate this idea. Okay, they might say, we're machines in the sense that our bones and muscles and blood have to obey the laws of physics. Our enzymes and DNA follow the laws of chemistry. These gray blobs of protoplasm in our skulls are simply massive tangles of neurons. "But *I* am not a machine. I'm here. I'm *me*. I'm alive."

It may be a reaction to the thought of becoming cold, rigid, and machinelike. Given voice, the feeling is often expressed as something like, "Computers are reason and logic; you can simulate *that* part of the mind. But people are also intuition, sensuality, and emotion; that is the essence of humanity, and that is something you cannot simulate."

In *Computer Power and Human Reason*, a 1976 attack on AI, former AI researcher Joseph Weizenbaum of MIT put it like this: "Sometimes when my children were still little, my wife and I would stand over them as they lay sleeping in their beds. We spoke to each other in silence, rehearsing a scene as old as mankind itself. It is as Ionesco told his journal: 'Not everything is unsayable in words, only the living truth.' "

But MIT computer scientist Marvin Minsky isn't so sure that emotions are somehow more mysterious and ineffable than reason. "It is a mistaken idea in our culture that feeling and emotion are deep, whereas intelligence, how we get ideas, how we think is easy to understand," he told *Psychology Today* in 1983. "If you ask someone, 'Why are you mad at your wife?' they might say, 'Well, it's really because my boss was mean to me, and I can't get mad at him.' It seems to me that people understand the dynamics of emotions quite well. But they have no idea at all . . . how thought works."

Philosopher John Searle of the University of California at Berkeley thinks of the computer as "an immensely useful tool in the study of language and the study of the mind." But it can't really think, he maintains, because all it does is manipulate symbols—and those symbols don't mean anything to the computer. It simply has no attribute that corresponds to consciousness or awareness.

Not surprisingly, the people who work in AI tend to find these arguments less than compelling. While opinions differ widely as to whether machines will ever *really* think, researchers tend to be more comfortable thinking of themselves as machines.

No one has a really good answer to the question of consciousness in a machine, because no one really knows what consciousness is. In fact, given the enormous amount of hidden processing that goes on in our brains, it almost seems presumptuous to think that *we* are self-aware. But be that as it may, at least some people in the AI community argue that self-awareness is an "emergent" property of complex systems. The idea is that no one element in the mind is aware of conscious by itself, just as no one atom or enzyme in a cell is alive by itself. Yet when those atoms are

---

TERRY WINOGRAD: ENGLISH AS A COMPUTER LANGUAGE

In the early 1970s, Terry Winograd tried to program computers to understand natural languages—English or French as opposed to programming languages such as Pascal and Basic. While at MIT, he developed a reasonably successful program called SHRDLU. Given the command, "Put the blue pyramid on top of the red block," SHRDLU would translate the words into short program fragments. Using the sentence structure as a guide, it would then arrange these fragments into a complete program. Finally it would pick up the blue pyramid and move it into place. Thus, SHRDLU showed that it "understood" the command.

A decade later Winograd's approach has changed profoundly. He now spends most of his hours trying to understand language as a social act, as a web of commitments between one person and another. He has been working with the Center for the Study of Language and Information, founded at Stanford in late 1983. The center is an attempt, probably the first, to bring together researchers in artificial intelligence with those in language-related fields—linguistics, philosophy, psychology, and computer science.

Winograd sees much value in getting such people talking to each other; programming, like language, embodies many formal concepts still imperfectly understood. But he isn't so sure that all of this analytic firepower will be the key to natural language programming. "The idea is that language and thought can be modeled by such things as formal logic," he says. "But I think that that is grossly oversimplified." Winograd feels that a great deal of what goes on when people talk happens at a deep, perhaps unconscious level we don't yet comprehend. "What people actually do has very little in common with formal logic," he says. "And what's missing is the social dimension. Once you take into account what you are using a word for, what part it plays in discourse, there is no boundary to the meaning of that word."

---

brought together in an exquisitely ordered patterns, they *are* life.

And if one day we do build machines that think, that are aware . . .? In 1514, Nicholaus Copernicus moved the Earth from the center of the universe and made it one planet among many—and changed humankind's relationship with God. In 1859 Charles Darwin published *On the Origin of Species* and made *Homo sapiens* one animal among many—and gave us a far less exalted view of our own significance. And now the creation of an artificial consciousness could change our very ideas of "self." The consequences will surely be just as profound.

And that's not necessarily a threatening thought. What if we are machines? If so, we are marvelously complex and surprising machines. Perhaps the human mind is only a processor of neuronal symbols. Perhaps a snowflake is only a collection of water molecules. Perhaps *The Magic Flute* is only a sequence of sound waves.

And perhaps, in trying to emulate the essence of the human mind, AI will only reaffirm how unique and precious it really is.

4

Matthew Zeidenberg

Modeling the Brain

The idea of simulating the brain formed the foundation for much of the early work in artificial intelligence. The brain was seen as a "neural network," that is, a set of nodes, or neurons, connected by communication lines. Lately, there has been a substantial revival in the use of neural-network models, or connectionism, as the field is often called (see reference 1). Connectionist models are applicable to a variety of cognitive-science problems, including natural-language processing, speech processing, and vision.

One major advocate of connectionism is Daniel W. Hillis. His Connection Machine is more brain-like than a traditional computer. Hillis points out that in a conventional computer, most of the silicon lies inactive most of the time. At any given time, only the CPU [central processing unit] and a very small part—a few bytes—of the memory are active (see reference 2). The Connection Machine is composed of many processor/memory units, most of which are active at the same time. Douglas R. Hofstadter (see references 3 and 4) has long been an advocate of a similar view of cognition, with interacting actors in a cognitive process exchanging messages.

On the simplest level, the brain functions as follows: Neurons activate or inhibit the firing of other neurons. Whether or not a particular neuron fires depends on the inhibitory or excitatory inputs from all the neurons connected to it. Somehow, the activations of all the neurons, how they communicate with one another, and the nervous system's interactions with the environment determine your memories and thoughts—at least as far as philosophical materialists are concerned.

Of course, neurophysiologists, while still largely in the dark as to the operation of higher cognitive functions, have learned a great deal more about the brain than is evident in this simple model. Neverthe-

THE PERCEPTRON CONTROVERSY

The 1950s brought substantial interest in what neural networks could do. After all, if we understood their behavior, we would be able to understand the brain and the mind. That was the hope. One of the most popular variants of the neural network was the "perceptron," invented by Frank Rosenblatt. The perceptron was a "perception machine."

Perception has always been the most difficult area in AI, and the area in which the least progress has been made. The ability to decipher the world, to break it up into meaningful parts, is a human ability of astonishing complexity.

Ironically, areas that people view as difficult—like playing chess or solving a chemical structure—are areas in which AI programs have had the most success, although they seldom equal the abilities of the best human experts.

Yet, the computer has not been programmed that can learn a language the way any infant does, or given a scene of any room, can recognize all the objects in the room. Thus, machines that can perceive have always held special interest.

What Is a Perceptron?

A perceptron is a neural-network model with an array of input units, each of which can take on the value 0 or 1. This array is called the *retina*, in analogy to human vision.

The perceptron also has another array of units called the *predicates*. Each predicate can be connected to any subset of the units in the retina and can compute any linear function of the values of these units.

Finally, the predicate units are connected to one or more decision units, which return a single answer—yes or no—depending on the values of the units in the retina. Thus, a perceptron can perform an elementary classification task—that is, it can classify input patterns by some property. Since perception is basically a classification problem (i.e., classifying objects as chairs, tables, or whatever), the hope was that the perceptron model, properly elaborated, could account for complex perception.

The Great Debate

The controversy over perceptrons continued for some time, and in 1969, Marvin Minsky and Seymour Papert wrote a formal analysis of perceptrons (see reference 7), or, more precisely, the single-layer perceptron, which squelched interest in them.

Minsky and Papert proved, mathematically, that there were certain functions of input that the single-layer perceptron could not compute. One of the simplest was the parity function, which tells if the number of ones in the input is even or odd. If the perceptron could not compute such a simple function, they reasoned, it could hardly perform the complex tasks required for perception and intelligence.

At the time, Minsky and Papert's work appeared to have destroyed perceptrons and perceptron-like models as viable lines of AI research. Little attention was paid to the fact that they directed their criticism at a very simple system, the single-layer perceptron.

If you add one more layer of units between the input units and the predicates, the computational power of the machine rises abruptly, and Minsky and Papert's critique no longer applies. And if you add multiple layers, it is difficult to characterize formally the network's behavior.

This difference was not well understood at the time, and Minsky and Papert's work put a strong damper on research. It didn't discourage everyone, however: Throughout this time, Steven Grossberg of Boston University continued detailed studies of brain-like systems.

---

less, scientists in the 1950s were amazed at what simple systems of nodes with excitatory and inhibitory connections could do. (See the text box "The Perceptron Controversy.")

In 1943, Warren S. McCulloch and Walter Pitts proved that any neural-network model in which a finite amount of information could define the state of an individual neuron could be modeled on a standard computer. The "fi-

nite amount of information" assumption is a big one: The number of bits needed to describe the state of a given neuron may be so large that it makes the simulation slow and impractical.

IS THE BRAIN RELEVANT?

A strong school in AI [artificial intelligence] feels that studying the brain is not the most fruitful road to understanding thought. The brain represents just one way of making a thinking machine, and certainly not the optimal way. Traditional AI sees thought as a series of problems to solve, and believes strongly that there is no philosophical reason why a computer can't solve them. The basis for this belief is the Church-Turing thesis, which roughly states that if a function is computable, you can compute it with a conventional computer—formally, a Turing machine. This thesis cannot be proved, but it is widely accepted because no one can think of a counterexample.

Daniel Dennett of Tufts University argues that neurophysiologists, working from the "bottom up"—that is, from the minute details up to the overall problem to be solved—in an attempt to understand human cognition, and computer scientists, working from the "top down," may ultimately both reach their goal. But he thinks the computer scientists will reach it first (see reference 5). The argument is: If I take a computer running a spreadsheet, and try to figure out what the program is doing by looking at the electrical currents inside, I won't progress as quickly as I would if I tried to write another program that also runs a spreadsheet.

In an approach that is in between those of the neurophysiologists and the more traditional AI researchers, David E. Rumelhart, James L. McClelland, and their colleagues don't dismiss the brain as irrelevant to the functioning of the mind. Rather, they feel that, by experimenting with neural networks, they can gain insight into how the brain copes with the problems it has to solve.

PARALLELISM

Another reason for studying brain-like models is their parallelism. The "circuitry" of the brain is much slower than a computer's. In order for the brain to work as fast as it does—psychologists have shown that we can recognize objects in a split second—many neurons must work in parallel. In contrast, many AI programs run very slowly. The hope is: If we can find ways to run AI programs in parallel, they will run in a reasonable amount of time.

Parallel computation has been a busy area in computer science over the past 10 years. Most mainstream research on parallel computing is quite different from the neural-network approach. Researchers have studied algorithms for mesh-connected arrays of processors, pipelines, processors arranged in a tree-like fashion, and distributed systems of interconnected processors, to cite just a few.

Neural networks represent only one line of research in parallel computation. Basically, you must answer two fundamental questions in designing a parallel computer system: How do you connect the processors for communication purposes? And how much computing power and memory do you put in each processor? Many researchers find no reason to restrict themselves to neural-network models, which represent a very small subset of the possible parallel-computing models.

Nevertheless, neural-network researchers think that their models, by being most faithful to what we know about the brain, will show the most success. Unfortunately, neural networks have seldom been built in hardware; normally, they must be simulated in software. These simulations have typically been very slow, since one processor had to do the work of many. Until we build effective parallel-processing hardware, connectionist models are unlikely to provide computationally efficient solutions to AI problems.

THE CONNECTION MACHINE

One attempt to build a parallel computer is Hillis's Connection Machine, which has many small processors, each containing a small amount of memory. The machine has a fixed architecture—that is, certain processors are physically connected to certain others. Any pair of processors not physically connected can communicate in software via special processors called "routers," which exist to forward messages. It is critical that connections between processors be programmable so that the machine is not limited in the types of networks it can realize.

Hillis's machine can realize a wide variety of network models. It can adapt itself to the mesh-like architecture used in image processing, as well as to conventional semantic networks for knowledge representation. Recently, the Connection Machine has shown that it is well suited to database tasks, which are closely related to semantic networks. Hillis's company, Thinking Machines Corporation, has built a prototype of the machine, which it is marketing. The company provides a version of the popular AI programming language, LISP, that allows you access to the power of parallelism without having to know the details of the machine. On the Connection Machine, you can implement a neural network in hardware rather than in software, so the network will run much faster.

VARIETIES OF NEURAL NETWORKS

Most neural-network models owe something to perceptrons but are more general. The typical neural-network model consists of a set of nodes, or neurons, and connections (see figure 1). Each node contains a real number, which is its *activation*. Each connection also contains a real number, its *weight*. These numbers are usually positive and usually have a maximum value. Some of the units are connected to input and output. The weights represent the strength of the connection between two neurons.

Generally, a neural network is a dynamic system, moving from one state to the next. As such, it has a mathematical rule that takes the system from one state to the next. An infinite number of such rules are possible. However, we usually want to constrain our models to those that influence the activation of a given node based only on the activations of the nodes connected to it and the weights of the connections to those nodes.

Neural networks are not explicitly programmed like a conventional computer. Rather, they obey laws, or rules, like a physical system. You must program a conventional computer, but a neural network simply behaves. Neural-network designers view this as an advantage, since it provides a mechanism whereby intelligence can arise from physical law.

Figure 1 _____

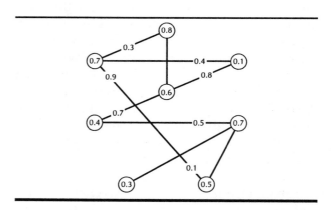

In a typical neural network, every node has an activation, and every connection between nodes has a weight. A rule, which varies from network to network, governs the way in which weights and activations change over time.

One of the simplest of these rules is a linear rule. You compute the activation of a given node as the sum of the products of the weight of each node it is connected to and the strength of that connection. Often such a rule is *thresholded:* Values that go above a certain threshold are cut off, to avoid arbitrarily large activation values. There are many variants of linear rules.

Another rule, suggested by D. O. Hebb (see reference 6) strengthens the connection between two nodes that are highly activated at the same time. Some versions of the Hebbian learning rule allow inputs, called teaching inputs, to influence the change in weight. This type of rule is a formalization of associationist psychology, which holds that associations are built up between things that occur together.

COMPETITIVE LEARNING

Learning is, perhaps, the most important phenomenon in psychology. Early neural-network researchers were anxious to show how networks could learn patterns in the input presented to them—that is, how they could come to perceive these patterns *on their own.*

One of the methods that various researchers have devised over the years is *competitive learning.* This method has a bottom level of input units that contains the pattern to be input to the system. The level above the input units consists of clusters of units. Each unit in a cluster competes with the other units in the cluster for the right to recognize an input pattern. Over a learning period, each unit in a cluster comes to recognize a subset of the patterns presented to it. Thus, each cluster represents a classification, or group, of input patterns.

In competitive learning, each unit in each cluster is connected to all the input units. The weights of the connections are initially set to random values. The random weights cause certain units in clusters to start responding more to particular input patterns, since the weights of the connections to particular input units are stronger to some than to others.

As the learning proceeds, the weights change. As particular units in the cluster become sensitive to particular units in the input pattern, the weights connecting the associated pairs of units increase, at the expense of unassociated pairs of units. Different units in the same cluster inhibit each other, so that only one unit in a cluster "wins" the right to recognize a given pattern.

Thus, over time, different units in a cluster come to "recognize" different properties of input patterns. For instance, a cluster of two units might separate all the input patterns into those that are mostly on (i.e., have most of their units highly activated) and those that are mostly off. Larger clusters would make more discriminating classifications.

There may be an additional level of clusters that uses the first level of clusters as its input pattern. This level could extract more complex features from the bottom-level input pattern.

Rumelhart and David Zipser applied the competitive-learning paradigm to letter and word recognition. Letters were represented by bits on a grid, which was the input pattern for the competitive-learning system. The system came to spontaneously recognize an "A" and a "B" in a fixed position on the grid.

This is very interesting, for it illustrates a potential mechanism by which people may have learned to recognize letters. This mechanism is completely general, since it presupposes nothing about the letters except that they can be distinguished from one another.

BOLTZMANN MACHINES

An important class of neural networks simulates the behavior of physical systems. Physical systems have a tendency to move into states of minimum potential energy. A simple example of this is a ball rolling into the valley between two hills. At the top of the hill, potential energy is high; in the valley, it is low.

This process is called *relaxation.* John Hopfield has shown that a certain simple evolutionary rule for a neural network will lead to relaxation. Systems such as Hopfield's, which resemble thermodynamic systems like the atoms in a room, are called Boltzmann Machines, after Ludwig Boltzmann, a physicist who made major contributions to thermodynamics. Boltzmann Machines are widely used in a variety of neural-network applications.

In vision and in playing games, you can often formulate solutions to problems, such as recognizing a set of objects or discovering the best move, as constraint-satisfaction problems. For instance, in chess, the constraints are the possible ways that a piece can move, and the total "goodness" of the move, as measured by some formula, taking into account pieces captured, board position, and so on. Relaxation can correspond closely to constraint-satisfaction—a Boltzmann Machine can satisfy constraints automatically.

DISTRIBUTED REPRESENTATIONS

One important feature of many neural-network models is their *distributed* nature. A standard semantic network, like those used in early knowledge-representation schemes, consists of a set of nodes connected in some fashion. Each node represents a single word or concept. If the network is "thinking" of the word "cat," the node for "cat" is activated, and all other nodes are not. This is a *local* representation.

In contrast, in a distributed network, nodes don't have a simple meaning; rather, an individual concept is represented by a pattern over all the nodes. For instance, if there are 10 nodes, activating nodes 1, 3, 4, and 7 might represent the concept "gorilla," while activating nodes 2, 4, 5, and 7 might represent the closely related concept "chimp." Concepts that are closely related have similar representations.

A parallel distributed-processing (PDP) network, a neural network that uses distributed representation, offers the advantage of *automatic generalization*. If I want to represent the concept "gorillas are hairy," I strengthen the connection between all the nodes composing the concept "gorilla" and all the nodes composing the concept "hairy." As a result, since most of the nodes in "gorilla" are also used in "chimp," an association is also made between "chimp" and "hairy." This is how automatic generalization works. In a local representation, where "gorilla" and "chimp" are represented by separate nodes, a connection between "gorilla" and "hairy" would not imply a connection between "chimp" and "hairy."

Another advantage of a distributed representation is its insensitivity to damage. In a local representation, if the system loses the node representing "grandmother," it loses its concept of grandmother. People don't display disorders like this; there are no people who are completely normal except that they have lost their concept of grandmother. This has led to the opinion that the brain doesn't use local representation.

In a distributed representation, in order to lose a concept, you must lose *all* the nodes representing it. If you lose only one or two of the nodes, the concept may be degraded, but it's still there. This is closer to the type of memory loss seen in older adults: Memory is degraded in a uniform fashion.

SCHEMATA

One criticism of neural-network models is that they're not as flexible at representing knowledge as standard methods are. The standard methods include the local semantic network, of which Marvin Minsky's *frame* and Roger

Schank's *script* are varieties. For instance, a frame description of a bedroom would contain information about all the objects in that room and how they relate to one another. The relations between objects are represented by labeled links.

Cognitive psychologists, notably developmental psychologists like Jean Piaget, use the concept of a *schema*. A schema is a mirror—in the mind—of a real situation. As children, and as adults, we learn new associations and relations between objects and integrate them into our schemata.

It's not immediately clear how a neural-network model can account for knowledge represented in a schema; however, Rumelhart, Paul Smolensky, McClelland, and Geoffrey Hinton have shown that it's possible. They first gathered data from subjects about rooms—kitchens, bedrooms, offices, living rooms, and bathrooms. They took 40 words associated with rooms and asked each subject whether each word was associated with each room. Then, they set up a network that had each of the 40 words represented by a single node. They set the weight of a connection between two nodes to correspond to the extent to which the two tended to be used together when a single subject described a single room.

The network uses Hopfield's energy-minimization rule. When a single descriptor is "clamped on" (i.e., when its activation is permanently set to its maximum value), the system relaxes into one of five states, or rooms, since each room implies a constraint as to which words can occur together.

In the network, don't explicitly define the schemata; you only set the associations between pairs of descriptors. The schema emerges out of the network as a natural consequence of its behavior. Thus, the schemata are not explicitly represented in the network, but rather are simply patterns of activation across a set of descriptors.

This system has several nice properties. First, it explains how schema are activated when you have incomplete information—that is, why you think "kitchen" when you see "refrigerator." This corresponds to the "clamping on" of a single descriptor.

Since schemata are patterns rather than single units, this system allows for more flexibility in representing things. A slightly different version of a particular object can correspond to a slight change in the weights. And closely related schemata, such as "woman" and "girl," can overlap. In a more elaborate scheme, each descriptor in a schema can itself be a schema. The number of connections you need, however, rises quickly.

COGNITIVE HIERARCHIES

Often neural-network models are ordered into hierarchies. Several levels exist in such a hierarchy, each composed of a set of units. Typically, units that receive input are at the bottom of the system, and units that give output are at the top. In a bottom-up system, units at each level connect to other units on their own level and influence units on levels above them. In a top-down system, units again connect to units on their own level but influence units on levels below.

Top down and bottom up are familiar concepts in cognitive science. For instance, in sentence perception, these terms refer to how different-size linguistic elements, the phoneme (sound), morpheme (word element), word, phrase, and sentence, interact with one other. The HEARSAY-II speech-recognition program from Carnegie Mellon was one of the first AI programs to integrate knowledge from several levels, storing its results in a global data structure called the blackboard.

Does the overall perception of a word help you to perceive all the letters in it, individually, in a top-down fashion? Most psychologists would say yes. For instance, psychologists have done experiments in which they show subjects non-words like BCAK and PLAM; the subjects interpret these words as BACK and PALM. The theoretical explanation is that the units representing letters activate the units representing words in a manner that is somewhat insensitive to the letter's position in the word. The unit for the whole word actually influences the perception of the individual sound. Neural-network models exist that model this process and others like it.

For example, in McClelland's programmable blackboard model of reading, units for letters and units for words are connected by a grid. A connection in the grid between a letter and a word is set to a positive value if the letter is in the word, and to zero if it isn't. The letter units reinforce the word units in a bottom-up fashion, and the word units influence the activation of the letter units in a top-down fashion. Thus, the network converges to the perception of a single word at a time.

The programmable blackboard model does not handle the perception of individual letters, but you could readily add a third level to the system, a level of letter subfeatures. Information would pass up and down in the network, from letter subfeature to letter to word, and back down again.

A PARALLEL READING NETWORK

One problem in creating a reading network is that people tend to read more than one word at a time. Since a single network reads only one word, it can't handle this. If the network tries to read more than one word, you get "cross-talk"; that is, if the input words are "bank" and "lane," the network will perceive both the two inputs and "lank" and "bane" as well. As a solution, McClelland proposes duplicate copies of networks. Duplicate individual word-recognition networks would have programmable connections instead of hard-wired connections between letters and words.

In addition to programmable networks, you could have a hard-wired network that represents the relationships between letters and words. This network programs all the programmable networks via connections to them. Thus, you could represent knowledge centrally instead of having to duplicate it several times. You can save memory space by loading a programmable network with only knowledge relevant to processing the word it currently encounters. McClelland has worked out the details of his model thoroughly.

The programmable blackboard model accounts for psychological data concerning such things as parallelism in reading and word misperception. It shows how useful the psychological modeling approach to AI is: In explaining a good deal of psychological data with a model, we get a system that is quite good at the job at hand. McClelland has constructed a similar model of speech recognition and built a model of a higher-level process.

PROCESSING SENTENCES

One important aspect of sentence understanding involves determining the various roles that the different parts of a sentence play. For instance, consider the following two sentences:

The house rented for $2000.
The man rented the car.

In the first sentence, the house is the thing rented; in the second, the man is the agent of the rental. Yet in the two sentences, the nouns "man" and "house" are in the same position. Somehow, the model must discern their different roles.

McClelland and Alan Kawamoto have developed a connectionist system to do this role assignment. Words are described by "semantic microfeatures"—basic dimensions that describe many objects and actions. For instance, two of the microfeatures describing nouns are *human* and *softness*, which have the values "human, nonhuman" and "soft, hard," respectively. Words are not directly represented in the system's networks, but in terms of the activations of units representing microfeatures.

The model has a group of units for each of the major roles that different nouns can play in an action. These roles are Agent (actor) Patient (acted upon), Instrument (thing used), and Modifier (adverbial word or clause). For instance, the sentence "The man ate the sandwich" would activate the microfeatures of "ate" and "man" in the set of units that corresponds to the Agent; this represents the fact that the Agent for the verb "ate" is "man."

The system is trained on a series of sentences. The correct role assignments for the training sentences are shown to the system. These assignments correspond to the activations of particular nodes. The system adjusts the connections between these nodes so that they reinforce one another.

After being trained on a sufficient number of sentences, the system can make correct role assignments for new sentences. It can even make accurate role assignments for sentences with some syntactic ambiguity. For instance, in the sentence "The man hit the boy with the mallet," the system figures out that "mallet" is the Instrument of "hit" instead of belonging to "boy," since "mallet" has microfeatures that fit in well with it being an Instrument.

The system also handles a number of other problems well, and generally does a good job in assigning roles. McClelland and Kawamoto are currently considering ways of expanding their system into a more complete language-understanding model—for instance, one that includes a network to parse sentences.

THE PROMISE FOR THE FUTURE

Neural networks are good for a variety of natural-language processing tasks, including letter recognition, reading, and sentence understanding. They are also useful in storing knowledge in schemata and in retrieving items from memory. They are not a cure-all for what ails AI and cognitive psychology, but they do bring a strong and biologically plausible new direction to many important problems.

Eventually, a connectionist model will probably be built of the natural-language-understanding process, since, as psychologists have shown, it involves integrating knowledge from many domains, including phonetics, morphology, syntax, and semantics. Connectionist models are particularly good at integrating these types of knowledge.

ACKNOWLEDGMENT

I would like to thank Greg Oden of the psychology department at the University of Wisconsin for introducing me to the subject of connectionism.

REFERENCES

1. Rumelhart, David E., James L. McClelland, et al. *Parallel Distributed Processing: Explorations in the*

Microstructures of Cognition, vols. 1 and 2. Cambridge, MA: MIT Press, 1986.

2. Hillis, W. Daniel. *The Connection Machine,* Cambridge, MA: MIT Press, 1986.

3. Hofstadter, Douglas R. *Godel, Escher, Bach: An Eternal Golden Braid.* New York: Basic Books, Inc., 1979.

4. Hofstadter, Douglas R. *Metamagical Themas.* New York: Basic Books Inc., 1985.

5. Dennet, Daniel. *Brainstorms.* Cambridge, MA: MIT Press, 1981.

6. Hebb, D. O. *The Organization of Behavior.* New York: John Wiley and Sons, 1949.

7. Minsky, Marvin, and Seymour Papert. *Perceptrons.* Cambridge, MA: MIT Press, 1969.

PART · TWO

MEMORY AND MENTAL REPRESENTATION

Sally P. Springer and Georg Deutsch

❖

Christine M. Temple

❖

Hans Wallach and Virginia Slaughter

❖

K. Anders Ericsson, William G. Chase,
and Steve Faloon

❖

Roger N. Shepard

❖

William Raft Kunst-Wilson
and R. B. Zajonc

❖

Ulric Neisser

❖

Elizabeth F. Loftus and Geoffrey R. Loftus

Memory and Mental Representation

T he study of memory is the core of psychology because memory is fundamental to mental life. In some deep way, we are our memories. Memory is necessary for essentially all of our behavior and thought. Bereft of memory, we could not type, eat, fantasize, read, watch television, listen to a friend's story, or boil rice. Furthermore, there is no known limit to memory. By contrast, no computer comes close to having the memory capacity and flexibility of humans.

VARIOUS QUESTIONS CAN BE ASKED ABOUT MEMORY—WHAT IS IT, ARE THERE different kinds, how does it develop, how is it controlled, and so on. The first two articles in this section treat memory from a neurological perspective. Sally P. Springer and Georg Deutsch, in an extended excerpt from their book *Left Brain/Right Brain*, discuss the research done on people who had severe cases of epilepsy and underwent as treatment for their condition a surgical procedure in which the corpus callosum, the major neural conduit between the two cerebral hemispheres, was cut. Springer and Deutsch present some of the history of the research on the corpus callosum and split-brain operations and then describe some of the findings from specific test cases. For example, a stimulus presented to the right visual field (to the right of the visual fixation point) could be verbally described, but a stimulus presented to the left visual field (to the left of the visual fixation point) could not, the reason being that the right visual field projects information to the left hemisphere, which for most people contains Broca's area, the speech center. However, these surgical subjects could respond appropriately to left visual field presentations—nude figures elicited a smile—and they could select objects, sight unseen, with their left hand (controlled primarily by the right hemisphere) in correspondence with the stimuli presented in the left visual field. Springer and Deutsch also describe the *cross-cuing* phenomenon, in which one hemisphere would "cue" the other about a stimulus when only one hemisphere had the information. In addition to exploring the laboratory findings on split-brain patients, Springer and Deutsch report on some of the everyday experiences of some of the subjects, including incidences of temporary muteness, neglect of the left side of the body, and more long-term problems in learning associations between names and faces.

SPLIT-BRAIN RESEARCH HAD A MAJOR IMPACT ON psychology. It helped to effect a rapprochement between psychology and neurology, it motivated psychologists to study cerebral asymmetries, and it led to some interesting speculation about consciousness and personal identity. Is consciousness a unitary phenomenon because introspection makes it seem that way, or are there separate aspects to consciousness that work together to produce an illusion of integrated consciousness? Is consciousness of self something that is more than the sum of its (neurophysiological) parts?

The view that the mind contains specialized mechanisms or modules receives support in Christine M. Temple's article "Developmental Memory Impairment: Faces and Patterns." Temple tells the fascinating saga of Dr. S, a highly intelligent woman and a medical doctor by training, who has had a lifelong problem in recognizing faces. Problems in recognizing faces are a form of visual agnosia (recognition disorder) known as *prosopagnosia*. Temple reports the results of various tests that were given to Dr. S in an attempt to pin down the precise nature of her problem. For example, Dr. S performed quite well on the Weschler Adult Intelligence Scale (WAIS) test; indeed, she showed exceptional verbal abilities. But she also performed well on perceptual tests, mental rotation tests, tests of common object recognition, and even face recognition tests for which testing was done after a very short retention interval. However, Dr. S performed poorly on tests of visual memory for designs and had problems recognizing the faces of famous people. Temple concludes that "there are brain mechanisms which are specific to face recognition." For the student, this article provides an engaging entry into the world of neuropsychology, an area that is linking up with cognitive psychology.

SEVERAL PAPERS IN THIS SECTION TAKE UP THE topics of long-term memory (and how its organizing influence can affect perception), short-term memory, and language comprehension. Hans Wallach and Virginia Slaughter, in "The Role of Memory in Perceiving Subjective Contours," examine a subject's tendency to perceive subjective, or illusory, contours. Such contours are not actually present in the stimulus, but subjects often report that they are. The authors' rationale was that if subjects were made familiar with the actual stimulus pattern, they would be more likely to see the pattern in an inducing, or "containing," pattern, where the latter was designed to promote the perception of the illusory contour. In two separate experiments, this is what they found. Wallach and Slaughter explain this result by framing it within the Gestalt view that perception is inherently organizational and that a perceptual set can facilitate this process.

K. Anders Ericsson, William G. Chase, and Steve Faloon, in "Acquisition of a Memory Skill," consider whether or not short-term memory performance can be expanded. The usual finding with normal adults is that short-term memory span is about 7 items, plus or minus 2. Over the course of a year and a half, Ericsson et al. gave the subject (S. F.) 230 hours of practice at recalling digits. His memory span went from an initial 7 digits to an incredible 80 digits, an accomplishment equivalent to some of the feats performed by the best-known mnemonist. Ericsson et al. provide evidence that S. F. used his expert knowledge of runners' times (he was a track and field enthusiast) to organize the digits and that he used a strategy of grouping the chunks of digits into bigger groups and adding more subgroups to the higher-level groups. The authors argue that S. F. did not actually increase his short-term memory capacity—his recall of letters was normal. Rather, he was able to recruit long-term memory knowledge and strategies to improve his short-term memory skill.

S. F.'s skill was of a verbal-propositional sort. What of short-term memory skills that involve nonverbal information in the form of mental images? Before 1960 the topic of mental imagery was largely ignored because the behaviorists felt that it was too "soft" and incapable of being studied in an objective way. However, the role of imagery in facilitating long-term memory for simple verbal materials became clear in the early 1960s. With the advent of information-processing models in the 1960s, some investigators sought to get at the imagery process in real time, or as it occurred in short-term memory. One such investigator was Roger N. Shepard, who discusses various questions about imagery in "The Mental Image." Apparently, visual imagery has played a crucial role in scientific and literary genius, as well as a more practical everyday role in clinical situations. But what is imagery? Shepard's answer is that it is not necessarily a picture in the head but a process that shares certain properties with perception. The trick is how to study it, and Shepard describes some of his own research, in which responses to imagined stimuli were similar to responses to real stimuli and that reaction time to judge rotated stimuli increased linearly with degrees of rotation. Shepard concludes that these results strongly suggest that mental imagery operates as an analog code that has evolved to process spatial structures and that this code is different from the more "logical" codes used in abstract reasoning.

IF THERE ARE ANALOG AND LOGICAL/PROPOSITIONAL codes, what of emotion and feeling codes? Until recently, cognitive psychology treated the topic of emotion in much the same way that behaviorists treated imagery: as something not worth considering. The next two papers in Part 2 address this topic. The study reported by William Raft Kunst-Wilson and R. B. Zajonc in "Affective Discrimination of Stimuli That Cannot Be Recognized" suggests that if a stimulus makes even minimal contact with long-term memory, it may take on some emotional significance, even if it does not arouse more explicit, and presumably conscious, recognition processes. The authors presented irregular octagons five times, each for a period of 1 millisecond (enough time to effect chance recognition), with the added instruction to subjects that they would not be able to see what was presented. In the second part of the experiment, subjects were asked which of a pair of octagons (old and new) they preferred, and then which they judged to be old. The results indicated that recognition performance was at chance but that old (originally shown) stimuli were preferred 60 percent of the time. The authors concluded that "individuals can ap-

parently develop preferences for objects in the absence of conscious recognition." Familiarity, even if unavailable to normal memorial routes to recollection, seems to promote a warm, cozy feeling.

Such results raise questions about the separability of affective/emotional and conscious/ cognitive systems in the mind. Questions about subliminal processing also come to mind. While the data in this area are controversial, it is nevertheless an interesting and viable area of research. There are other literatures in psychology that have touched upon this question—"incidental learning," "learning without awareness," "subception," and some attention studies come to mind here. More recently this general topic has been dubbed "implicit memory," in which experience is seen to affect performance on a task that does not seem to require conscious processing. Thus, the issue concerning the effect of minimally processed stimuli simply will not go away. Indeed, it seems to raise important theoretical and methodological questions (some of these are also addressed by the National Research Council in Part 5, the Applications section).

THE ROLE OF LONG-TERM MEMORY IN LANGUAGE comprehension is a central topic in cognitive psychology. Clearly there is no comprehension without memory, and, more to the point, there is no coherence to what we hear or read unless we can establish sensible connections between the linearly given inputs. That is, spoken language is spoken one word and one utterance at a time; written language is laid out in a spatial pattern that can only be accessed a little at a time. How, then, do people make language sequences coherent?

One popular answer to this question is that people construct "mental models" of the linguistic inputs. That is, they build a mental structure that connects important elements of the input in such a way that, given the current structure of long-term memory (what people know and what they believe is important), the elements form a personally meaningful pattern.

Clearly this is the case for autobiographical memory. But how accurate is it? For example, what do people remember of conversations they have had just a minute ago? Two days ago? Several years ago? In an article published in the journal *Cognition*, Ulric Neisser examines the case of John Dean's memory for two conversations he had in the presence of President Richard Nixon during the time of the Watergate fiasco. Watergate involved a break-in at the Democratic party headquarters at the Watergate Hotel in Washington, D.C., just before the presidential election of 1972, the eventual cover-up of which led to Nixon's resignation. It also led to a congressional investigation in 1973, in which John Dean, special counsel to the president, became the star witness. Nixon had taped a number of conversations and was forced to hand over the tapes to the congressional committee. Neisser reasoned that this was an ideal opportunity to compare Dean's testimony against what was actually said on the tapes. In this intriguing essay, Neisser concludes that Dean "remembered how he felt himself and what he had wanted, together with the general state of affairs; he didn't remember what anyone had actually said. His testimony had much truth in it, but not at the level of 'gist.' It was true at a deeper level." Neisser argues that motives anchor memories and that these memories can be "repisodic," the result of repetitions of several episodes rather than the recall of a particular episode.

THE FINAL SELECTION, "ON THE PERMANENCE OF Stored Information in the Human Brain," by Elizabeth F. Loftus and Geoffrey R. Loftus, raises a fitting question to conclude this section—is information in long-term memory in a permanent, unalterable, pristine form? The authors provide evidence that most psychologists hold this view, with the corollary assumption that special techniques such as electrical stimulation of the brain, hypnosis, or psychoanalysis can provide access to memory in its original, untainted form. Loftus and Loftus take two tacks in dispelling what they consider to be the myth of permanent memory. They first examine the evidence that comes from the special techniques and find it to be woefully inadequate: Brain surgeon Wilder Penfield's patients' reports of long-remembered experiences during electrical stimulation of the brain were rare, and many of these may have been inferences rather than the original memories; hypnosis may produce many fabrications and an uncritical willingness to report; and psychoanalysis may lead people to report a variety of fantasies, hunches, etc., that may be hard to distinguish from original memories. Second, the authors report experimental evidence that indicates that misleading information can be incorporated into a memory in such a way that it blends with it. The original memory is thereby lost as a distinct structure. In general, this is a sobering paper that makes us think deeply about our beliefs about long-term memory and about the faithfulness of recall in particular.

5

Sally P. Springer and Georg Deutsch

The Human Split Brain: Surgical Separation of the Hemispheres

In 1940, an article appeared in a scientific journal describing experiments on the spread of epileptic discharge from one hemisphere to the other in the brains of monkeys.[1] The author concluded that the spread occurred largely or entirely by way of the corpus callosum, the largest of several *commissures*, or bands of nerve fiber connecting regions of the left brain with similar areas of the right brain. Earlier, other investigators had observed that damage to the corpus callosum from a tumor or other problem sometimes reduced the incidence of seizures in human epileptics.[2] Together, these findings paved the wave for a new treatment for patients with epilepsy that could not be controlled in other ways: the split-brain operation.

Split-brain surgery, or *commissurotomy*, involves surgically cutting some of the fibers that connect the two cerebral hemispheres. The first such operations to relieve epilepsy were performed in the early 1940s on approximately two dozen patients. The patients subsequently gave scientists their first opportunity to study systematically the role of the corpus callosum in humans, a role that had been speculated on for decades.

The corpus callosum was a puzzle for researchers who expected to find functions commensurate with its large size and strategic location within the brain. Animal research had shown the consequences of split-brain surgery on a healthy organism to be minimal. The behavior of split-brain monkeys, for example, appeared indistinguishable from what it was before the operation. The apparent absence of any noticeable changes following commissurotomy led some scientists to suggest facetiously that the corpus callosum's only function was to hold the halves of the brain together and keep them from sagging.

Speculations on the philosophical implications of split-brain surgery go back to the nineteenth century and the writings of Gustav Fechner, considered by many to be the father of experimental psychology. Fechner considered consciousness to be an attribute of the cerebral hemispheres, and he believed that continuity of the brain was an essential condition for unity of consciousness. If it were possible to divide the brain through the middle, he speculated, something like the duplication of a human being would result. "The two cerebral hemispheres," he wrote, "while beginning with the same moods, predispositions, knowledge, and memories, indeed the same consciousness generally, will thereafter develop differently according to the external relations into which each enter."[3] Fechner considered this "thought experiment" involving separation of the hemispheres impossible to achieve in reality.

Fechner's views concerning the nature of consciousness did not go unchallenged. William McDougall, a founder of the British Psychological Society, argued strongly against the position that unity of consciousness depends on the continuity of the nervous system. To make his point, McDougall volunteered to have his corpus callosum cut if he ever got an incurable disease. He apparently wanted to show that his personality would not be split and that his consciousness would remain unitary.

McDougall never got the opportunity to put his ideas to the test, but the surgery Fechner thought an impossibility took place for the first time almost a century later. The issues these men raised have been among those explored by scientists seeking a fuller understanding of the corpus callosum through the study of split-brain patients.

CUTTING 200 MILLION NERVE FIBERS: A SEARCH FOR CONSEQUENCES

The First Split-Brain Operations on Humans

William Van Wagenen, a neurosurgeon from Rochester, New York, performed the first split-brain operations on humans in the early 1940s. Postsurgical testing by an investigator named Andrew Akelaitis showed surprisingly little in the way of deficits in perceptual and motor abilities.[4] The operation seemed to have had no effect on everyday behavior. Unfortunately, for some patients the surgery also seemed to do little to alleviate the condition responsible for the surgery in the first place. Success in relieving seizures seemed to vary greatly from patient to patient.

In retrospect, this variability seems attributable to two causes: (1) individual differences in the nature of the epilepsy in the patients and (2) variations in the actual surgical procedures used with each patient. Figure 1 shows the corpus callosum and the adjacent smaller commissures. Van Wagenen's operations varied considerably but usually included sectioning of the forward (anterior) half of the corpus callosum. In two patients, he also sectioned a separate fiber band known as the anterior commissure.

At the time, the importance of these factors was not known, and Van Wagenen soon discontinued the commissurotomy procedure in cases of intractable epilepsy. Clearly, it was not producing the dramatic results he had hoped for. Despite these discouraging findings, other investigators continued to study the functions of the corpus callosum in animals. A decade later, in the early 1950s, Ronald Myers and Roger Sperry made some remarkable discoveries that marked a turning point in efforts to study this enigmatic structure.

Myers and Sperry showed that visual information presented to one hemisphere in a cat with its corpus callosum cut would not be available to the other hemisphere.[5] In most higher animals, the visual system is arranged so that each eye normally projects to both hemispheres. But by cutting into the optic-nerve crossing, the *chiasm*, experimenters can limit where each eye sends its information. When this cut is made, the remaining fibers in the optic nerve transmit information to the hemisphere on the same side. Visual input to the left eye is sent only to the left hemisphere, and input to the right eye projects only to the right hemisphere.

Figure 1

The Major Interhemispheric Commissures

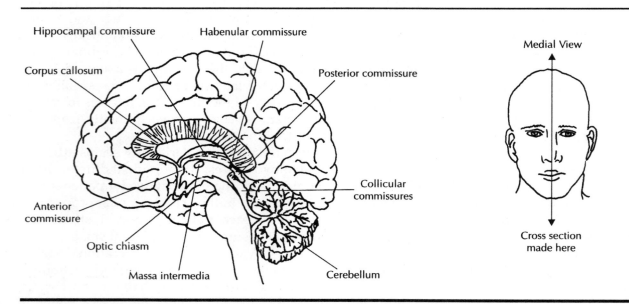

This is a sectional view of the right half of the brain as seen from the midline. [From Sperry, *The Great Cerebral Commissure*, Scientific American, 1964. All rights reserved.]

Myers performed this operation on cats and subsequently taught each animal a visual-discrimination task with one of its eyes patched. A discrimination task involves, for example, an animal's pressing a lever when it sees a circle but not pressing it when it sees a square. Even if this training is done with one eye covered, a normal cat can later perform the task using either eye. Myers found that cats with the optic chiasm cut were also able to perform the task using either eye when tested after the one-eyed training. However, when he cut the corpus callosum in addition to the optic chiasm, the results were dramatically different.

The cat trained with one eye open and one eye patched would learn to do a task well; but when the patch was switched to the other eye, the cat was unable to do the task at all. In fact, it had to be taught the same task over again, taking just as long to learn it as it had the first time. Myers and Sperry concluded that cutting the corpus callosum had kept information going into one hemisphere isolated from the other hemisphere. They had, in effect, trained

only half of a brain. Figure 2 schematically illustrates the different conditions of their experiment.

These findings, as well as some further studies, led two neurosurgeons working near the California Institute of Technology, in Pasadena, to reconsider the use of split-brain surgery as a treatment for intractable epilepsy in human beings. The surgeons, Philip Vogel and Joseph Bogen, reasoned that some of the earlier work with human patients had failed because the disconnection between the cerebral hemispheres was not complete. As we have mentioned, Van Wagenen's operations varied considerably from patient to patient. Some parts of the corpus callosum as well as several smaller commissures were usually not included in his operations, and these remaining fibers may have connected the hemispheres sufficiently to mask the effects of the fibers that were cut. On the basis of this logic, coupled with new animal data showing no ill effects from the surgery, Bogen and Vogel performed a complete commissurotomy on the first of what was to be

Figure 2

Split-Brain Experiment With Animals

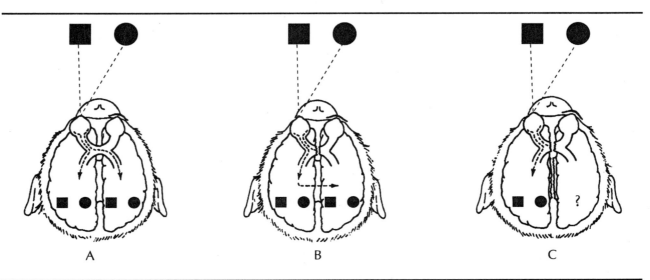

In a control situation, both eyes and both hemispheres see the stimuli. Experimental conditions alter this in the following ways: A. When one eye is patched, the other eye continues to send information to both hemispheres. B. When one eye is patched and the optic chiasm is cut, the visual information is transmitted to both hemispheres by way of the corpus callosum. C. When one eye is patched and both the optic chiasm and corpus callosum are cut, only one hemisphere receives visual information.

a new series of two dozen patients suffering from intractable epilepsy.

Bogen and Vogel's reasoning proved to be correct. In some of the cases, the medical benefits of the surgery even appeared to exceed expectations. In striking contrast to its consequences for seizure activity, the operation appeared to leave patients unchanged in personality, intelligence, and behavior in general, just as had been the case with Van Wagenen's patients. More extensive and ingenious testing conducted in Roger Sperry's California Institute of Technology laboratory, however, soon revealed a more complex story, for which Sperry was awarded the 1981 Nobel Prize in Physiology or Medicine.

Testing for the Effects of Disconnecting Left from Right

Split-brain patient N. G., a California housewife, sits in front of a screen with a small black dot in the center. She is asked to look directly at the dot. When the experimenter is sure she is doing so, a picture of a cup is flashed briefly to the right of the dot. N. G. reports that she has seen a cup. Again, she is asked to fix her gaze on the dot. This time, a picture of a spoon is flashed to the left of the dot. She is asked what she saw. She replies, "No, nothing." She is then asked to reach under the screen with her left hand and to select, by touch only, from among several items the one that is the same as the one she has just seen. Her left hand palpates each object and then holds up the spoon. When asked what she is holding, she says, "Pencil."

Once again the patient is asked to fixate on the dot on the screen. A picture of a nude woman is flashed to the left of the dot. N. G.'s face blushes a little, and she begins to giggle. She is asked what she saw. She says, "Nothing, just a flash of light," and giggles again, covering her mouth with her hand. "Why are you laughing, then?" the investigator inquires. "Oh, doctor, you have some machine!" she replies.

The procedure just described is frequently used in studies with split-brain patients and is

Figure 3

The Basic Testing Arrangement Used to Lateralize Visual and Tactile Information and Allow Tactile Responses

illustrated in Figure 3. The patient sits in front of a tachistoscope, a device that allows the investigator to control precisely the duration for which a picture or pattern is presented on a screen. The presentations are kept brief, about one- or two-tenths of a second (100 to 200 milliseconds), so that the patient does not have time to move his or her eyes away from the fixation point while the picture is still on the screen.* This procedure is necessary to ensure that visual information is presented initially to only one hemisphere. Stimuli presented to only one hemisphere are said to be *lateralized*.

*the rapid eye movements that occur when gaze is shifted from one point to another are known as *saccadic eye movements* or saccades. Although once started, saccades are extremely rapid, they take about 200 milliseconds to initiate with the eye at rest. If a stimulus is presented for less than 200 milliseconds, the stimulus is no longer present by the time an eye movement can occur.

The design of the human nervous system is such that each cerebral hemisphere receives information primarily from the opposite half of the body. This contralateral rule applies to vision and hearing as well as to body movement and touch (somatosensory) sensation, although the situation in vision and hearing is more complex.

In vision, the contralateral rule applies to the right and left sides of one's field of view (visual field), rather than to the right and left eyes per se. When both eyes are fixating on a single point, stimuli to the right of fixation are registered in the left half of the brain, while the right half of the brain processes everything occurring to the left of fixation. This split and crossover of visual information results from the manner in which the nerve fibers from corresponding regions of both eyes are divided

Figure 4

Visual Pathways to the Hemispheres

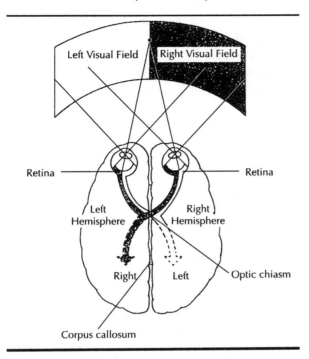

When fixating on a point, each eye sees both visual fields but sends information about the right visual field only to the left hemisphere and information about the left visual field only to the right hemisphere. This crossover and split is a result of the manner in which the nerve fibers leading from the retina divide at the back of each eye. The visual areas of the left and right hemisphere normally communicate through the corpus collosum. If the callosum is cut and the eyes and head are kept from moving, each hemisphere can see only half of the visual world.

between the cerebral hemispheres. Figure 4 shows both the optics and the neural wiring involved.

In animal studies, as we have seen, visual information can be directed to one hemisphere by cutting the optic chiasm so that the remaining fibers in the optic nerve are those transmitting information to the hemisphere on the same side as the eye. This allows experimenters to present a stimulus easily to either hemisphere alone by simply presenting the stimulus to the appropriate eye. The procedure is used only with animals, however, because cutting the chiasm substantially reduces peripheral vision, eliminates binocular depth perception, and plays no part in the rationale for the split-

brain operation on humans. For these reasons, investigators wishing to transmit visual information to one hemisphere at a time in a human split-brain patient must do so through a combination of controlling the patient's fixation and presenting information to one side of space.

With this as background, let's return to an analysis of the tests administered to patient N. G. In those tests, the patient saw the left half of the screen (everything to the left of the fixation point) with the right side of her brain and everything to the right with her left hemisphere. The split in her brain prevented the normal interchange of information between the two sides that would have occurred before her surgery. In effect, each side of her brain was blind to what the other side was seeing, a state of affairs dramatically brought out by the knowledge that only one hemisphere controls speech.

As a consequence, the patient reported perfectly well any stimuli falling in the right visual field (projecting to the verbal left hemisphere), although she was unable to tell anything about what was flashed in her left visual field (sent to the mute right hemisphere). The fact that she "saw" stimuli in the left visual field is amply demonstrated by the ability of her left hand (basically controlled by the right brain) to select the spoon from among several objects hidden from view. It is also demonstrated by her emotional reaction to the nude picture, despite her claim not to have seen anything.[6]

The patient's response to the nude picture is particularly interesting. She seemed puzzled by her own reactions to what had appeared. Her right hemisphere saw the picture and processed it sufficiently to evoke a general, nonverbal reaction—the giggling and the blushing. The left hemisphere, meanwhile, did not "know" what the right had seen, although its comment about "some machine" seems to be a sign that it was aware of the bodily reactions induced by the right hemisphere. It is very common for the verbal left hemisphere to try to make sense of what has occurred in testing situations where information is presented to the right hemisphere. As a result, the left brain sometimes comes out with erroneous and often elaborate rationalizations based on partial cues.

EVERYDAY BEHAVIOR AFTER SPLIT-BRAIN SURGERY

It is natural to wonder what evidence of disconnection effects there is in the everyday behavior of split-brain patients. Some instances of bizarre behavior have been described by both patients and onlookers and are frequently mentioned in popular articles on split-brain research. One patient, for example, described the time he found his left hand struggling against his right when he tried to put his pants on in the morning: one hand was pulling them up while the other hand was pulling them down. In another incident, the same patient was angry and forcibly reached for his wife with his left hand while his right hand grabbed the left in an attempt to stop it.[7]

The frequency with which such stories are mentioned would lead one to believe that they are commonplace events. In fact, the frequency of such events is low in most patients. However, there are exceptions. One example is P. O. V., a female patient operated on by Dr. Mark Rayport of the Medical College of Ohio. The patient reported frequent dramatic signs of interhemispheric competition for at least three years after surgery. "I open the closet door. I know what I want to wear. As I reach for something with my right hand, my left comes up and takes something different. I can't put it down if it's in my left hand. I have to call my daughter."[8]

Another case is a young man in Georgia who continued to show some profound problems two years after his operation.[9] In working at his father's grocery store he had tremendous difficulty performing stocking and shelving tasks. For example, in stocking canned goods, one hand would place a can in its proper spot on a shelf and the other hand would remove it. These conflicting hand movements persisted even when he thought he was "really" concentrating on the task. His physical and occupational therapists tried many times to practice similar tasks with him, but were unable to stop the problem in real life contexts.

Cases such as these support the concept that the cerebral commissures transmit a good deal of information that is inhibitory in nature— that is, activity in one hemisphere leads to callosal transmissions that serve to moderate, decrease, or stop certain activity in the other. Creating efficient new function through the balance of competitive or "opponent" processes is very common in biological systems. All locomotion, for instance, is based on the action of opposing muscle groups, and all postures depend on a careful balance of such muscle groups. In the central nervous system, opponent processes seem to underlie, for example, geometric illusions where the same drawing can be viewed in two different ways and appears to alternate dramatically between them.

With respect to hemispheric interaction, research with animals has indicated that the cerebral commissures pass information that can either excite or inhibit activity.[10] Colwin Trevarthen reported that split-brain baboons at times reached for an object with both forelimbs at the same time, presumably because no inhibitory processes were available to establish unilateral control over the action.[11] Other work demonstrated that monkeys whose corpus callosum was cut reached to grasp presumably hallucinated objects when the occipital region of one hemisphere was electrically stimulated.[12] This did not occur in animals with the commissures intact, suggesting that in normal animals the unstimulated hemisphere would "disconfirm" the hallucination through inhibitory information passed via the callosum.

It seems likely, thus, that inhibition mediated by the corpus callosum is an important process in maximizing efficiency in behavioral performance and perhaps even in producing new kinds of functions. It is very apparent, however, that these functions are quickly masked by some compensatory mechanisms in most split-brain patients. In fact, in a large majority of cases the two sides of the body appear to work in a coordinated fashion. Perhaps the rarity of patients with persistent disconnection effects indicates that more than callosal damage is necessary in order for the patient to be unable to adjust to the commissurotomy.

For the most part, a battery of sophisticated tests specifically designed to identify a commissurotomy patient would be needed for anyone to know the operation had occurred. Much more common, however, are reports of subtle changes in behavior or ability after surgery. Although some of the reported changes have not held up when carefully studied, others do appear to be verifiable consequences of the operation.

Subtle Deficits Following Surgery

Several patients have reported great difficulty learning to associate names with faces after surgery. Verification of this came from a study in which subjects had to learn first names for each of three pictures of young men.[13] This procedure was only incidental to the main purpose of the study, but it proved to be a major stumbling block for the subjects. The investigators reported that subjects eventually learned the name–face associations by isolating some unique feature in each picture (for example, "Dick has glasses") rather than by associating the name with the face as a whole. This suggests that the deficit in the ability to associate names and faces may be due to the disconnection of the verbal naming functions of the left side of the brain from the facial-recognition abilities of the right side.

Deficits in the ability to solve geometrical problems have been anecdotally linked to the absence of the corpus callosum. Patient L. B., a high school student with an IQ considerably above average, was transferred out of geometry into a class in general math after he experienced inordinate difficulty with the course. Another report told of a college student who had exceptional difficulty with geometry despite average grades in other courses. Research with split-brain patients studying the ability of each hemisphere to match two- and three-dimensional forms on the basis of common geometrical features showed the right hemisphere to be markedly superior, especially on the most difficult matches.[14] Thus, as in the preceding example, the patient's deficits may be the result of the disconnection of the speaking left hemisphere from the right-hemisphere regions specialized for such tasks.

Another complaint of some split-brain patients is that they no longer dream. Because dreaming is primarily a visual-imaging process, investigators have speculated that it might be the responsibility of the right half of the brain. The operation would serve to disconnect this aspect of the patient's mental life from the speaking left hemisphere and would result in verbal reports that the patient does not dream.

This idea, however, has not been confirmed by further research. Split-brain patients were monitored for brain-wave activity while sleeping and were awakened whenever the recordings indicated they were dreaming. They were then asked to describe the dreams they had just been having. In contrast to the prediction that they would be unable to do so, the patients provided the experimenters with descriptions of their dreams.[15]

Other anecdotal evidence has pointed to poorer memory after surgery. These reports were apparently supported by a study of memory abilities in which several split-brain patients were compared with other epilepsy patients and were found to have poorer scores on a variety of memory tests.[16] A major problem with this type of study, though, is that we really do not know much about split-brain patients' preoperative memory abilities. We can compare their performance after surgery with that of epileptic control subjects who have not had surgery, but we have no way of knowing if the memory skills of the split-brain patients before their surgery were really comparable to the memory skills of the control group. Perhaps they had poorer memories to begin with!

The best approach is to compare memory abilities before and after surgery in the same patient. This was done informally in five patients in the Rayport series. When tested for attention, memory, and sequencing abilities, four showed noticeably impaired performance when tested five to 38 months after surgery. A male patient, J. A. C., reportedly prepared for a shower by removing his clothes, only to put them on again without getting wet. P. O. V., the female patient mentioned earlier, became forgetful to the point of being unable to keep track of her own medication or remember simple directions and arrangements even for a few hours.[17]

This pattern apparently is not found in all or even most patients, however. In the case of patient D. H. operated on by Dr. Donald Wilson of the Dartmouth Medical School, memory performance improved considerably after surgery.[18]

The most likely explanation for this finding is that D. H.'s true abilities were suppressed by drugs and his general condition before surgery. The operation did not miraculously improve his memory; instead, it allowed his true abilities to emerge. In any case, this single-subject study shows that memory deficits do not *necessarily* follow split-brain surgery, and it indicates that further work will be needed to answer the question of whether the operation affects memory and, if so, in which way. It also points to the importance of appropriate controls in studies looking for changes in split-brain patients.

Overall, it is not clear why a few patients seem to show persistent patterns of deficit after commissurotomy, whereas the majority of patients do not. Important differences among patients in their preoperative condition and surgical treatment probably exist, although we do not yet know what they are. There are some consequences of commissurotomy, however, that are dramatic and quite consistent across patients but are short lived.

Acute Disconnection Syndrome

The *acute disconnection syndrome* is probably due to the surgical division of the commissures as well as to the general trauma resulting from the surgeon's having to squeeze or compress the right hemisphere to gain access to the nerve tracts between the hemispheres.

Patients are often mute for a time after surgery and sometimes they have difficulty controlling the left side of the body, which may at first seem almost paralyzed and then work very awkwardly. As the patient recovers use of the left hand, competitive movements between the left and right hands sometimes occur. This problem usually passes quickly.

After recovering from the initial shock of major brain surgery, most patients report an improved feeling of well-being. Less than two days after surgery, one young patient was well enough to quip that he had a "splitting headache." Within a few weeks, the symptoms of the acute disconnection syndrome subside, making it necessary to use carefully contrived laboratory tests to reveal what had taken place earlier in the operation.

CROSS CUING

As the study of split-brain patients continued, certain inconsistencies in the findings began to occur with greater frequency. Patients previously unable to identify verbally objects held out of sight in the left hand began to name some items. Some pictures flashed in the left visual field (to the right hemisphere) were also correctly identified verbally. One interpretation of these results is that over time, the right hemispheres of the patients acquired the ability to talk. Another is that information being transmitted between the hemispheres by way of pathways other than those that were cut.

Although these were interesting and exciting possibilities, Michael Gazzaniga and Steven Hillyard were able to pinpoint a much simpler explanation for their findings.[19] They coined the term *cross cuing* to refer to patients' attempts to use whatever cues are available to make information accessible to both hemispheres. Cross cuing is most obvious in the case where a patient is given an object to hold and identify with his or her left hand, which is out of the line of vision and thus disconnected from the verbal left hemisphere. If, for example, the left hand is given a comb or a toothbrush to feel, the patient will often stroke the brush or the surface of the comb. The patient will then immediately identify the object because the left hemisphere hears the tell-tale sounds.

Cross cuing provides a way for one hemisphere to provide the other with information about what it is experiencing. The direct channels of information transfer are eliminated by the surgery in most instances leaving the patient with indirect cues as the only means of interhemispheric communication. Cross cuing can often be quite subtle, testing the ingenuity of investigators seeking to eliminate it from the experimental situation.

A good example of this is the patient who was able to indicate verbally whether a 0 or a 1 had been flashed to either hemisphere. The same patient was unable to identify verbally pictures of objects flashed to the right hemisphere, nor was he able to identify most objects held in his left hand. This suggested that he lacked the ability to speak from the right hemisphere. Instead, the investigators proposed that cross cuing was involved when the patient reported the numbers flashed to the right hemisphere. They hypothesized that the left hemisphere would begin counting "subvocally" after a presentation to the left visual field and that these signals were picked up by the right hemisphere. When the correct number was reached, the right hemisphere would signal the left to stop and report that digit out loud.

To test this idea, the patient was presented with an expanded version of the task: the digits 2, 3, 5, and 8 were added without his knowledge. At first the subject was very surprised when a new number was presented. His response to the first unexpected number presented to the right hemisphere was, "I beg your pardon." With a little practice, however, he was able to give the correct answer for all the numbers presented to the right hemisphere, but with hesitation when the number was high. In contrast, responses to the same digits presented in the right visual field (to the left hemisphere) were quite prompt.

These findings fit well with the idea that the left hemisphere began counting subvocally after a digit was presented to the right hemisphere. The larger the number of potential digits, the longer the list of numbers the left hemisphere had to go through before reaching the correct one.

Cross cuing generally is not a conscious attempt by the patient to trick the investigator. Instead, it is a natural tendency by an organism to use whatever information it has to make sense of what is going on. This tendency, in fact, contributes further insight into why the common, everyday behavior of split-brain patients seems so unaffected by the surgery.

Careful testing procedures that prevent cross cuing, however, can lead to striking "disconnection" effects, such as those described in the case of patient N. G. In these situations, the patient is unable to tell what picture was flashed to the right hemisphere, although the left hand can point to the correct object. If blindfolded, the patient cannot verbally identify an object held in the left hand but can select with that hand other objects related to it (for example, selecting a book of matches after having held a cigarette).

To an observer unfamiliar with the patient's surgical history, these findings give the impression that the left arm has a mind of its own. They are less mysterious when we realize that the split-brain operation has disconnected the patient's right hemisphere from the centers in the left hemisphere that control speech. The left hand, thus, is the primary means through which the right hemisphere can communicate with the outside world.

NOTES

1. T. C. Erikson, "Spread of Epileptic Discharge," *Archives of Neurology and Psychiatry* 43 (1940): 429–452.

2. W. Van Wagenen and R. Herren, "Surgical Division of Commissural Pathways in the Corpus Callosum," *Archives of Neurology and Psychiatry* 44 (1940): 740–759.

3. G. Fechner (1860), cited in O. Zangwill, "Consciousness and the Cerebral Hemispheres," in *Hemispheric Function in the Human Brain*, ed. S. Dimond and G. Beaumont (New York: Halsted Press, 1974).

4. J. Akelaitis, "Studies on the Corpus Callosum. II: The Higher Visual Functions in Each Homonymous Field Following Complete Section of the Corpus Callosum," *Archives of Neurology and Psychiatry* 45 (1941): 789–796.

A. J. Akelaitis, "The Study of Gnosis, Praxis and Language Following Section of the Corpus Callosum and Anterior Commissure," *Journal of Neurosurgery* 1 (1944): 94–102.

5. R. E. Myers, "Function of Corpus Callosum in Interocular Transfer," *Brain* 79 (1956): 358–363.

R. E. Myers and R. W. Sperry, "Interhemispheric Communication Through the Corpus Callosum.

Mnemonic Carry-Over Between the Hemispheres," *Archives of Neurology and Psychiatry* 80 (1958): 298–303.

6. R. W. Sperry, "Hemisphere Deconnection and Unity in Conscious Awareness," *American Psychologist* 23 (1968): 723–733.

7. M. S. Gazzaniga, *The Bisected Brain* (New York: Appleton-Century-Crofts, 1970).

8. S. M. Ferguson, M. Rayport, and W. S. Corrie, "Neuropsychiatric Observations on Behavioral Consequences of Corpus Callosum Section for Seizure Control," in *Epilepsy and the Corpus Callosum*, ed. A. G. Reeves (New York: Plenum Press, 1985).

9. M. White, Personal Communication.

10. F. Bremer, "An Aspect of the Physiology of Corpus Callosum," *Journal of Electroencephalography and Clinical Neurophysiology* 22 (1967): 391.

11. C. B. Trevarthen, "Manipulative Strategies of Baboons, and the Origins of Cerebral Asymmetry," in *Hemispheric Asymmetry of Function*, ed. M. Kinsbourne (London: Tavistock, 1974).

12. R. W. Doty, "Electrical Stimulation of the Brain in Behavioral Cortex," *Annual Review of Psychology* 20 (1969): 289–320.

13. J. Levy, C. Trevarthen, and R. W. Sperry, "Perception of Bilateral Chimeric Figures Following Hemispheric Disconnection," *Brain* 95 (1972): 61–78.

14. L. Franco and R. W. Sperry, "Hemisphere Lateralization for Cognitive Processing of Geometry," *Neuropsychologia* 15 (1977): 107–114.

15. P. Greenwood, D. H. Wilson, and M. S. Gazzaniga, "Dream Report Following Commissurotomy," *Cortex* 13 (1977): 311–316.

16. E. Zaidel and R. W. Sperry, "Memory Impairment Following Commissurotomy in Man," *Brain* 97 (1974): 263–272.

17. Ferguson, Rayport, and Corrie, "Neuropsychiatric Observations on Behavioral Consequences of Corpus Callosum Section for Seizure Control."

18. J. E. LeDoux, G. Risse, S. P. Springer, D. H. Wilson, and M. S. Gazzaniga, "Cognition and Commissurotomy," *Brain* 100 (1977): 87–104.

19. M. S. Gazzaniga and S. A. Hillyard, "Language and Speech Capacity of the Right Hemisphere," *Neuropsychologia* 9 (1971): 273–280.

6

Christine M. Temple

Developmental Memory Impairment: Faces and Patterns

Children with developmental dyslexia have selective difficulty in learning to read despite normal intelligence. It could be something unusual about reading itself, which makes it particularly problematic, but it is also possible that these reading difficulties are only one of a range of different types of selective learning problems. Our attention may be particularly attracted to reading difficulties because of their obvious educational implications. Can fluent and articulate people who read well, and pass exams easily, nevertheless have other cognitive weaknesses? The answer to this question is important in understanding the extent to which different systems in the brain are dependent upon each other as the child develops. Is it possible for one system in the brain to function poorly whilst the rest functions well? If different systems are independent this provides information about the brain's underlying organization.

The traditional view is that there can be 'plasticity' in brain development, which means that if a system is not working well the developing brain may have the capacity to reorganize and compensate for the problem. According to this view, selective problems in cognitive skills should not occur in otherwise normal and healthy children and adults. The common existence of developmental dyslexia (see Snowling and Goulandris, chapter 6) suggests that plasticity and compensation fail to correct for potential reading difficulty. Are there comparable non-verbal disorders which show similar resistance to compensation?

Dr S came to our attention because of the life-long difficulty she reported in recognizing people's faces. When I first met her this, of course, was not obvious, as I did not expect her to recognize me.

Instead, two other characteristics were instantly apparent. First, she became completely lost trying to find me. Given the complexity of the university buildings, this in itself might have been unsurprising but, as we moved between offices and laboratories, it became apparent that she was quite unable to find her way around. Even relatively simple routes appeared to be a mystery, and at the end of the day when I left her by the station I had to ensure that she had actually noted the entrance or she would walk the wrong way down the street, away from the station itself. Secondly, I was struck by the speed and quantity of her speech. She remains the most fluent talker I have ever encountered. So rapid is her speech output, that at times it becomes a challenge to decipher the individual words. The continuous flow of speech, as Dr S herself knows, is tiring for the listener and, because of her capacity to inflict headaches, she carries aspirin with her to hand out in cases of need!

On my second encounter with Dr S, and as I continued to see her, the face recognition problem became obvious. She failed to recognize me as I went to meet her, looking blankly through me until I said her name. She would also report that as she knew I had blond hair, she had moved expectantly towards several other people before I arrived, thinking them to be me.

Face recognition impairment is documented in the neurological literature; it was given the name *prosopagnosia* by Bodamer in 1947. Prosopagnosia is one of a range of recognition disorders for visually presented material termed visual agnosias. However, in the case of Dr S the difficulty does not result from any neurological injury but has been present since birth.

An intelligent and perceptive lady, Dr S has clear insight about the nature of her difficulties as her own description illustrates:

> There are two problems. I meet somebody who I totally feel I have never seen before, like I told you happened with you, after one or two encounters with you. I had absolutely no idea what you look like and yet know that you are a lovely person, and have the embarrassment of the feeling that I have never seen you before. Also sometimes, I know I have met this person but I do not know where.

> I do this game with people to whom I try to explain . . . I say 'Close your eyes', and then I ask them can you see (visualize) my face, and 99 per cent of them say they can. When I close my eyes, I see virtually nothing. In your case, I know that you have blonde hair because I have fixed that verbally. But if asked what do you wear, I haven't got the faintest idea . . . I know that you have lovely blonde hair but the rest I wouldn't have known at all.

Dr S is also aware of her rapid speech:

> I may be overfluent . . . I talk too much. I overexplain, and all this I'm conscious of. I find it difficult to get out of . . . Most people complain about me. The most striking thing is she talks too much and too fast.

Dr S was happy to be our guinea-pig and we decided particularly to investigate her face recognition problems but also to explore her intelligence, her verbal fluency and her memory. Before discussing the way in which the studies developed, I shall give a little of Dr S's personal history.

BIOGRAPHICAL HISTORY

Dr S is now in her sixties and lives in London. She was born in Germany, into a prosperous Jewish family, and lived there and in Austria as a child, coming to the UK at the age of fifteen. In the UK she qualified as a doctor of medicine, in 1945, from the London School of Medicine for Women, at the Royal Free Hospital. Further qualifications included training as a pathologist; a diploma in tropical medicine and hygiene; a diploma in family planning; and a BA in psychology. The latter was taken in evening classes at Birkbeck College, London. For many years, Dr S worked as a family planning specialist in Mauritius. She has also travelled widely.

Dr S speaks fluent German, English, French and some Danish. She reports that she was very good at Latin at school. She has had difficulty in mastering both Russian and Greek, possibly relating to problems in mastering the Cyrillic alphabet. She is highly motivated to learn Hebrew but continues to have difficulty with the script.

Dr S has been married twice. Her first husband was a university professor. Her second husband was a medical doctor. She has four children, three boys and a girl, all of whom have university degrees. None of the children is left-handed. All of the boys are colour blind. Dr S has a first cousin who also has difficulty in recognizing faces.

Dr S is in good health. She has had no major illnesses, has never had an accident with loss of consciousness and has had no seizures. In addition to the difficulties discussed here, Dr S complains of clumsiness; difficulty with figures; excessive anxiety about using machines and appliances; and that she is tone deaf.

INTELLIGENCE AND VERBAL FLUENCY

Dr S was obviously intelligent because of the formal qualifications she had attained, and her sharp, alert and thoughtful mind was also apparent in conversation. To assess her intelligence more formally, we used the Weschler Adult Intelligence Scale, in its revised format, and the scores she attained are given in table 1. The Weschler contains a range of verbal sub-tests and also non-verbal sub-tests involving puzzles, designs and pictures, which are called performance tests. We were interested in whether Dr S would have much better verbal than non-verbal intelligence. However, the scores revealed that her non-verbal abilities were just as good as her verbal abilities. Thus, any difficulty in face recognition can be attributed neither to a general intellectual problem, nor to a general problem in dealing with pictorial or visual material. Dr S had an exceptionally high IQ. Her scores would be attained by fewer than 1 in a 1000 women in their sixties.

Another feature which struck us about her performance was the exceptionally high score which she attained on the vocabulary sub-test. In fact, her ability to give definitions of words was perfect for all those which we gave to her. This was particularly impressive given that English was not Dr S's first language. However, it was consistent with our informal observations of her extensive speech production.

Another way in which verbal production skills can be measured is to look at the ease

Table 1

Scores on the Intelligence Test

Verbal sub-tests		Performance sub-tests	
Information	14	Picture completion	12
Digit span	12	Picture arrangement	13
Vocabulary	19	Block design	10
Arithmetic	13	Object assembly	13
Similarities	16	Digit symbol	17

10 is an average sub-test score. Possible scores are 1–19. The standard deviation is 3, which means that about two-thirds of people score between 7 and 13 on sub-tests.

Verbal IQ	136	Performance IQ	147
Full-scale IQ	147		

100 is an average IQ. Two-thirds of people have an IQ between 85 and 115. Only one in a thousand has an IQ as high as 147.

with which words in the vocabulary can be found. A standard clinical measure is a fluency task. The subject is asked to generate as many words as possible in one-minute time slots for particular categories. Here we used animals, household objects, words beginning with 'f' and words beginning with 's'. We compared Dr S's performance with that of six other healthy women in their sixties, who acted as normal 'controls'. Results were consistent on all the categories. Dr S generated significantly more items than the other women. For example, the other women generated on average 14 animals in a minute; Dr S generated 35 on one occasion and 42 on another. The animals that she and a typical control subject named are given in table 2.

From these investigations, we conclude that Dr S is of exceptionally high intellectual ability and that her vocabulary and verbal fluency are also exceptionally highly developed. If abnormality is defined in terms of distance from the average, then Dr S's fluency is abnormal in its extreme quality. Later, we will examine the difficulty which this extremely highly developed skill creates for Dr S in everyday life. It is not simply impairments which create prob-

Table 2 _____

Animals Generated in the Fluency Tasks

Subject	Named animals
Typical control	cat dog horse goat sheep elephant leopard lion monkey parrot donkey snake mouse
Dr S	monkey bear walrus whale dog cat hen mouse rat lion tiger leopard wolf hyena eagle owl swan duck goose chicken elephant buffalo cow ox sheep lamb horse donkey sparrow ram dove heron pelican ostrich polar bear

lems. However, first we will discuss the way in which we explored her face recognition problems.

NORMAL MODELS OF VISUAL PERCEPTION AND FACE RECOGNITION

Cognitive neuropsychologists have discussed the recognition disorders, both visual agnosias and prosopagnosias, in relation to information-processing models of object and face recognition. Such models incorporate elements of Marr's theory of visual perception. According to Marr (1976, 1980, 1982), there are at least three levels of description involved in the recognition of objects. The first level is the primal sketch in which texture, gradations of light and discontinuities are coded. The second level is called the '2½-D level'. This incorporates descriptions of the structures of objects but these are said to be *viewer-centred*, in that they are entirely dependent upon the angle of sight of the observer. Thus, if you are looking at a chair from one angle and you get up and move and look at it from a different angle the 2½-D representation changes completely. At the third level in Marr's model, there is a 3-D representation which is said to be *object-centred*, in that it is independent of the view of the observer. At the 3-D level there must be stored descriptions of the variable appearances of objects. The 3-D level is essential for object constancy and in order for us to deal effectively

with unusual or partially obscured views of objects.

A functional model for face processing, against which subjects can be interpreted has been proposed by Bruce and Young (1986) (see figure 1). This model does not make explicit the distinction between initial representations, viewer-centred representations and object-centred representations. Instead, it describes a general process of *structural encoding*, which includes these processes and which can gain access to *face recognition units*. Each face recognition unit corresponds to a particular person's face and these units are established in the course of our daily life and encounters. In a way analogous to the biologist's discussion of the 'firing' of a nerve cell, face recognition units are said to have thresholds of activation. When a face is seen, there will be an increase in activity in all the units representing faces which resemble it but only the unit which corresponds to the viewed face will be fully

Figure 1 _____

Model for Face Processing

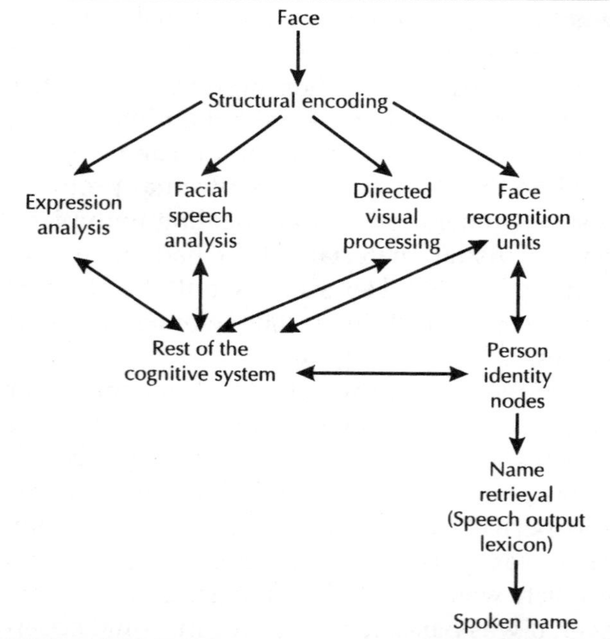

Adapted from Bruce and Young, 1986, and reproduced with permission.

activated. This unit will reach threshold and will 'fire'.

Following the structural encoding of a face's appearance, several types of information are extracted simultaneously. Expression is analysed, providing information about the mood and affect of the speaker or his/her message. Facial speech analysis monitors the mouth and tongue movements involved in producing speech. Lip-readers exploit this system which also reduces ambiguity in normal processes of speech comprehension. Directed visual processing is used, for example, to see the similarities and differences between the faces of unfamiliar people. These inputs all feed into a semantically structured cognitive system. When a face recognition unit fires, it will trigger a corresponding *person identity node* which contains information which specifically identifies an individual, for example, their occupation and their personal characteristics.

In order to retrieve a person's name, it is necessary to first activate a person identity node. Thus, it is an explicit prediction of this model that one should never be able to name a person from their appearance unless one also knows something about the person (i.e. their profession or partner). But one can know something about the person without being able to name him/her.

Face recognition disorders may arise from impairments at several different levels within the face recognition system, and a number of these have been described in patients following neurological injury. In Bodamer's original paper (1947), one patient had a deficit in structural encoding. He appeared to have difficulty perceiving faces and even considered that a dog's face was an unusually hairy human being. Most forms of prosopagnosia in neurological patients will result in difficulties in gaining access to or utilizing face recognition units.

Patients with amnesia, who have generalized memory loss, may have lost or be unable to gain access to the person identity nodes themselves. Patients with language problems may have intact person identity nodes but may have difficulty in generating names.

The model of Bruce and Young (1986) clearly implies that faces are 'special' in the sense that there are specialized brain mechanisms for processing them. This would make sense in terms of the importance of both face recognition and expression analysis in our social interaction.

In our investigation of Dr S we wished to determine whether there was a difficulty with her basic visual perceptual or spatial skills or whether there was a difficulty with a particular component of the face recognition system.

VISUAL PERCEPTION

To assess Dr S's basic perceptual skills and her capacity to make judgements about simple components of the visual scene, we tested her ability to make judgements about the orientations of lines. We modified the Benton et al. (1978) line orientation task. Subjects are presented with an array of 31 lines displayed on the lower part of a booklet. On the upper part are two lines of different orientations and varying lengths. The subject must select from the response array, the two lines whose angles match those of the stimulus pair (see figure 2).

The performance of Dr S was compared with that of 12 other healthy women in their sixties, who acted as controls. Unless mentioned otherwise, these women acted as controls for all tests. This line orientation task is not easy, as figure 2 may indicate. The control subjects averaged ten correct. Dr S got 12 correct. Thus her performance was normal. She also performed normally on a tactile version of this task. Thus there is no unusual difficulty in making basic perceptual judgements about orientations of lines.

As mentioned above, Marr's model emphasizes the importance of being able to integrate different viewpoints and recognize things from different angles. We tested Dr S's ability mentally to rotate an abstract shape and recognize it in a different angle. The Mental Rotation task used was a shortened version of a task (Vandenburg and Kuse, 1978) requiring the internalized spatial rotation of 3-D structures depicted by 2-D drawings. The drawings appear to represent 3-D structures composed of multiple cubes (see figure 3). The subjects are

Figure 2

Line Orientation Test

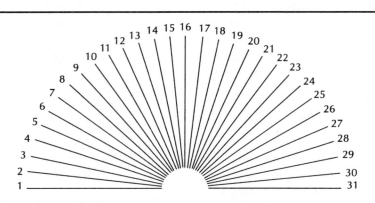

told that they may mentally rotate the structure in any direction and they must then select, two identical structures from an array of four. The score out of 20, represents the number of correct selections.

Once again Dr S's performance was compared with the controls. They averaged nine correct and Dr S averaged 14 correct. Thus Dr S can perform this complex spatial manipulation. She can recognize shapes from different angles. In these tests and others we gave we could find no problem with basic perceptual processes and no reason for difficulty in Marr's terms in establishing either viewer-centred or object-centred representations.

FACE PROCESSING

In order to recognize that a face is a face it is necessary to integrate its features. Sometimes this must be done in conditions of poor lighting or when the face is partially obscured. Dr S says that she does realize that a face is a face but could she have difficulty with the 'gestalt' processes involved in integrating features? To assess this we tested her with Mooney faces. The Mooney faces (Lansdell, 1968) present patterns of light and shadow in black and white, depicting faces for which sex and appropriate age are judged. The subject is told that all the pictures are faces but she will only be able to assess the face correctly if she can integrate the blocks of black and white (see figure 4). Dr S was able to make these judgements as easily as

the control subjects. Thus she has intact gestalt integrative skills and she is also able to make correct judgements of age and sex about faces.

We had established that Dr S could match an unfamiliar structure in different rotations but we wanted to see if she could do the same things with faces. We also wanted to see if she could match identical pictures of faces. To test these skills we used Benton's Facial Recognition task (Benton et al., 1983). This involves matching a target face with an identical face in the same or a differing orientation. The faces are black and white and are photographed partially in shadow. Both in comparison to the controls and in comparison to the published test norms Dr S performed normally on these tasks. Although she has difficulty in recognizing faces in real life, she is able to match unfamiliar faces seen at different angles. The results of the Mooney faces and the Benton task indicate that Dr S's structural encoding of faces and directed visual processing (see figure 1) have developed normally. Difficulties in face recognition have a basis elsewhere in the face-processing system.

We decided to investigate Dr S's ability initially to register face recognition units by teaching her some new faces. For this we used the Warrington Recognition Memory Battery (Warrington, 1984). The test is in two matched sections. In the first section, the subject is shown a pack of 50 words. Each word is exposed for three seconds and the subject is required to make a judgement of whether or not the asso-

Figure 3

Mental Rotation

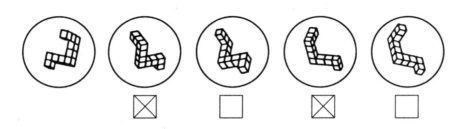

ciations of the word are pleasant. This encourages some degree of encoding of meaning or semantics. Immediately after the stimulus cards have all been exposed, the subject is required to make a forced choice judgement between pairs of words, one of which has appeared in the stimulus pack and one of which is novel. The faces section is identical except that the stimulus cards consist of unfamiliar faces of men. The forced choice responses are made to pairs of faces, one of which has been shown in the stimulus pack.

Unsurprisingly, on the word section, Dr S had a perfect score. On the faces section, she was correct on 43/50 items which was slightly better than the controls. Thus Dr S is able to set new face recognition units and gain access to these in a choice situation a few minutes later. Her problems must therefore either lie in a failure of these units to become permanently established in memory or in difficulty in using the units to gain access to person identity information and names.

By this stage we were beginning to wonder what Dr S would be unable to do with faces. She seemed to be able to do all our face tasks yet she still failed to recognize us. We wanted to get another measure of these recognition problems so we tested her on her recognition of famous faces. This would indicate her ability to gain access to person identity information (see figure 1) and names.

We showed her two sets of pictures of famous people. There were 45 pictures in total, though a few people appeared on both picture sets. Dr S was able to identify 14 pictures (31 per cent). She was significantly poorer than the

six healthy women in their sixties with whom we compared her. It appears that she has difficulty in accessing person identity information from faces. One uninteresting interpretation of these results would be that, although these people seem famous, Dr S simply does not know them. We were particularly concerned about this possibility since she had spent time overseas and some of the figures were British. In order to see whether she knew the people and whether there was a genuine difficulty in identifying people from their faces, we gave her the names of 37 of the people who had appeared in the picture sets. For each name, we asked who they were and what was their occupation to determine whether Dr S had person identity information for these people which was accessible from their spoken name. Dr S could give identifying information for 27 of the 37 people (73 per cent). Thus there were many people whom she knew but whom she had been unable to identify from their faces.

However, we then wondered whether giving somebody's occupation was a less specific task than naming them. You could, after all, identify someone as a politician without knowing exactly who they are. We therefore decided to do a more balanced experiment, with another set of faces. Here we took 40 faces and asked Dr S to give us the occupation of each person from their face. Then, much later, we took the 40 names of these people and spoke them aloud, again asking her to give us their occupations. Dr S could give the occupations for 12 of the faces but 28 of the names. Thus she can gain access to person identity information more easily from spoken names than faces.

Figure 4 _____

Mooney Face

Many faces failed to elicit the person identity information which we know Dr S possesses.

In terms of the model in figure 1, it would appear that there is intact structural encoding and that the initial registration of face recognition units is normal, but we have found that there is a significant impairment in accessing person identity information from faces in order to recognize the face. Either the face recognition units have failed to consolidate and despite their initial registration they are lost over time or there is difficulty in using the units to activate the person identity information.

RECOGNIZING OTHER PICTURES

As mentioned above, there is a theoretical debate about whether faces are 'special' and have special brain mechanisms devoted to them or whether they are very complex visual stimuli when it comes to identifying individuals. We believed that despite Dr S's difficulty in recognizing faces she did not have generalized recognition difficulties for other visually presented stimuli but we wanted to test this

more formally. We therefore gave her the Boston naming test which is a standardized test of object recognition. It consists of a graded set of line drawings of objects: the earlier items are common, e.g. toothbrush, whistle, octopus; the later items are more unusual, e.g. palette, trellis, sphinx. Dr S performed normally on this task.

As another test of object recognition, in comparison to face recognition, we gave her a test constructed by Edward De Haan. It consists of three sets of photographs: familiar (famous) and unfamiliar (novel) faces; familiar (real) and unfamiliar (novel) objects; and familiar and unfamiliar names of people. The novel objects are actually real but rare objects like specialist hardware tools, unfamiliar to any one except an expert. In each group the subject must indicate whether the items are familiar or not. Thus this test permits a direct comparison of recognition skills for faces, objects and names. There are 16 familiar and 16 unfamiliar items in each set. Results are given in table 3. Only with the familiar faces was performance abnormal. Yet on all other sections, performance was good. Dr S can discriminate between familiar and unfamiliar objects. She can also correctly categorize the names of the famous people whose faces she cannot recognize. The deficit is thus specific to faces of people. This supports the view that there are brain mechanisms which are specific to face recognition.

VISUAL MEMORY

We had established that the face recognition problems did not generalize to problems in

Table 3 _____

Scores on Familiarity Decision

	%
Familiar faces	44
Unfamiliar faces	100
Familiar objects	100
Unfamiliar objects	88
Familiar names	82
Unfamiliar names	94

Table 4

Scores on the Weschler Memory Battery

	Dr S	Controls (mean ± s.d.)
Personal and current information	6	5.7 ± 0.48
Orientation	5	5.0 ± 0.0
Mental control	7	6.5 ± 2.55
Logical memory (story recall)		
Immediate recall	13.5	9.5 ± 3.08
		[age-matched controls 8.4 ± 2.7]
Delayed recall	10	8.15 ± 2.64
Digits forward and back	10	9.6 ± 1.96
Associate learning (of pairs of words)		
Immediate recall	20	16.9 ± 2.95
Delayed recall	9	9.5 ± 1.08
Visual memory (for designs)[1]		
Immediate recall	4	10.5 ± 1.9
Delayed recall	3	9.9 ± 1.9
Copy of designs	13	12.5 ± 1.27
Overall Memory Quotient	132	

[1] Significant impairment.

recognizing objects. However, in view of Dr S's difficulty with topographical orientation we decided to explore whether she had other visual memory problems.

We therefore gave her the Weschler Memory battery which contains a range of different types of memory tasks, including both verbal and visual memory. Her overall score gave a memory quotient of 132, which is in line with her IQ. This result indicated that there was no generalized memory impairment. We did not have control data on the sub-tests from the controls used above, but we had control data from another study we had been doing, which came from 15–16-year-olds. The performance of Dr S is compared to the teenagers in table 4. Her logical memory, which involves the recall of stories, is somewhat better than the teenagers, as is her ability to learn new associations between words in the paired associates sub-test. On other tasks her performance is at approximately the control level except for the visual memory items. On both immediate and delayed recall of simple designs she is significantly impaired. This difficulty in drawing the

designs from memory cannot be attributed to any difficulty with the motor control of drawing as her copying is at a normal level.

This impairment in visual memory for designs was confirmed using another, more complex, figure, known as the Figure of Rey. Here, Dr S's recall of the figure was at a 4-year-old level. Thus visual memory is poor.

MEMORY FOR FACES AND PATTERNS

When Dr S had seen something many, many times she may learn to recognize it. She is able to recognize her family and familiar friends and she recognizes the faces of Margaret Thatcher and Princess Anne. She is also able to recognize everyday objects. However, she seems to be unable to register, and gain access to after a few minutes, memories for complex visual information which is novel. Just as she fails to recognize me, she fails to recall designs, and fails to recognize the house in which she lives, which is identified only by number, despite familiarity with the building for several years. In relation to our model of face recognition (see figure 1), she cannot gain access to person identity information from faces.

LIVING WITH THESE PROBLEMS

Dr S has had a career with professional success, has four healthy children and many friends. Nevertheless, her life has often been difficult and her pattern of cognitive strengths and weaknesses have contributed to her problems. In excerpts from our conversations with her she gives these examples from her life.

On faces
There was a very striking example in America [Dr S had just returned from a lengthy visit] of a lady who took me home, when I was trying to find my way home, and I had noticed her in the synagogue every Saturday. I met her in an unexpected place. If I had met her in the synagogue I would have made a probably word-based recognition . . . but by meeting her in the unexpected place I have the feeling dimly that I have seen her a few years ago when I was in the same town and I asked her

'Excuse me, have we met?' which is what I tend to do. I then fish from the conversation. And she couldn't believe it, because the week before she had shown me the way and we had had an intense conversation several times in the synagogue. And I was absolutely totally unable to know who she is. The moment she said 'But we walked home together' I remembered the conversation, I remembered how many children she had, I remembered details which sometimes surprise people, based on verbal memory . . . I have a kind of photographic memory for conversations . . . but as to the visual I was sure that I had perhaps seen her when I was there a year ago and was absolutely unaware that I had seen her every Saturday . . . She thought I was peculiar . . .

. . . In Cambridge now, I kept on getting lost, and . . . it's very embarrassing because I kept on getting lots of lifts and I met lots of people. I had very intense conversations and I didn't recognize them, even though they had been helpful by giving me lifts . . . I look, but the only person I recognize is a lady with a big wart on her nose, that is very striking. It is very embarrassing because they say, you know the fellow with the glasses or whatever they say, I have no idea if they have got glasses. It just doesn't register. People don't like not to be remembered. So I always say, 'You beautiful ladies, I don't recognize you, excuse me, have we met before?'

I warn people now. If we have a wonderful exchange and are going to be friends for life. I say, look if we meet again outside . . . and I wouldn't recognize you, just give me the code word. The code word is something we talked about and then I would recall what we talked of.

People complain, I don't greet them. So I warn them beforehand. It is very embarrassing. I live in this active community . . . and I ask now after four years in the community, 'Who is this?' Now people, cannot understand it. I ask friends of mine who do not know that I have this problem, 'Who is this?' They are amazed. 'Of course, she is so and so.'

On houses
My own house, I can't recall what it looks like. If I had to draw it, I'm not even sure if it's three storeys. I'm on top so it must be three storeys.
[CMT: You can't conjure up a picture in your own mind of what your own house looks like?]
No, no. I only know it's got three storeys because I am in the attic.

[CMT: How long have you known this house?]
Four and a half years, I've been there. First, I lived in the house next door. I rather think it looks similar. It may not be similar.

On talking
I have extremely low self-confidence. I feel very concerned about mutual thoughtfulness. And I feel very upset that I make a lot of effort hoping, wishing, trying, to talk less and even tell people 'give me feedback'. The amazing thing is that people I do talk a lot to don't complain. But the vast majority of people who know me, do complain that I talk too much. They mostly say I am quite interesting but I talk too much. I give more than they want. I overexplain, and all this I'm conscious of. I find it difficult to get out of . . . Most people complain about me. 'The most striking thing is she talks too much and too fast'. I am deeply hurt, not offended because of this valid comment, but I am hurt that I do this to people because I have such a love for people and I want to be mutually constructive and mutually helpful. I don't give others enough chance to get their word in edgeways and I say please interrupt me. I go on too much. I am now talking to you like a psychologist, a psychotherapist, but it is a problem . . . The Jews are a fast-speaking people but I am in the front line of the Jews, I think.

Dr S is eager that problems such as hers should be investigated further and that people should have greater awareness of these types of developmental difficulty. Lack of awareness, in her view, increases the difficulty which people have in tolerating her behaviour. To this end, she has requested from us a written document explaining her problems which she can show to those who become exasperated with her. To her, both this and a copy of this chapter have been of benefit.

ACKNOWLEDGEMENTS

This research was supported by a research award from the Wolfson Foundation. On sections of data, research assistance was given by Kim Cornish, Joanne Ilsley and Metke Shawe-Taylor.

FURTHER READING

Bruce, V. (1988) *Recognising Faces*. London: Lawrence Erlbaum.

Stiles-Davis, J., Kritchevsky and Bellugi, U. (ed.)

(1988) *Spatial Cognition: Brain Bases and Development.* London: Erlbaum.

Temple, C. M. (1992) Developmental pathologies and developmental disorders. In I. Rapin and S. J. Segalowitz (eds) *Handbook of Neuropsychology: Child Psychology.* Amsterdam: Elsevier.

REFERENCES

Benton, A. L., Hamsher, K. des, Varney, N. R. and Spreen, O. (1983) *Facial Recognition.* New York: Oxford University Press.

Benton, A. L., Varney, N. R. and Hamsher, K. des (1978) Visuospatial judgement: a clinical test. *Archives of Neurology, 35,* 364–7.

Bodamer, J. (1947) Die Prosopagnosie. *Archiv für Psychiatrie und Nervenkrankbeiten, 179,* 6–53.

Bruce, V. and Young, A. (1986) Understanding face recognition. *British Journal of Psychology, 77,* 305–27.

Ellis, A. W. and Young, A. W. (1988) *Human Cognitive Neuropsychology.* Hove, East Sussex: Lawrence Erlbaum.

Lansdell, H. (1968) Effect and extent of temporal lobe ablation on two lateralised deficits. *Physiology and Behaviour, 3,* 271–3.

Marr, D. (1976) Early processing of visual information. *Philosophical Transactions of the Royal Society (London), 275B,* 483–524.

Marr, D. (1980) Visual information processing: the structure and creation of visual representations. *Philosophical Transactions of the Royal Society (London), 290B,* 199–218.

Marr, D. (1982) *Vision.* San Francisco: W. H. Freeman.

Vandenburg, S. G. and Kuse, A. R. (1978) Mental rotation, a group test of three dimensional spatial visualization. *Perceptual and Motor Skills, 47,* 599–604.

Warrington, E. K. (1984) *Recognition Memory Battery.* Windsor: NFER-Nelson.

7

Hans Wallach and Virginia Slaughter

The Role of Memory in Perceiving Subjective Contours

In the variety of subjective contours that are structured like Kanizsa's triangle, shapes consist partly of edges of elements that make up the patterns that give rise to the subjective contours and partly of the subjective contours. It was found that familiarity with the shape that fit the subjective-contour-inducing pattern in this fashion increased the likelihood that subjective contours were perceived when the "containing" pattern was shown. Six containing patterns were constructed that did not readily yield subjective contours when the fitting shapes were not familiar. It was found that these containing patterns yielded subjective contours considerably more often when their fitting shapes had been made familiar than when they had not been. This result was obtained even though all subjects were acquainted with subjective contours before the containing patterns were shown, and even though they were asked whether or not they saw subjective contours when they saw the containing patterns. In a second experiment, subjects had no such set to experience subjective contours. When two of the containing patterns that had been used in the first experiment were shown, no subjective contours were perceived. However, after subjects had been familiarized with a drawing of one of the fitting shapes, they saw that shape in the pattern that contained it and along with it the subjective contours.

In recent years, subjective contours, also called illusory contours, have been given much attention, and that is as it should be. Whenever percepts have features that do not have their counterparts in proximal stimulation, they are likely to reveal something about the perceptual processes involved. Subjective contours take many forms. They are discussed in a recent review of the large literature by Parks

Figure 1 _____

Kanizsa's Display, Yielding Subjective Contours

(1984). Our investigation deals with the kind of patterns that yield subjective contours most reliably when viewed by naive subjects, that is, by those who have not been specifically aware of subjective contours before. In these patterns, subjective contours are more or less straight connections between aligned edges in cutouts that are readily perceived as cutouts, where the subjective contours are parts of edges of simple shapes, such as the upright triangle in Figure 1. The outline of the triangle consists of real contours where it shares the edges of the cutouts in the three black disks. Where the outline of the triangle is not provided by stimulation—that is, in the straight connections between the ends of the real contours—subjective contours are seen. These parts of the triangle's outline are the perceived features that have no counterpart in stimulation. The pattern that gives rise to subjective contours—in the case of Figure 1 the three black disks and the interrupted outline of the upside-down triangle—has been called a subjective-contour-inducing array and will be referred to as a *containing pattern*. The figure that is composed in part of subjective contours, here the upright triangle, has been called subjective figure; its shape will be referred to as the *fitting shape*.

When a percept has features not given in proximal stimulation, as in the case of shapes partly composed of subjective contours, it is possible that a memorial representation contributes to them. That happens, for instance,

when in the absence of binocular vision or of head movements, tridimensional shapes are perceived although only the projections of such shapes are given on a retina. Strong evidence for such effects of memories were obtained by Wallach, O'Connell, and Neisser (1953), who demonstrated that memorial representations created within an experiment could cause retinal patterns that normally evoke flat shapes to be perceived as tridimensional shapes. The authors experimented with tridimensional shapes so chosen that their projections resulted in the perception of flat shapes. In the course of that experiment, the tridimensional shapes were made to turn so that their projections changed form and evoked tridimensionally perceived shapes. When later stationary projections were displayed again, they were often perceived as tridimensional shapes. A stringent criterion for perceived tridimensionality was used; spontaneous reports of inversion served as evidence that now tridimensional shapes were being perceived.

Analogous experiments will be reported here that show that memorial representations contribute to the perceptions of shapes that, like the upright triangle in Figure 1, are partially composed of subjective contours. Instead of employing displays in which the subjective figures were simple familiar shapes, we, too, created, in the course of our experiments, the memorial representations that we believed were needed for the perception of subjective contours. Six unfamiliar shapes were designed to serve as fitting shapes, and for each of them a containing pattern was constructed (Figure 2). The containing patterns were so designed that the fitting shapes were not readily seen. But after subjects were made familiar with outline drawings of the fitting shapes (Figure 3), the fitting shapes were seen more frequently in the containing patterns, as were the subjective contours.

It was not easy to construct the containing patterns so that no subjective contours would be reported when the fitting shapes were not familiar to the subjects but would emerge from the containing patterns when the fitting shapes had been made familiar to them. This ideal outcome could be obtained only when subjects

Figure 2 ——

Six Containing Patterns Employed in Experiment 1

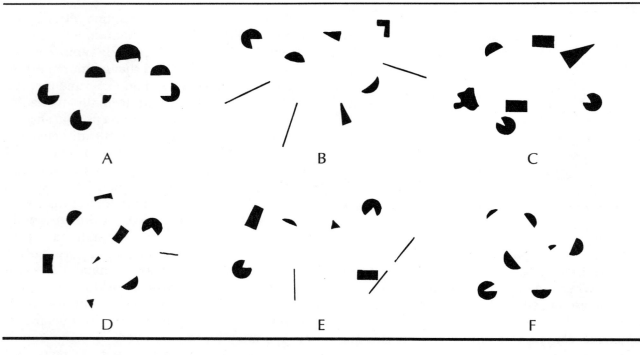

had no set to perceive subjective contours and as long as no set developed in the course of the experiment; otherwise, this outcome could only be approximated. Often, subjects who have a set to perceive subjective contours look for alignments between edges of different cutouts and other enclosing pattern elements; when they find them, they perceive the connection between the aligned edges as subjective contours. If they do, they will report subjective contours, even though they may not perceive the whole subjective figure.

EXPERIMENT 1

Initially, we felt that we had to acquaint our subjects with the experience of subjective contours so that we could be sure whether or not they perceived them. The result we hoped for was that subjective contours would be perceived in those containing patterns for which the fitting shapes had been made familiar, and that they would not be perceived in patterns for which that had not been done. Both results

involved hazards. For familiarization to be effective, the resulting memorial representation of the fitting shape had to become operational when the containing pattern was displayed. That would not happen when that pattern did not make contact with the memory of the shape that fitted it. Some process akin to recognition had to take place; otherwise, even when the fitting shape had been learned, subjective contours would not be perceived. On the other hand, subjects might report seeing subjective contours in containing patterns for which the fitting shapes had not been made familiar, because they had looked for alignments between edges of the cutouts and other edges of pattern elements. The two hazards diminished the difference between the results for the containing pattern for which the fitting shapes had been made familiar (experimental condition) and the results for the containing patterns for which this had not been done (control condition).

The experiment consisted of three steps. First, three of the six fitting shapes were made

Figure 3

Drawings of the Fitting Shapes of the Six Containing Patterns

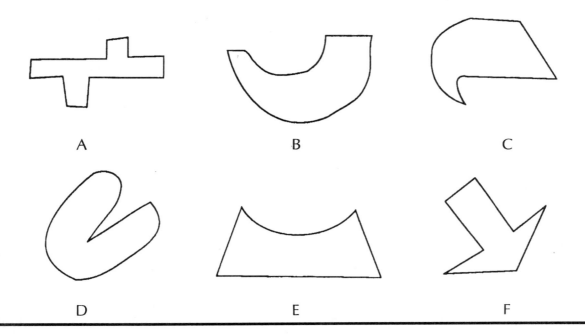

A   B   C

D   E   F

familiar to the subject. Then the subject was made acquainted with subjective contours. Finally, all six containing patterns were shown to the subject, one after the other, and the subject had to report, in each case, whether he or she saw subjective contours.

Method

Subjects.

Fifty-four undergraduates were paid for serving as subjects.

Equipment.

In addition to the six containing patterns shown in Figure 2 and the six outline drawings of the fitting shapes (Figure 3), there were four patterns that resembled the containing patterns but could not yield subjective contours because none of the edges of the pattern elements were aligned. They will be called N patterns. Finally, there was the containing pat-

tern that was used to make the subjects familiar with the experience of subjective contours (Figure 4). It was chosen for this purpose because its fitting shape was not immediately seen by naive subjects but yielded impressive subjective contours when it was. All these figures were drawn on 20 × 20 cm cards and were observed from a distance of 152 cm.

Procedure.

All subjects were first made familiar with three of the outline drawings of fitting shapes (Figure 3). First they learned to associate each of the three drawings with its letter name, and then they had to draw each from memory and supply its name. Odd-numbered subjects learned in this fashion the fitting shapes A, B, and C; even-numbered subjects learned the shapes D, E, and F.

Next, all subjects were shown Figure 4. They were asked what they saw and were made to look at the pattern until they reported seeing a cross. Then the experimenter pointed to an area where the subject presumably saw a sub-

Figure 4 _____

Containing Pattern Employed to Acquaint Subjects With Subjective Contours

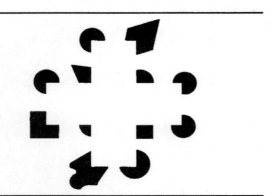

jective contour. Calling it an "illusory contour," the experimenter said: "Even though you may feel that you are perceiving a line here, surrounding and defining the cross, there is not any such line. Such an illusory contour seems to be a line enclosing a whole cohesive figure." The experimenter then explained that the subject would be shown some charts similar to that of the cross, and that some would contain illusory contours while others would not. The subject was instructed to "yes" if he or she saw an illusory contour and "no" if he or she did not.

During the subsequent test presentation, each chart was shown for approximately 4 sec, sufficient time for every subject to arrive at a decision. All six containing patterns were presented, the three for which the fitting shapes had been made familiar and the three for which they had not. In addition to the six critical patterns, all subjects were shown the N patterns. All subjects saw the six containing patterns and the four N patterns in the same order: N1, N2, A, D, N3, B, E, N4, C, F. This was our way of controlling for an order effect. A particular pattern whose fitting shape had been made familiar to one group of subjects occupied exactly the same position in the presentation sequence when, for the other group, its fitting shape was unfamiliar. Although randomization of the order of the containing patterns would have provided information about an order effect, the fixed-order procedure was

used because it provided optimal conditions for dealing with the effect of familiarity.

Results

Table 1 lists the number of subjects who reported seeing a subjective contour in the case of each of the containing patterns when its fitting shape was familiar (first row) or when it was not (second row) and in the case of the four N patterns combined (third row). The 162 containing patterns whose fitting shapes had been made familiar elicited a total of 115, or 71.0%, "yes" responses. The 162 containing patterns whose fitting shapes were unfamiliar elicited 66, or 40.7%, "yes" responses. Altogether, the 216 presentations of N patterns elicited 23 "yes" responses, providing an estimate of random "yes" responses of 10.6%. This rate of random "yes" responses cannot account for a rate of 40.7% of "yes" responses that were given in the control condition; a high proportion of these cases were caused by a set. However, the difference between the 66 cases in which the unfamiliar fitting shapes (control condition) produced "yes" responses and the 115 cases in which the familiar fitting shapes (experimental condition) produced "yes" responses can be ascribed to the familiarity of the fitting shapes. If one takes into account that nothing was done to facilitate containing patterns' making contact with memorial representations of the fitting shapes, the rate of 71.0% "yes" responses in the experimental condition seems quite satisfactory.

Table 1 _____

Number of Subjects Who Reported Seeing Subjective Contours When Viewing Containing Patterns Representing Familiar or Unfamiliar Shapes and When Viewing N Patterns

Pattern Category	Patterns						
	A	B	C	D	E	F	Totals
Familiar	26	16	14	14	21	24	115
Unfamiliar	16	7	14	5	14	10	66
N pattern							23

An analysis of subjects' "yes" responses in the experimental and control conditions, using Wilcoxon's matched-pairs signed-ranks test, yielded $z = -4.34$ and $p = .00006$.

This result encouraged us to try to experiment with subjects who had not been made acquainted with subjective contours in the course of the experiment. With such subjects, the frequency with which subjective contours would be reported in the control condition should be greatly diminished. In this experiment, a subject was presented with only one containing pattern whose fitting shape was familiar and was familiarized with only two fitting shapes.

EXPERIMENT 2

Method

Subjects.

Twenty-six undergraduates were paid for serving as subjects.

Equipment.

The containing patterns A and F were selected from those of Experiment 1 because they most resembled conventional subjective contour patterns. They served as critical items, that is, the outline drawings of their fitting shapes were also used. The outline drawing of shape E served as a filler.

Procedure.

First, every subject was shown the containing patterns A and F and, in each case, asked to describe it (first presentation). The order in which these patterns were shown was varied. If, in either one of the two cases, the subject reported seeing the fitting shape, for example, an arrow or a white figure on the black circles, he or she was disqualified. There were 4 so-disqualified subjects. Thus, 22 subjects completed the experiment.

Then the subject was made familiar with the outline drawing of either fitting shape A or

fitting shape F and with the outline drawing E. When the subject felt ready, after being shown the two drawings alternately several times, he or she drew the shapes and gave their names. When it came to the test, 11 subjects were familiar with the fitting shape A but not with fitting shape F and 11 were familiar with the fitting shape F but not the fitting shape A.

In the test, all subjects were shown both containing patterns, A and F, with one of the patterns always serving as control. As before, the subject was asked to describe what he or she saw. A subject was always first presented with the containing pattern whose fitting shape had *not* been made familiar. (Because it turned out that the fitting shape was never seen in that containing pattern, subjects had still not seen subjective contours during the experiment when the critical containing pattern was presented.)

Results

When the containing pattern whose fitting shape had not been made familiar was shown, all subjects gave a description similar to the one they had given at the first presentation; the fitting shapes never occurred in these descriptions. When next they were shown the other, critical containing pattern, 15 subjects reported seeing the fitting shape, 6 of them immediately and 9 after looking at the pattern for a brief time. The other 7 subjects saw the fitting shape after they had been asked: "Can you see one of the figures you have learned before?" This caused them to see the fitting shape. (This question could not be asked in Experiment 1, and this probably accounts in large part for the 162 minus 115 cases in which no subjective contours were reported in the experimental conditions.)

After the subject had seen the fitting shape, either spontaneously or after being prompted, we made sure that he or she also saw its subjective contour. Twelve of the subjects were asked to follow the edge of the shape they saw with a finger. They all traced the outline correctly and answered positively to the question: "Do you see it as if there were a line around the figure, even in the white spaces?" The other 10 subjects were then shown a compelling subjective contour pattern (Figure 4), and the experimenter said: "This is what we call an illusory contour; there seems to be an outlined shape even though there isn't actually a line surrounding it. Did you see the same thing in the figure I just showed you?" All 10 subjects answered "yes" to this question.

The probability that all 22 subjects saw the subjective figure where the fitting shape had been made familiar and none where that was not the case is 2.4×10^{-7}.

This experiment demonstrated that only subjects familiar with the fitting shape reported seeing it in the containing pattern, that these subjects did so either spontaneously (15) or when associative access to the memorial representation was provided (7), and that all subjects who saw the fitting shape in the containing pattern also saw subjective contours.

SUMMARY AND DISCUSSION

An important condition for the perception of subjective contours is familiarity with the fitting shape and a coming into play of the memories that represent the familiarity. In fact, it may well be the only condition that, in the absence of a perceptual set, results in a perception of subjective contours, unless a stereoscopic depth effect provides the fitting shape. . . . In Experiment 1, in which all subjects were made acquainted with subjective contours and in which instructions caused a set to look for them, subjective contours were still 1.74 times as frequently perceived when the fitting shapes had been made familiar than when they had not been. When, in Experiment 2, subjects were free of a set to look for subjective contours and remained so until the critical exposure, no subjective contours were perceived unless the subject had been made familiar with the fitting shape. When the memorial representation of the fitting shape came into play, subjective contours were perceived in every case.

In the usual demonstrations of subjective contours, the fitting shapes are simple geometric forms that are highly familiar, such as equi-lateral triangles and squares. Sixty or 90° cutouts in elements of the containing patterns serve to make contact with the memorial representations of these simple shapes. In the most reliable demonstration, that using Kanizsa's triangle (Figure 1), the relevant memory, that of a triangle, is brought into play by the outline triangle that is part of the display.

That the emergence of subjective contours may be favored by a perceptual set has occasionally been noted, but formal experimental evidence has been presented only recently. Coren, Porac, and Theodor (1986) published two experiments that demonstrated the effectiveness of set. Their Experiment 2 demonstrated a general set produced by prior exposure to subjective-contour-inducing patterns. This is comparable to the general set that operated in our Experiment 1, in which subjects were first made acquainted with a subjective-contour-producing pattern and were under instruction to report subjective contours when they saw them. Coren et al.'s (1986) Experiment 1 is more relevant to this discussion. Their test figure consisted of four thin lines forming an upright cross with a gap where the crossing point would have been. Upon suggestion that this gap may be seen as a white form and that subjects should draw a line around the form if they saw it, 90 out of 161 subjects did so. This set was thus 56% effective. However, the important finding was that naming the shape of the white form was also partially effective. When the white form was referred to as "figure," the result was 20 drawings of a circular outline, 2 of a square, and 4 amorphous outlines by 51 subjects; when it was referred to as a circle, the result was 39 circular outlines from the 58 subjects; and when it was called a square, the result was 5 circular and 20 square outlines from 52 subjects.

Coren et al. (1986) found these results "consistent with cognitive explanations of subjective-contour formation" and compatible with several theoretical positions: Subjective contours may be "a form of problem solving, . . . a form of Gestalt closure," or arise from a "reorganization of the configuration on the basis of implicit depth cues" (p. 332). Our experiments, on the other hand, support the view that subjective figures are manifestations of memorial representations coming into play and being part of the form process. Coren et al.'s finding that instructions containing the words "circle" and "square" often influenced the shape of the subjective figure if one was seen is in agreement with our conclusion. Such instructions may bring memorial representations of these shapes into play and thereby determine the shapes of the subjective figures.

That subjective contours occur when information carried by stimulation is incomplete and when memory supplies the missing pieces shows that their perception is similar to that of a tridimensional form that, in the absence of depth cues from stimulation, also results from the operation of memorial representations. But there is a difference. In the perception of tridimensional form, memorial representation merely gives shape to what is given on the retina. In the case of subjective contours, memorial representations add material features to perception. This suggests imagery. But we hesitate to regard the subjective figure with its completed contours as an image fitted into the containing pattern; mental images are not known to fit themselves into percepts.

There are two conditions under which subjective contours are seen that are not completions of edges in stationary patterns. They are discussed here because they fit with our findings in various ways. One of the conditions involves dot-matrix stereograms, as designed by Julesz (1960), that give rise to a segregation of a part of the dot pattern. The segregation may be achieved by dichoptic presentation of the stereograms causing stereoscopic depth to be perceived, with the inner region appearing in front of the outer region. Before Kanizsa's subjective contours became widely known, White (1962) noted that the inner region seems to have an edge that "lies *between* the rows and columns of dots. . . . This is a rare instance of visual contour-formation in the absence of a brightness gradient in the field" (p. 411). Later, Lawson and Gulick (1967) produced a whole subjective figure stereoscopically by omitting the dot pattern in the inner region. The other way to bring about such segregation and to cause such subjective contours to form is by

alternately projecting the left-eye and the right-eye matrix into the same area in rapid sequence. The inner region will then appear to move horizontally back and forth slightly in front of the outer region (White, 1962). The finding that in both cases segregation is an antecedent of the perception of subjective contours agrees with the notion that is implicit in our findings: Subjective contours result when shapes are perceived whose edges are not given or are only partly given in stimulation. In Kanizsa-type displays, memorial representations furnish the shapes, and in Julesz-type stereograms, stereoscopic depth or White's stroboscopic motion result in segregation which provides the shapes.

The other condition for subjective contours involves moving line patterns. When a pattern of parallel and regularly spaced oblique lines moves behind a screen and is seen through an aperture in the screen, even though the objective direction of the motion of the pattern is not given, the perceived motion has a definitive direction, and that has interesting consequences (Wallach, 1935; see also Wallach, 1976, chap. IX, 1). When, for instance, such line-pattern motion is given in a square aperture, the perceived motion is parallel to the aperture edges. Since there are two pairs of aperture edges, two motion directions are possible, one vertical and the other horizontal. Perception that results from such ambiguous stimulation conditions as a rule yields to perceptual satiation; the two possible versions are experienced in alternation. The line motion is no exception: the pattern appears to move alternately vertically and horizontally. Satiation has a strong effect. Motion direction changes even when cues for the objective motion are present. When a line pattern with a vertical gap (Figure 5) moves vertically downward, vertical motion is seen for much longer than it is in the ambiguous arrangement, because the visible ends of the lines serve as cues for the objective motion direction. When eventually the lines are seen to move horizontally, the gap is perceived as a vertical white strip with subjective contours on either side where the lines objectively have their ends. These ends are no longer seen; the line pattern seems to be whole and to be

Figure 5 ─────────────────

Moving-line Display With Vertical Gap in Line Pattern

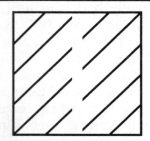

Figure 6 ─────────────────

Moving-line Display With Lines Ending on the Right Side, Inside the Frame

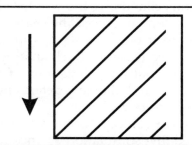

moving behind the strip. This case fits our explanation of the subjective contours that are structured like Kanizsa's triangle. In this case, too, memory supplies the shape that fits into the pattern, into the gap between the end of the lines, the memory of objects that conceal part of a pattern. It appears that the strip results from two process steps, the development of horizontal motion of the pattern and a recall step that causes perception of the strip. Wallach (1935, 1976) investigated a similar arrangement, in which, instead of a gap in the line pattern, the pattern ended laterally. With this arrangement (Figure 6), many subjects saw the pattern move horizontally several times before they "saw clearly" what happened at the right side of the pattern where the lines seemed to disappear under a vertical strip. Prior to the formation of the strip, the line seemed to vanish unaccountably. The two process steps often took place at different times.

REFERENCES

Coren, S., Porac, C., & Theodor, L. H. (1986). The effects of perceptual set on the shape and apparent depth of subjective contours. *Perception & Psychophysics*, **39**, 327–333.

Julesz, B. (1960). Binocular depth perception of computer-generated patterns. *Bell System Technical Journal*, **39**, 1125–1162.

Lawson, R. B., & Gulick, W. L. (1967). Stereopsis and anomalous contour. *Vision Research*, **7**, 271–297.

Parks T. E. (1984). Illusory figures: A (mostly) atheoretical review. *Psychological Bulletin*, **95**, 282–300.

Wallach, H. (1935). Über visuell wahrgenommene Bewegungsrichtung. *Psychologische Forschung*, **20**, 325–380.

Wallach, H. (1976). *On perception*. New York: Quandrangle/The New York Times Book Co.

Wallach H., O'Connell, D. N., & Neisser, U. (1953). The memory effect of visual perception of three-dimensional form. *Journal of Experimental Psychology*, **45**, 360–368.

White, B. W. (1962). Stimulus-conditions affecting a recently discovered stereoscopic effect. *American Journal of Psychology*, **75**, 411–420.

This work was supported by Grant BSN-8318772 from the National Science Foundation to Swarthmore College, Hans Wallach, principal investigator.

8

K. Anders Ericsson, William G. Chase, and Steve Faloon

Acquisition of a Memory Skill

Abstract: *After more than 230 hours of practice in the laboratory, a subject was able to increase his memory span from 7 to 79 digits. His performance on other memory tests with digits equaled that of memory experts with lifelong training. With an appropriate mnemonic system, there is seemingly no limit to memory performance with practice.*

One of the most fundamental and stable properties of the human memory system is the limited capacity of short-term memory. This limit places severe constraints on the human ability to process information and solve problems (1). On the other hand, this limit (about seven unrelated items) stands in apparent contrast to documented feats of memory experts (2). Whether these memory skills are the result of extensive practice or of exceptional ability has often been disputed. The goal of this research is to analyze how a memory skill is acquired.

An undergraduate (S.F.) with average memory abilities and average intelligence for a college student engaged in the memory span task for about 1 hour a day, 3 to 5 days a week, for more than 1½ years. S.F. was read random digits at the rate of one digit per second; he then recalled the sequence. If the sequence was reported correctly, the next sequence was increased by one digit; otherwise it was decreased by one digit. Immediately after half the trials (randomly selected), S.F. provided verbal reports of his thoughts during the trial. At the end of each session, he also recalled as much of the material from the session as he could. On some days, experiments were substituted for the regular sessions.

During the course of 20 months of practice (more than 230 hours of laboratory testing), S.F.'s digit span steadily improved from 7 to al-

Figure 1

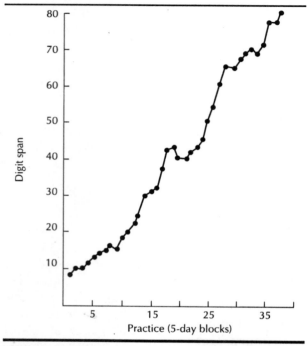

Average Digit Span for S. F. as a Function of Practice

Digit span is defined as the length of the sequence that is correct 50 percent of the time; under the procedure followed, it is equivalent to average sequence length. Each day represents about 1 hour's practice and ranges from 55 trials per day in the beginning to 3 trials per day for the longest sequences. The 38 blocks of practice shown here represent about 190 hours of practice; interspersed among these practice sessions are approximately 40 hours of experimental sessions (not shown).

most 80 digits (Figure 1). Furthermore, his ability to remember digits after the session also improved. In the beginning, he could recall virtually nothing after an hour's session; after 20 months of practice, he could recall more than 80 percent of the digits presented to him. On one occasion (after 4 months of practice), we tested S.F.'s memory after the session with a recognition test (because recognition is a much more sensitive measure of retention than recall is); he not only recognized perfectly 3- and 4-digit sequences from the same day, but also recognized sequences from earlier in the week.

With only a few hundred hours of practice, S.F. would be classified as a beginner at most skills. However, in his field of expertise, memory for random digits, he compares favorably with the best-known mnemonists, such as Lu-

ria's S. and Hunt and Love's V.P. (2). For example, after about 6 months of practice, we set S.F. the task of recalling a matrix of 50 digits because data on this task are available for both S. and V.P. S.F.'s study times and recall times were at least as good as those of the lifetime memory experts.

The key to understanding this skill comes from analyses of S.F.'s verbal reports and his performance on various experimental tests. We will first describe two essential components of this skill: (i) his mnemonic associations and (ii) his retrieval structures. Then we will address the question of whether or not S.F. was able to increase his short-term memory capacity.

The most essential part of S.F.'s skill is his mnemonic associations, which he described in great detail in his verbal reports. The principle of a mnemonic is to associate unknown material with something familiar; the advantage is that it relieves the burden on short-term memory because recall can be achieved through a single association with an already-existing code in long-term memory. What S.F. did was to categorize 3- and 4-digit groups as running times for various races (3). For example, 3492 was recoded as "3 minutes and 49 point 2 seconds, near world-record mile time" (4). During the first 4 months, S.F. gradually constructed an elaborate set of mnemonic associations based initially on running times and then supplemented with ages (893 was "89 point 3, very old man") and dates (1944 was "near the end of World War II") for those sequences that could not be categorized as times. Running times (62 percent) and ages (25 percent) account for almost 90 percent of S.F.'s mnemonic associations.

There are several lines of evidence concerning the mnemonic associations. On the basis of S.F.'s verbal reports, we were able to simulate his mnemonic associations, that is, to abstract a set of rules that categorizes a sequence of digits as 3- and 4-digit running times. When we compared the simulation to the verbal reports, between 85 and 95 percent of the time the computer categorized the digit sequences as S.F. did. By means of the simulation, we were also able to determine which sequences of digits would be categorized as running times and which would not. On the basis of this analysis, we presented S.F. with sequences that could not be associated with running time categories. (This was before S.F. started to use ages to supplement his running times, after about 2 months of practice.) When S.F. was faced with these uncodable sequences, his performance dropped almost to his beginning level. In another experimental session we did the opposite: We presented him with sequences that could all be coded in terms of running times. His performance jumped by 22 percent (from an average of 16 to an average of 19.5 digits).

The mechanism whereby S.F. recodes single digits into 3- and 4-digit units is not sufficient to account for his performance. If S.F. originally had a digit span of 7 digits, and he then learned to recode digits into 4-digit groups, how could he remember the order of more than seven groups of digits—that is, more than 28 digits? The answer to this question comes from an analysis of his retrieval structures.

Like most people, S.F. initially tried to hold everything in a rehearsal buffer, which stored material in a phonetic code. When he first used his mnemonic associations (session 5), he demonstrated the first rudimentary use of a retrieval structure. He recoded the first 6 digits as two running times, if possible, and he held the last 4 to 6 digits in his rehearsal buffer. He then tried to recall the two running times in order while rehearsing the last few digits. This strategy worked well, and he gradually perfected it over the course of the first 30 sessions until he could recall as many as 18 digits by recoding three groups of 4 digits each as running times and holding the last 6 digits in his rehearsal buffer. At this point, he began to experience real difficulty in keeping the order straight for more than three or four running times (Figure 1, blocks 8 and 9).

The next important advance came when S.F. introduced organization into his retrieval structure by segmenting his groups into subgroups: He used two 4-digit groups followed by two 3-digit groups and the rehearsal group. From this point, S.F. improved his performance rapidly by increasing the number of groups within each subgroup, until he began to experience

the same difficulty as before. The second plateau in his performance curve (around block 21 in Figure 1) is associated with difficulty in remembering the order of more than four groups within a supergroup. Introducing another level of organization by subdividing these supergroups allowed S.F.'s performance to improve rapidly so that he now averages almost 80 digits. His current retrieval organization can be described as a hierarchy with three levels, and his retrieval structure for 80 digits can be illustrated in the following way, with spaces corresponding to levels in the hierarchy:

444 444   333 333   444   333   444   5

Besides the verbal descriptions, there is a great deal of additional evidence that S.F. uses hierarchical retrieval structures. Probably the most straightforward evidence comes from his speech patterns during recall, which almost invariably follow the same pattern. Digit groups are recalled rapidly at a normal rate of speech (about 3 digits per second) with pauses between groups (about 2 seconds between groups, on average, with longer pauses when he has difficulty remembering). At the end of a supergroup, however, there is a falling intonation, generally followed by a longer pause (5).

In several experiments, we verified that groups are retrieved through the hierarchical structure rather than through direct associations between groups. In one experiment, instead of asking for recall after presenting the digits, we presented S.F. with a 3- or 4-digit group and asked him to name the group that preceded it or followed it in the sequence. He required more than twice as long, on the average, if the preceding or following group crossed a supergroup boundary (10.0 seconds) than if it did not (4.4 seconds). In another experiment, after an hour's session, we presented S.F. with 3- and 4-digit groups from that session and asked him to recall as much as he could about each group. He invariably recalled the mnemonic associations he had generated, and he often recalled a great deal about the location of the group within the hierarchy, but he was virtually never able to recall the preceding or following group.

After all this practice, can we conclude that S.F. increased his short-term memory capacity? There are several reasons to think not. (i) The size of S.F.'s groups were almost always 3 and 4 digits, and he never generated a mnemonic association for more than 5 digits (6). (ii) He almost never allowed his rehearsal group to exceed 6 digits. (iii) He generally used three groups in his supergroups and, after some initial difficulty with five groups, never allowed more than four groups in a supergroup. (iv) In one experimental session, S.F. was switched from digits to letters of the alphabet after 3 months of practice and exhibited no transfer: His memory span dropped back to about six consonants.

These data suggest that the reliable working capacity of short-term memory is about three or four units, as Broadbent has recently argued (7), and that it is not possible to increase the capacity of short-term memory with extended practice. Rather, increases in memory span are due to the use of mnemonic associations in long-term memory. With an appropriate mnemonic system and retrieval structure, there is seemingly no limit to improvement in memory skill with practice.

REFERENCES AND NOTES

1. G. A. Miller, *Psychol. Rev.* **63**, 81 (1956); A. Newell and H. A. Simon, *Human Problem Solving* (Prentice-Hall, Englewood Cliffs, N.J., 1972).

2. A. R. Luria has documented the case history of one exceptional person, S., who seemed to remember large amounts of trivial information for years by means of visual imagery [*The Mind of a Mnemonist* (Avon, New York, 1968)], and E. Hunt and T. Love have described another exceptional person, V.P., who could remember large amounts of material by means of elaborate linguistic associations in several languages [in A. W. Melton and E. Martin, Eds., *Coding Processes in Human Memory* (Winston, Washington, D.C., 1972), p. 237].

3. S.F. is a good long-distance runner who competes in races throughout the eastern United States. He classifies running times into at least 11 major categories, from half-mile to marathon, with several subcategories within each.

4. The category label by itself was not sufficient to retrieve the exact digits presented. A complete understanding of the precision of mnemonic associations will require an answer to the more general question of how meaningful associations work.

5. Pauses, intonation, and stress patterns are well-known indicators of linguistic structures [M. A. K. Halliday, *Intonation and Grammar in British English* (Mouton, The Hague, 1967); K. Pike, *The Intonation of American English* (Univ. of Michigan Press, Ann Arbor, 1945)]. In one memory span study, we compared the grouping patterns indicated by the prosodic features in recall with the grouping patterns reported by S.F. in his verbal protocols, and agreement was virtually perfect.

6. The mnemonic associations of lightning calculators appear to be limited to 3 or 4 digits [G. E. Müller, *Z. Psychol. Ergänzungsband* 5 (1911)].

7. D. A. Broadbent, in *Studies in Long Term Memory*, A. Kennedy and A. Wilkes, Eds. (Wiley, New York, 1975), p. 3.

8. Supported by contract N00014-78-C-0215 from the Advanced Research Projects Agency and by grant MH-07722 from the National Institute of Mental Health. We thank J. R. Anderson, M. T. H. Chi, W. Jones, M. W. Schustack, and H. A. Simon for their valuable comments.

9

Roger N. Shepard

The Mental Image

Abstract: *Although neglected by cognitive psychologists, mental imagery appears to have played a crucial role in far-reaching scientific developments. Without assuming anything about the internal processes underlying visual images, we can study such images as defined solely in relation to their corresponding external objects. The results indicate that mental imagery is remarkably able to substitute for actual perception: Subjects make the same judgments about objects in their absence as in their presence; subjects who imagine a particular object are uniquely fast and accurate in discriminatively responding to related external test stimuli; and, in the process of imagining a spatial transformation, subjects pass through states with a demonstrable one-to-one relation to corresponding states in the external world. Possibly, rules governing spatial structures and transformations, having been incorporated into our perceptual machinery by eons of evolution in a three-dimensional world, are now at the service of creative thought.*

Cognitive psychology has long been preoccupied with processes that are verbal or at least readily verbalizable. I attribute the origin of this preoccupation to the former ascendancy of behaviorism, with its preference for responses that are overt or, if not overt, that could directly be made so. Thoughts embodied in words and propositions have this property; mental images often do not. Despite a general weakening of behavioristic strictures, this preoccupation continues, reinforced now by the dazzling emergence from linguistics of the inherently discrete formalisms of generative grammar and semantics, by the almost total dependence of work in artificial intelligence on computers designed for sequential manipulation of discrete symbols, and perhaps by the antimentalistic writings of such philosophers as Wittgenstein (1953) and Ryle (1949).

IS MENTAL IMAGERY OF ANY IMPORTANCE?

If mental images are at most subjective epiphenomena that play little or no functional role in significant processes of human thought, as some articulate commentators such as Pylyshyn (1973) have been suggesting, then the scientific study of imagery might be judged of little consequence. Still, I for one am uneasy about proceeding on the assumption that mental imagery is merely epiphenomenal—especially since visual imagery seems to have played such a central role in the origin of the most creative of my own ideas, and since so many other, more illustrious scientists, inventors, and writers have made similar claims concerning *their* thought processes. From a recent survey of a variety of introspective reports of this kind (Shepard, in press) I shall here select, for illustration, just two of the many lines of scientific and technological development of far-reaching significance in which mental imagery appears to have played a prominent role—namely, those concerning electromagnetic fields and molecular structures.

Visual Imagery in the Origin of the Theory and Application of Electromagnetic Fields

The modern conception of electric and magnetic fields had its origin in the mind of Michael Faraday, who, without the benefit of any mathematical education beyond "the merest elements of arithmetic" (Tyndall, 1868), was able to find a large number of general results requiring of others, as Helmholtz later observed with great astonishment, "the highest powers of mathematical analysis." And he succeeded in doing this, according to Helmholtz, "by a kind of intuition, with the security of instinct, without the help of a single mathematical formula" (quoted in Kendall, 1955). What kind of "intuition" or "instinct" was this? A clue may be discerned in the claim that the invisible lines of force, which Faraday visualized as narrow tubes curving throughout

space, "rose up before him like things" (Koestler, 1964; Tyndall, 1868).

The culmination of classical electromagnetic theory was achieved by Faraday's towering successor, James Clerk Maxwell, who brilliantly crystallized the fundamental relationships governing electric and magnetic fields, and the propagation of electromagnetic waves, in the form of a beautifully symmetrical set of equations universally known simply as "Maxwell's equations." What is significant here is that although Maxwell has been regarded as a prime example of an abstract theoretician, he is reported to have "developed the habit of making a mental picture of every problem" (Beveridge, 1957, p. 76). He, in fact, arrived at his formal equations only at the end of a long series of more and more elaborately visualized concrete hydrodynamic and mechanical models of the underlying "ether"—models that he ultimately discarded, as Sir Edmund Whittaker once put it, in much the same way that one might discard a temporary "scaffolding" used in the erection of a permanent edifice (Newman, 1955).

The present-day relativistic reformulation of electromagnetic theory had its inception when Albert Einstein performed his epochal Gedanken experiment of imagining himself traveling alongside a beam of light (at 186,000 miles per second). It was then that he confronted the paradox that the stationary spatial oscillation that he mentally "saw" corresponded neither to anything that could be perceptually experienced as light nor to anything described by Maxwell's equations (Einstein, 1949; Holton, 1972). As is well known, Einstein later stated quite explicitly that he "very rarely" thought in words at all (Wertheimer, 1945, p. 184). Indeed, he explained that his "particular ability" did not lie in mathematical calculation either, but rather in *visualizing . . . effects, consequences, and possibilities*" (Holton, 1972, p. 110). He could not even undertake the difficult business of finding words and mathematical symbols to communicate his new insights into the nature of space and time, he said, until he had already worked out his conceptualization of the physical situation by means of "more or less clear images which can be 'voluntarily' reproduced and combined" (Hadamard, 1945, Appendix 2).

Many applications of electromagnetism evidently arose in a similar way. The simultaneous conception of the self-starting induction motor and the now universally adopted polyphase electrical distribution system upon which that motor depends reportedly came to the prolific visionary Nikola Tesla with hallucinatory intensity, in the form of a kinetic visual image of a rotating magnetic field (Hunt & Draper, 1964; Tesla, 1956). And spatial visualization seems to have figured heavily in the geometrical conceptions of the complex electric and magnetic fields underlying the inventions of the original cyclotron, which led to a Nobel Prize for Ernest O. Lawrence, and of the later and vastly more powerful alternating gradient synchroton, which overnight "elevated" the obscure Greek elevator-engineer Nicholas Christofilos to international scientific prominence (Livingston, 1966, 1969; Shepard, in press).

Visual Imagery in the Development of the Theory and Biological Application of Molecular Structures

The German chemist Friedrich A. Kekulé said that many of his early insights into the nature of chemical bonds and of molecular structure arose out of idle reveries in which he spontaneously experienced kinetic visual images of the dancing atoms hooking up to form chainlike molecules. Kekulé's cultivation of this visionary practice culminated in his celebrated dream in which one of these snakelike, writhing chains suddenly twisted into a closed loop as if seizing its own tail; thus was the startled Kekulé provided with his long-sought answer to the problem of the structure of benzene—a structure fundamental to all of modern organic chemistry (Findlay, 1948).

The demands that certain branches of chemistry place on spatial imagery apparently are no less today. When the first of the studies that my students and I carried out on "mental rotation" appeared in the journal *Science* (Shepard & Metzler, 1971), the letters we received

from stereochemists, particularly, recognized in the mental process we were studying something that was crucial to their own everyday work. In fact, according to the account of the "cracking" of the genetic code in Watson's (1968) *The Double Helix*, mental rotation may even have played a significant role in that Nobel-Prize-winning discovery. After studying the three-dimensional molecular models that he and Crick had been developing, it suddenly occurred to Watson that there might be "profound implications of a DNA structure in which . . . each adenine residue would form two hydrogen bonds to an adenine residue related to it by a 180-degree rotation" and later, as he came still closer to the truth, that "an adenine-thymine pair . . . was identical in shape to a guanine-cytosine pair" (Watson, 1968, pp. 116; 123). Since the shapes he refers to are themselves quite complex and hard to describe, it seems likely that the processes leading to this sudden awareness were not so much atomistic and logical as holistic and analogical. The importance of such analogical processes is further suggested when Watson (1968) then speaks of coming into the lab to find Crick "flipping the cardboard base pairs about an imaginary line" (p. 128).

Other Roles of Visual Imagery

Even when we turn to lines of work in which words themselves rather than spatial configurations that are difficult to put into words constitute the core of the matter, we still find those who emphasize the importance of imagery in the creative process. The most famous parallel, in the field of belles lettres, to Kekulé's dream-discovery of the structure of benzene, is undoubtedly the one in which the poem "Kubla Khan" involuntarily and effortlessly came to the dozing Samuel Taylor Coleridge. Of particular relevance to the question of the role of visual imagery is Coleridge's explicit statement that, in parallel with the production of the corresponding verbal expressions, "all of the images rose up before him as *things*" (Ghiselin, 1952, p. 85).

The contemporary American novelist Joan Didion has asserted that none of the novels that she has written began with any notion of "character" or "plot" or even "incident." Instead, each developed out of what she calls "pictures in my mind"—some of which she describes in vivid detail. Indeed, Didion claims that the very syntax and arrangement of the words of her sentences is dictated by the image: "The arrangement you want can be found in the picture in your mind" (Didion, 1976, p. 2). Similarly, in a very recent interview, Judith Guest, whose first novel *Ordinary People* is a current best-seller, reports that her novel began as a "mental image" of the leading character sitting on a stone bench in the garden of a mental hospital. The character of the psychiatrist also appeared to Guest as a mental image—but this time in a dream: "I saw him in the dream—exactly what he looked like, everything" (Friedman, 1977, p. 3).

The above sampling of merely anecdotal reports from the fields of physics, chemistry, and literature does not of course establish that mental images actually played the crucial *functional* role that the various scientists and authors attributed to them. These reports nevertheless suggest that, until we possess a much more complete and satisfactory theory of the creative process, we run the risk of missing something of potential importance if we take it for granted that visual imagery is of no significance (also see Ferguson, 1977; Sloman, 1971).

And finally, it is not only those engaged in creative work who may be powerfully affected by their own mental imagery. Witness, today, the widespread clinical attention to the role of imagery in the control of autonomic and affective states and, consequently, to its use in procedures for the reduction of stress or the deconditioning of phobias. As an indication of how effectively an imagined thing can substitute for the real thing, consider how often behavior seems to be governed more by how vividly one pictures a desired or feared event, such as winning a lottery or being dismembered by a shark, than by the probability that one would otherwise assign to the event by purely logical or statistical reasoning.

WHAT IS A MENTAL IMAGE?

Current controversy concerning mental imagery seems to have focused on two closely related questions: (a) Do the mental images that some of us undeniably experience play a significant functional role in our thinking or are they merely epiphenomenal accompaniments of underlying processes of a very different, less pictorial character? and (b) What exactly are mental images or, more specifically, what sort of physical processes underlie them in the brain, and to what extent are these processes, like pictures, isomorphic to the external objects that they represent? Before we can go much beyond the merely anecdotal evidence relevant to the first of these two questions, we need to attempt some logical clarification with respect to the second.

Gedanken Experiments on the Externalization of Visual Images

What makes a mental image such a difficult thing to study empirically or even to clarify conceptually is that it is inherently internal. True, some artists and psychological subjects have attempted to externalize particularly vivid images, dreams, or hallucinations by means of drawing or painting; and I myself have recently presented detailed color reconstructions of some of my own entoptic, hypnagogic, and dream images (Shepard, in press). However, such reconstructions are generally too time-consuming and dependent on the graphical skills of the subject to be of wide use in the parametric investigation of mental imagery. Before considering some laboratory techniques that do permit a kind of externalization adequate to support such an investigation, we might profitably follow Einstein's example and seek conceptual clarification, in this case of what it would mean to "externalize" a mental image, by performing a kind of futuristic Gedanken experiment.

Suppose that we have, as in Figure 1, a device that is able to detect the intricate pattern of cortical activity in the brain of Creature A

Figure 1 _____

A Device for the Externalization of Visual Images

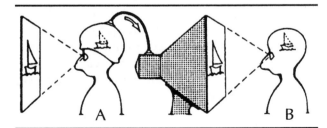

Figure 2 _____

The Same Device Used for the Externalization of a Purely Mental Image

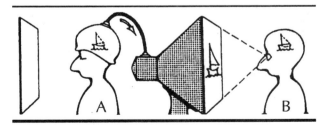

and, from an analysis of this pattern, to reconstruct the external physical stimulus that must have given rise to this pattern. To the extent that the reconstruction is accurate, Creature B, who looks at the reconstruction, could enjoy much the same perceptual experience as Creature A.

Essential here is the realization that, so far, we need assume no structural isomorphism between the pattern of activity in the brain and the external objects that it represents. That mental images have been drawn, within each creature's head, as a dotted outline with the same shape as the corresponding external object should be taken only figuratively—not literally. All that is really required in order for the device to be able to decode the pattern of brain activity, and thus to reconstruct a corresponding external picture, is that there be a unique one-to-one correspondence between the external stimulus and the resulting inner pattern of neural activity—whatever that pattern may be.

Suppose now that Creature A, instead of actually perceiving the external object, merely imagines or remembers the appearance of that same object. To the extent that internally generated mental imagery uses the same neural circuits that are externally excited in perception, our hypothetical device would again reconstruct an external likeness of the object imagined, as shown in Figure 2. And, again, this would not imply that the pattern of brain activity underlying the mental image had itself the shape of the external object.

Already our little thought experiment has indicated two things: First, although the brain processes that underlie a mental image need

not themselves be like any sort of a picture, they must necessarily contain the information that could in principle permit the reconstruction of a picture with a high degree of isomorphism to the external object imagined. And second, what is behind the common tendency to think of a mental image as some sort of a picture may be the fact, schematizied in Figures 1 and 2, that the brain process that underlies a purely mental image is very much like the brain process that is produced by looking at a corresponding picture (Shepard, 1975; Shepard & Chipman, 1970; Smart, 1959).

This thought experiment does not in any way contradict earlier arguments that I have made that there may sometimes be some abstract kind of isomorphism between the brain process and the corresponding external object (Shepard, 1975). Very likely, the neural activity underlying the mental image of a square has some multiple of four functionally isolable subparts. Certainly one can attend to, imagine, or perceive just one side or corner of a square with the rest.

There is, however, a significant limitation of our hypothetical device. The limitation is brought out most sharply by consideration of ambiguous figures such as Figure 3, which I have redrawn on the basis of a sketch that Arnheim (1969) attributes to one of his students. Running the risk of seeming to reveal one or more of my own proclivities, I refer to this as the Martini-Bikini reversible figure.[1]

1. The possibility of a conveniently mnemonic rhyme dictated the choice of "martini" over, say, "champagne," though the small size of the oval above the glass might otherwise suggest a rising bubble more than a dropping olive. Its interpretation as a small onion should present no problem for Gibsonians.

An Ambiguous Figure

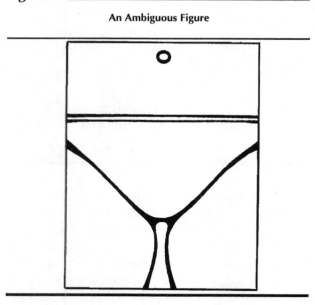

What such a figure demonstrates is that not all of what is perceived or imagined is contained in the concrete picture that is externally presented or reconstructed. Thus, while Creature A may see the drawing as a martini, this "deep structure" interpretation may not be adequately preserved in the "surface structure" reconstruction, with the consequence that Creature B may see the reconstruction of Creature A's martini as a bikini, or vice versa.

Moreover, the seeing of something *as* something is not limited to such contrived oddities as ambiguous figures. It pervades our everyday perception. As the demonstrations of Ames and others so dramatically bring home, we perceive a room as rectangular and a face as convex even though our retinal image may be consistent with an infinity of grossly different external situations in which the ceiling, walls, and floor are wildly askew and the "face" is a concave mask (Gregory, 1970). Or, we see that our train is beginning to pull out of the station when in reality it is only that the adjacent train is backing up. And, of course, we perceive an apple as edible, a pair of pliers as squeezable, and an ice cube as cold and wet (Gibson, 1950).

What distinguishes the "seeing as" in the perception of ambiguous figures from "the seeing as" in the more usual sort of perception is the prevailing tendency toward seeing the same ambiguous stimulus in two or more distinctly different ways. The case of ambiguous figures thus falls somewhere between the case of normal perception, in which most subjects see essentially the same thing, and the case of completely unconstrained imagery, in which some subjects may be able to "see" virtually anything. Of course, this is all a matter of degree; even when presented with a "normal" scene, different individuals may attend to different aspects, and particularly creative individuals may "see" radically different potentialities.

Since the deep-structure interpretation can not always be captured by the surface-structure pattern that is externally reconstructable, we must take a step beyond the externalization device depicted in Figures 1 and 2 if we are to ensure that the perceptual or imaginal experience of Creature A is fully recreated in Creature B. From my basic premise that any aspect of an internal representation—whether it be of the nature of deep or surface structure—must correspond to some physical process in the brain, I deduce that it would in principle be possible to detect the total pattern of that process and to recreate it by artificially exciting the functionally equivalent pattern in the brain of a second individual, as envisioned in Figure 4. Since Creature B's experience is then reconstructed, directly and internally to match Creature A's experience in its entirety, Creature B will always perceive or imagine the martini or the bikini, say, in agreement with Creature A.

The same will be true whether Creature A's experience is perceptual, as in Figure 4, or merely imaginal, as it was in Figure 2. In fact, although I align myself with those who suppose that imaginary and direct perception have much in common (for example, Brooks, 1968; Neisser, 1967; Weber & Harnish, 1974), the two kinds of experience are quite discriminable, except in extreme cases in which external stimulation is very weak (Perky, 1910) or is shut out or overridden as the result of an altered internal state (as in dreaming or hallucination). In comparison with the ordinary waking images of memory and imagination, perceptual images are generally characterized as more vivid, compelling, and rich in detail, texture, and color. Along with Hebb (1968), I suspect that

Figure 4

A Device for Recreating the Deep as Well as the Surface Structure of a Mental Image

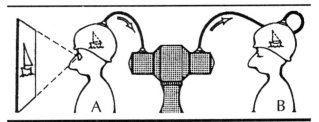

discrimination between the two kinds of images is based on the degree of engagement of the lowest or most concrete units of the sensory system. But, whatever its neurophysiological basis, this discrimination would be preserved in the reconstruction provided by the device in Figure 4. That is, Creature B's experience would be perceptual or merely imaginal depending on Creature A's.

However, the principal thing that this further thought experiment has now made clear is this: Not only is it unnecessary to suppose that the brain process underlying a mental image is like some sort of picture, but in some situations it is unjustified to assume even that an externally reconstructed picture can fully capture what is represented in that brain process. A mental image has a deep as well as a surface structure, whereas a picture as such is just its own surface structure.

A Metaphor of Lock and Key

The relation of a mental image to its corresponding object is in some ways analogous to the relation of a lock to a key. Generally, a lock and its key do not have any obvious resemblance. They nevertheless can have a unique one-to-one relationship defined by the fact that the lock can be externally operated only by its corresponding key. It may also be possible to operate the lock, at least partially, by direct manipulation of its mechanism from the inside, in the absence of its external key. This latter case provides a possible analogy to imagining an object in the absence of the object—whether voluntarily or by forced excitation of the sort

suggested in Figure 4. But to externalize such a mental image in the sense envisioned in Figures 1 and 2 is not, according to this metaphor, to achieve the external reconstruction of the internal lock itself. Rather, it is analogous to taking a wax impression and thereby reconstructing the external key that will operate the hidden lock.

We can extend the metaphor in several significant ways: (a) Just as there presumably exists some partial complementarity between the visible shape of a key and the invisible conformation of the corresponding lock's internal mechanism, the neural representation of a square probably has itself a four-fold structure. (b) Just as a skeleton key can operate two or more structurally different locks, an ambiguous figure can evoke two or more distinct perceptual interpretations. (c) And just as some locks (such as one designed for the front door of an office building) can be operated by a variety of keys sharing certain basic features, there are internal representations that can be evoked by a variety of stimuli sharing some common property.

This last extension of the analogy shows how, contrary to the well-known pronouncement of the good Bishop Berkeley, one can have the "abstract idea" of a triangle without having either to think the word "triangle" or to image any particular, concrete triangle, be it acute, obtuse, right-angled, equilateral, or scalene (Shepard, 1975). Furthermore, as experiments such as those of Klatzky and Stoy (1974) indicate, the fact that an internal representation is more abstract than a picture does not entail that such a representation is nonvisual. So-called "imageless thought" may constitute just one end of a continuum of representational processes ranging from the most concrete and pictorial to the most abstract and conceptual. And the thinking of those who claim to experience little imagery may simply tend to be less concretely imagistic in this sense (except, perhaps, in the state of dreaming).

Relations Between Mental Images, Percepts, and Pictures

Clearly, the closer parallel is between a mental image and a perceptual image rather than between a mental image and a concrete picture (just as the closer parallel is between the internal and external operation of a lock rather than between a lock and a key). Recognizing this, we are less likely to tumble to certain erroneous conclusions. If I am asked to imagine a zebra but then turn out to be unable to report the number of its stripes, this does not make a lie of my claim that I had a mental image of the zebra. I may well have trouble in answering the question even when I am looking at an actual zebra or a picture of one. In both the imaginal and perceptual conditions, my stripe-representing circuits may well be activated, but to determine the *number* of those stripes will require additional internal and possibly, external operations. To be accurate, I may need to move my physical finger along the picture while counting—an operation that is more difficult with a purely internal image.

At the same time, I believe it would be undesirably restrictive to draw the conclusion, implicit in some recent attacks on the "picture metaphor" for visual imagery, that concrete pictorial reconstructions of the sort envisioned in Figures 1 and 2 are necessarily wholly inadequate. To the extent that a scene is normally perceived in essentially the same way by most subjects, a colored, moving, and stereoscopic display reconstructed by a device of this sort would constitute a sufficient externalization of the corresponding internal image in the specific sense that the decoding process is, by hypothesis, essentially invertible: Given either the internal or the external representation (that is, the brain state or the display), the corresponding other representation could in principle be satisfactorily reconstructed. Even in the case of ambiguous figures, the set of different internal representations corresponding to the same externally reconstructed picture will generally consist of no more than a small number of distinct and well-defined alternatives. And, possibly, subtle shifts occurring in the surface structure of the reconstruction might sometimes suffice to determine the appropriate deep-structure interpretation (as, say, a martini or bikini).

I acknowledge, then, that concrete external representations of mental images are limited

by their inherent concreteness—so that it is, for example, difficult to represent the presence of stripes without implicitly representing their number. Yet I believe this limitation has been overdrawn of late. In fact, the unifying aspect of the experiments I am about to review is that, in all of them, the corresponding concrete external object is in one way or another taken as the "key" to the mental image, I remain hopeful that the marked degree of functional substitutability that these experiments demonstrate between internally and externally generated images will not be dismissed on the grounds that these experiments *merely* scratch the surface (or "surface structure") of mental imagery.

HOW CAN MENTAL IMAGES BE STUDIED?

Typically, past studies of mental imagery have used a largely correlational methodology and have relied heavily on the subjects' introspective ratings of their own mental imagery. The results confirm that imagery varies from individual to individual and is more helpful in some kinds of tasks than in others. The results do not, however, tell us much about the nature of a mental image itself or about its relation to a perceptual image. In the remainder of this article I try to indicate some ways in which my students and I have been trying to come closer to this goal by comparing the performance of subjects in conditions that are as nearly identical as possible, with the exception that in one condition the relevant stimuli are physically present, whereas in another they are only remembered or imagined (also see Shepard & Podgorny, in press).

The Paradigm of Second-Order Isomorphism

I have argued that there need not be a concrete or "first-order" isomorphism between an external object and the corresponding representational process within the physical brain. Nevertheless, the proposed equivalence between perception and imagination implies a more abstract or "second-order" isomorphism in which the functional relations among objects as imagined must to some degree mirror the functional relations among those same objects as actually perceived. Thus, to the extent that mental images can substitute for perceptual images, subjects should be able to answer questions about objects as well when those objects are merely imagined as when they are directly perceived (cf. Baylor, 1972; Kosslyn, 1975). Of the types of questions that might be asked, one of the most instructive concerns the perceived similarities between the objects. For in this way, we can obtain information about global, holistic relations without having to make any assumptions in advance about what local, particularistic features may be important in any one object. Moreover, in comparison with the reaction-time paradigms that follow, this paradigm has the advantage that we do not limit our investigation to the concretely externalizable component of mental images. The subjects may well base their judgments on the inherently internal, more abstract components as well.

We have now carried out experiments of this kind with diverse sets of objects, including two-dimensional shapes (Shepard & Chipman, 1970), spectral colors (Shepard & Cooper, Note 1), one-digit numbers represented in such visual forms as Arabic numerals, printed English names, and patterns of dots (Shepard, Kilpatric, & Cunningham, 1975), and even such more difficult-to-describe objects as familiar faces, musical sounds, and distinctive odors (see Shepard, 1975). Typically, for any one set of objects, the similarity data were statistically indistinguishable between the two conditions in which the objects were physically presented or only imagined. Moreover, multidimensional scaling analyses have indicated that, in both conditions alike, the subjects based their judgments on identifiable physical properties of those objects—for example, vertical versus horizontal elongation and degree of irregularity, for shapes; hue for colors; and straightness versus curvature and degree of closure, for Arabic numerals.

These results suggest, first, that the subjects were performing very similar mental processes in the perceptual and imaginal conditions and, second, that these processes operated on properties of the relevant objects even when those objects were not physically present. Despite the introspective claims of the subjects, however, a critic could argue that these results do not conclusively establish that the properties being compared were represented visually rather than in the form of some at least crudely isomorphic verbal description. For more direct and objective evidence on this point, we have turned to paradigms in which the speed of the subjects' responses to visual test stimuli seems to rule out the possibility that those responses were mediated by verbally encoded processes.

The Paradigm of Reaction Time to a Corresponding External Test Stimulus

If perception and imagination use much of the same neural circuitry, then to imagine a particular object is to place oneself in a unique state of readiness for the actual perception of that particular object. In terms of our metaphor, to imagine a particular object is like moving a particular lock into position for the insertion of its corresponding key. This state of special readiness should reveal itself most sensitively in the reaction time to the corresponding test stimulus. Accordingly, my associates and I have compared the time required to respond discriminatively to a test stimulus under conditions in which the subject has or has not already formed a preparatory visual image of the relevant stimulus.

Quite uniformly we have found that when an appropriate visual image has already been formed, subjects are able to make the required discriminative response with great speed and accuracy (typically within a half-second or less, and with an error rate on the order of 5% or so), whereas when no image or an inappropriate image has been formed, subjects show a very consistent increase in reaction time which, depending on the condition, may amount to another half-second or to as much as several full seconds. We have now obtained results of this kind with a variety of different sets of visual stimuli, including perspective views of three-dimensional objects (Shepard & Metzler, 1971), random polygons (Cooper, 1975), and alphanumeric characters and pictures of human hands (Cooper & Shepard, 1973, 1975). And supportive results with various other visual configurations have been obtained by others of my associates (Shepard & Feng, 1972; Bassman, Note 2; Glushko & Cooper, Note 3) as well as by other colleagues working independently (see, for example, Nielsen & Smith, 1973).

In many of our experiments, in order to ensure that subjects did not make their responses on the basis of any one local feature, we required a discrimination between enantiomorphic (mirror-image) stimuli that had the same local features and differed only in global structure. In one of the experiments, Cooper and Podgorny (1976) ensured that a subject's image retained virtually all of the complex structural information in the corresponding stimulus by forcing a discrimination between test stimuli differing in extremely subtle, random perturbations. In many of the experiments, an "inappropriate" preparatory image was one corresponding to the very same object but as viewed in a different orientation. Two results emphasize the highly concrete, template-like character of the preparatory image: (a) the great speed and precision of the discriminative response when the preparatory image was appropriate, and (b) the marked increase in reaction time when it became inappropriate by a rotation of as little as 20° or 30°.

Perhaps the most direct evidence for a functional equivalence between imagery and perception in these experiments is the finding that a purely mental image that is internally generated and transformed into the "appropriate" orientation is virtually as effective as an external comparison stimulus already provided in that orientation. Thus, Cooper and Shepard's (1973) subjects responded to a test character in a rotated orientation with about the same speed and accuracy when they prepared for the test by merely imagining the appropriate character in the appropriately rotated orientation as when an actual outline of the character was physically presented, already rotated into the appropriate orientation, just before test.

Strictly, in these experiments the effectiveness of the internally generated preparatory image was contrasted with the effectiveness of an externally shaped *memory* image—not with the effectiveness of a true *perceptual* image. For, when the test stimulus consists of the object itself, a true perceptual condition would degenerate into the trivial task of detecting whether or not any change occurred in the external stimulus at time of test. For this reason, we have more recently turned to a paradigm that permits a more direct comparison between imagery and perception.

The Paradigm of Reaction Time to a Spatially Localized Probe

Instead of testing an image with the corresponding external stimulus as a whole, Peter Podgorny and I have been testing the image with a small, spatially localized probe. In this way we can test images of perception, memory, or imagination in exactly the same way. For a small, colored probe dot can be superimposed on a physically presented stimulus just as well as on a blank field where the stimulus is merely being imagined. In order to control the placement of the probe with respect to the image, however, we have to provide subjects with a fixed external reference frame within which each image is presented or imagined. We used a square, 3 × 3 or 5 × 5 grid within which, in the perceptual condition, certain squares were actually shaded in to form the "figure" or, in the memory or imagery conditions, the same squares were merely remembered or imagined as shaded in. In all cases, the subject was instructed to operate one of two switches as soon as possible upon the appearance of any colored test dot (or dots) according to whether or not at least one dot fell on the portion of the grid defined as figure (Podgorny & Shepard, 1978; Podgorny & Shepard, Note 4).

Figure 5 illustrates a case in which the figural portion formed a block letter F and the probe consisted of a single dot. When the subject indicated a state of full preparation for test, we

Figure 5 _____

A Perceptual Field (A), Imaginal Field (B), and Probe Field (C)
from an Experiment by Podgorny and Shepard

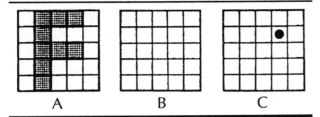

presented the probe dot (C) superimposed on the actual shaded stimulus (A) in the perceptual condition, or on the blank grid (B) in the imagery condition. The imagery condition can in turn be further classified as a memory condition or an imagination condition depending upon whether the figure itself had preceded the blank grid or whether only the blank grid was presented while the squares to be imagined as shaded were orally designated, by means of a previously learned verbal code. Notice that this kind of imagery, constrained as it is by an external framework, constitutes another intemediate case between unconstrained imagery and normal perception (cf. Shepard & Cermak, 1973, p. 374). The blank 5 × 5 grid can even be thought of as a highly ambiguous figure that can be "seen as," among a great number of other alternatives, the block letter F. The results provided objective evidence that the appropriate figure was in fact seen in the grid in much the same way in the imagery as in the perceptual conditions.

First, reaction times were generally short, ranging from 300 to 500 msec in all three conditions. And, although responses in the true perceptual condition sometimes showed an approximately 50-msec advantage, this relatively small difference was essentially independent of other factors. The results thus seem consonant with the already-expressed possibility that the most concrete representational units are more fully activated in the perceptual condition but that, otherwise, the representational processes operate in the same way in the imaginal and perceptual conditions.

Second, error rates were generally low, averaging between 4% and 7% in different experiments. This implies that the internal rep-

resentation of the figure against which the subject compared the test probe preserved much of the structure of the external object. In fact, by darkening those squares of an empty grid for which a subject made the "on" response to the probe, we can rather directly (though tediously) achieve a concrete externalization of the subject's mental image in the sense of Figures 1 and 2.

Third, reaction times did not show any consistent dependence on the absolute position of the probe within the grid of the sort that would be expected if subjects, in searching for the colored dot, carried out a systematic left-to-right or top-to-bottom scan of the grid.

And fourth, reaction times did, however, depend in a highly orderly way on the relative position of the probe with respect to the pattern of squares forming the figure on any one trial: (a) On-figure responses were consistently faster than off-figure responses; (b) off-figure responses consistently decreased in reaction time with the distance of the probed square from the figural portion of the grid; and (c) on-figure responses were consistently faster to probes with more dots falling on the figure, falling on more different bars of the figure or on intersections of such bars, and falling on more "compact" figures with a smaller total number of such bars. We argue that these highly orderly dependencies are supportive of a model in which the probe is detected and classified as "on" or "off" by a kind of limited-resource parallel watch process organized around the figural portion of the grid in exactly the same way whether the figure is physically present or only remembered or imagined (Podgorny & Shepard, 1978; Podgorny & Shepard, Note 4).

Thus, in addition to providing evidence that the very same mechanisms are operative in imagery as in perception, these experiments are beginning to provide some rather specific indications as to what some of these mechanisms may be.

Paradigms of Mental Transformation

All of the paradigms considered so far have treated the mental images as static entities. Yet, if we are to believe the introspective reports of the scientists quoted at the beginning of the article, it is the possibility of performing dynamic operations with such images that confers on them much of their creative power. Einstein emphasized the role that imagined operations seemed to play in his thinking, and Tesla, Lawrence, Kekulé and Watson have all referred to the visualization, specifically, of rotations in space. Helmholtz was even more explicit: "Without it being necessary, or even possible to describe [an object] in words . . . we can clearly imagine all the perspective images which we may expect upon viewing from this or that side" (Warren & Warren, 1968, pp. 252–254).

It was partly on the basis of my recognition of the importance in my own thinking of such dynamic kinds of imagery that I first undertook the study of mental operations on objects in space and, particularly, of "mental rotation." Since Lynn Cooper and I have recently reviewed this now-extensive line of work in some depth (Cooper & Shepard, in press), I shall confine myself to a summary of two of the most directly relevant findings, obtained principally by Cooper, Metzler, and myself.

First, then, under a broad range of conditions we have established that the time required to carry out an imagined operation in space increases—often in a remarkably linear manner—with the extent of the spatial transformation; for example, with angle in the case of a rotation. And this is equally true whether the mental operation is performed in the presence of a transformed stimulus in order to make a discriminative response to it or in the absence of the stimulus in order to prepare for its expected presentation. We have taken this dependence of transformation time on the extent of the transformation as supportive of the notion that the mental transformation is carried out over a path that is the internal analog of the corresponding physical transformation of the external object (Cooper, 1975; Cooper & Shepard, 1973; Metzler & Shepard, 1974; Shepard & Metzler, 1971).

Second, by measuring reaction times to variously oriented test stimuli presented during the course of a mental rotation, we have estab-

lished, more directly, that the intermediate states of the internal process do indeed have a one-to-one correspondence to intermediate orientations of the external object. Our results, in fact, show that there is actually something rotating during the course of a mental rotation—namely, the orientation in which the corresponding external stimulus, if it were to be presented, would be most rapidly discriminated from other possible stimuli (Cooper, 1976; Cooper & Shepard, 1973; Metzler & Shepard, 1974). Still more recently, Clive Robins and I have obtained a different kind of support for this conclusion in an experiment on the illusion of "apparent" rotational movement between the two orientations in which an object is alternately displayed. Subjects' reports of whether a spatio-temporally localized probe dot flashed before or after the object appeared to pass through the tested location exhibited a highly orderly pattern consistent with the assumption that the subjects were comparing the external probe against an internally constructed representation of the intervening rotation (Robins & Shepard, 1977).

Most basically, what I am arguing for here is the notion that the internal process that represents the transformation of an external object, just as much as the internal process that represents the object itself, is in large part the same whether the transformation, or the object, is merely imagined or actually perceived. The phenomenon of apparent rotational movement that we have most recently been investigating represents an instructive intermediate case in which the transformation, although a purely internal construction, is experienced perceptually (Robins & Shepard, 1977; Shepard & Judd, 1976).

CONCLUDING REMARKS

I submit that there are both logical and analogical processes of thought, and that processes of the latter type, though often neglected in psychological research, may be comparable in importance to the former. By an analogical or analog process I mean just this: a process in which the intermediate internal states have a natural one-to-one correspondence to appropriate intermediate states in the external world. Thus, to imagine an object such as a complex molecule rotated into a different orientation is to perform an analog process in that half way through the process, the internal state corresponds to the external object in an orientation half way between the initial and final orientations. And this correspondence has the very real meaning that, at this half-way point, the person carrying out the process will be especially fast in discriminatively responding to the external presentation of the corresponding external structure in exactly that spatial orientation. The intermediate states of logical computation do not in general have this property. Thus, a digital computer may calculate the coordinates of a rotated structure by performing a matrix multiplication. But the intermediate states of this row-into-column calculation will at no point correspond to—or place the machine in readiness for—an intermediate orientation of the external object.

By thus defining analog processes in terms of conditional relations to possible external objects, I do not need to commit myself with respect to the much-debated issue of whether the format of the internal process itself is more felicitously characterized as pictorial or propositional (cf., Attneave, 1974; Kosslyn & Pomerantz, 1977; Paivio, 1976; Palmer, 1975; Pylyshyn, 1973; Reed, 1974). I take this as an advantage since I, apparently along with Anderson (Note 5), suspect that this particular issue will wane in significance as the two contrasting types of theories, in striving to account for the same growing body of results, become more and more isomorphic to each other. In the meantime, by defining mental images in terms of the concrete external objects to which they correspond, we can continue to move ahead with our empirical investigations of such images and of the analog processes that operate upon them.

These analog processes seem to be particularly effective in dealing with complex spatial structures and operations on such structures. As Sir Francis Galton long ago remarked, "A visual image is the most perfect form of mental representation wherever the shape, position, and relations of objects in space are concerned" (Galton, 1883, p. 113). By imagining various objects and their transformations in space, moreover, one can explore many possibilities without, as Metzler and I once put it, "taking the time, making the effort or running the risk" of carrying the operations out in physical reality (Metzler & Shepard, 1974, p. 198). Moreover, even when scientists, such as Watson or Crick, construct external supports for their mental operations in the form of sketches, diagrams, or three-dimensional models, their acts of drawing, construction, and spatial manipulation are very likely guided by covert acts of an analogical nature. Indeed, as writers such as Didion and Guest as well as the mathematician Hadamard have suggested, even the construction of verbal or symbolic outputs may be similarly guided by nonverbal images or schemata that capture what Hadamard (1945) suggestively termed the "physiognomy" of the problem.

The question of what controls the construction and transformation of the purely internal images, models, or schemata themselves poses a major challenge to those of us who seek to understand the dynamics of human thought. Before concluding, I can only point to two as yet vaguely formulated ideas that may be of some relevance. The first idea is that mental imagery comes increasingly into play as more concrete representational units become entrained by related associative processes ongoing at more abstract, conceptual levels of the representational hierarchy. Presumably this happens most fully when the more concrete units are released from the preemptive control of external stimulation. The most striking examples in my own experience have occurred in the process of falling asleep, when my abstract thoughts of a piece of music or of a geometrical problem have suddenly verged over into the hallucinatory fullness and richness of a hypnagogic image or a dream (Shepard, in press). The second idea is that once these more concrete representational units have thus been activated, they exert their own constraining influence back on the more abstract process by virtue of our eons of prelinguistic evolution in a three-dimensional world populated with semirigid moveable and often animate bodies. For the system of constraints that governs the projections and transformations of such bodies in space must long ago have become internalized as a powerful, though largely unconscious, part of our innate perceptual machinery.

I conclude that as we probe still further into either the processes of perception or the processes of imagery, we are likely to gain a deeper understanding of both—and, just possibly, some significant insights into the sources of creative thought.

REFERENCE NOTES

1. Shepard, R. N., & Cooper, L. A. *Representation of colors in normal, blind, and color-blind subjects.* Paper presented at the annual meeting of the American Psychological Association, Chicago, September 2, 1975. (A more complete report is now in preparation.)

2. Bassman, E. S. *Chronometric analysis of the sequence of folding a cube.* Paper presented at the annual meeting of the American Psychological Association, San Francisco, August 27, 1977. (A more complete report is now in preparation as a doctoral dissertation).

3. Glushko, R. J., & Cooper, L. A. *Spatial comprehension and comparison processes in verification tasks.* Manuscript submitted for publication, 1977.

4. Podgorny, P., & Shepard, R. N. *The distribution of visual attention over space.* Manuscript in preparation, 1977.

5. Anderson, J. R. *The status of arguments concerning representations for mental imagery.* Manuscript submitted for publication, 1977.

REFERENCES

Arnheim, R. *Visual thinking.* Berkeley: University of California Press, 1969.

Attneave, F. How do you know? *American Psychologist,* 1974, *29*, 493–511.

Baylor, G. W. *A treatise on the mind's eye: An empirical investigation of visual memory.* Unpublished doctoral dissertation, Carnegie-Mellon University, 1972. (Available as a technical report, Institute of Psychology, University of Montreal, Canada.)

Beveridge, W. I. B. *The art of scientific investigation* (3rd ed.). New York: Vintage, 1957.

Brooks, L. R. Spatial and verbal components of the act of recall. *Canadian Journal of Psychology,* 1968, *22*, 349–368.

Cooper, L. A. Mental transformation of random two-dimensional shapes. *Cognitive Psychology,* 1975, *7*, 20–43.

Cooper, L. A. Demonstration of a mental analog of an external rotation. *Perception & Psychophysics,* 1976, *19*, 296–302.

Cooper, L. A., & Podgorny, P. Mental transformations and visual comparison processes: Effects of complexity and similarity. *Journal of Experimental Psychology: Human Perception and Performance,* 1976, *2*, 503–514.

Cooper, L. A. & Shepard, R. N. Chronometric studies of the rotation of mental images. In W. G. Chase (Ed.), *Visual information processing.* New York: Academic Press, 1973.

Cooper, L. A., & Shepard, R. N. Mental transformation in the identification of left and right hands. *Journal of Experimental Psychology: Human Perception and Performance,* 1975, *1*, 48–56.

Cooper, L. A., & Shepard, R. N. Transformations on representations of objects in space. In E. C. Carterette & M. P. Friedman (Eds.), *Handbook of perception* (Vol. 8). New York: Academic Press, in press.

Didion, J. Why I write. *The New York Times Book Review,* December 5, 1976, pp. 2; 98–99.

Einstein, A. Autobiographical notes. In P. A. Schlipp (Ed.), *Albert Einstein: Philosopher-scientist.* Evanston, Ill.: Library of Living Philosophers, 1949.

Ferguson, E. S. The mind's eye: Nonverbal thought in technology. *Science,* 1977, *197*, 827–836.

Findlay, A. *A hundred years of chemistry* (2nd ed.). London: Duckworth, 1948.

Friedman, M. Every author's perfect dream comes true. *San Francisco Sunday Examiner & Chronicle,* August 7, 1977, p. 3 of "Scene."

Galton, F. *Inquiries into human faculty and its development.* London: Macmillan, 1883.

Ghiselin, B. *The creative process.* New York: New American Library, 1952.

Gibson, J. J. *Perception of the visual world.* Cambridge, Mass.: Riverside Press, 1950.

Gregory, R. L. *The intelligent eye.* London: Weidenfeld & Nicolson, 1970.

Hadamard, J. *The psychology of invention in the mathematical field.* Princeton, N.J.: Princeton University Press, 1945.

Hebb, D. O. Concerning imagery. *Psychological Review,* 1968, *75*, 466–477.

Holton, G. On trying to understand scientific genius. *American Scholar,* 1972, *41*, 95–110.

Hunt, I., & Draper, W. W. *Lightning in his hand: The life story of Nikola Tesla.* Denver, Colo.: Sage Books, 1964.

Kendall, J. *Michael Faraday, man of simplicity.* London: Faber & Faber, 1955.

Klatzky, R. L., & Stoy, A. M. Using visual codes for comparison of pictures. *Memory & Cognition,* 1974, *2*, 727–736.

Koestler, A. *The act of creation.* New York: Macmillan, 1964.

Kosslyn, S. M. Information representation in visual images. *Cognitive Psychology*, 1975, 7, 341–370.

Kosslyn, S. M., & Pomerantz, J. R. Imagery, propositions, and the form of internal representations. *Cognitive Psychology*, 1977, 2, 52–76.

Livingston, M. S. (Ed.). *The development of high-energy accelerators.* New York: Dover, 1966.

Livingston, M. S. *Particle accelerators: A brief history.* Cambridge, Mass.: Harvard University Press, 1969.

Metzler, J., & Shepard, R. N. Transformational studies of the internal representation of three-dimensional objects. In R. Solso (Ed.), *Theories in cognitive psychology: The Loyola Symposium.* Potomac, Md.: Erlbaum, 1974.

Neisser, U. *Cognitive psychology.* New York: Appleton-Century-Crofts, 1967.

Newman, J. R. James Clerk Maxwell. *Scientific American*, 1955, 192(6), 58–71.

Nielsen, G. D., & Smith, E. E. Imaginal and verbal representations in short-term recognition of visual forms. *Journal of Experimental Psychology*, 1973, 101, 375–378.

Paivio, A. Images, propositions, and knowledge. In J. M. Nicholas (Ed.), *Images, perception and knowledge* (The Western Ontario Series in the Philosophy of Science). Dordrecht, Netherlands; Reidel, 1976.

Palmer, S. E. Visual perception and world knowledge: Notes on a model of sensory-cognitive interaction. In D. A. Norman & D. E. Rumelhart (Eds.), *Explorations in cognition.* San Francisco: Freeman, 1975.

Perky, C. W. An experimental study of imagination. *American Journal of Psychology*, 1910, 21, 422–452.

Podgorny, P., & Shepard, R. N. Functional representations common to visual perception and imagination. *Journal of Experimental Psychology: Human Perception and Performance*, 1978, 4, 21–35.

Pylyshyn, Z. What the mind's eye tells the mind's brain: A critique of mental imagery. *Psychological Bulletin*, 1973, 80, 1–24.

Reed, S. K. Structural descriptions and the limitations of visual images. *Memory & Cognition*, 1974, 2, 329–336.

Robins, C., & Shepard, R. N. Spatio-temporal probing of apparent rotational movement. *Perception of Psychophysics*, 1977, 22, 12–18.

Ryle, G. *The concept of mind.* New York: Barnes & Noble, 1949.

Shepard, R. N. Form, formation, and transformation of internal representations. In R. Solso (Ed.), *Information processing and cognition: The Loyola Symposium.* Hillsdale, N.J.: Erlbaum, 1975.

Shepard, R. N. Externalization of mental images and the act of creation. In B. S. Randhawa & W. E. Coffman (Eds.), *Visual learning, thinking, and communication.* New York: Academic Press, in press.

Shepard, R. N., & Cermak, G. W. Perceptual-cognitive explorations of a toroidal set of free-form stimuli. *Cognitive Psychology*, 1973, 4, 351–377.

Shepard, R. N., & Chipman, S. Second-order isomorphism of internal representations: Shapes of states. *Cognitive Psychology*, 1970, 1, 1–17.

Shepard, R. N., & Feng, C. A chronometric study of mental paper folding. *Cognitive Psychology*, 1972, 3, 228–243.

Shepard, R. N., & Judd, S. A. Perceptual illusion of rotation of three-dimensional objects. *Science*, 1976, 191, 952–954.

Shepard, R. N., Kilpatric, D. W., & Cunningham, J. P. The internal representation of numbers. *Cognitive Psychology*, 1975, 7, 82–138.

Shepard, R. N., & Metzler, J. Mental rotation of three-dimensional objects. *Science*, 1971, 171, 701–703.

Shepard, R. N., & Podgorny, P. Cognitive processes that resemble perceptual processes. In W. K. Estes (Ed.), *Handbook of learning and cognitive processes.* Hillsdale, N.J.: Erlbaum, in press.

Sloman, A. Interactions between philosophy and artificial intelligence: The role of intuition and non-logical reasoning in intelligence. *Artificial Intelligence*, 1971, 2, 209–225.

Smart, J. J. C. Sensations and brain processes. *Philosophical Review*, 1959, 68, 141–156.

Tesla, N. *Nikola Tesla: Lectures, patents, articles.* Beograd, Yugoslavia: Nikola Tesla Museum, 1956.

Tyndall, J. *Faraday as a discoverer.* London: Longmans, Green & Co., 1868.

Warren, R. M., & Warren, R. P. *Helmholtz on perception: Its physiology and development.* New York: Wiley, 1968.

Watson, J. D. *The double helix.* New York: The New American Library, 1968.

Weber, R. J., & Harnish R. Visual imagery for words: The Hebb test. *Journal of Experimental Psychology*, 1974, 102, 409–414.

Wertheimer, M. *Productive thinking.* New York: Harper, 1945.

Wittgenstein, L. *Philosophical investigations* (G. E. M. Anscombe, trans.). New York: Macmillan, 1953.

This article was presented as a Distinguished Scientific Contribution Award address at the meeting of the American Psychological Association, San Francisco, August 29, 1977.

The reported research has been supported by the National Science Foundation (principally through Grants GS-1302, GB-31971X, and BNS-75-02806). I am greatly indebted, also, to the many students, past and present, who have contributed so much to the work reviewed here, most especially to Lynn Cooper and to Peter Podgorny.

10

William Raft Kunst-Wilson and R. B. Zajonc

Affective Discrimination of Stimuli That Cannot Be Recognized

Abstract: *Animal and human subjects readily develop strong preferences for objects that have become familiar through repeated exposures. Experimental evidence is presented that these preferences can develop even when the exposures are so degraded that recognition is precluded.*

A substantial body of evidence demonstrates that the mere repeated exposure of a stimulus object increases its attractiveness (1). Both human (2) and animal subjects (3) exhibit the exposure effect with a variety of stimuli, exposure methods, and outcome measures of stimulus attractiveness.

In addition to its effects on preferences, exposure experience also allows the individual to learn a great deal about the stimulus object, so that the ability to recognize, discriminate, and categorize the object generally improves. Traditionally, theorists have assumed that this cognitive mastery resulting from experience with the stimulus mediated the growth of positive affect [for example, Harrison's response competition theory (4) and Berlyne's theory of optimal arousal (5)]. Thus, as the individual comes to "know" the stimulus better, his affective reaction to it is likely to become increasingly positive. For example, much of the literature on esthetic reactions to music suggests that experience leading to the recognition of familiar patterns and the ability to anticipate development is pleasurable and makes the composition attractive (6).

Recent research, however, suggests that overt affective responses may be unrelated to prior cognitive outcomes which result from stimulus exposure. For example, Moreland and Zajonc (7) have shown by a correlational analysis that repeated exposure increases preference for stimuli even when recognition is held constant, and Wilson (8) has demonstrated by experimental methods that auditory stimuli gain in attractiveness by virtue of repeated exposure, even when their registration and subsequent recognition had been considerably impaired in the course of a dichotic listening task.

In the present experiment, a more stringent test was used to determine whether the exposure effect could be obtained when recognition was drastically reduced. Through preliminary studies, the conditions of stimulus exposure were systematically impoverished until recognition performance was brought down just to a chance level. A new group of subjects was then exposed to stimuli under these impoverished conditions, and judgments of attractiveness and measures of recognition memory for these stimuli and for stimuli not previously exposed were obtained. The results revealed clear preferences for exposed stimuli, even though subjects in a recognition memory test could not discriminate them from novel stimuli.

The experiment consisted of an exposure phase and of a test series. The stimuli were 20 irregular octagons constructed by a random process. Octagons of this type were used previously in exposure research, and subjects found no difficulty in making clear cognitive and affective discriminations among them (9). The 20 stimuli were divided into two sets of ten, sets A and B. In the exposure phase, half of the subjects saw set A and half set B. All subjects saw sets A and B in the test series. During the exposure phase, subjects fixated the center of a 23 by 17 cm rear projection screen mounted at the end of a viewing tunnel 91 cm long. Five exposures of each stimulus from the set of ten stimuli were shown in a random sequence. The octagons were solid black on white background; because of their high contrast, chance recognition could be obtained only after exposures were reduced to a 1-msec duration and illumination was lowered by a neutral density (ND8X) and a red gelatin filter. The instructions to subjects at the beginning of the expo-

sure phase were that the experiment consisted of two parts and that during the first part slides would be shown on the screen at durations so brief that one could not really see what was being presented. Nevertheless, the subject was instructed to pay close attention to the flashes, even if nothing could be distinguished, and to acknowledge verbally the occurrence of each flash.

The second part of the experiment required subjects to make paired comparisons between slides from set A and set B. Now the slides were presented under adequate viewing conditions (exposure time was extended to 1 second). For each of the ten pairs, all containing one octagon previously exposed and one new, the subjects had to indicate (i) the one they liked better and (ii) the one they thought had been shown previously. For both judgments, confidence ratings were obtained on a three-point scale: "sure" (3 points), "half-sure" (2 points), and "guess" (1 point). Two groups of 12 subjects were studied, one making affective judgments of the ten stimulus pairs first and recognition judgments of the same pairs afterward, and another for whom the order of these judgments was reversed.

Recognition performance was very close to chance (48 percent accuracy). Affect responses, however, did reliably discriminate between old and new stimuli: old stimuli were liked better than new ones 60 percent of the time ($x^2 = 8.44$, $P < .01$). Overall, 16 of the 24 subjects preferred old to new stimuli, but only 5 of the 24 recognized old stimuli as such at better than the chance level. Of the 24 subjects, 17 discriminated better between old and new stimuli in their affective judgments than in their recognition responses, while only 4 showed superiority of recognition memory over affective judgments.

Subjects' confidence ratings show an interesting pattern (Figure 1). When they reported they were just guessing, recognition accuracy and affective discrimination were both at chance levels (47 and 48 percent, respectively). Recognition accuracy did not improve when subjects were either "half-sure" or "sure" of their recognition judgments (49 and 45 percent). In contrast, at these levels of confidence, affective

Figure 1

Proportion of Correct Recognition and Affective Discriminations
for First Judgments in Each Category

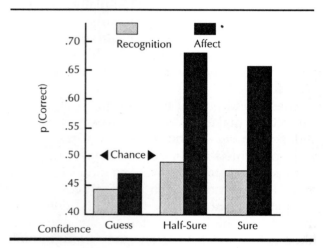

discrimination was considerably more accurate (63 and 60 percent).

These effects are slightly more pronounced when the affective and recognition judgments were obtained first, and were therefore unbiased by prior responses to the test stimuli. Accuracy for affective judgments made prior to recognition judgments tended to be higher than the overall levels, while accuracy for recognition-first judgments tended to remain about the same.

Confidence in affective preferences was substantially higher than in recognition judgments. Mean confidence in affective discrimination was 2.29, while confidence in recognition judgments was 1.60 [$t(23) = 6.66$, $P < .01$] (10). The tendency for affective preferences to be rendered more rapidly than recognition judgments (2.76 and 2.97 seconds, respectively) was not significant.

Individuals can apparently develop preferences for objects in the absence of conscious recognition and with access to information so scanty that they cannot ascertain whether anything at all was shown. The results thus suggest that there may exist a capacity for making affective discriminations without extensive participation of the cognitive system (11). In fact, evidence of this sort, together with data

on the influence of affective judgments on recall and recognition (12, 13), has been taken to indicate that partially independent systems may encode and process affect and content (12, 14).

The fact that with minimal stimulus information, some forms of discrimination can be performed while others are not possible is not new. Studies of perceptual vigilance and defense have yielded findings obtained with modern methods and under conditions that satisfy the most stringent experimental criteria—findings that can no longer be seriously ignored (15). The large number of clear subliminal effects reported warrant the belief that various forms of affect-linked reactions are possible with only minimal access to the content. Shevrin (16), for example, found physiological and behavioral effects with 1-msec exposures. The recent work of Blum and Barbour (17), using hypnosis, confirms that affective reactions of various forms can take place with the content almost entirely suppressed.

Evidence for processing that occurs without an apparent access to the physical properties of verbal stimuli has been repeatedly reported. For example, subjects can identify a word sooner than they are able to identify its letters (18), and they can identify the semantic category of a word without being able to identify the word itself (19). Of course, what stimulus cues or internal processes allow the subject to make affective discriminations on the basis of what must surely be minimal processing of stimulus information cannot be established on the basis of what is now known. Perhaps from the point of view of survival value, however, it should not be entirely surprising that these affective discriminations can be made with so little stimulus information (20). Since affective reactions to a stimulus may readily change without any changes in the stimulus (as a result of repeated exposure, for example), these reactions must be based not only on the properties of the stimulus itself, but on information related to some internal states of the individual. Further empirical work may reveal the different bases of affective and cognitive judgments, should they indeed be partially separate and independent.

REFERENCES AND NOTES

1. R. B. Zajonc, *J. Pers. Soc. Psychol. Monogr. Suppl.* **9,** 1 (1968).

2. A. A. Harrison, in *Advances in Experimental Social Psychology,* L. Berkowitz, Ed. (Academic Press, New York, 1977), vol. 9, pp. 218–252.

3. W. F. Hill, *Psychol. Bull.* **85,** 1177 (1978); R. B. Zajonc, in *Man and Beast: Comparative Social Behavior,* J. F. Eisenberg and W. S. Dillon, Eds. (Smithsonian Institution Press, Washington D.C., 1971), pp. 48–73.

4. A. A. Harrison, *J. Pers. Soc. Psychol.* **9,** 363 (1968).

5. D. E. Berlyne, *Percep. Psychophys.* **8,** 279 (1970); *Aesthetics and Psychobiology* (Appleton, New York, 1971).

6. H. K. Mull, *J. Psychol.* **43,** 155 (1957).

7. R. L. Moreland and R. B. Zajonc, *J. Pers. Soc. Psychol.* **35,** 191 (1977).

8. W. R. Wilson, *ibid.* **37,** 811 (1979).

9. P. H. Hamid, *Br. J. Psychol.* **64,** 569 (1973).

10. Unlike recognition, preferences cannot be construed as right or wrong. In an attempt to correct for this source of bias, subjects in another experiment were led to believe that their affect judgments would be compared with those of art critics, and "subjective impressions of familiarity" were requested in the place of recognition judgments. Even under these conditions, subjects' confidence in their affect judgments remained significantly higher.

11. Explanations involving response bias, such as that individuals use less stringent criterion for liking than for recognition judgments, cannot be readily invoked because a forced-choice procedure eliminated response biases of this kind.

12. N. H. Anderson and S. Hubert, *J. Verb. Learn. Verb Behav.* **2,** 379 (1963).

13. G. H. Bower and M. B. Karlin, *J. Exp. Psychol.* **103,** 751 (1974); K. E. Patterson and A. D. Baddeley, *J. Exp. Psychol. Hum. Learn. Mem.* **3,** 406 (1977).

14. M. I. Posner and C. R. R. Snyder, in *Attention and Performance,* V. P. M. A. Rabbitt and S. Dornic, Eds. (Academic Press, New York, 1975), pp. 87–103; R. B. Zajonc, paper presented at the First Ontario Symposium of Personality and Social Psychology, London, Ontario, 27 August 1978.

15. M. H. Erdelyi, *Psychol. Rev.,* **81,** 1 (1974).

16. H. Shevrin and D. E. Fritzler, *Science* **161,** 295 (1968).

17. G. S. Blum and J. S. Barbour, *J. Exp. Psychol. Gen.* **108,** 182 (1979).

18. J. C. Johnston and J. L. McClelland, *Science* **184,** 1192 (1974).

19. A. J. Marcel and K. E. Patterson in *Attention and Performance,* J. Requin, Ed. (Erlbaum, Hillsdale, N.J., 1978), vol. 7, pp. 209–226.

20. There is no implication that one of these processes is more accessible to awareness. Either the affective or the cognitive process can become consciously available, depending on a variety of factors.

21. Supported in part by a fellowship from the John Simon Guggenheim Foundation and by HEW grant 5RO2-NU00572.

11

Ulric Neisser

John Dean's Memory: A Case Study

Abstract: *John Dean, the former counsel to President Richard Nixon, testified to the Senate Watergate Investigating Committee about conversations that later turned out to have been tape recorded. Comparison of his testimony with the actual transcripts shows systematic distortion at one level of analysis combined with basic accuracy at another. Many of the distortions reflected Dean's own self-image; he tended to recall his role as more central than it really was. Moreover, his memory for even the "gist" of conversations was quite poor except where that gist had been rehearsed in advance or frequently repeated. But while his testimony was often wrong in terms of the particular conversations he tried to describe, Dean was fundamentally right about what had been happening: the existence of a "cover-up" and the participation of various individuals in it. His testimony was accurate at a level that is neither "semantic" (since he was ostensibly describing particular episodes) nor "episodic" (since his accounts of the episodes were often wrong). The term "repisodic" is coined here to describe such memories: what seems to be a remembered episode actually represents a repeated series of events, and thus reflects a genuinely existing state of affairs.*

"Have you always had a facility for recalling the details of conversations which took place many months ago?" Senator Inouye of Hawaii asked this question of John Dean with more than a trace of disbelief. Dean, the former counsel to President Richard M. Nixon, was testifying before the "Watergate" Committee of the United States Senate in June, 1973. His testimony had opened with a 245-page statement, in which he described literally dozens of meetings that he had attended over a period of several years. The meetings were with John Mitchell, Robert Haldeman, Charles Colson, Gordon Liddy, and others whose names became American household words as the Watergate scandal brought down the Nixon administration. Some were with Nixon himself. Dean's testimony seemed to confirm what many already suspected: that these high officials were engaged in a "cover-up" of White House involvement in the original Watergate burglary. But was he telling the truth? How much did he really remember?

In a psychological experiment, it is relatively easy to determine whether what the subject says is true. The experimenter knows what really happened because she staged it in the first place, or because she kept a record with which the subject's report can be compared. Because life does not keep such records, legal testimony is usually evaluated in more indirect ways: corroborative witnesses, cross-examination, circumstantial evidence. For some of Dean's testimony, however, it is now possible to compare what he said with a factual record: the *Presidential Transcripts*. This comparison will enable us to assess the accuracy of his memory rather precisely. In addition, it may clarify our theoretical conceptions of memory itself.

When Dean first testified, his "facility for recalling details" seemed so impressive that some writers called him "the human tape recorder." Ironically, a very real tape recorder had been tuned in to some of the same "details." Not long after its interrogation of Dean, the Senate Committee discovered that all conversations in Nixon's Oval Office were routinely (but secretly) recorded. The result of this discovery was a sharp legal struggle for possession of the tapes. When the President realized that he would not be able to keep the tapes out of the hands of the prosecutors indefinitely, he decided to transcribe some of them and release the transcripts himself. Although he did this reluctantly, he also thought it possible that they might actually help his cause. The published version of the *Presidential Transcripts* (1974) includes a lengthy foreword reiterating Nixon's claim that he knew nothing of the cover-up. (It does admit that there are " . . . possible ambiguities that . . . someone with a motive to discredit the President could take out of context and distort to suit his own purposes,"—p. 5.) The foreword explicitly insists that the transcripts discredit Dean's testimony. Dean himself, however, saw them as substan-

tiating *his* side of the story. In his autobiography (Dean, 1976) he describes himself as "ecstatic" (p. 332) to learn of the tapes' existence, because they would prove he had told the truth.

The testimony and the transcripts are now in the public domain. I propose to treat them as data, as if they had resulted from a deliberately conducted memory experiment. The analysis of these data will be somewhat unorthodox, however, because we know its outcome in advance. If Dean had actually perjured himself—if the transcripts had proved him to be fundamentally mistaken or dishonest—the defense lawyers in the subsequent Watergate trials would surely have seized the opportunity to discredit his testimony. Instead, the outcome of those trials has vindicated him: the highest-placed members of the White House staff all went to prison for doing what John Dean said they had done. Nixon, of course, was forced to resign. If history has ever proven anything, it surely proves that Dean remembered those conversations and told the truth about them. I will not quarrel with that assessment here, but we shall see that "truth," "accuracy," and "memory" are not simple notions. Dean's testimony was by no means always accurate. Yet even when he was wrong, there was a sense in which he was telling the truth; even when he was right, it was not necessarily because he remembered a particular conversation well.

These are levels of analysis with which psychology has rarely been concerned. Although there have been many demonstrations of the fallibility of testimony (Stern, 1904; Buckhout, 1974), none has dealt with a situation as complex as Dean's: with such significant material, such long spans of time, or such ambiguous motives. We will find it hard to do full justice to John Dean's memory within the conceptual framework of the psychology of memory. Nevertheless, that framework is not irrelevant. It includes a number of valuable ideas: that memory is influenced by mental "scripts" or "schemata" for familiar events (Bartlett, 1932; Bransford & Franks, 1972; Bower, Black & Turner, 1979); that distortions of memory are often motivated by the needs and character of the individual (Freud, 1899); and that a person's general knowledge ("semantic memory") must be distinguished from his recollection of specific events ("episodic memory," Tulving, 1972). Most obviously, we will have to make a distinction that has been familiar at least since Bartlett: to contrast *verbatim* recall with memory for the *gist* of what was said.

Verbatim recall is word-for-word reproduction. It is not something that we expect of ourselves in everyday life. Dean did not claim to be able to recall conversations verbatim, and indeed he could not. (We shall see that even the few phrases that he seemed to recall exactly may owe their fidelity to frequent repetition.) Memory for gist, on the other hand, occurs when we recall the "sense" of an original text in different words. To remember the gist of a story or a conversation is to be roughly faithful to the argument, the story line, the underlying sequence of ideas. Psychologists have developed a number of methods of evaluating memory for gist. One can divide the text and the recall protocol into so-called "idea units," and count how many of them match. With somewhat more trouble, one can make a structural analysis of the original, perhaps guided by theoretical ideas about "story grammars" and "schemata"; then one can determine how much of the structure reappears in the reproduction (e.g., Mandler & Johnson, 1977). These methods have worked well in the laboratory, where there is nothing to remember except an originally presented text. They are not as easily applied to the recall of actual conversations that take place in a context of real events: The events may be remembered even when the gist of the conversation is not.

Analysis of Dean's testimony does indeed reveal some instances of memory for the gist of what was said on a particular occasion. Elsewhere in his testimony, however, there is surprisingly little correspondence between the course of a conversation and his account of it. Even in those cases, however, there is usually a deeper level at which he is right. He gave an accurate portrayal of the real situation, of the actual characters and commitments of the people he knew, and of the events that lay behind the conversations he was trying to remember. Psychology is unaccustomed to analyzing the truthfulness of memory at this level, because we usually work with laboratory material that has no reference beyond itself. One of my purposes in analyzing John Dean's testimony is to call attention to this level of memory, and perhaps to devise ways in which it can be studied.

DEAN'S OWN ACCOUNT OF HIS MEMORY

It is impossible to survey all of Dean's testimony here; there is far too much of it. Moreover, most of his conversations were not recorded at all (so far as we know); it was only in the President's Oval Office that tape recorders ran night and day. Not even all of the taped material is fully reproduced in the available transcripts. We will only be able to analyze the two conversations reported in his testimony for which an apparently unedited transcript has been published. The reader should bear in mind that we are dealing with only a small fraction of what Dean said. The present paper is not an effort to assess his overall contribution to the Watergate investigations or to the course of justice; it is a psychological study aimed at clarifying the nature of memory for conversations.

The two conversations we will examine are those of September 15, 1972 and March 21, 1973. These two meetings with the President were crucial for the Senate Committee, which was trying to determine the extent of Nixon's involvement in the Watergate cover-up. Accordingly, Dean was cross-examined about both of them at length. He had already described each conversation in his long opening statement to the Committee: it was that statement which aroused Senator Inouye's incredulity. The interchange between Dean and Inouye is interesting in its own right: it may be the only discussion of mnemonics and metamemory in the Congressional Record.

Senator Inouye Your 245-page statement is remarkable for the detail with which it recounts events and conversations occurring over a period of many months. It is particularly remarkable in view of the fact that you indicated that it was prepared without benefit of note or

daily diary. Would you describe what documents were available to you in addition to those which have been identified as exhibits?
Mr. Dean What I did in preparing this statement, I had kept a newspaper clipping file from roughly June 17 [June 17, 1972 was the date of the Watergate break-in], up until about the time these hearings started when I stopped doing any clipping with any regularity. It was by going through every single newspaper article outlining what had happened and then placing myself in what I had done in a given sequence in time, I was aware of all the principal activities I had been involved in, the dealings I had with others in relationship to those activities. Many times things were in response to press activities or press stories that would result in further activities. I had a good memory of most of the highlights of things that had occurred, and it was through this process, and being extremely careful in my recollection, particularly of the meetings with the President (*Hearings*, pp. 1432–1433).

Note that Dean has spontaneously invented the temporal equivalent of an ancient mnemonic device: the famous "method of loci." In that method, one mentally moves through a familiar series of places in order to recall images that were previously assigned to them. Dean apparently used newspaper clippings in a similar way, to pinpoint moments in time rather than loci in space; then he tried to recall what he had been doing at those moments. Senator Inouye's next questions (I am omitting some additional comments by Dean) indicate that he failed to grasp this point:

Senator Inouye Are you suggesting that your testimony was primarily based upon press accounts?
Mr. Dean No sir, I am saying that I used the press accounts as one of the means to trigger my recollection of what had occurred during given periods of time.

Inouye still does not understand:

Senator Inouye Am I to gather from this that you had great faith in the reporting in the press?
Mr. Dean No, I am saying what was happening is that this sequentially—many times White House activities related to a response to a given press activity. I did not have the benefit—in fact, the statement might be even more detailed, Senator, if I had had the benefit of all the Ziegler briefings where some of these questions came up very specifically in

press briefings as to given events at that time, but I didn't have the benefit of those (*Ibid.*).
Senator Inouye In addition to the press clippings, the logs, what other sources did you use in the process of reconstruction?
Mr. Dean Well Senator, I think I have a good memory. I think that anyone who recalls my student years knew that I was very fast at recalling information, retaining information. I was the type of student who didn't have to work very hard in school because I do have a memory that I think is good (*Ibid.*).

A moment later Inouye asks the question I have already quoted, encouraging Dean to say more about his memory:

Senator Inouye Have you always had a facility for recalling the details of conversations which took place many months ago? (*Ibid.*).

Dean responds with examples of things he would certainly never forget, beginning with conversations in the Oval Office:

Mr. Dean Well, I would like to start with the President of the United States. It was not a regular activity for me to go in and visit with the President. For most of the members of the White House staff it was not a daily activity. When you meet with the President of the United States it is a very momentous occasion, and you tend to remember what the President of the United States says when you have a conversation with him. (Dean goes on to mention several other salient events that he remembers well, and concludes . . .) . . . . So I would say that I have an ability to recall not specific words necessarily but certainly the tenor of a conversation and the gist of a conversation (*Ibid.*, pp. 1433–1434).

We shall see later that Dean recalls the "gist" of some conversations and not of others; the determinants of memory are more complicated than he believes them to be. In particular, he did *not* remember what the President said in their first prolonged and "momentous" meeting. But there is no doubt about his confidence in his own testimony: at the end of the exchange with Inouye, he expresses it again:

Mr. Dean I cannot repeat the very words he (the President) used, no, sir. As I explained to Senator Gurney, my mind is not a tape recorder, but it certainly receives the message that is being given (*Ibid.*).

THE MEETING OF SEPTEMBER 15

On June 17, 1972, five men were arrested in the offices of the Democratic National Committee in the Watergate Office Building. They had planned to tap the Committee's telephones as part of an illegal "political intelligence" operation, mounted on President Nixon's behalf in the 1972 presidential elections. High White House officials then began a major effort to conceal their involvement in the affair, even to the point of paying "hush money" to some of those who had been arrested. John Dean was centrally involved in the cover-up. His chief task was to "contain" the legal investigation of the Watergate break-in, concealing every link between the underlings already caught and the White House. On September 15 this aim seemed achieved, because on that day the Grand Jury handed down indictments against only seven men: the five burglars plus Howard Hunt and Gordon Liddy. Since Hunt and Liddy were "small fish," and the Justice Department said it had no evidence to indict anyone else, Dean felt victorious. When the President summoned him to the Oval office that afternoon, he expected to be praised.

The transcript indicates that the meeting lasted 50 minutes. It begins with the following interchange among the President (P), Dean (D), and Robert Haldeman (H), Nixon's "Chief of Staff." Note that Dean and Haldeman are both obviously pleased by the events of the day, while the President has little to say about them.

> P Hi, how are you? You had quite a day today, didn't you? You got Watergate on the way, didn't you?
> D We tried.
> H How did it all end up?
> D Ah, I think we can say well, at this point. The press is playing it just as we expected.
> H Whitewash?
> D No, not yet—the story right now—
> P It is a big story.
> H Five indicted plus the WH former guy and all that.
> D Plus two White House fellows.
> H That is good; that takes the edge off the whitewash, really. That was the thing Mitchell kept saying, that to people in the country Liddy and Hunt were big men. Maybe that is good.
> P How did MacGregor handle himself?

> D I think very well. He had a good statement, which said that the Grand jury had met and that it was now time to realize that some apologies may be due.
> H Fat chance.
> D Get the damn (inaudible)
> H We can't do that.
> P Just remember, all the trouble we're taking, we'll have a chance to get back one day. How are you doing on your other investigation? (*Presidential Transcripts*, p. 32).

The next few exchanges are about other details of the Watergate "bugs" (telephone taps), and then about the scope of the investigations being conducted. It all seemed "silly" to them, especially since they believed that "bugging" was common in politics:

> P Yes (expletive deleted). Goldwater put it in context when he said "(expletive deleted) everybody bugs everybody else. You know that."
> D That was priceless.
> P It happens to be totally true. We were bugged in '68 on the plane and even in '62 running for Governor—(expletive deleted) thing you ever saw.
> D It is a shame that evidence to the fact that that happened in '68 was never around. I understand that only the former director (J. Edgar Hoover, former head of the FBI) had that information.
> H No, that is not true.
> D There was evidence of it?
> H There are others who have information (*Ibid.*, p. 34).

This interchange about "bugging" is noteworthy not only because of the light it sheds on the attitudes of the participants, but also because it stuck in Dean's mind. It is one of the few parts of the conversation which will be recognizable in his testimony nine months later.

The conversation continues from this point with more talk about "bugging," plans for action against White House enemies, questions about another pending legal action. It is interrupted briefly when Nixon takes a phone call. As soon as he hangs up, Dean speaks. He wants to point out how well things are going:

> D Three months ago I would have had trouble predicting there would be a day when this would be forgotten, but I think I can say that 54 days from now [i.e., on election day in November] nothing is going to come crashing down to our surprise.
> P That what?

D Nothing is going to come crashing down to our surprise (*Ibid.*, p. 36).

He finally gets a bit of Presidential praise in return:

P Oh well, this is a can of worms as you know, a lot of this stuff that went on. And the people who worked this way are awfully embarrassed. But the way you have handled all this seems to me has been very skillful, putting your fingers in the leaks that have sprung here and sprung there. The Grand Jury is dismissed now?

D That is correct . . . (*Ibid.*).

The conversation goes on to cover many other areas—McGovern's campaign finances, a list of "enemies" that Dean offers to keep, more political strategy. Later on Dean and Haldeman (but not Nixon) seize another opportunity to congratulate each other on the success of the cover-up.

P You really can't sit and worry about it all the time. The worst may happen but may not. So you just try to button it up as well as you can and hope for the best, and remember basically the damn business is unfortunately trying to cut our losses.

D Certainly that is right and certainly it has had no effect on you. That's the good thing.

H No, it has been kept away from the White House and of course completely from the President. The only tie to the White House is the Colson effort they keep trying to pull in.

D And of course the two White House people of lower level—indicated—one consultant and one member of the domestic staff. That is not very much of a tie.

H That's right (*Ibid.*, p. 40).

DEAN'S TESTIMONY ABOUT SEPTEMBER 15

Nine months later, Dean devoted about two pages of his prepared statement to the September 15 meeting. The first paragraph purports to describe the way the meeting began. It is an important bit of testimony because the remarks Dean ascribes to Nixon would indicate full knowledge (and approval) of the cover-up. This is his account:

On September 15 the Justice Department announced the handing down of the seven in-dictments by the Federal Grand Jury investigating the Watergate. Late that afternoon I received a call requesting me to come to the President's Oval Office. When I arrived at the Oval Office I found Haldeman and the President. The President asked me to sit down. Both men appeared to be in very good spirits and my reception was very warm and cordial. The President then told me that Bob—referring to Haldeman—had kept him posted on my handling of the Watergate case. The President told me I had done a good job and he appreciated how difficult a task it had been and the President was pleased that the case had stopped with Liddy. I responded that I could not take credit because others had done much more difficult things than I had done. As the President discussed the present status of the situation I told him that all I had been able to do was to contain the case and assist in keeping it out of the White House. I also told him there was a long way to go before this matter would end and that I certainly could make no assurances that the day would not come when this matter would start to unravel (*Hearings*, p. 957).

Comparison with the transcript shows that hardly a word of Dean's account is true. Nixon did not say *any* of the things attributed to him here: he didn't ask Dean to sit down, he didn't say Haldeman had kept him posted, he didn't say Dean had done a good job (at least not in that part of the conversation), he didn't say anything about Liddy or the indictments. Nor had Dean himself said the things he later describes himself as saying: that he couldn't take credit, that the matter might unravel some day, etc. (Indeed, he said just the opposite later on: "nothing is going to come crashing down.") His account is plausible, but entirely incorrect. In this early part of the conversation Nixon did not offer him any praise at all, unless "You had quite a day, didn't you," was intended as a compliment. (It is hard to tell from a written transcript.) Dean cannot be said to have reported the "gist" of the opening remarks; no count of idea units or comparison of structure would produce a score much above zero.

Was he simply lying to the Senators? I do not think so. The transcript makes it quite clear that Nixon *is* fully aware of the cover-up: Haldeman and Dean discuss it freely in front of him, and while he occasionally asks questions he never seems surprised. Later on he even praises Dean for "putting his fingers in the leaks." Because the real conversation is just as incriminating as the one Dean described, it seems unlikely that he was remembering one thing and saying another. His responses to Senator Baker during cross-examination (see below) also indicate that he was doing his best to be honest. Mary McCarthy's assessment of Dean has stood the test of time: she wrote in 1973 of her overpowering impression " . . . not so much of a truthful person as of someone resolved to tell the truth about this particular set of events because his intelligence has warned him to do so" (McCarthy, 1971, pp. 40–41).

If Dean was trying to tell the truth, where did his erroneous account of the September 15 meeting come from? Some of it might be explained by the currently popular notion that everyone knows certain "scripts" for common events, and that these scripts are used in the course of recall (Bower, Black, and Turner, 1979). Dean's recollection of the very beginning of the meeting may have been constructed on the basis of an "entering-the-room script." People do often ask their guests to sit down, though Nixon apparently did not ask Dean. It is also possible, however, that Dean's recollection of such a request is a case of non-verbal gist recall rather than a script-based construction. Perhaps Nixon *did* ask Dean to sit down, but with a gesture rather than a word—a brief wave of a commanding presidential hand. To recall such a gesture as if it had been a verbal request would not be much of an error. Current theoretical interest in the recall of written texts should not blind us to the non-verbal components of real conversation.

Although familiar scripts and non-verbal cues explain a few of Dean's errors, most of them seem to have deeper roots. They follow, I believe, from Dean's own character and especially from his self-centered assessment of events at the White House. What his testimony really describes is not the September 15 meeting itself but his fantasy of it: the meeting as it should have been, so to speak. In his mind Nixon *should* have been glad that the indictments stopped with Liddy, Haldeman *should*

have been telling Nixon what a great job Dean was doing; most of all, praising him *should* have been the first order of business. In addition, Dean *should* have told Nixon that the cover-up might unravel, as it eventually did, instead of telling him it was a great success. By June, this fantasy had become the way Dean remembered the meeting.

Almost. But Dean was not really as confident of his recollection as the tone of his statement suggested; not as sure of himself as he claimed in the exchange with Senator Inouye. This becomes clear in a very sharp interrogation by Senator Baker:

Senator Baker I am going to try now to focus entirely on the meeting of September 15.
Mr. Dean Right.
Senator Baker And I have an ambition to focus sharply on it in order to disclose as much information as possible about the September 15 meeting. What I want to do is to test, once again, not the credibility of your testimony but the quality of the evidence, that is, is it direct evidence.
Mr. Dean I understand (*Hearings*, p. 1474).

Dean does understand: Baker wants vivid details and exact wording. The next few exchanges show how he struggles to reconcile the vagueness of his actual recollection with Baker's demands for specificity, dodging some questions and eventually committing himself on others. After an uncontroversial account of how he learned that Nixon wanted to see him that evening, Dean begins with his physical entrance into the office:

Mr. Dean When I entered the office I can recall that—you have been in the office, you know the way there are two chairs at the side of the President's desk.
Senator Baker You are speaking of the Oval Office?
Mr. Dean Of the Oval Office. As you face the President, on the left-hand chair Mr. Haldeman was sitting and they had obviously been immersed in a conversation and the President asked me to come in and I stood there for a moment. He said "Sit down," and I sat in the chair on the other side.
Senator Baker You sat in the right-hand chair?
Mr. Dean I sat on the right-hand chair.
Senator Baker That is the one he usually says no to, but go ahead.
Mr. Dean I was unaware of that. (Laughter).

Senator Baker Go ahead, Mr. Dean (*Ibid.*, p. 1475).

Now Dean plunges into the conversation, giving almost exactly the same account of it that he had presented in his prepared statement a few days before. Indeed, his opening phrase suggests that he is remembering that statement rather than the meeting itself:

Mr. Dean As I tried to describe in my statement, the reception was very warm and cordial. There was some preliminary pleasantries, and then the next thing that I recall the President very clearly saying to me is that he had been told by Mr. Haldeman that he had been kept posted or made aware of my handling of the various aspects of the Watergate case and the fact that the case, you know, the indictments had now been handed down, no one in the White House had been indicted, they had stopped at Liddy (*Ibid.*).

Senator Baker is not satisfied with this response; he wants to know how accurate Dean is really claiming to be:

Senator Baker Stop, stop, stop just for one second. "That no one in the White House had been indicted": is that as near to the exact language—I don't know so I am not laying a trap for you, I just want to know (*Ibid.*).

It is now clear that the right answer to Baker's question would have been "no." Nixon did not use anything remotely like the "exact language" in question; the conversation did not go that way at all. Dean's answer is cautious:

Mr. Dean Yes, there was a reference to the fact that the indictments had been handed down and it was quite obvious that no one in the White House had been indicted on the indictments that had been handed down (*Ibid.*).

Notice that although Dean's answer begins with "Yes," he now avoids attributing the critical words to Nixon. He hides behind ambiguous phrases like "There was a reference to the fact that . . ." and "It was quite obvious . . ." Baker is unsatisfied with these evasions and continues to press for a straight answer:

Senator Baker Did he say that, though? (*Ibid.*).

Dean decides to be honest about it:

Mr. Dean Did he say that no one in the White House had been handed down? I can't recall it. (*Ibid.*).

This is the answer which suggests to me that Dean was being as truthful as he could. After all, he might easily have answered "yes" instead of "I can't recall it." But he doesn't want to give up the points he has already scored, so he repeats them:

Mr. Dean (continuing) I can recall a reference to the fact that the indictments were now handed down and he was aware of that and the status of the indictments and expressed what to me was a pleasure to the fact that it had stopped with Mr. Liddy (*Ibid.*).

This paragraph is a nice summary of what Dean remembers of the conversation, and it is phrased so carefully that everything in it is true. There *was* reference to the indictments (by Haldeman and Dean); Nixon *was* aware of that (though he didn't say so); and somehow he did express what Dean *interpreted* as pleasure in the outcome. It is fair to say that Dean here captures the "tenor," though not the gist, of what went on in the Oval Office that afternoon. But Baker notices that he still hasn't committed himself to any exact statements by Nixon, and tries again:

Senator Baker Tell me what he said.
Mr. Dean Well, as I say, he told me I had done a good job—
Senator Baker No, let's talk about the pleasure. He expressed pleasure the indictments had stopped at Mr. Liddy. Can you just for the purposes of our information tell me the language that he used? (*Ibid.*).

Dean ducks once more:

Mr. Dean Senator, let me make it very clear: the pleasure that it had stopped there is an inference of mine based on, as I told Senator Gurney yesterday, the impression I had as a result of the, of his, complimenting me (*Ibid.*).

Baker hangs tough:

Senator Baker Can you give us any information, can you give us any further insight into what the President said?
Mr. Dean Yes, I can recall he told me that he appreciated how difficult a job it had been for me.
Senator Baker Is that close to the exact language?
Mr. Dean Yes, that is close to the exact language (*Ibid.*, p. 1476).

Finally Dean gives in, and puts words into Nixon's mouth. He may just have felt he had no choice: if he didn't claim to remember *any* of Nixon's remarks his whole testimony might be discredited. But also he may have believed it. Nixon's compliment was what he had most yearned for, and his invented version of it may have been the most compelling thing in his memory. Either way, the exchange seems to have hardened his willingness to testify to exact language. He and Baker went at it again a few minutes later when Dean said he had told Nixon "that the matter had been contained." Baker repeatedly asked whether he had used that very word, and Dean repeatedly asserted that he had done so. When Baker questioned him closely about how the President had reacted to "contained," however, Dean said he did not recall. He certainly didn't: the word "contained" appears nowhere in the transcript.

In summary, it is clear that Dean's account of the opening of the September 15 conversation is wrong both as to the words used and their gist. Moreover, cross-examination did not reveal his errors as clearly as one might have hoped. The effect of Baker's hard questioning was mixed. Although it did show up the weakness of Dean's verbatim recall, the overall result may have been to increase his credibility. Dean came across as a man who has a good memory for gist with an occasional literal word stuck in, like a raisin in a pudding. He was not such a man. He remembered how he had felt himself and what he had wanted, together with the general state of affairs; he didn't remember what anyone had actually said. His testimony had much truth in it, but not at the level of "gist." It was true at a deeper level. Nixon was the kind of man Dean described, he had the knowledge Dean attributed to him, there was a cover-up. Dean remembered all of that; he just didn't recall the actual conversation he was testifying about.

So far I have concentrated on the first few minutes of the meeting, covered in a single paragraph of Dean's prepared statement. The next paragraph is interesting because (unlike the first) it refers to a bit of conversation that actually occurred.

> Early in our conversation the President said to me that former FBI Director Hoover had told him shortly after he assumed office in 1969

that his campaign had been bugged in 1968. The President said that at some point we should get the facts out on this and use this to counter the problems that we were encountering (*Ibid.*, p. 958).

As we have already seen, an exchange about Hoover and bugging in previous campaigns did take place, a little after the beginning of the conversation. But although it was indeed Nixon who raised the subject, it was Dean, not Nixon, who brought Hoover's name into it: "I understand that only the former director had that information." Dean may have forgotten this because Haldeman had put him down so sharply ("No, that is not true"), or he may have preferred to put the words into Nixon's mouth for other reasons. In any case, he isn't quite right.

The remainder of Dean's testimony about the meeting is no better than the parts we have examined. He mentions topics that were indeed discussed, but never reproduces the real gist of anything that was said. Surprisingly, he does *not* remember the President's actual compliment to him ("putting your fingers in the leaks") although it is a fairly striking phrase. At the end of his statement he presents the following summary:

> *Mr. Dean* "I left the meeting with the impression that the President was well aware of what had been going on regarding the success of keeping the White House out of the Watergate scandal, and I also had expressed to him my concern that I was not confident that the cover-up could be maintained indefinitely (*Ibid.*, p. 959).

The first part of this summary is fair enough: Nixon was surely " . . . well aware of what had been going on." The conclusion is less fair; Dean seriously—perhaps deliberately—misrepresents the optimistic predictions he had made. In fact he was *not* wise enough or brave enough to warn Nixon in September, though by June he was smart enough to wish he had done so.

THE MEETING OF MARCH 21

The cover-up was only temporarily successful. Although Nixon was re-elected overwhelmingly in November of 1972, Dean's problems increased steadily. There were more blackmail demands by the indicted Watergate defendants, and more investigations moving closer to the White House. Dean met frequently with Nixon, Haldeman, and the others, but their strategems were unsuccessful. Dean began to realize that he and the others were engaging in a crime ("obstruction of justice"), and might eventually go to prison for it. He was not sure whether Nixon understood the gravity of the situation. Finally he resolved to ask the President for a private meeting at which he could lay out all the facts. This meeting took place on March 21, 1973.

Dean's autobiography (1976) relates an incident that occurred on the day before the critical meeting. When he was trying to describe the relentlessly increasing complexity of the Watergate affair to Richard Moore, another White House aide, Moore compared it to the growth of a tumor. The metaphor attracted Dean, and he resolved to use it in his report the next day: to tell Nixon that there was a "cancer" growing on the presidency. The transcript of the meeting shows that he did so. After a few minutes of conversation about the day's events, Dean and the President continue as follows:

> D The reason I thought we ought to talk this morning is because in our conversations I have the impression that you don't know everything I know, and it makes it very difficult for you to make judgments that only you can make on some of these targets, and I thought that—
> P In other words, I have to know why you feel that we shouldn't unravel something?
> D Let me give you my overall first.
> P In other words, your judgment as to where it stands, and where we will go.
> D I think there is no doubt about the seriousness of the problem we've got. We have a cancer within, close to the presidency, that is growing. It is growing daily. It's compounded, growing geometrically now because it compounds itself. That will be clear if I, you know explain some of the details of why it is. Basically it is because (1) we are being blackmailed; (2) people are going to start perjuring themselves very quickly that have not had to perjure themselves to protect other people in the line. And there is no assurance—
> P That that won't bust?

> D That that won't bust (*Presidential Transcripts*, pp. 98–99).

In this first part of the March 21 meeting, Dean was alone with the President. They remained alone for about an hour, then Haldeman came in to join the discussion for another 45 minutes or so. Haldeman's entrance proved to be a critical turning point in Dean's later memory of that morning: he forgot the rest of the conversation almost completely. What he said about the first hour, in contrast, was quite accurate. Comparison of the transcript with Dean's subsequent testimony shows clear recall of the gist of what was said. One's admiration for his memory is somewhat diminished, however, by the realization that the March 21 meeting was less a conversation than the delivery of a well-prepared report. Dean did most of the talking, taking 20 minutes to describe the events before the break-in and 40 more for the cover-up. Although Nixon interjected occasional remarks, questions, or expletives, the hour stayed quite close to the script Dean had prepared for it in advance.

The difference between this meeting and that of September 15 is instructive. This one fulfilled Dean's hopes as the earlier one had not: he really did give a personal lecture to the President of the United States, talking while Nixon listened. His testimony, too long to reproduce here, highlights the meeting's didactic quality. Almost every statement begins with "I told him . . . ," "I proceeded to tell him . . . ," "I informed the President . . ." or some similar phrase. He was remembering a report that he had rehearsed ahead of time, presented as planned, and probably continued to rehearse afterwards. It became John Dean's own story; March 21 had merely been his first opportunity to tell it.

Dean's testimony includes a fragment of nearly verbatim recall that later achieved some notoriety: he quoted his own remark about the "cancer on the presidency" to the Senate Committee. This, too, was a well-rehearsed passage. We know that he prepared it in advance, and the transcript shows that he used it repeatedly. (He probably used it on other occasions as well; why let such a good phrase go to waste?) His first presentation of the simile, early in the meeting, has been quoted above. Twenty minutes later he refers back to it:

> D . . . When I say this is a growing cancer, I say it for reasons like this . . . (*Ibid.*, p. 111).

and still later he brings it in obliquely:

> D . . . we should begin to think . . . how to minimize the further growth of this thing . . . (*Ibid.*, p. 119).

Interestingly, Dean's self-quotation to the Senators was not faithful to any of these occasions:

> I began by telling the President that there was a cancer growing on the presidency and that if the cancer was not removed the President himself would be killed by it. I also told him that it was important that this cancer be removed immediately because it was growing more deadly every day (*Hearings*, p. 998).

A glance back at the excerpt from the transcript shows that Dean is once again giving himself the benefit of hindsight. He did *not* say that the President would be *killed* by the cancer, for example. By June he probably wished he had done so; I don't know whether he altered the wording in his testimony deliberately or whether his memory had already accommodated itself slightly to his self-image.

In Dean's mind, the significance of the March 21 meeting must have lain in the degree to which he dominated it. That may explain why he barely mentioned the second half of the meeting in his Senate testimony; Haldeman's entrance spoiled his private command performance. The rest of the session was by no means uninteresting, however. What actually happened was that Nixon, Haldeman, and Dean considered various options, trying to find the best way to deal with their Watergate dilemma. One of those options was to raise money to meet the blackmail demands of the men who had already been convicted. This possibility seemed to attract Nixon; he returned to it again and again. He had already discussed it in the first hour, when only Dean was with him:

> D I would say these people are going to cost a million dollars over the next two years.
> P We could get that. On the money, if you need the money you could get that. You could get a million dollars. You could get it in cash. I know where it could be gotten. It is not easy

but it could be done . . . (*Presidential Transcripts*, p. 110).

He seemed more enthusiastic about it than Dean himself:

> P Just looking at the immediate problem, don't you think you have to handle Hunt's financial situation damn soon?
> D I think that is—I talked with Mitchell about that last night and—
> P It seems to me we have to keep the cap on the bottle that much or we don't have any options (*Ibid.*, p. 112).

Later he makes it as explicit as he possibly can:

> D The blackmailers. Right.
> P Well I wonder if that part of it can't be—I wonder if that doesn't—let me put it frankly: I wonder if that doesn't have to be continued? Let me put it this way: let us suppose you get the million bucks, and you get the proper way to handle it. You could hold that side?
> D Uh-huh.
> P It would seem to me that would be worthwhile (*Ibid.*, p. 117).

Remarks like this continue to sprinkle the conversation after Haldeman joins them:

> P . . . First, it is going to require approximately a million dollars to take care of the jackasses who are in jail. That can be arranged . . . (*Ibid.*, p. 127).
> . . . P Now let me tell you. We could get the money. There is no problem in that . . . (*Ibid.*, p. 129).
> . . . P I just have a feeling on it. Well, it sounds like a lot of money, a million dollars. Let me say that I think we could get that . . . (*Ibid.*, p. 130).*

These are quite remarkable things for a President to say. They would certainly seem to be memorable, and indeed Dean did not forget them. He just assigned them to a different day! Although he makes no reference to them in his testimony about March 21, his statement includes the following description of a meeting with Nixon on March 13, eight days before:

> . . . It was during this conversation that Haldeman came into the office. After this brief

---

*Nixon never expressed any hesitation about making these payments, or any reluctance to meet the burglars' demands for money. He did, however, agree with Dean that their demands for *executive clemency* should not be met. At one point he said "No—it is wrong, that's for sure" about the possibility of clemency. The transcript shows no analogous statement about the blackmail payments.

interruption by Haldeman's coming in, but while he was still there, I told the President about the fact that there was no money to pay these individuals to meet their demands. He asked me how much it would cost. I told him that I could only make an estimate that it might be as high as $1 million or more. He told me that that was no problem, and he also looked over at Haldeman and made the same statement . . . (*Hearings*, p. 995).

Dean amplifies this account later during cross-examination:

. . . We had also had a discussion on March 13 about the money demands that were being made. At the time he discussed the fact that a million dollars is no problem. He repeated it several times. I can very vividly recall that the way he sort of rolled his chair back from his desk and leaned over to Mr. Haldeman and said "A million dollars is no problem" (*Ibid.*, p. 1423).

It is hardly surprising that Dean remembered these million-dollar statements, especially since Nixon repeated them so often. It *is* a little surprising that he put them into the wrong conversation. (There is a transcript of the March 13 meeting, and it shows no such remarks by the President.) Evidently Dean's improvised method of temporal loci, based on newspaper clippings, did not work as well as his exchange with Senator Inouye had suggested. His ego got in the way again. The March 21 meeting had been the occasion for his own personal report to the President; he could not suppose that anything else worth mentioning had happened. Other memories were shifted to another day if they survived at all.

Nixon's eagerness to pay the blackmail money was not the only part of the conversation to suffer this fate. Dean even displaced one of his own jokes; a joke that had drawn a response from Haldeman if not from Nixon. They were discussing various illegal ways of "laundering" the blackmail money so it could not be traced:

D And that means you have to go to Vegas with it or a bookmaker in New York City. I have learned all these things after the fact. I will be in great shape for the next time around!
H (Expletive deleted) (*Presidential Transcripts*, p. 134).

That may not have been the only time Dean used this wisecrack; he probably enjoyed describing himself as increasingly skilled in underworld techniques. Certainly he didn't mind repeating it to the Senators, though his statement assigns it, too, to March 13 rather than March 21:

. . . I told him I was learning about things I had never had before, but the next time I would certainly be more knowledgeable. This comment got a laugh out of Haldeman (*Hearings*, p. 996).

It isn't very funny.

IMPLICATIONS FOR THE PSYCHOLOGY OF MEMORY

Are we all like this? Is everyone's memory constructed, staged, self-centered? And do we all have access to certain invariant facts nevertheless? Such questions cannot be answered by single case histories. My own guess—and it is only a guess—is that reconstruction played an exaggerated part in Dean's testimony. The circumstances and the man conspired to favor exaggeration. The events *were* important; his testimony *was* critical; its effect *was* historic. Dean was too intelligent not to know what he was doing, and too ambitious and egocentric to remain unaffected by it. His ambition reorganized his recollections: even when he tries to tell the truth, he can't help emphasizing his own role in every event. A different man in the same position might have observed more dispassionately, reflected on his experiences more thoughtfully, and reported them more accurately. Unfortunately, such traits of character are rare.

What have we learned about testimony by comparing "the human tape recorder" with a real one? We are hardly surprised to find that memory is constructive, or that confident witnesses may be wrong. William Stern studied the psychology of testimony at the turn of the century and warned us not to trust memory even under oath; Bartlett was doing experiments on "constructive" memory fifty years ago. I believe, however, that John Dean's testimony can do more than remind us of their work. For one thing, his constructed memories were not altogether wrong. On the contrary, there is a sense in which he was altogether right; a level at which he was telling the truth about the Nixon White House. And sometimes—as in his testimony about March 21—he was more specifically right as well. These islands of accuracy deserve special consideration. What kinds of things did he remember?

Dean's task as he testified before the Senate Committee was to recall specific well-defined conversations, " . . . conversations which took place months ago." This is what witnesses are always instructed to do: stick to the facts, avoid inferences and generalizations. Such recall is what Tulving (1972) called *episodic*; it involves the retrieval of particular autobiographical moments, individuals episodes of one's life. Tulving contrasted episodic memory only with what he called *semantic* memory, the individual's accumulated store of facts and word meanings and general knowledge. That concept seems inadequate as a description of data such as these. Dean's recollection of Nixon's remarks about the million dollars was not merely semantic: he talked as if he were recalling one or more specific events. I doubt, however, that any of those events was being recalled uniquely in its own right. A single such episode might not have found its way into Dean's testimony at all. What seems to be specific in his memory actually depends on repeated episodes, rehearsed presentations, or overall impressions. He believes that he is recalling one conversation at a time, that his memory is "episodic" in Tulving's sense, but he is mistaken.

He is not alone in making this mistake. I believe that this aspect of Dean's testimony illustrates a very common process. The single clear memories that we recollect so vividly actually stand for something else; they are "screen memories" a little like those Freud discussed long ago. Often their real basis is a set of repeated experiences, a sequence of related events that the single recollection merely typifies or represents. We are like the subjects of Posner and Keele (1970) who forgot the individual dot patterns of a series but "remembered" the prototypical pattern they had never

seen. Such memories might be called *repisodic* rather than episodic: what seems to be an episode actually *re*presents a *re*petition. Dean remembers the million-dollar remark because Nixon made it so often; he recalls the "cancer" metaphor because he first planned it and then repeated it; he remembers his March 21 lecture to the President because he planned it, then presented it, and then no doubt went over it again and again in his own mind. What he says about these "repisodes" is essentially correct, even though it is not literally faithful to any one occasion. He is not remembering the "gist" of a single episode by itself, but the common characteristics of a whole series of events.

This notion may help us to interpret the paradoxical sense in which Dean was accurate throughout his testimony. Given the numerous errors in his reports of conversations, what did he tell the truth about? I think that he extracted the common themes that remained invariant across many conversations and many experiences, and then incorporated those themes in his testimony. His many encounters with Nixon were themselves a kind of "repisode." There were certain consistent and repeated elements in all those meetings; they had a theme that expressed itself in different ways on different occasions. Nixon wanted the cover-up to succeed; he was pleased when it went well; he was troubled when it began to unravel; he was perfectly willing to consider illegal activities if they would extend his power or confound his enemies. John Dean did not misrepresent this theme in his testimony; he just dramatized it. In memory experiments, subjects often recall the gist of a sentence but express it in different words. Dean's consistency was deeper; he recalled the theme of a whole series of conversations, and expressed it in different events. Nixon hoped that the transcripts would undermine Dean's testimony by showing that he had been wrong. They did not have this effect because he was wrong only in terms of isolated episodes. Episodes are not the only kinds of facts. Except where the significance of his own role was at stake, Dean was right about what had really been going on in the White House. What he later told the Senators was fairly close to the mark: his mind was not a tape recorder, but it certainly received the message that was being given.

REFERENCES

Bartlett, F. C., (1932) *Remembering*. Cambridge University Press.

Bower, G. H., Black, J. B., and Turner, T. J. (1979) Scripts in memory for text. *Cog. Psychol., 11*, 177–220.

Bransford, J. D. and Franks, J. J. (1972) The abstraction of linguistic ideas: A review, *Cog., 1*, 211–249.

Buckhout, R. (1974) Eyewitness testimony. *Sci. Amer., 231* (6), 23–31.

Dean, J. W. (1976) *Blind Ambition*. New York, Simon and Schuster.

Freud, S. (1899) Screen memories. Reprinted in *Collected Papers of Sigmund Freud, Vol. V*. London: Hogarth Press, 1956.

Hearings before the Select Committee on Presidential Campaign Activities of the United States Senate, Ninety-third Congress, First Session, 1973.

Mandler, J. M. and Johnson, N. (1977) Remembrance of things parsed: story structure and recall. *Cog. Psychol., 9*, 111–151.

McCarthy, M. (1975) *The Mask of State: Watergate Portraits*. New York, Harcourt Brace Jovanovich (Harvest).

Posner, M. J. and Keele, S. (1970) Retention of abstract ideas. *J. Exper. Psychol., 83*, 304–308.

The Presidential Transcripts (1974). New York, Dell.

Stern, W. (1904) Wirklichkeitsversuche (Reality Experiments). *Beitrage zur Psychologie der Aussage, 2*, No. 1, 1–31.

Tulving, E. (1972) Episodic and semantic memory. In E. Tulving and W. Donaldson (Eds.), *Organization and Memory*. New York, Academic Press.

The first annual Delos D. Wickens Lecture, presented at Ohio State University on October 14, 1980.

12

Elizabeth F. Loftus and Geoffrey R. Loftus

On the Permanence of Stored Information in the Human Brain

Abstract: *Many people believe that information that is stored in long-term memory is permanent, citing examples of "retrieval techniques" that are alleged to uncover previously forgotten information. Such techniques include hypnosis, psychoanalytic procedures, methods for eliciting spontaneous and other conscious recoveries, and—perhaps most important—the electrical stimulation of the brain reported by Wilder Penfield and his associates. In this article we first evaluate the evidence and conclude that, contrary to apparent popular belief, the evidence in no way confirms the view that all memories are permanent and thus potentially recoverable. We then describe some failures that resulted from attempts to elicit retrieval of previously stored information and conjecture what circumstances might cause information stored in memory to be irrevocably destroyed.*

Few would deny the existence of a phenomenon called "forgetting," which is evident in the common observation that information becomes less available as the interval increases between the time of the information's initial acquisition and the time of its attempted retrieval.

Despite the prevalence of the phenomenon, the factors that underlie forgetting have proved to be rather elusive, and the literature abounds with hypothesized mechanisms to account for the observed data. In this article we shall focus our attention on what is perhaps the fundamental issue concerning forgetting: Does forgetting consist of an actual loss of stored information, or does it result from a loss of access to information, which, once stored, remains forever?

It should be noted at the outset that this question be impossible to resolve in an absolute sense. Consider the following thought experiment. A person (call him Geoffrey) observes some event, say a traffic accident. During the period of observation, a movie camera strapped to Geoffrey's head records the event as Geoffrey experiences it. Some time later, Geoffrey attempts to recall and describe the event with the aid of some retrieval technique (e.g., hypnosis or brain stimulation), which is alleged to allow recovery of any information stored in his brain. While Geoffrey describes the event, a second person (Elizabeth) watches the movie that has been made of the event. Suppose, now, that Elizabeth is unable to decide whether Geoffrey is describing his memory or the movie—in other words, memory and movie are indistinguishable. Such a finding would constitute rather impressive support for the position held by many people that the mind registers an accurate representation of reality and that this information is stored permanently.

But suppose, on the other hand, that Geoffrey's report—even with the aid of the miraculous retrieval technique—is incomplete, sketchy, and inaccurate, and furthermore, suppose that the accuracy of his report deteriorates over time. Such a finding, though consistent with the view that forgetting consists of information loss, would still be inconclusive, because it could be argued that the retrieval technique— no matter what it was—was simply not good enough to disgorge the information, which remained buried somewhere in the recesses of Geoffrey's brain.

Thus, the question of information loss versus retrieval failure may be unanswerable in principle. Nonetheless it often becomes necessary to choose sides. In the scientific arena, for example, a theorist constructing a model of memory may—depending on the details of the model— be forced to adopt one position or the other. In fact, several leading theorists have suggested that although loss from short-term memory does occur, once material is registered in long-term memory, the information is never lost from the system, although it may normally be inaccessible (Shiffrin & Atkinson, 1969; Tulving, 1974). The idea is not new, however. Two hundred years earlier, the German philosopher Johann Nicolas Tetens (1777) wrote: "Each idea

does not only leave a trace or a consequent of that trace somewhere in the body, but each of them can be stimulated—even if it is not possible to demonstrate this in a given situation" (p. 751). He was explicit about his belief that certain ideas may seem to be forgotten, but that actually they are only enveloped by other ideas and, in truth, are "always with us" (p. 733).

Apart from theoretical interest, the position one takes on the permanence of memory traces has important practical consequences. It therefore makes sense to air the issue from time to time, which is what we shall do here.

The purpose of this paper is threefold. We shall first report some data bearing on people's beliefs about the question of information loss versus retrieval failure. To anticipate our findings, our survey revealed that a substantial number of the individuals queried take the position that stored information is permanent—or in other words, that all forgetting results from retrieval failure. In support of their answers, people typically cited data from some variant of the thought experiment described above, that is, they described currently available retrieval techniques that are alleged to uncover previously forgotten information. Such techniques include hypnosis, psychoanalytic procedures (e.g., free association), and— most important—the electrical stimulation of the brain reported by Wilder Penfield and his associates (Penfield, 1969; Penfield & Perot, 1963; Penfield & Roberts, 1959).

The results of our survey lead to the second purpose of this paper, which is to evaluate this evidence. Finally, we shall describe some interesting failures that have resulted from attempts to elicit retrieval of previously stored information. These failures lend support to the contrary view that some memories are apparently modifiable, and that consequently they are probably unrecoverable.

BELIEFS ABOUT MEMORY

In an informal survey, 169 individuals from various parts of the U.S. were asked to give their views about how memory works. Of these, 75 had formal graduate training in psychology, while the remaining 94 did not. The nonpsychologists had varied occupations. For example, lawyers, secretaries, taxicab drivers, physicians, philosophers, fire investigators, and even an 11-year-old child participated. They were given this question:

Which of these statements best reflects your view on how human memory works?
1. Everything we learn is permanently stored in the mind, although sometimes particular details are not accessible. With hypnosis, or other special techniques, these inaccessible details could eventually be recovered.
2. Some details that we learn may be permanently lost from memory. Such details would never be able to be recovered by hypnosis, or any other special technique, because these details are simply no longer there.
Please elaborate briefly or give any reasons you may have for your view.

We found that 84% of the psychologists chose Position 1, that is, they indicated a belief that all information in long-term memory is there, even though much of it cannot be retrieved; 14% chose Position 2, and 2% gave some other answer. A somewhat smaller percentage, 69%, of the nonpsychologists indicated a belief in Position 1; 23% chose Position 2, while 8% did not make a clear choice.

What reasons did people give for their belief? The most common reason for choosing Position 1 was based on personal experience and involved the occasional recovery of an idea that the person had not thought about for quite some time. For example, one person wrote: "I've experienced and heard too many descriptions of spontaneous recoveries of ostensibly quite trivial memories, which seem to have been triggered by just the right set of a person's experiences." A second reason for a belief in Position 1, commonly given by persons trained in psychology, was knowledge of the work of Wilder Penfield. One psychologist wrote: "Even though Statement 1 is untestable, I think that evidence, weak though it is, such as Penfield's work, strongly suggests it may be correct." Occasionally respondents offered a comment about hypnosis, and more rarely about psychoanalysis and repression, sodium pentothal, or even reincarnation, to support their belief in the permanence of memory.

Admittedly, the survey was informally conducted, the respondents were not selected randomly, and the question itself may have pressured people to take sides when their true belief may have been a position in between. Nevertheless, the results suggest a widespread belief in the permanence of memories and give us some idea of the reasons people offer in support of this belief.

Evidence People Use

Brain Stimulation.
The most impressive evidence for the notion of permanent storage seems to come from the reports that events long forgotten are vividly recalled during electrical stimulation of certain regions of the human cortex. Wilder Penfield, who is best known for this work, was operating on epileptic patients during the 1940s, removing the damaged areas in their brains (Penfield, 1969; Penfield & Perot, 1963; Penfield & Roberts, 1959). To guide himself in pinpointing the damage, Penfield stimulated the surface of the brain with a weak electric current in the hope of discovering, in each of his patients, the particular area in the brain that was related to the epileptic attacks. During this electrical invasion of their brains, Penfield discovered that certain placements of the stimulating electrode apparently caused some of the patients to re-experience events from their past.

If one looks at accounts of Penfield's work written by others, one gets a clear impression of a phenomenon that is extremely vivid and rather widespread. For example, the following remarks are found in popular textbooks of introductory psychology:

Dr. Wilder Penfield, a Canadian brain surgeon, has reported that he was able to produce vivid memories in some of his patients by stimulating certain areas of the temporal lobes with weak electric currents. One patient reported hearing a song; in his words, " . . . it was not as though I were imagining the tune to myself. I actually heard it." Other patients suddenly relived long-forgotten childhood experiences. Stimulation of the same cerebral area always produced the same episode. (Kendler, 1968, p. 185)

We are in the operating room of the Montreal Neurological Institute observing brain surgery on Buddy, a young man with uncontrollable epileptic seizures. The surgeon wants to operate to remove a tumor, but first he must discover what the consequences will be of removing various portions of the brain tissue surrounding the tumor. . . . Suddenly, an unexpected response occurs. The patient is grinning; he is smiling; eyes opening when that area is stimulated. "Buddy, what happened, what did you just experience?" "Doc, I heard a song, or rather a part of a song, a melody." "Buddy, have you ever heard it before?" "Yes, I remember having heard it a long time ago, but I can't remember the name of the tune." When another brain site is stimulated, the patient recalls in vivid detail a thrilling childhood experience.

In a similar operation, a woman patient "relived" the experience she had during the delivery of her baby. As if by pushing an electronic memory button, the surgeon, Dr. Wilder Penfield, has touched memories stored silently for years in the recesses of his patients' brains. (Zimbardo & Ruch, 1975, pp. 48–49)

Acceptance of the power of Penfield's stimulating electrode has reached a far wider audience than the students of introductory psychology courses. The following example appeared in an article that reached millions of Americans—through the *New York Times*—just a couple of years ago:

One of Penfield's patients was a young woman. As the stimulating electrode touched a spot on her temporal lobe, she cried out: "I think I heard a mother calling her little boy somewhere. It seemed to be something that happened years ago . . . in the neighborhood where I live." Then the electrode was moved a little and she said, "I hear voices. It is late at night, around the carnival somewhere—some sort of traveling circus. I just saw lots of big wagons that they use to haul animals in."

There can be little doubt that Wilder Penfield's electrodes were arousing activity in the hippocampus, within the temporal lobe, jerking out distant and intimate memories from the patient's stream of consciousness. (Blakemore, 1977/1978, p. 88)

It is of interest to examine Penfield's own writings. In his 1969 work, he expressed a belief in the relatively permanent nature of memory:

It is clear that the neuronal action that accompanies each succeeding state of consciousness leaves its permanent imprint on the brain. The imprint, or record, is a trail of facilitation of neuronal connections that can be followed again by an electric current many years later with no loss of detail, as though a tape recorder had been receiving it all.

Consider now what happens in normal life. For a short time, a man can recall all the detail of his previous awareness. In minutes, some of it has faded beyond the reach of his command. In weeks, all of it seems to have disappeared, as far as voluntary recall is concerned, except what seemed to him important or wakened in him emotion. But the detail is not really lost. During the subconscious interpretation of later contemporary experience, that detail is still available. This is a part of what we may call perception. (p. 165)

On what did Penfield base these conclusions? Apparently on his observation of "flashback" responses.

The flashback responses to electrical stimulation . . . bear no relation to present experience in the operating room. Consciousness for the moment is doubled, and the patient can discuss the phenomenon. If he is hearing music, he can hum in time to it. *The astonishing aspect of the phenomenon is that suddenly he is aware of all that was in his mind during an earlier strip of time.* It is the stream of a former consciousness flowing again. If music is heard, it may be orchestra or voice or piano. Sometimes he is aware of all he was seeing at the moment; sometimes he is aware of only the music. It stops when the electrode is lifted. It may be repeated (even many times) if the electrode is replaced without too long a delay. This electrical recall is completely at random. Most often, the event was neither significant nor important. (Penfield, 1969, p. 152; emphasis ours)

In sum, Penfield concluded that memories are highly stable, that the brain contains a complete record of past experience that preserves an individual's past perceptions in astonishing detail. In this conclusion, he has provided the strongest version of a memory-permanence hypothesis—a view that might be dubbed the "videorecorder model." The videorecorder concept is clearly an exciting one, and the science-fiction quality of Penfield's findings seems to have engendered a remarkable degree of excitement over the past 20 years.

Hypnosis.

Hypnosis is also viewed as a retrieval technique that is capable of reactivating detailed memories that have lain dormant in a person for many years. The technique enjoys sufficient popular credibility for various U.S. law agencies to have used hypnosis as an aid to criminal investigation since the early 1960s. Many of the apparent successes deriving from hypnosis have been reported in a recent book by Eugene Block (1976) called: *Hypnosis: A New Tool in Crime Detection*. There, for example, the reader will learn how hypnosis was used by the Israeli National Police Force in solving scores of cases. Also in Block's book are descriptions of the successful role that hypnosis played in other investigations, for example, in the case of the Boston Strangler, of the San Francisco cable-car nymphomaniac, and of Cleveland's Dr. Sam Sheppard, accused of killing his pregnant wife, Marilyn.

If one looks at what the "experts" are saying about hypnosis, one gets a clear impression that some of them believe it works because of the permanence of memory. For example, two hypnotherapists, Cheek and LeCron (1968), wrote in their book *Clinical Hypnotherapy*,

> It seems that everything that happens to us is stored in memory in complete detail. Conscious recall is limited to a very tiny part of total memory. Regression under hypnosis can bring out completely forgotten memories. It is also possible to bring them out merely by suggesting that they will be recalled. In this situation the patient remembers but doesn't relive the event. (p. 54)

Acceptance of the power of hypnosis has reached an audience far wider than that made up of researchers in the field. An example is an article that found its way into the homes of millions of Americans—through the *TV Guide* (Stump, 1975). There readers learned of the case of a 38-year-old woman whose boyfriend had been murdered. She saw it happen, but the shock—and heavy drinking—almost totally blocked her memory. She was brought to the police station, where a hypnotist, speaking soothingly, explained to her that the mind is like a videotape machine. What we observe is recorded, stored in the subconscious, and available for recall through hypnosis. Information that she provided, previously unreported, helped crack the case.

The article went on to report the enormous success that the Los Angeles police department has had with hypnosis. One spokesman said it had provided valuable leads and evidence in an impressive 65% of the cases. He further said,

> Frequently when someone is shot, raped, beaten or otherwise attacked, he or she performs a defensive maneuver. They throw up a guard against fright, anxiety, and other traumas. Acting on survival instinct, they hide the hurt. Through hypnosis, we make the conscious mind passive and communicate with the subconscious to release what's buried there. (Stump, 1975, p. 34)

In sum, many proponents of hypnosis have used successful memory recoveries to support a version of a memory-permanence hypothesis. These views, along with widely publicized examples in which hypnosis was apparently successful, have been passed on to laypersons through the popular press.

Spontaneous and Prompted Recoveries.

The phenomenon of spontaneous recovery, namely, the fact that some items that seem to have been forgotten can and do reappear spontaneously, is well documented (Crowder, 1976). A spontaneous recovery can be a striking phenomenon that would be desirable to study in the laboratory. However, because that would be very difficult to do—the experimenter might be forced to wait all week for a spontaneous recovery to emerge—psychologists have tended to do experiments in which particular cues are provided in an attempt to recover certain memories. For example, Tulving and Pearlstone (1966) discovered that in a categorized free-recall situation, providing category cues elicited words that had not been recalled in the absence of the cues. Thus, prior to being given the cues, the subjects must have had stored in memory words that were available but not accessible. This experiment, together with others that followed it (e.g., Tulving & Thomson, 1971, 1973), indicates that retrieval cues are instrumental in eliciting a desired item from memory.

A different body of evidence suggests that initially unreported elements of a stimulus tend to emerge in subsequent dreams, daydreams, doodles, free associations, and other fantasy activities. Furthermore, recollections following certain fantasy activities yield a similar recovery of initially unreported stimulus elements (Erdelyi, 1970). Such recoveries, whether spontaneous or prompted, are offered as evidence for the notion that memories are stored permanently.

Psychoanalysis.

Psychotherapists use various techniques to help their patients bring their anxieties and conflicts into the open in order to determine where they came from and how to deal with them. Psychoanalysis is a type of psychotherapy that concentrates on dreams, fantasies, and other material from the unconscious that patients reveal through free association. This sort of treatment has apparently enjoyed some success in treating repression of traumatic events. Repression is characterized by a curious forgetfulness. The amnesia that results from repression is curious because "the affect surrounding the idea remains in consciousness and because the repressed idea has an uncanny way of returning—albeit in disguised form" (Vaillant, 1977, p. 128).

The purpose of psychoanalysis is to help the patients dig under the layer of repression, develop new insights into their behavior, and find more flexible ways to cope with their anxiety. It is premised on the idea that some emotional experiences in childhood are so traumatic that to allow them to enter into consciousness many years after they occurred would cause one to be totally overwhelmed by anxiety. It is thought that such traumatic experiences are stored in the unconscious, or repressed, but that with proper therapeutic techniques they can be unleashed. Repression is thus conceptualized in terms of a retrieval failure, with access to the critical memories being temporarily blocked.

The primary evidence for repression comes from clinical patients, and numerous reports exist in the literature. Often recoveries from amnesias of unbearable memories occur through the use of therapy, hypnosis, or drugs (see Erdelyi & Goldberg, 1979). Patients have, through interventions of this sort, recovered memories of such experiences as being accidently buried alive or surviving an airplane crash, about which they had been hitherto amnesic. The vividness with which these memories are reported can indeed be impressive.

Evaluation of the Evidence

These phenomena seem to offer impressive support for the belief that information is permanently stored. However, careful evaluation of the evidence in each case raises substantial doubts. As we shall see, reports of "memories" that occur either spontaneously or as a result of memory probes, such as electrical stimulation, hypnosis, or psychotherapy, may not involve memories of actual past events at all. Rather, there is good reason to believe that such reports may result from reconstruction of fragments of past experience or from constructions created at the time of report that bear little or no resemblance to past experience. Furthermore, secondary sources and popular accounts tend to distort the evidence so as to lend more credence to the notion of memory permanence than is really warranted.

Brain Stimulation.

As noted, the work of Penfield captured the imagination of psychologists and has provided perhaps the most widely cited support for the connection that memories are permanent. But let us look more closely at what Penfield actually found. Penfield began with 1,132 patients, and by his own admission, the patient responses that might have indicated a memory recovery occurred in only 40 cases out of the total of 1,132 cases surveyed, or only 3.5% of the time (Penfield, 1969, p. 154). (In an earlier publication, however, Penfield and Perot, 1963, noted that electrical stimulation produced what they labeled "experiential responses" only when the electrodes were applied to the cortex of the temporal lobe. This region was explored in 520 of the patients; thus the 40 patients exhibiting experiential responses constituted 7.7% of this group.) But in any event, production of these responses by the stimulating electrode was relatively rare to begin with.

In their 1963 article in *Brain*, Penfield and Perot reviewed all 40 cases in which stimulation of the cortex of conscious patients produced experiential responses. Of the 40 patients, 24 claimed to have had an auditory experiential response; that is, they heard a voice, voices, music, or a meaningful sound. For example, upon stimulation, one patient (Case 9) said in a subdued voice, "Oh, a kind of sound in the distance like people singing." When asked what they were singing, she replied, "I don't know. It was like a bunch of old folks in the background, probably some hymns." Nineteen patients claimed to have a visual experiential response, seeing a person or a group of people, a scene, or a recognizable object. For example, one patient (Case 19) claimed to have seen a familiar man grabbing a stick. Twelve patients reported combined visual and auditory experiential responses; that is, they experienced scenes with appropriate sounds. Penfield and Perot (1963) seemed to be most impressed with the 22 responses observed in these 12 people, for they argued that many of these responses "consisted of an experience which the patient could easily recognize and identify as having been part of a previous experience" (p. 672). Finally, five patients made responses that were described vaguely; for example, patients referred to having had "a thought," "a memory," "a flash-back," or they may have said "that reminded me of something."

When we eliminate the patients who heard only music or voices and those whose responses were too vague to classify, we find that less than 3% of the patients contributed the lifelike experiential responses for which Penfield's work is so famous. And a detailed examination of even these patient protocols leaves one with the distinct feeling that they are reconstructions or inferences rather than actual memories. For example, one patient

(Case 1) said upon stimulation that she suddenly saw herself as she had appeared in childbirth, and that she felt as if she were reliving the experience. Another (Case 36) said, "I think I heard a mother calling her little boy somewhere. It seemed to be something that happened years ago." She said it was "somebody in the neighborhood where I live." When the same spot was stimulated 18 minutes later, she said, "Yes, I hear the same familiar sounds, it seems to be a woman calling. The same lady. That was not in the neighborhood. It seemed to be at the lumberyard." She added that she had never in her life been around a lumberyard. When a patient under stimulation sees herself from the sidelines engaged in a particular act, or experiences people in locations in which she has never been, there is clear indication that the individual is not "reliving" the experience but rather constructing it. A similar interpretation of brain-stimulation work has been offered by Neisser (1967):

> In short, the content of these experiences is not surprising in any way. It seems entirely comparable to the content of dreams, which are generally admitted to be synthetic constructions and not literal recalls. Penfield's work tells us nothing new about memory. (p. 169)

In sum, Penfield would have us believe that stimulation of the brain "causes previous experience to return to the mind of a conscious patient" and that "there is within the adult brain a remarkable record of the stream of each individual's awareness or consciousness" (Penfield & Perot, 1963, p. 692). But these conclusions (and the videorecorder model), based as they are on the dubious protocols of a handful of patients, seem unwarranted. A reconstruction or construction hypothesis seems much more viable. A hint as to what is likely to go into such reconstructions was provided by Mahl, Rothenberg, Delgado, and Hamlin (1964) in their examination of a 27-year-old housewife who underwent brain stimulation; they concluded that a strong determinant of the content of these "memories" is "the patient's 'mental content' at the time of stimulation" (p. 358). These so-called memories, then, appear to consist merely of the thoughts and ideas that happened to exist just prior to and during the stimulation.

Hypnosis.

Despite apparent successes in using hypnosis to recover memories, the technique is subject to a variety of criticisms. First, when it does work to revive a temporarily inaccessible memory, hypnosis does not necessarily involve the awesome, mysterious power that many apparently attribute to it. Rather, it may simply be that hypnosis encourages people to relax more, to cooperate more, or to concentrate more than they otherwise would. Put another way, the argument is that hypnosis is best understood in terms of the interpersonal relationship existing between hypnotist and subject. A good relationship results in the subject's behaving in a way that is pleasing to the hypnotist, that is, in a way in which the subject perceives a good hypnotic subject should behave (Hilgard, 1977; Evans & Kihlstrom, Note 1). The net result may well be simply a *criterion shift* rather than improved access to stored information. That is, rather than being more able, the subject may simply be more willing to report information in the hypnosis setting than under ordinary circumstances.

In support of this criterion-shift hypothesis is the fact that although hypnotized subjects who are asked to recall or relive former experiences often produce a wealth of recollections, much of this material is fabricated. There exists no evidence to support the view that recall during a state of hypnosis is any more accurate or complete than recall under ordinary waking conditions (Barber, 1965; Neisser, 1967). Even more dramatic, several experiments have shown that subjects under hypnosis will confidently recall events not only from the past but from the future as well (Kline, 1958; Rubenstein & Newman, 1954). In response to this somewhat muddied state of affairs, many researchers have voiced strong objections to the use of hypnosis in the legal arena. An article in the *American Bar Association Journal* recently argued:

> People can flat-out lie under hypnosis, and the examiner is no better equipped to detect the hypnotic lie than any other kind. Even more serious, a willing hypnotic subject is more pliable than he normally would be, more anxious to please his questioner. Knowing even a few details of an event, often supplied in early contacts with police, may provide the subject with enough basis to create a highly detailed "memory" of what transpired, whether he was there or not. ("Hypnotized Man Remembers Too Much," 1978, p. 187)

Spontaneous and Prompted Recoveries.

The recovery of items that appear to have been forgotten certainly does happen, but this does not, of course, constitute evidence that all or even many memories are recoverable. If we traveled to Holland and saw one yellow tulip, that obviously would not provide evidence that all tulips are yellow. Even after seeing an acre of yellow tulips, we would not be surprised to walk a mile down the road and find a field of tulips that were red. Similarly, in the case of memory, the existence of examples of successful recoveries should not imply that all memories are potentially recoverable.

Thus the vast evidence that fantasy activities can result in the emergence of initially unreported elements of a stimulus does not imply that all memories are potentially recoverable. In fact, from a thoughtful application of signal-detection analysis, Erdelyi (1970) concluded that fantasy activities did nothing to intensify the memory for the stimulus but, rather, affected the response rates: "While fantasy generation increases the extent to which information is outputted from memory storage, the input traces in memory storage do not themselves become intensified" (p. 111). Fantasy activities apparently induce people to adopt a less stringent criterion for reporting, so that low-confidence memory items are recalled when otherwise they might not have been reported.

Psychoanalysis.

Our remarks on the subject of memory recovery also apply to psychoanalysis. In fact, Erdelyi's (1970) conclusions were based largely on work involving free-association techniques, one of the principal methods used in psychoanalysis.

In terms of the recovery of repressed memories, even some of those who believe in the concept of repression have argued that it is possible that subjects purportedly recovering lost memories are in fact generating not memories of true events but fanciful guesses, fantasies, or plain confabulations (Erdelyi & Goldberg, 1979). The major methodological problem is that for the most part, independent verification of the accuracy of the "memory" produced by the subject can never be obtained. In reviewing the available evidence, Neisser (1967) has flatly stated that these recoveries are "not a fully accurate copy of earlier experience" (p. 169).

SOME RETRIEVAL FAILURES

Our emphasis thus far has been on the use of different techniques designed to produce recovery of memories that have at one time or another been temporarily unavailable. What we have tried to illustrate is that the results of these techniques must be viewed with a highly jaundiced eye. They do not, contrary to popular belief, provide support for anything like a videorecorder memory.

On the other side of the coin, we cannot deny that successful recoveries can and do occur. Our argument is with the contention that all memories are potentially recoverable. In this section, we shall offer some speculations about the circumstances under which a particular memory trace may be altered or obliterated.

Memory Distortion in the Laboratory

One of us (EL) has, over the past several years, been investigating circumstances under which reports of real-world, complex events can undergo systematic and predictable distortions (Loftus, 1975, 1977, 1979a, 1979b; Loftus & Palmer, 1974). To get an idea of the flavor of this research, consider the following experiment reported by Loftus, Miller, and Burns (1978). The subjects viewed a series of 30 color slides depicting successive stages in an auto-pedes-

trian accident. The auto was a red Datsun seen traveling along a side street toward an intersection with a stop sign for half of the subjects, and toward an intersection with a yield sign for the remaining subjects. The remaining slides show the Datsun turning right and knocking down a pedestrian who is crossing at the crosswalk. Immediately after viewing the slides, the subjects answered a series of 20 questions. For half of the subjects, Question 17 was "Did another car pass the red Datsun while it was stopped at the stop sign?" The remaining subjects were asked the same question with the words "stop sign" replaced by "yield sign." The assignment of subjects to conditions produced a factorial design in which half of the subjects received consistent or correct information, whereas the other half received misleading or incorrect information. After a short filler activity, a two-forced-choice recognition test was administered. Two slide projectors were used to present 15 pairs of slides, each pair being presented for about 8 seconds. For each pair of slides, the subjects were asked to select the slide they had seen earlier. The critical pair consisted of a slide depicting a red Datsun at a stop sign and another slide, nearly identical, except that it depicted the Datsun at a yield sign. The results showed that when the intervening question contained misleading information, recognition performance was hindered. In one condition, for example, over 80% of the subjects who received misleading information responded incorrectly on the forced-choice recognition test. They indicated that they had seen the slide that corresponded to what they had been told rather than the slide that they had actually seen.

A major thrust of this and related research has been a practical one: It provides a warning, for example, that eyewitness accounts occurring in such situations as courtroom trials and insurance investigations can be highly suspect. Of interest in the present essay, however, is the relation between the eyewitness report and the memorial information that underlies it. Three hypotheses seem viable. The first, relatively uninteresting, might be termed a "supplementation of nothing" hypothesis. According to this hypothesis, many subjects simply fail to store information about the critical object (say the stop sign) at the time of original viewing. The postperceptual (misleading) information (corresponding to the yield sign in this example) is then added to the memory representation of the event and thereby forms the basis for the subsequent report.

A variety of data allow us to reject this possibility. First, when given no misleading information, and when tested immediately after the incident, over 90% of the subjects correctly identified the sign they had seen. The result suggests that the information did register itself in long-term memory. Second, one group of subjects viewed the incident and then filled in a diagram with all the details they could remember; more than half of them drew in the correct sign. This finding suggests that at least half of the subjects encoded the sign to the point of including it in their diagram. In fact, it underestimates the actual number who encoded the sign, since others may have encoded it but not bothered to draw it in their diagram (Loftus, Miller, & Burns, 1978). Taken together, these results indicate that at least some of those subjects whose recollection changed as a result of misleading information actually did store the critical information in the first place.

The other two hypotheses about the relation between the eyewitness report and the underlying memorial information bear directly on the permanence issue. A coexistence (permanence) hypothesis would hold that the postperceptual information is added to the memory representation, where it coexists with the original information. The test report then rests on a choice between these two competing alternatives. A substitution hypothesis, on the other hand, would claim that the postperceptual information replaces the original information and that in the process, the original information is forever banished from the subject's memory.

Evidence for Substitution

Can we distinguish between these two hypotheses? As noted earlier, it is not possible to

unequivocally reject the coexistence hypothesis, since failing to find a member of a supposedly coexisting pair does not logically imply that the elusive member does not exist. We can, however, provide circumstantial evidence against the coexistence hypothesis by devising experiments that attempt, in as rigorous a way as possible, to uncover the original information. If such attempts fail, then we can conclude that the information may have vanished—and that for all practical purposes, it has vanished. What follows is a brief description of some rigorous attempts to recover the original information. None of them succeeded in finding it once it had been tampered with.

Testing Method.
As we have said, it is not at all difficult to take someone who has seen one object, say a stop sign, and cause him or her to recollect actually seeing another object, in this case a yield sign. The method of probing for a recollection seems to matter very little. We can ask, "Did you see a yield sign?" and obtain the response "yes." We can ask, "What type of traffic sign did you see?" and obtain the response "a yield sign." We can ask, "Was it a stop sign or a yield sign?" and obtain the answer "yield." And, what is most impressive, we can present, side by side, pictures of the two signs and find that the yield sign is the choice. This last recognition test is particularly compelling, for the subject rejects the stimulus that is identical to the one actually seen. If recognition were assumed to be a relatively passive process of matching stimuli to specific locations in a content-addressable storage system, one would expect that a representation of the actual and true scene would result in a match and that an alteration would fail to match. This does not occur.

Also relevant is the finding that warning people just prior to a test that some misinformation may have been presented earlier does not enable them to reject that misinformation in favor of their original memory. Put another way, once the misinformation has been incorporated into memory, a later warning is unable to help in the recovery of what was initially seen (Loftus, 1979a).

Demand Characteristics.

It is natural to ask whether these results are due to demand characteristics. Perhaps observant subjects discern the experimental hypothesis. Obliging subjects may then try to confirm that hypothesis. In the context of the stop sign/yield sign study, it is possible that some or all of the subjects not only remembered which traffic sign they had observed but also remembered what they had been "told" and then went along with what they believed to be the experimental hypothesis, choosing the sign that they had heard about rather than the one they had actually seen. Loftus, Miller, & Burns (1978, Experiment 2) devised a way to test this notion. Subjects who had participated in the sign-altering experiment were told, just before leaving the experiment, the exact purpose of the experiment. They were told that they had seen either a stop sign or a yield sign and that their questionnaire had presupposed the existence of one sign or the other. Their task was to guess which condition they had been in. In other words, this final debriefing activity gave the subjects the opportunity to be completely insightful about their condition in the experiment. Of those who had been given misleading sign information and had been fooled by it, nearly 90% still insisted they had seen the sign that corresponded to what they had been told.

Incentives.

It could be argued that the reason so many people go along with misleading information is that they are not highly motivated to be accurate. If high incentive were provided for accurate responding, perhaps people would show evidence that their memories were accurate. For example, if subjects were offered $1, or $5, or even $25 for correct responding, would their choice still be for the yield sign that they had read about over the stop sign that they had actually seen? Loftus (1979a) found the answer to be yes. When no reward was offered, 75% of the subjects chose the incorrect sign; with a $1 reward, 80%, with a $5 reward, 70%, and with a $25 reward, 85% of the subjects rejected the true sign in favor of the incorrect alternative. In sum, subjects actually performed slightly less accurately when an incentive was provided.

Second Guesses.

A second-guess technique is particularly well suited for investigating whether original information and new information coexist in memory or whether original information is altered by what occurs subsequently. The logic of this technique is as follows: At the time subjects are asked for their recollections of an event, they first guess among fixed alternatives, and if they guess incorrectly, they choose among the remaining uncommitted alternatives; if they choose correctly on the second guess at a level higher than chance, then they must have had some information available about the correct response, in spite of the error on the first guess. A variation of this technique has been used successfully in the study of psychophysical thresholds (Swets, Tanner, & Birdsall, 1961), tachistoscopic recognition (Bricker & Chapanis, 1953), and paired-associate learning (Bregman, 1966).

Loftus (1979a) performed a second-guess experiment using memory for colors. In one study, the subjects viewed a series of slides depicting a complex incident involving several people. Some subjects saw one slide that showed a man sitting down and reading a book with a green cover. Subsequently, these individuals were exposed to information indicating that the cover was a different color, say yellow. Later all the subjects were tested on their memory for the details of the slides; they picked colors that best represented their recollection of critical objects. For each object, they were also asked to indicate their second choice, assuming that the first choice was incorrect. In brief, the results showed that the subjects did not choose correctly on the second guess at a level higher than chance.

The same result was obtained in an experiment using memory for objects. The subjects looked at the stop/yield sequence, viewing either a stop sign or a yield sign. They returned to the laboratory after one week, at which time a questionnaire subtly told them that they had seen either a stop sign, a yield sign, or a no-parking sign. After a filler activity, they were tested. The critical test item asked them to indicate their recollection of the type of sign they had seen on the corner by choosing among fixed alternatives. They also indicated their second choice. Here, too, we found that when subjects were initially wrong, and 90% of them were, their second guesses showed basically chance performance. In short, the pattern of responses in these experiments suggests that the subjects had completely lost the original information about the correct alternative.

Hypnosis.

Despite the fact that hypnosis can result in the "recollection" of facts that never occurred, there are those who are still impressed with its power to reveal original memory traces. To determine whether this technique could enable an individual whose memory had been altered to "return to the truth," Putnam (1979) conducted a study in which the subjects were first shown a videotape of an accident involving a car and a bicycle. After some delay, the subjects received a questionnaire that asked some objective questions and some that contained misleading information. Some of the subjects were questioned under hypnosis whereas others were not. The hypnotized subjects were told that "under hypnosis it would be possible for them to see the entire accident again just as clearly as they had seen it the first time, only this time they would be able to slow it down or zoom in on details if they chose to" (p. 442). Putnam found more errors were made by the subjects in the hypnosis condition, particularly on the leading questions. He interpreted these results to indicate that hypnosis does not reduce retrieval difficulties and allow subjects to retrieve a veridical memorial representation. Quite the contrary, subjects appear to be "more suggestible in the hypnotic state and are, therefore, more easily influenced by the leading questions" (p. 444). Suggesting the existence of a license plate, when in fact none had been visible at all, not only induced hypnotic subjects to say they had seen it but prompted them to offer partial descriptions of the license number. One subject said it was a California plate which began with W or V, and this obviously constructed information was not obtained under any duress. Suggesting that the major character's hair was blond, when actually it was

black, caused hypnotized subjects to "remember" blond hair. Showing these subjects the videotape again caused some consternation. One subject said, "It's really strange because I still have the blond girl's face in my mind and it doesn't correspond to her (pointing to the woman on the videotape) . . . it was really weird" (p. 444).

Implications

The net result of these studies is a strong suspicion that substitution has occurred—that the misleading information has irrevocably replaced the original information in the subject's brain. The suggestion is that some aspects of the original representation of a complex event are fragile indeed. When the memory of an event is called to consciousness, there appears to be a potential for substitution to occur. It is reasonable to suppose that memory is not necessarily permanent.

What then of the coexistence possibility? Implicit in our remarks has been the notion that substitution and coexistence are not mutually exclusive mechanisms of the mind. Classical interference-theory experiments have certainly indicated that A–B and A–C responses can be simultaneously maintained in memory (cf. Crowder, 1976). And instances of coexistence are abundant in everyday life; few have lost the information that Jacqueline Onassis was once Jacqueline Kennedy.

Assuming then that both substitution and coexistence are possible, a major question then confronts the memory theorist: Under what circumstances does one process rather than the other occur? As a start toward answering this question, we suggest that the mechanism responsible for updating memory both seeks efficiency and takes account of real-world constraints. In a situation that permits logical (real-world) coexistence, memorial coexistence is likewise allowed. Thus, the Stimulus A may be attached to both B and C, and similarly, to illustrate, allowance is made for the fact that the former First Lady may undergo a name change in accord with her marital status. Often, however, real-world coexistence is logically forbidden. The automobile that was involved in the accident that we recently experienced stopped either at a stop sign or at a yield sign, but it did not stop at both. The shirt worn by the thief was not simultaneously green and blue. In such instances, the most economical procedure may be to dismiss one memory in favor of the other, much as a computer programmer will irrevocably destroy an old program instruction when a new one is created.

The implication of the notion of nonpermanent memory is that it should give pause to all who rely on obtaining a "truthful" version of an event from someone who experienced that event in the past. Clinical psychologists, counselors, and psychiatrists who use the anamnestic interview to gain information about the prior events in someone's life typically do so to be able to make intelligent decisions about what kind of help should be given. Anthropologists, sociologists, and some experimental psychologists query people about their past in the course of studying some particular problem of interest to social science. It is important to realize that the statements made during such interviews may not be particularly accurate as reports of prior events. The contents of an interview may not reflect a person's earlier experiences and attitudes so much as his or her current picture of the past. It may not be possible, in some instances, to ever discover from interviewing someone what actually happened in that person's past. Not only might the originally acquired memory have departed from reality in some systematic way, but the memory may have been continually subject to change after it was initially stored.

REFERENCE NOTE

1. Evans, F. J. & Kihlstrom, J. F. *Contextual and temporal disorganization during posthypnotic amnesia.* Paper presented at the meeting of the American Psychological Association, Chicago, September 1975.

REFERENCES

Barber, T. K. The effect of "hypnosis" on learning and recall: A methodological critique. *Journal of Clinical Psychology*, 1965, *21*, 19–25.

Blakemore, C. The unsolved marvel of memory. *The New York Times Magazine*, Feb. 6, 1977. (Reprinted in *Readings in Psychology, 78/79.* Guilford, Conn.: Annual Editions, Dushkin Publishing Group, 1978.)

Block, E. B. *Hypnosis: A new tool in crime detection.* New York: McKay, 1976.

Bregman, A. S. Is recognition memory all or none? *Journal of Verbal Learning and Verbal Behavior*, 1966, *5*, 1–6.

Bricker, P. D., & Chapanis, A. Do incorrectly perceived tachistoscopic stimuli convey some information? *Psychological Review*, 1953, *60*, 181–188.

Cheek, D. B., & LeCron, L. M. *Clinical hypnotherapy.* New York: Grune & Stratton, 1968.

Crowder, R. F. *Principles of learning and memory.* Hillsdale, N.J.: Erlbaum, 1976.

Erdelyi, M. H. Recovery of unavailable perceptual input. *Cognitive Psychology*, 1970, *1*, 99–113.

Erdelyi, M. H., & Goldberg, B. Let's now sweep repression under the rug: Towards a cognitive psychology of repression. In J. Kihlstrom & F. Evans (Eds.), *Functional disorders of memory.* Hillsdale, N.J.: Erlbaum, 1979.

Hilgard, E. R. *Divided consciousness: Multiple controls in human thought and action.* New York: Wiley, 1977.

Hypnotized man remembers too much, *American Bar Association Journal*, February 1978, *64*, 187.

Kendler, H. H. *Basic psychology* (2nd ed.). New York: Appleton-Century-Crofts, 1968.

Kline, M. V. The dynamics of hypnotically induced anti-social behavior. *Journal of Psychology*, 1958, *45*, 239–245.

Loftus, E. F. Leading questions and the eyewitness report. *Cognitive Psychology*, 1975, *7*, 560–572.

Loftus, E. F. Shifting human color memory. *Memory & Cognition*, 1977, *5*, 696–699.

Loftus, E. F. *Eyewitness testimony.* Cambridge, Mass.: Harvard University Press, 1979. (a)

Loftus, E. F. Reactions to blatantly contradictory information. *Memory & Cognition*, 1979, *7*, 368–374. (b)

Loftus, E. F., Miller, D. G., & Burns, H. J. Semantic integration of verbal information into a visual memory. *Journal of Experimental Psychology: Human Learning and Memory*, 1978, *4*, 19–31.

Loftus, E. F., & Palmer, J. C. Reconstruction of automobile destruction: An example of the interaction between language and memory. *Journal of Verbal Learning and Verbal Behavior*, 1974, *13*, 585–589.

Mahl, G. F., Rothenberg, A., Delgado, J. M. R., & Hamlin, H. Psychological responses in the human to intracerebral electrical stimulation. *Psychosomatic Medicine*, 1964, *26*, 337–368.

Neisser, U. *Cognitive psychology.* New York: Appleton-Century-Crofts, 1967.

Penfield, W. Consciousness, memory, and man's conditioned reflexes. In K. Pribram (Ed.), *On the biology of learning.* New York: Harcourt, Brace & World, 1969.

Penfield, W., & Perot, P. The brain's record of auditory and visual experience. *Brain,* 1963, *86,* 595–696.

Penfield, W., & Roberts, L. *Speech and brain mechanisms.* Princeton: Princeton University Press, 1959.

Putnam, B. Hypnosis and distortions in eyewitness memory. *International Journal of Clinical and Experimental Hypnosis,* 1979, *27,* 437–448.

Rubenstein, R., & Newman, R. The living out of "future" experiences under hypnosis. *Science,* 1954, *119,* 472–473.

Shiffrin, R. M., & Atkinson, R. C. Storage and retrieval processes in long-term memory. *Psychological Review,* 1969, *76,* 179–193.

Stump, A. That's him—the guy who hit me! *TV Guide,* October 4–10, 1975, pp. 32–35.

Swets, J. A., Tanner, W. P., & Birdsall, T. G. Decision processes in perception. *Psychological Review,* 1961, *68,* 301–340.

Tetens, J. N. *Philosophische Versuche über die menschliche Natur und ihre Entwicklung* [Philosophical essays on human nature and its development]. Leipzig: Weidnanns Erben und Reich, 1777.

Tulving, E. Cue-dependent forgetting. *American Scientist,* 1974, *62,* 74–82.

Tulving, E., & Pearlstone, Z. Availability versus accessibility of information in memory for words. *Journal of Verbal Learning and Verbal Behavior,* 1966, *5,* 381–391.

Tulving, E., & Thomson, D. M. Retrieval processes in recognition memory: Effect of associative context. *Journal of Experimental Psychology,* 1971, *87,* 116–124.

Tulving, E., & Thomson, D. M. Encoding specificity and retrieval processes in episodic memory, *Psychological Review,* 1973, *80,* 353–373.

Vaillant, G. E. *Adaptation to life.* Boston: Little, Brown, 1977.

Zimbardo, P. G., & Ruch, F. L. *Psychology and life* (9th ed.). Glenview, Ill.: Scott, Foresman, 1975.

This article was written while E. Loftus was a fellow at the Center for Advanced Study in the Behavioral Sciences, Stanford, California, and G. Loftus was a visiting scholar in the Department of Psychology at Stanford University. James Fries generously picked apart an earlier version of this article. Paul Baltes translated the writings of Johann Nicolas Tetens (1777).

The following financial sources are gratefully acknowledged: (a) National Science Foundation (NSF) Grant BNS 76–2337 to G. Loftus; (b) NSF Grant BNS 77–26856 to E. Loftus; and (c) NSF Grant BNS 76–22943 and an Andrew Mellon Foundation grant to the Center for Advanced Study in the Behavioral Sciences.

PART ◆ THREE

THOUGHT: CATEGORIZATION, EXPERTISE, AND METAKNOWLEDGE

Susan A. Gelman

❖

Mary Kister Kaiser, John Jonides,
and Joanne Alexander

❖

Richard P. Honeck, Michael Firment,
and Tammy J. S. Case

❖

Richard E. Mayer

❖

John H. Flavell

❖

Daniel M. Wegner and David J. Schneider

Thought: Categorization, Expertise, and Metaknowledge

The topic of higher-order thinking skills—solving problems, reasoning, making decisions, categorizing, and so on—is an important one for the cognitive psychologist. For some cognitivists, it is *the* topic, since, unlike perception or motor skills or even emotion, it seems less relatable to physiology on the one hand and isolable from social processes on the other. The articles in this section fall into two natural divisions of thinking: how people construe things that originate "outside the skin," or in the environment, and how people construe things that originate "inside the skin" and, in particular, in their own minds. The first division leads to questions about how knowledge is represented and used, whether or not knowledge can be taught so that it can be used in new situations, how people with different degrees of expertise differ, etc. The second division fosters questions about metaknowledge, or how people think about their own and others' minds, and about whether or not these thoughts show patterns like those for externally derived knowledge.

How people think has become a hot topic in American education. Educators from grade school to college have sought to incorporate the teaching of critical thinking and reasoning skills into their curriculums. However, there is little agreement about how and when it should be done, and the issue of whether general thinking skills can be taught or whether such skills are task-specific remains controversial. Can thinking skills be taught in a critical thinking course without regard to subject matter, or do these skills have to be taught on a subject-by-subject basis?

This debate has been further fueled by recent developments in artificial intelligence (AI). Researchers in AI have attempted to develop systems that can mimic the complex abilities of experts in many technical fields, such as diagnostic medicine and physics. As a result, it has become increasingly clear that experts in a given field have both extensive domain-specific knowledge as well as an abstract hierarchical rule system that allows them to recognize, organize, and act on new information with great speed and accuracy.

Of course, this thinking-as-content-specific versus thinking-as-content-free issue has not escaped the attention of psychologists. In the early twentieth century, psychologists such as Edward Lee Thorndike (1874–1949) began to look for evidence that people's thinking skills involved the use of a formal rule system, as the Greek philosopher Plato suggested over 2,000 years ago. However, Thorndike's work did not substantiate the claim that training in a formal discipline (e.g., Latin or Greek) would transfer to other tasks. Instead, transfer of training effects appeared to be dependent upon concrete task attributes rather than on abstract rules, a result that is consistent with the content-specific view.

But in recent years, psychologists doing research in categorization, expertise, and reasoning have garnered support for the idea that some abstract, content-free knowledge is transferrable; that is, certain abilities transfer to certain situations but not to others. So, not surprisingly, the answer to the question we posed earlier, about whether or not thinking skills can be taught on their own without regard to subject matter, is not yes or no but sometimes yes and sometimes no. The articles in this section present both perspectives.

IN THE FIRST ARTICLE, "CHILDREN'S EXPECTATIONS Concerning Natural Kind Categories," Susan A. Gelman challenges the view that children's categories are restricted to a simple perceptual level. Gelman reports a series of studies that showed that 4-year-old children were more likely to make inferences based on category membership than on perceptual similarity. These results were obtained utilizing an innovative methodology that probed children's knowledge of categories rather than their ability to construct categories. In one study, children were shown three pictures at a time, a flamingo, a blackbird, and a bat, for example, and the experimenter labeled the objects for the children and told them a new fact about two of the pictures (the flamingo and the bat). The experimenter then questioned the children about the blackbird, which was visually similar to the bat: "Does this bird give its baby mashed-up food, like this bird, or milk, like this bat?" It was found that 68 percent of the time children assumed that objects with the same name shared underlying similarities even

when perceptually dissimilar. Contrary to some other researchers' findings, Gelman concluded that children can form mature concepts.

AN INTERESTING COUNTERPOINT TO GELMAN'S findings is the second article in this section, which indicates that even certain concepts held by some adults may not be mature (conceptually based). Mary Kister Kaiser, John Jonides, and Joanne Alexander, in "Intuitive Reasoning About Abstract and Familiar Physics Problems," examine people's reasoning about curvilinear motion in both familiar and abstract domains. They suggest that people solve problems in familiar domains by drawing on specific experiences in those domains rather than by reasoning via underlying physical laws. Evidence for this was obtained in two experiments. In the first experiment, Kaiser et al. asked subjects to indicate the path that a ball would take when exiting a spiral tube that was elevated at one end (the abstract problem). Subjects were also asked to indicate the path that a stream of water would take if a hose were connected to the tube (the familiar problem). Half the subjects received the ball problem first and half received the water problem first. Kaiser et al. found that subjects produced far more correct predictions for the water problem than the ball problem, regardless of the order in which they attempted to solve the problems. Moreover, successfully completing the water problem first did not enhance performance on the ball problem. A second experiment introduced another familiar problem—a bullet exiting a curved rifle barrel—in order to more fully explore the effects of solution transfer to the abstract problem. Again, subjects gave more accurate predictions for solving the familiar problems, and there was no transfer from the familiar to the abstract. This supports Kaiser et al.'s conclusion that the familiar problems were so realistic that subjects could solve them by drawing on concrete experiences rather than on reasoning skills.

A DIFFERENT VIEW OF EXPERTISE, ONE THAT EMPHA-sizes the role of abstract interpretation, is presented in "Expertise and Categorization," by Richard P. Honeck, Michael Firment, and

Tammy J. S. Case. The article begins with the premise that expertise is due in part to skill in categorization, and Honeck et al. delineate several aspects of this skill thusly: As compared to nonexperts, experts develop categories that are more abstract, more sensitive to deep aspects of a problem, more informationally dense, more coherent, and more finely graded. Honeck et al. then present the basics of three current views of categorization—the exemplar, probabilistic, and classical views—as well as their own conceptual base view. In comparing the ability of the three current views to handle the categorization phenomena with their own view's ability, the authors find that their own view does better, largely because it makes interpretation the driving force behind the categorization process. The other views place more emphasis on the stimulus; they consider categorization to be more "data-driven" than do Honeck et al., who emphasize that experts extract the significance of inputs by relating them to well-learned mental representations that are abstract and schema-like.

IF THE ABILITY TO REASON AND CATEGORIZE EFFECtively is dependent on domain, experience, and clues of various kinds, then there may still be only a limited set of problem-solving processes, and *these* are abstract, general, and domain free. This certainly seems to be the assumption in the standard information-processing model of problem solving. Briefly, this model holds that problems are represented, mental operations are performed on the representation, and problem solution occurs. These steps all seem to occur in a serial, mechanical way in the model. However, Richard E. Mayer, in "Human Nonadversary Problem Solving," presents evidence that challenges this model. In the course of problem solving, according to Mayer, people may distort problems, attend to irrelevant aspects of the problems, change representations, are often rigid, are sometimes creative, and are affected by their beliefs. Mayer finds that these phenomena violate the atomistic, mechanical, discrete aspects of the information-processing model.

IF MAYER IS CORRECT, MIGHT THESE ABSTRACT AND idealized aspects of the standard problem-

solving model be too abstract and too idealized? Is a more modest model called for, one that reflects the range of behaviors in reasoning and problem-solving situations?

Moreover, it is one thing to ask young children questions about categories such as birds and to ask adults to make predictions about the paths of balls, bullets, and water, and quite another to ask how people conceive of and reason about mental events. This intriguing question is taken up in the last two articles in this section.

In "Young Children's Understanding of Thinking and Consciousness," John H. Flavell reports some of the results of recent developmental experiments on young children's theories of mind. For example, if what looks like a box of candy turns out to have some crayons in it, a 3-year-old may believe that other people will think that the box contains crayons, whereas a 5-year-old is likely to understand that people will usually assume a candy box contains candy. The 3-year-old seems unable to understand that other people could have what amounts to a false belief. According to Flavell, very young children begin to see others as having goals and intentions and as being responsive to the child, and later, during the preschool years, children come to recognize deception, illusions, and false beliefs. Flavell describes young children's ability to discriminate thinking from seeing, acting, knowing, and the like. However, children have less appreciation of the stream of consciousness, a situation that may change as they begin to experience negative thoughts that persist in memory, including dream memories and thoughts of monsters.

There is an easy progression from the dawning of children's recognition and introspection about their own minds to the final article in this section, "Mental Control: The War of the Ghosts in the Machine," by Daniel M. Wegner and David J. Schneider. The topic of their paper is unwanted thoughts and what people do about them. What do we do in order to not think about an upcoming need for surgery, a frustrating interpersonal situation, a dying relative, or a recurring negative memory from childhood? Wegner and Schneider argue that we control such thoughts in order to demonstrate self-control, to keep the thoughts secret, and to keep mental peace. The mechanism of control is one of *primary suppression*, by which attention is purposely kept away from the negative thought, and *auxiliary concentration*, by which a different thought is focused on. Experimental work on the topic involved having subjects verbalize their thoughts for five minutes, then do it again with the instruction "Try not to think of a white bear" (and ring a bell if they did), and do it one more time while specifically thinking about a white bear. In general, bell ringing tended to decrease during the second period, but compared to control groups, the experimental group showed more bell ringing in the last five-minute period. In other words, once the subjects who had tried to suppress the thought were free to think about the white bear, the thought "rebounded" and the subjects seemed more preoccupied with it. Follow-up studies on this rebound effect showed that *unfocused distraction* strategies, in which subjects thought about a variety of things in order to suppress, tended to guarantee a rebound because a multiplicity of mental cues had become associated with the unwanted thought. *Focused distraction*, in which a single thought was used to suppress, was a more successful strategy. This very interesting article is at the boundaries of cognition and emotion.

13

Susan A. Gelman

Children's Expectations Concerning Natural Kind Categories

Abstract. *Research examining the early emergence of beliefs about natural kinds is described, and implications for theories of category development are considered. The research challenges three assumptions implicit in many studies: that children cannot form mature concepts, that categories do not differ substantially from one another, and that classification tasks are the best measure of children's category knowledge. Categories, it is argued, allow and even encourage children to extend their knowledge beyond the obvious, thus serving as a mechanism of information acquisition.*

A few years ago, a first-grade child said something that captured an important insight about categories. She and I were in the midst of an experiment, and I showed her a picture of two snakes: one was small and brown, the other was a large, gray cobra. She looked at the snakes, then turned to me and said, 'All snakes should be a little bit the same and a little bit different. Inside, they should be the same.' What this child seemed to realize was that things can appear to be different on the surface, yet still share deeper, less obvious similarities. The present paper examines this belief that categories can extend knowledge beyond what is perceptually salient. I will suggest that children expect categories to share underlying similarities that go beyond what is obvious or already known.

Psychologists have long regarded categories as basic to human cognition [Bruner et al, 1956], and a great deal of research has centered on describing their structure and function [Mervis and Rosch, 1981]. Most traditional accounts of categories in psychology focus on their importance in organizing what is obvious and well known. From this perspective, the important, definitional information about 'dogs', for example, includes that they have fur, four legs, and the ability to bark. This traditional view, though accurate, has limited the scope of questions that can be addressed, in two respects. First, researchers often study simple perceptual attributes of category members to the exclusion of other information people might have about a category (e.g., theoretical beliefs or expert knowledge). Second, categories tend to be seen as fixed and unchanging.

In contrast, nonobvious properties can be viewed as crucial to adult classification systems. Quine [1969] points out that many of our categories have a theoretical basis and incorporate more than intuitive similarities. Although often we do form categories based on intuitive similarities (much as a pigeon does when learning to peck at a colored disk), it is also the case that we can readily extend beyond such groupings. We can deliberately overlook salient properties such as color, size, and shape. We form theory-based categories to understand the exceedingly complex nature of the world. Looking beyond the obvious has two important consequences: (a) we are not limited by misleading appearances, so categories can have a more theoretical basis, and (b) we can make inductive inferences, that is, we can generalize from known facts to what is not yet known [Skyrms, 1975].

An example of a category shaped by theoretical beliefs is the legless lizard. Although it resembles a snake, it is classified as a lizard because it has a cluster of features in common with other lizards. Its diet, life expectancy, DNA structure, and so forth, are just like others of the same kind. Similarly, the musky rat kangaroo strongly resembles a mouse, but is actually a marsupial and so is classified as a kind of kangaroo. And tassel-eared squirrels are squirrels, despite their long, rabbit-like ears. The point of these examples is that categories may go beyond intuitive similarity, to capture deeper underlying properties. In fact, many categories—not just these unusual examples—reflect a richly correlated structure, especially categories of things found in nature, or *natural kinds*.

There is a critical developmental issue here. Children start to learn natural kind terms at a very young age, beginning with their first few words. Yet preschool children do not have the scientific knowledge to understand why these categories extend beyond appearances. Moreover, young children are often misled by appearances. On a wide range of cognitive tasks —including memory, quantitative reasoning, and perspective-taking—children have a strong perceptual bias [Flavell, 1985; Mansfield, 1977]. So how do children understand natural kind terms? Do they expect these words to capture underlying similarities? Or is there a developmental shift in how these terms function over time? After reviewing research examining early-emerging beliefs about natural kinds, I will discuss some implications of the work for theories of category development.

CATEGORY IDENTITY VERSUS APPEARANCES

Ellen Markman and I [Gelman and Markman, 1986] conducted a series of studies to explore the question of whether preschoolers believe that members of a category share nonobvious features. This work was conducted with 4-year-old children, as they were the youngest that could be tested on the procedure we developed.

In the task we used, children saw different sets of pictures, one at a time. Within each set, children saw three pictures at a time, for example, a bird (flamingo), a bat, and a bird (blackbird). Two of the pictures were from the same category (e.g., the blackbird and the flamingo); two of the pictures looked alike (the blackbird and the bat). The experimenter first labeled the pictures. Then children heard a new fact about each of two of the pictures, and a question about the third, for example, 'This bird (pointing to the flamingo) gives its baby mashed-up food; this bat gives its baby milk.' (Pointing to the blackbird:) 'Does this bird give its baby mashed-up food, like this bird, or milk, like this bat?'

Another set we used consisted of a dinosaur (brontosaurus), a rhinoceros, and a dinosaur (triceratops). Children learned that the first dinosaur has cold blood, and that the rhinoceros has warm blood. We also used a bar of gold, a lump of clay, and a lump of gold ore that resembled the clay. Children learned that if you put the first piece of gold in a hot oven, it melts, and if you put the clay in a hot oven, it burns. Altogether we included 20 different natural kind categories. We used properties that were true of each category as a whole. All questions were pretested to make sure that children did not already know these facts. The question was whether children would base their inductions on the category label or on the appearances.

Results

In our first study we found that the category label in fact had a powerful effect. Sixty-eight percent of the time, 4-year-olds preferred to draw inferences on the basis of category membership, even though it was pitted against striking perceptual similarity. For example, they claimed that the blackbird gives its young mashed-up food, like the flamingo. We replicated the study with a second group of 4-year-olds, who based their inferences on category membership 73% of the time. Performance in both studies was well above chance. Furthermore, individual children were remarkably consistent. Only 1 child of over 60 relied on appearances for drawing inferences. Over one third relied on category membership (on at least 15 of 20 trials). So, by the age of 4 children assume that objects with the same name share underlying similarities. Clearly, children are sensitive to the power of language for organizing and extending knowledge. This means that much knowledge is passed down implicitly through the system of categories encoded in language.

Children's comments were particularly revealing, as they often appealed to category membership to justify within-category inferences. In the following examples the child's age is given in years and months in parentheses: A swatch of cotton comes from a plant, as does a cotton ball, because, 'They're both

cotton' (4–0); a flower has tubes for water inside, because, 'Every flower has tubes inside, so it does have tubes inside!' (4–2); a large chunk of salt helps make snow melt, as does a heap of fine-grained salt, 'Because it's the same kind as this' (4–9), a triceratops has cold blood, as does a brontosaurus, because, 'Both are dinosaurs so both have to have cold blood' (4–9). Children have not reached the level of sophistication or abstraction found in some adult justifications (e.g., 'Usually animals of the same species have similar characteristics'), yet the category is salient and explicitly mentioned.

We have also conducted several control studies showing that these effects are not due simply to hearing the category label. Preschool children attend to the category even when they hear no labels at all. For example, even when none of the pictures are named, children tend to draw more inferences from a black beetle to a green leaf-insect, than from a leaf to a leaf-insect [Gelman and Markman, 1987]. We also replicated these findings with younger children, using a simpler presentation but the same task [Gelman and Markman, 1987]. The most interesting result was that there were no developmental differences. Categories are a powerful source of information for children, even by age 3.

In sum, the results of these studies suggest that young children certainly realize that categories share more than surface similarities. They assume that basic-level categories capture enduring features that cannot be observed, even among category members that are superficially dissimilar.

IMPLICATIONS FOR THEORIES OF CATEGORY DEVELOPMENT

In the remainder of the paper I discuss the implications of our findings for theories of category development. In particular, I argue that these data challenge three assumptions that are implicit in many studies: that children cannot form mature concepts, that categories do not substantially differ from one another, and that classification (grouping) tasks are the best vehicle for tapping children's knowledge about categories.

Coherence of Young Children's Categories

The first assumption is that children have a fundamental difficulty in forming coherent categories, and that the categories children do learn are perceptually (rather than conceptually) based. It has even been suggested that children fail to have 'true' concepts until age 6 or 7 [Inhelder and Piaget, 1964]. Even when such a strong position is not taken, it is generally agreed that young children focus almost exclusively on outward, perceptual features for classifying [Bruner et al., 1966; Tversky, 1985], and that children do not realize that categories are stable across time [De Vries, 1969].

In contrast, the present work demonstrates that children readily form stable categories that extend beyond superficial perceptual features. Children accept category labels in which category membership and outward appearance do not perfectly coincide. They draw inductive inferences based on category membership even when to do so conflicts with appearance-based judgments, and even when the inferences concern nonobvious properties. In short, children assume that category labels are the key to uncovering deeper similarities among objects. There is even some evidence that this belief is stronger among younger than older children, at least concerning basic-level categories. In a recent study [Gelman and O'Reilly, in press] we asked preschoolers and second graders (age 8) to describe the insides of various objects (e.g., 'Do you think all dogs [or spiders, dolls, vacuums, etc.] have the same kinds of stuff inside? Why? What do they have inside?'). We found that preschoolers were significantly *more* likely than second grades to report that all category members have a particular internal structure (83 vs. 51%). Preschool children typically asserted that all category members have the same internal parts, whereas older children noted individual differences with a category.

These patterns were supported by children's explanations: On over 80% of all trials, children

Table 1

Sample Descriptions of Internal Parts

Preschool	'All flowers have nectar in 'em.' 'Caterpillars have liquidy stuff inside.' 'Because blocks are wood--most blocks are wood. All blocks are wood.' 'They (dolls) all have cotton.' 'Vacuums all have just foam inside 'em.' 'Teddy bears have feathers inside.'
Second grade (age 8)	'There's all different kinds of apples, and I think some are from different kinds of seeds.' 'Some (carrots) are white and some are orange, and that probably changes the minerals.' 'Some spiders are smaller than others. Smaller spiders have to have smaller hearts.' 'All chairs aren't the same. Some of 'em have metal, some of 'em have wood. Some of 'em have iron.' 'Some of them (dolls) have feathers and some of them have cotton.' 'Some ties can be leather, some ties can be soft.'

gave explanations that were consistent with their yes/no response. For example, younger children tended to talk about each category as a whole, whereas older children discussed individual differences (Table 1). Of all subjects, it was the youngest who most strongly assumed that category members are alike inside. This finding is reminiscent of overgeneralization in language development, when children apply a particular linguistic rule even in cases that require exceptions (e.g., -s as plural, yielding 'foots' instead of 'feet'). Young children may have formulated a general principle that members of a category share deep similarities, a principle which is then resistant to counterexamples.

Distinctions Among Categories

A second common assumption is that categories do not differ substantially from one another. If this were true, then the study of one sort of category should readily generalize to all the child's classification schemes and abilities. How children classify geometric shapes should be as revealing as how children classify natural kinds. Yet categories differ tremendously as to whether they tie into richly organized world knowledge. Boxes do not share deep underlying similarities. Green things have just one feature in common: their color. A study that concerns itself with just arbitrary groupings [e.g., blue circles and red squares; see Inhelder and Piaget, 1964] is unlikely to reveal any of the beliefs about category structure delineated above. It is thus important to study categories that are meaningful, and that potentially reflect underlying theories.

There is an empirical basis as well for asserting that not all categories promote inferences equally. In recent work [Gelman, 1984], I hypothesized that category domain should be critical to an eventual understanding of the role that categories play in induction. In particular, natural kind categories should promote more inferences concerning internal parts and substance than artifact categories. For example, we might expect all rabbits to have roughly the same internal parts, but we do not expect all dolls to do so—some are filled with cotton, others with air, others with plastic. The natural-kind/artifact distinction does not reflect an absolute dichotomy, as there are many unclear and borderline cases. For example, computers are artifacts but generally have the same internal parts as one another; domesticated animals are naturally occurring but affected by human intervention. Nonetheless, it is generally true that natural kinds capture sameness of internal structure, whereas artifact categories do not.

To examine this distinction, I presented preschool and second-grade children (age 8) with an induction task [Gelman, 1984]. For each set of pictures the experimenter first presented the target picture, labeled it, and taught the child a new fact about it. Then the child saw various test pictures and for each was asked whether it, too, had the new property. For example, children learned that one apple had pectin inside and were asked whether other apples did also. Altogether 18 categories were tested, nine natural kinds and nine artifacts. By age 8, children drew significantly more inferences within natural kind categories (e.g., apple, rabbit) than within artifact categories (e.g., bicycle, coat). However, preschool children did not distin-

guish between natural kinds and artifacts in their inductions. For example, they were as likely to say that a ceramic cup and a styrofoam cup are made out of the same substance, as to say that two different pieces of gold are made out of the same substance. They overgeneralized the importance of category membership for promoting inferences.

In addition, there are several other developmental changes concerning which categories promote the most inductions. For example, although superordinate-level categories (e.g., animals, furniture) are an important basis for inferences by adults, children rarely draw inferences at this level [Gelman, 1984], and preschoolers draw even fewer superordinate-level inferences than second-grade children [Gelman and O'Reilly, in press]. These results are consistent with a sizable literature showing that superordinates are especially difficult for children to learn [Mervis and Rosch, 1981; Markman and Callanan, 1984]. Similarly, substances (e.g., water, gold) promote relatively few inferences for children [Gelman, 1984], but many inferences for adults [Gelman and Markman, unpubl. data].

Thus, what is developmentally constant is that children grasp the function of categories and expect basic-level categories to capture rich similarities. What is developmentally in flux are the distinctions that are made among categories.

Constructing a Classification Versus Drawing Category-Based Inferences

The third assumption is a methodological one. Category knowledge is often measured by asking children to sort or classify objects. For example, often children are asked to 'put the things together that go together'. What this means is that children are asked to *construct* a classification—to decide on the category membership of an object or objects, often when there are competing possible bases of classification [e.g., taxonomic vs. thematic, color vs. form; see Markman and Callanan, 1984, for a review]. Yet concepts comprise more than knowledge of which instances belong together. It is at least as important to ask what the consequences are of having a category. I stress that the method I have used differs from the standard classification task. In my work, children are explicitly told what the category is, then are asked to draw inferences from it. When the two tasks—classification vs. category-based induction—are compared directly [Gelman et al., 1986], children perform significantly better on the latter. Although children cannot always determine which objects belong in a category, once the category is established they treat it as having a privileged status for promoting inferences.

CONCLUSION

Altogether the results of these studies suggest that preschool children certainly realize that category members share more than surface similarities. For basic-level categories, this assumption may be stronger among younger than older children, since younger children are more likely to report that *all* category members have a particular internal structure, and younger children also do not as clearly distinguish between natural kinds and artifacts in their inductions. In sum, categories allow and even encourage children to extend their knowledge beyond the obvious, thus serving as a mechanism for the acquisition of new information.

REFERENCES

Bruner, J. S., Goodnow, J. J., & Austin, G., A. (1956). *A study of thinking.* New York: Wiley.

Bruner, J. S., Olver, R. R., & Greenfield, P. M. (1966). *Studies in cognitive growth.* New York: Wiley.

De Vries, R. (1969). Constancy of generic identity in the years three to six. *Society for Research in Child Development Monographs, 34,* No. 127.

Flavell, J. H. (1985). *Cognitive development.* 2nd ed. Englewood Cliffs, NJ: Prentice Hall.

Gelman, S. A. (1984). Children's inductive inferences from natural kind and artifact categories. Ph.D. dissertation, Stanford University.

Gelman, S. A., Collman, P., & Maccoby, E. E. (1986). Inferring properties from categories versus inferring categories from properties: The case of gender. *Child Development, 57,* 396–404.

Gelman, S. A., & Markman, E. M. (1986). Categories and induction in young children. *Cognition, 23,* 183–209.

Gelman, S. A., & Markman, E. M. (1987). Young children's inductions from natural kinds: The role of categories and appearances. *Child Development, 58,* 1532–1541.

Gelman, S. A., & O'Reilly, A. W. (in press). Children's inductive inferences within superordinate categories. The role of language and category structure. *Child Development.*

Inhelder, B., & Piaget, J. (1964). *The early growth of logic in the child.* New York: Norton.

Mansfield, A. P. (1977). Semantic organization in the young child. *Journal of Experimental Child Psychology, 23,* 57–77.

Markman, E. M., & Callanan, M. A. (1984). An analysis of hierarchical classification. In R. Sternberg (Ed.), *Advances in the psychology of human intelligence* (pp. 325–365). Vol. 2. Hillsdale, NJ: Erlbaum.

Mervis, C. B., & Rosch, E. (1981). Categorization of natural objects. In M. Rosenzweig & L. Porter (Eds.), *Annual Review of Psychology.* Vol. 32 (pp. 89–115). Palo Alto, CA: Annual Reviews.

Quine, W. V. (1969). Natural kinds. In W. V. Quine, *Ontological relativity and other essays* (pp. 114–138). New York: Columbia University Press.

Skyrms, B. (1975). *Choice and chance: An introduction to inductive logic.* 2nd ed. Encino, CA: Dickenson.

Tversky, B. (1985). The development of taxonomic organization of named and pictured categories. *Developmental Psychology, 21,* 1111–1119.

Preparation of this paper was supported by NIH grant 1-R29-HD23378-01.

14

Mary Kister Kaiser, John Jonides, and Joanne Alexander

Intuitive Reasoning About Abstract and Familiar Physics Problems

Previous research has demonstrated that many people have misconceptions about basic properties of motion. In two experiments, we examined whether people are more likely to produce dynamically correct predictions about basic motion problems involving situations with which they are familiar, and whether solving such problems enhances performance on a subsequent abstract problem. In Experiment 1, college students were asked to predict the trajectories of objects exiting a curved tube. Subjects were more accurate on the familiar version of the problem, and there was no evidence of transfer to the abstract problem. In Experiment 2, two familiar problems were provided in an attempt to enhance subjects' tendency to extract the general structure of the problems. Once again, they gave more correct responses to the familiar problems but failed to generalize to the abstract problem. Formal physics training was associated with correct predictions for the abstract problem but was unrelated to performance on the familiar problems.

Recent studies have demonstrated that many adults hold erroneous beliefs concerning fundamental laws of motion (McCloskey, 1983; McCloskey, Caramazza, & Green, 1980). For example, when asked to predict the trajectory of a ball exiting a curved tube, many college students respond that the ball will continue to curve, at least for some period of time. McCloskey and his colleagues explain such erroneous predictions as evidence that, when people are asked to reason abstractly about motion, their intuitive models frequently resemble a medieval impetus theory rather than a Newtonian model. The Newtonian model holds that, in the absence of external force, objects

From Mary Kister Kaiser, John Jonides, and Joanne Alexander, "Intuitive Reasoning About Abstract and Familiar Physics Problems," *Memory & Cognition*, vol. 14, no. 4 (1986), pp. 308–312. Copyright © 1986 by The Psychonomic Society, Inc. Reprinted by permission.

maintain a linear path. Alternatively, the impetus theory holds that setting an object in motion imparts to the object an internal energy, or impetus, that maintains the object's motion along its initial trajectory, be it linear or curvilinear.

Suppose people were asked to reason about problems that evoked actual motion events with which they are familiar. Would they make the same impetus-like error? Research in other cognitive domains raises the possibility that they would not: whereas many adults make errors in reasoning about abstract logic problems, performance is much better on problems that are logically equivalent to the abstract problems but that make reference to familiar situations. For example, in Wason's (1966) selection task, subjects were presented with cards showing a letter on one side and a number on the other. They were required to choose which cards needed to be examined to determine the validity of the statement: "If a card has an A on one side, then it has a 4 on the other." When presented four cards showing an "A," a "B," a "4," and a "7," many subjects responded that the "A" and "4" cards must be examined (instead of the logically correct "A" and "7"), an error termed "affirming the consequent." Other logical errors, such as insisting that all cards must be examined, were also observed. This would suggest that adults make systematic errors in logical reasoning, much as McCloskey's work suggests that adults make systematic errors in mechanical reasoning.

However, research has shown that subjects can solve problems that are formally identical to the selection task if they are presented in realistic, thematic contexts (see Evans, 1982). Drawing on the now-defunct British postal rule requiring more postage for sealed than unsealed envelopes, Johnson-Laird, P. Legrenzi, and M. S. Legrenzi (1972) asked subjects to examine letters for violations of the rule, "If the letter is sealed, then it has a 5d stamp on it." This problem is formally identical to Wason's (1966) selection task. Older subjects, familiar with the postal system, performed far better on the envelope task than on Wason's task. Younger subjects who had no previous experience with the postal rule performed no better on the envelope task.

Our Experiment 1 is concerned with the possibility that familiarity may breed success: We examined whether or not people would give more accurate trajectory predictions on a somewhat familiar motion problem than on a more abstract version of the problem. In addition to examining performance on the two problems, we were interested in whether or not subjects would recognize the similarity between the problems and perform better on the abstract problem if it was presented after the familiar one.

EXPERIMENT 1

Method

Subjects.
Eighty college students (40 males and 40 females) were recruited in the hallway of a classroom building at the University of Michigan. Half of the students (20 males and 20 females) had taken physics courses in either high school or college.

Materials and Procedures.
A clear plastic spiral tube was mounted on a 60 × 80 cm plywood board that lay flat on a level table. The tube was 2.2 cm in diameter and formed a spiral of 540° rotation with an interior diameter of 25 cm (see Figure 1a). One end of the tube was elevated such that it appeared that a ball or liquid inserted in the elevated end would travel through the tube at a moderate speed. Half of the subjects were given the following instructions: "Suppose I take this ball bearing and place it in this (the elevated) end of the tube. It would roll around the tube and come out here (indicate mouth of tube). I'd like you to draw the path that the ball would take when it exited the tube." Once the subject had produced a response, a second problem was presented: "Okay, now imagine that we connect a hose to the elevated end of the tube and send water through it. The water would flow through the tube and come out

Figure 1 _____

Schematics of Apparatus Employed in Experiment 1 (a) and Experiment 2 (a and b)

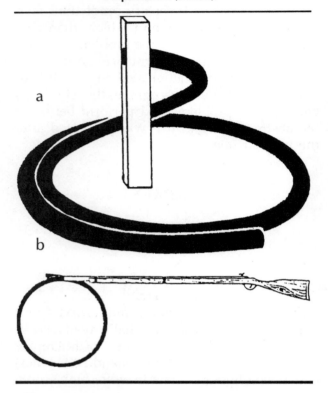

here (at the mouth of the tube). Could you draw the path that the main part of the stream of water would take when it came out of the tube?" The other half of the subjects were administered the problems in the opposite order.

The ball problem has been used by a number of researchers to investigate people's understanding of curvilinear motion (e.g., McCloskey et al., 1980). Typically, a sizable proportion of subjects' answers include references to non-existent forces and influences (e.g., curvilinear momentum). The water problem was chosen since water shooting from a curved garden hose is a closely related event that is familiar to most people. Since most subjects have seen that the curvature of the hose does not affect the water's path, we hoped that people would draw upon this experience in solving the problem.

Subjects made their predictions by drawing a path on a 28 × 55 cm piece of paper placed on the board at the mouth of the tube. Subjects

were asked to describe verbally the path they drew to clarify any ambiguity. The experimenter recorded the subject's gender, and inquired about his or her coursework in physics. Subjects were thanked and paid for their participation.

Results

A response was coded as correct if the path arced no more than 10° throughout its length and was tangent to the point of exit. Examples of correct and incorrect responses are illustrated in Figure 2. Subjects produced far more correct predictions for the water problem than for the ball problem. Fifty-three people (31 men and 22 women) drew linear paths for the water problem, compared with 31 subjects (22 men and 9 women) for the ball problem. This effect was highly significant ($x^2(1) = 12.13$, $p < .005$). Log-linear analyses demonstrated a strong gender effect for the ball problem [$x^2(1) = 9.45$, $p < .005$] and a lesser gender effect for the water problem [$x^2(1) = 4.59$, $p < .05$]. Physics training had a marginal effect on performance on the ball problem [$x^2(1) = 2.93$, $p < .10$] but no significant effect on performance on the water problem [$x^2(1) = 1.21$].

To examine whether or not subjects transferred their correct solutions on the water problem to the more abstract ball problem, we tested for a problem-order effect among those subjects who answered the water problem correctly. Were subjects who demonstrated a correct understanding of the water problem more likely to answer the ball problem correctly if it was administered second? Of the 53 subjects who gave a correct response to the water problem, 27 were administered the ball problem first. Ten of these subjects (37%) were correct on the ball problem. The other 26 subjects answered the ball problem after correctly answering the water problem. Fifteen of them (58%) were correct on the ball problem. This difference is not significant ($x^2 = 2.26$, $p > .10$). Thus, correctly solving a familiar problem on curvilinear motion immediately prior to attempting an abstract curvilinear problem did not significantly enhance performance on the latter.

Figure 2 _____

Examples of Correct and Incorrect Responses on the Water and Ball Problems in Experiment 1

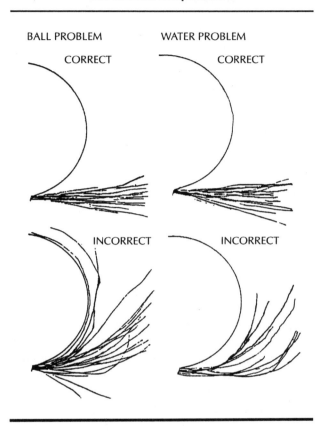

BALL PROBLEM   WATER PROBLEM

CORRECT   CORRECT

INCORRECT   INCORRECT

EXPERIMENT 2

The lack of transfer in Experiment 1 is quite striking, especially since the abstract problem was administered immediately after the common-sense problem and even used the same apparatus. Why did subjects fail to reason analogically from the water problem to the ball problem? Is it possible to improve subjects' transfer by offering more than one common-sense exemplar? These were addressed in Experiment 2.

The literature on analogical problem solving suggests that a critical obstacle to solution transfer is the failure to recognize the relevant similarities among problems (D. Gentner & D. R. Gentner, 1983; Holyoak, 1984). Providing multiple exemplars of a solution type often enhances people's ability to recognize abstract similarities (Holyoak, 1984). We investigated

whether providing a second common-sense motion problem increased the likelihood of solution transfer to the abstract problem. Furthermore, we asked subjects to justify their predictions, particularly when their solutions for the two types of problems differed.

Method

Subjects.

Eighty-one University of Michigan female students participated in the experiment. Forty-three of them had taken physics courses in either high school or college. Subjects were recruited from a subject pool at the university and were paid for their participation.

Materials and Procedure.

Subjects were administered one abstract and two familiar curvilinear motion problems. The ball problem from Experiment 1 was the abstract problem. One of the familiar problems was the water problem of Experiment 1. The other problem required subjects to predict the path of a bullet when fired from a rifle with a curved barrel. The rifle was oriented such that the curved barrel lay flat on a horizontal surface, similar to the curved-tube apparatus. A pilot study indicated that, although people had never used such a weapon, many insisted that they had seen them used (in cartoons and movies) and professed an intuitive understanding that bullets would have to travel straight regardless of the shape of the barrel. The experimental apparatus is schematized in Figures 1a and 1b.

Subjects were instructed to draw the path of the ball, the water, or the bullet upon exiting the curved tube or barrel. Forty of the subjects were given the two familiar problems (water and rifle) first, followed by the abstract (ball) problem. The other subjects were administered the abstract problem first. The order of presentation for the two familiar problems was counterbalanced across subjects. After they had made all three predictions, 41 of the subjects (every other subject) were asked to explain

Table 1

Patterns of Subjects' Responses for Abstract and Common-Sense Curvilinear Motion Problems (Experiment 2)

Pattern of Responses	Number of Subjects		
	Common-Sense Problems First	Abstract Problem First	Total
Accurate Predictions for all Problems	11(6)	17(14)	28(20)
More Accurate Predictions for Common-Sense Problems	10(7)	13(5)	23(12)
More Accurate Prediction for Abstract Problem	8(2)	3(2)	11(4)
Inaccurate Predictions for Common-Sense and Abstract Problems	13(3)	6(4)	19(7)

Note—Numbers in parentheses indicate number of subjects with formal physics training.

their predictions and to justify any discrepancies in the paths.

Results

Subjects' responses were coded as in Experiment 1. The patterns of subjects' predictions are shown in Table 1. It should be noted that a fairly conservative classification scheme was used for the familiar problems: Subjects had to produce correct predictions for both familiar problems to be classified as accurate on that problem type. Very few subjects (12) gave incorrect predictions for both familiar problems.

Even with such a classification scheme, subjects were found to give more accurate predictions for the familiar problems than for the abstract problem [$x^2(1) = 4.24$, $p < .05$]. As in Experiment 1, there was no evidence of transfer of correct solutions from the familiar to the abstract problems [$x^2(1) = 1.29\$7BC$. Having correctly solved two familiar curvilinear problems did not enhance subjects' performance on the abstract problem.

How did subjects who gave correct responses for the familiar problems justify their erroneous responses to the ball problem? Examination of these subjects' protocols indicated three basic justifications: First, in the case of the rifle, subjects noted that the barrel had less curvature (360°) than did the ball appa-

ratus (540°). Second, in the case of the water, subjects contended that liquids and solids had different motion properties; water would not acquire curvilinear "momentum" the way a ball would. Finally, subjects cited several irrelevant dynamic properties, notably speed, pressure, and weight. Speed was most often seen as a determining factor. Subjects reported that since the bullet (and sometimes the water) would travel faster than the ball, there would be less tendency for the bullet (and water) to "pick up" curvature from the tube. Two examples of subjects' protocols are given in the Appendix. Both of these subjects gave correct responses to the two common-sense problems but curvilinear responses to the abstract problem.

Most subjects who gave correct responses to all three problems noted the underlying similarity. Newton's first law of motion (or some more vernacular version) was often cited, as was the tendency of objects to move in a "natural" path (i.e., a straight line). The remainder of these subjects either were unable to justify their correct responses or acknowledged that they were just guessing.

Experience-based explanations were given for all problems, although more were given for the familiar problems than for the ball problem. Interestingly, incorrect responses were sometimes justified with inappropriate experiences, such as citing whirlpools as a basis for a curvilinear path for water.

GENERAL DISCUSSION

The data from both experiments indicate that people give more accurate predictions to some curvilinear motion problems than to others. Furthermore, a correct solution on one type of problem is not generalized to another, usually because irrelevant differences are noted in the problems.

One model that is generally consistent with the data holds that subjects apply formal physical principles to both kinds of problems, but that their principles are inaccurate and include such irrelevant factors as the object's velocity and the amount of tube curvature. Certainly, protocols indicate that subjects employ a number of inappropriate physical properties in their justifications. Subjects' allusions to specific experiences may merely reflect an attempt to provide concrete examples of their basic, abstract beliefs. However, if such a model is correct, it is not clear why these misconceptions should impact on subjects' ball predictions more often than on their water or rifle predictions. It would be rather serendipitous that the familiar problems we selected tapped more accurate formal physical principles than did the abstract problem we chose.

An alternative interpretation of the data is that people are able to reason more appropriately about motion problems when they are related to specific, concrete, familiar experiences. The facilitation of reasoning that results from placing an abstract problem in a familiar context has been examined in other cognitive domains, notably in the area of deductive reasoning. Context effects, or "facilitation by realism," have been found to affect performance on syllogistic reasoning (Wilkins, 1928) as well as on a number of variations of the Wason selection task (see Evans, 1982, for a summary). As in our motion problems, however, the facilitation did not generalize to subsequent abstract problems.

Evans (1982) has discussed context effects and the lack of solution transfer from the familiar to the abstract deductive reasoning problem. He argues that the studies that demonstrate the greatest context effects (e.g., Johnson-Laird et al., 1972) may present problems that are too

realistic. That is, they do not require subjects to reason at all, but rather allow for a solution based on specific experiences. Such a model would certainly explain the lack of transfer: the relevant similarity in the problems is not recognized since the familiar problem is never processed in formal terms.

We propose a similar model for our subjects' performance. Subjects draw on specific experiences to solve the common-sense problems, and need not employ formal reasoning. The abstract problem, evoking no specific memory, requires subjects to draw upon their formal understanding of physics (which is often erroneous). Thus, we suggest that subjects apply a two-stage approach to solving these problems. First, they search for a specific solution based on relevant experiences. If this search fails, they default to a reasoning process employing formal understanding of mechanics. Such default reasoning models have been proposed in many areas of cognitive psychology (e.g., Siegler, 1981) and artificial intelligence (e.g., Reiter, 1980).

The striking lack of transfer can also be accounted for by such a model. Reasoning by analogy is dependent upon recognizing the relevant similarities of the base problem and the target problem (D. Gentner, 1982). Since the relevant similarities of the common-sense and abstract problems exist only at the level of formal analysis, it is necessary that the common-sense problems be viewed in formal terms for transfer to occur. However, subjects' protocols suggest that most people are able to map the common-sense problem to experience-based solutions on a very concrete level. Since the common-sense problems are only considered on a concrete level, similarity recognition is not possible. The use of two common-sense problems in our Experiment 2 did not improve subjects' solution transfer, although other researchers have found the provision of multiple exemplars to enhance subjects' awareness of formal similarities among problems (Holyoak, 1984).

Finally, our model explains why people demonstrate inconsistency in their reasoning concerning motion problems. Many people who give impetus-type responses to one problem will provide a correct prediction on the next. We suggest that this is because people do not always draw upon their formal representation of physics, but only do so when they are unable to find an acceptable solution based on specific experiences in their memories. The problem of deciding what is or is not a relevant experience is still an issue, but our main point is that people draw on their formal models only after such a solution-by-analogy method fails. In the problems we employed, subjects usually failed to find a relevant experience for the abstract problem and dismissed the common-sense problems as irrelevant based on extraneous factors (e.g., velocity, substance). What we propose, therefore, is that reasoning by analogy is the default strategy most people apply to motion problems (particularly if they lack formal physics training). Only when people are unable to map the target problem to an appropriate base do they draw upon formal representations. It is then that errors reflecting an impetus model of physics emerge from many individuals.

REFERENCES

EVANS, J. ST. B. T. (1982). *The psychology of deductive reasoning.* London: Routledge & Kegan Paul.

GENTNER, D. (1982). Are scientific analogies metaphors? In D. S. Miall (Ed.), *Metaphor: Problems and perspectives* (pp. 106–132). Brighton, Sussex, England: Harvester Press.

GENTNER, D., & GENTNER, D. R. (1983). Flowing waters or teeming crowds: Mental models of electricity. In D. Gentner & A. Steven (Eds.), *Mental models* (pp. 99–130). Hillsdale, NJ: Erlbaum.

HOLYOAK, K. J. (1984). Analogical thinking and human intelligence. In R. J. Sternberg (Ed.), *Advances in the psychology of human intelligence* (Vol. 2, pp. 199–230). Hillsdale, NJ: Erlbaum.

JOHNSON-LAIRD, P. N., LEGRENZI, P., & LEGRENZI, M. S. (1972). Reasoning and a sense of reality. *British Journal of Psychology, 63,* 395–400.

McCLOSKEY, M. (1983). Intuitive physics. *Scientific American,* **248**(4), 122–130.

McCLOSKEY, M., CARAMAZZA, A., & GREEN, B. (1980). Curvilinear motion in the absence of external forces: Naive beliefs about the motion of objects. *Science,* **210,** 1139–1141.

REITER, R. (1980). A logic for default reasoning. *Artificial Intelligence,* **13,** 81–132.

SIEGLER, R. (1981). Developmental sequences within and between concepts. *Monographs of the Society for Research in Child Development,* **46**(2).

WASON, P. C. (1966). Reasoning. In B. M. Foss (Ed.), *New horizons in psychology I* (pp. 135–151). Harmondsworth, England: Penguin.

WILKINS, M. C. (1928). The effect of changed material on the ability to do formal syllogistic reasoning. *Archives of Psychology* (New York) No. 102.

Appendix

Sample Subject Protocols from Experiment 2

Subject 20

Q: Could you explain for each of the situations why you thought the objects took the paths you drew?

A: I guess when I think in terms of bullets, bullets always go straight; when it came out of the gun, I figure it would go straight. And the water, water also seems to go straight out, no matter how much like a garden hose is twisted around, so I imagine the water coming out straight. The ball, I imagine, staying next to the tube, like just following around the tube.

Q. Could you tell me how the speed of the object affects the path it takes?

A. If it were going really fast, it would go straighter than if it were going slow.

Q: Why is that?

A: When you roll a ball very slowly, it tends to go off to the side, where if you throw it faster, it takes a straighter path. I guess maybe it's the gravity behind it. . . . well, it's not even gravity, I guess; it's more like inertia, or the energy it has.

Q: Could you tell me your background in physics?

A: Two years in high school. I got As.

Subject 21

Q: Could you explain why you thought the objects took the paths you drew?

A: I'm going to assume that the ball's going to come out slower here, and because it's been going around and not going real fast, it's going to take the path it had, and curve around. With the gun, the curve was less on the tube, and there's more force, so it's going to be going more straight forward. I don't know the physics behind it, but since it hadn't been going real slow, it's going to take the most direct path, which will be straight. With the water, it's the same reasoning as with the shotgun, it's coming out faster, so it's going to take the direct path, and that's more out straight.

Q: How does the speed of the object affect the path it takes?

A: The faster the object goes, the straighter or more direct path it will take.

Q: Why is that? What about its going faster makes it take a straighter path?

A: Gravity's going to want to hold it in more to the circular path, but when it's going faster, then you get away from the effects of gravity.

Q: What's your physics background?

A: Very limited. Just reading on my own, and what they threw in chemistry. . . . I got an A in chemistry.

This research was supported in part by NIMH Training Grant T32-MH16892 to the first author and in part by a grant from AFOSR to the second author. Portions of this paper were presented at the Annual Meeting of the Midwestern Psychological Association, Chicago, May, 1985.

We would like to thank Michelene Chi, Alice Healy, and Michael McCloskey for their helpful comments.

15

Richard P. Honeck, Michael Firment, and Tammy J. S. Case

Expertise and Categorization

Experts exhibit various categorization phenomena, including category abstractness, use of second-order features, big chunks, category coherence, and category gradedness. Traditional views of categorization—the classical, prototype, and exemplar views—are variously successful in explaining these phenomena. We argue that our conceptual base view is more adequate.

We would like to juxtapose two areas of research that hitherto have passed like ships in the night: categorization and expertise. We are interested in these two topics for a simple enough reason: expertise stems, at least in part, from well-developed categorization processes. Thus, the question naturally arises as to whether current psychological views of categorization can elucidate expert categorization. In particular, we would like to assess the adequacy of three traditional views of categorization and of our own view.

To compare these several views of categorization, we must first ask what is known about experts' categories. At least five categorization issues can be identified. The issues are listed in Table 1.

CATEGORIZATION ISSUES

Abstract Categories

Experts develop categories that are more abstract than are novices'. For example, Larkin (1985) argues that expert physicists develop "scientific representations" that incorporate abstract principles of physics. In fact, Larkin argues that these scientific representations are

Table 1

A Scorecard for Various Views of Categorization

Issues	Views of Categorization			
	Exemplar	Proto-type	Classical	Conceptual Base
Abstract Representation	–	+	+	+
Second-Order Features	–	–	?	+
Big Chunks	?	?	?	?
Category Coherence	–	+	?	+
Gradedness	?	+	–	+

built on a "naive representation," which is only a short inferential distance from an initial literal representation of a verbal physics problem. Experts in chess (Chase & Simon, 1973; de Groot, 1965), baseball (Voss, Vesonder, & Spilich, 1980), X-ray reading (Lesgold, 1984), dinosaurs (Chi & Koeske, 1983), and even the videogame Star Wars (Means & Voss, 1985) have been shown to possess complex, abstract categories. To illustrate, expert physicists might group problems involving blocks on an inclined plane with problems involving pulleys with different weights on either end, because both problems are conservation of energy problems (Chi, Feltovich, & Glaser, 1981). Novices are more likely to sort problems on the basis of surface features; for example, problems are grouped because they all mention an inclined plane.

Second-Order Features

Experts and novices identify different aspects of a problem as relevant. Experts respond more to second-order features, which are a step or two removed from the literal situation. As Chi et al. (1981) noted, "experts perceive more in a problem statement than do novices. They have a great deal of tacit knowledge that can be used

to make inferences and derivations from the situation described by the problem statement" (pp. 148–149). Experts respond to what words might signify in terms of abstract principles rather than to the literal things mentioned.

A clear implication of the abstractness and second-order-features properties of experts' categories is that these categories are much more flexibly applied than are those of novices. An expert can spot an instance of a category regardless of its context and regardless of irrelevant surface-level cues in general. There is more breadth to the expert's categories, because they are both more abstract and decontextualized.

Big Chunks

Experts store information in bigger chunks than do novices, and these chunks are often hierarchically related (Chase & Simon, 1973; Chi & Koeske, 1983; McDermott & Larkin, 1978; Means & Voss, 1985).

Category Coherence

Expert knowledge is highly integrated and complete. For example, advanced students in political science show more awareness of the interrelatedness of problems and provide more extensive rationales for solutions to problems. Accurate medical diagnosis may also rely on complex, causally interrelated knowledge frames (Patel & Goren, 1986), as does an expert solution to hypothetical Soviet socioeconomic problems (Voss, Tyler, & Yengo, in press).

Gradedness of Categories

It is well known that some natural categories show gradedness rather than discreteness of category membership (Rosch, 1978). There is also some evidence that experts' categories can show gradedness. For example, Adelson (1985) found that expert programmers used sorting algorithms that yielded to a Roschian prototypical structure. We will return to this point later.

We have discussed five categorization issues as they arise in the area of expertise. How well do the various views of categorization explain these phenomena? By Smith and Medin's (1981) taxonomy, there are three general views of categorization—the classical, probabilistic (or prototype), and exemplar views. We add our own conceptual base view to this taxonomy.

VIEWS OF CATEGORIZATION

Exemplar View

The exemplar view holds that an input is categorized by matching it against a set of stored, disjunctively arranged exemplars. If the input is similar enough to the exemplars, or some subset of them, then it is categorized. The most radical form of the exemplar view disavows abstract representation. This view would explain successful recognition of a robin as due to a match of the features of the real-world robin with *particular* remembered features of *particular* robins. Unfortunately, the exemplar view fails to address most of the categorization issues. The general reason is that this view implicitly assumes a first-order isomorphism between the to-be-categorized input and the stored exemplars. That is, the *same kind of information* must be present in the input and in the stored exemplar even to initiate the categorization process. Thus, recognition of a real-world robin requires that features such as shape and feathers be coded in memory in direct analog form. This constraint prevents this view from engaging problems of abstract representation and second-order features. Big chunks could theoretically be big sets of instances, but category coherence is precluded on any reading of the exemplar view. In fact, because of this problem, Medin, the main proponent of the exemplar view, adopted a conceptualist point of view (Murphy & Medin, 1985). Finally, because the exemplar view must treat all category members as being on the same level, it also fails to handle hierarchicalness and rich interconnections between categories. In conclusion, the exemplar view's batting average is miserable.

Probabilistic View

The more formidable probabilistic, or prototype, view posits that a category is represented by a central tendency or ideal, the prototype is often not identical to any particular instance, the prototype is used to classify new instances, and category membership is graded rather than all-or-none. Actually, Smith and Medin (1981) consider prototypes only one aspect of the probabilistic view, but for present purposes we will equate the two.

The prototype view arises from experimental work on artificial stimuli such as dot patterns or geometric forms, although Rosch (1978) provided strong evidence that the "basic level" of natural categories (e.g., furniture, fruit) is organized around prototypes. Rosch states that a prototype shares the most features with other category members and the fewest features with other categories. How does the prototype view fare? As Table 1 indicates, it allows abstract representation and gradedness but runs into difficulty on the other issues. There are two reasons for this.

The first reason entails the first-order-isomorphism constraint. Even an ideal prototype retains the same kind of information as the inputs from which it is formed. An ideal tree is still somehow a tree. So construed, the prototype view is a sophisticated exemplar view—instead of several distinct exemplars in memory, there is at least one that aptly summarizes the information in previously encountered exemplars.

Because of the first-order-isomorphism constraint, there is no obvious way to combine information from dissimilar literal inputs to produce an effective, high-order prototype. Any combinatorial process would have to cancel pieces of information in each input and replace them with higher level information. Any combination of such generalities could not, by definition, be a prototype. This is not to say that the more general probabilistic view cannot accommodate superordinate categories, because it can, but these categories retain all the feature kinds of their nested subordinates, and the superordinates are not prototypes.

To illustrate, take Chi, Feltovich, and Glaser's (1981) finding that expert physicists group problems that have no literal similarity, either verbal or pictorial. The only way to connect the problems is through an abstract intermediary, in this case a principle of physics. These principles could not function as prototypes, because prototypes remain at the level of their inputs. Since such principles undoubtedly incorporate several categories, the prototype view suffers proportionately.

A second reason why the prototype view is inadequate concerns hierarchies. Experts' categories often use nested high-level information, yet, as our preceding analysis implies, prototypes do not operate at a level above their category members. Empirical confirmation of this point comes from studies that have found that observers list very few features, let alone common features, for superordinates (Adelson, 1985; Rosch, Mervis, Gray, Johnson, & Boyes-Braem, 1976).

A third and final reason why the prototype view is inadequate involves conceptual complexity. The phenomena in Table 1 bespeak a high order of conceptual complexity. There is a clear need to include part-whole, synonymy, contrast, case relations, and so on in the categorization process. Prototypes, however, generally entail only one or a few possibilities for conceptual combination, especially conjunction; but even conjunction is problematic for this view (Osherson & Smith, 1981).

We conclude that although the categories of experts may exhibit prototype phenomena there is little reason to believe that prototypes constitute the *basis* of these categories. Note the distinction between category structure and exemplariness (Armstrong, Gleitman, & Gleitman, 1983). Typicality phenomena, which prototypes demonstrate, may not tell us anything about category structure. We would be hard-pressed to argue that a prototype causes typicality. In fact, categories that exhibit gradedness could actually be relatively discrete at their core.

Classical View

This brings us to a third view of categorization, the classical view. Like the prototype view, this view holds that categories can be abstract, but it makes category membership all-or-none. More formally, the classical view holds that there are features whose presence is "singly necessary and jointly sufficient" to determine category membership. Since category membership is all-or-none, no member can be more representative than another.

With the investigation of prototypes, gradedness, and so on, the classical view fell into disfavor. These days it is largely a straw man. Should we reject it too? After all, Armstrong, Gleitman, and Gleitman (1983) showed that supposedly classical concepts such as odd number produced gradedness effects for college students who knew what an odd number was; for example, 3 was judged to be a better odd number than 65.

There is another slant on this issue, however. Expertise implies an ability to make fine-grained distinctions. The experienced chicken farmer can distinguish the sex of newborn chicks. The rest of us cannot. The expert X-ray reader can distinguish a collapsed lung from a lung tumor (Lesgold, 1984). The experienced baseball player can distinguish a good base runner from a runner who merely knows the rules of the game. What would have happened had Armstrong et al. (1983) asked mathematicians whether 3 or 65 was a better odd number? When they asked their college students whether it made sense to rate the oddness of odd numbers, the students said "no." Categories may look more or less dichotomous depending on the questions asked.

Another point is that expertise goes hand in hand with an individual-differences, as opposed to a normative, approach to issues. Many experts seem to see only dichotomies where novices see degrees of things. Ask a chemist whether something is more or less a hydrogen compound and see what happens. Ask a linguist whether grammaticality is a continuum. On the other hand, experts may see continuity where the novice sees discreteness. An evolutionary biologist can marshal good arguments for the continuity and relatedness of all animal forms, whereas the child or naive adult sees only distinct forms. Still, the biologist could be using discrete principles that result in judgments of continuity.

Perhaps, then, the book on the classical view should not be closed. Expertise, indeed learning, pushes us to act more in accordance with high-level rules that generate fine but momentous distinctions. Moreover, these rules may be deterministic and formal, thereby immediately implicating the classical view.

This view warrants mainly question marks on Table 1, not because this view is inconsistent with or incapable in principle of addressing the issues. Rather, there is too little empirical information relevant to the issues in relation to expertise, and there is no psychological theory that takes this viewpoint.

Conceptual Base View

This view is an outgrowth of our work on semantic memory and figurative language (see Honeck, Sugar, & Kibler, 1982; Honeck, Voegtle, Dorfmueller, & Hoffman, 1980). This view's key assumption is that people construct an amodal, nonlinguistic microtheory that serves to organize a category. A microtheory codes the significance or underlying message among exemplars, which are thereby made similar. We have called the microtheory a *conceptual base*. Most of the evidence for the microtheory stems from work on proverbs, or proverb families, to be more specific. For example, the proverb "A net with a hole in it won't catch any fish" has a figurative meaning that might be expressed as "A flawed instrument cannot perform its normal function." The figurative meaning, actually the conceptual base, is instantiated by events such as "The missionary who could not speak the natives' language converted none of them," "The astronaut's suit had a small hole, and he froze when he went outside the spaceship," and "The sleeping security guard failed to notice the thieves who ransacked the place." These are verbally expressed instances from vastly different semantic domains, but instances can be pictorial/visual as well. Furthermore, an interpretation of a conceptual base can be an abstract picture (Feldhaus, 1987;

Honeck, Case, & Firment, 1987). It is empirically clear that observers can make reliable connections, that is, they can match up proverbs with verbal and pictorial interpretations, proverbs with instances, literal pictures of proverbs with verbal instances, and even literal pictures of proverbs with abstract interpretive pictures (see Honeck & Kibler, 1985; Honeck, Kibler, & Sugar, 1985, for reviews). Note that all of these connections are nonliteral and that several are cross-modal. Thus proverbs, their interpretations, literal pictures of them, and their instances form a cohesive and, of necessity, abstractly mediated family.

In our admittedly biased opinion, the conceptual base view adequately addresses most of the categorization issues. Therefore, it explains expert categorization better than the other views. We have clear empirical evidence for abstract, nonliteral grouping of sentences, for selection of second-order features (the connections between family members are nonliteral), for gradedness, and for flexibility and breadth in category application (Honeck, Firment, & Kibler, 1987; Honeck, Kibler, & Sugar, 1985). It also seems necessary to believe that conceptual bases or microtheories are responsible for the coherence of the categories we have investigated. There is no other way of accounting for the "glue" that holds a proverb family together. They are also responsible for a variety of psychological functions, including recall of category members, generation of new exemplars, and "feelings of knowing" what a proverb means. Our observers were experts in language comprehension, but we have every confidence that our theorizing generalizes to some other forms of expertise.

In conclusion, it appears that the conceptual base view provides the best account of the phenomena listed in Table 1. We believe this is because this view places a premium on interpretation, whereas the three other views emphasize bottom-up learning processes at the expense of abstract thinking in the form of inferencing, making metaphorical connections, and so on. If there is any hope of accounting for the expert's high level of categorization skill, these sorts of cognitive processes will have to be given a predominant place in theorizing.

REFERENCES

ADELSON, B. (1985). Comparing natural and abstract categories: A case study from computer science. *Cognitive Science, 9,* 417–430.

ARMSTRONG, S. L., GLEITMAN, L. R., & GLEITMAN, H. (1983). On what some concepts might not be. *Cognition, 13,* 263–308.

CHASE, W. G., & SIMON, H. A. (1973). Perception in chess. *Cognitive Psychology, 4,* 55–81.

CHI, M. T. H., FELTOVICH, P. J., & GLASER, R. (1981). Categorization and representation of physics problems by experts and novices. *Cognitive Science, 5,* 121–152.

CHI, M. T. H., & KOESKE, R. D. (1983). Network representation of a child's dinosaur knowledge. *Developmental Psychology, 19,* 29–39.

DE GROOT, A. D. (1965). *Thought and choice in chess.* The Hague: Mouton.

FELDHAUS, R. (1987). *The conceptual base view of categorization.* Unpublished master's thesis, University of Cincinnati, Cincinnati, OH.

HONECK, R. P., CASE, T., & FIRMENT, M. (1987). *Conceptual connections between realistic and abstract pictures.* Manuscript submitted for publication.

HONECK, R. P., FIRMENT, M., & KIBLER, C. (1987). *Context and the generalizability of conceptually based categories,* Unpublished manuscript, University of Cincinnati.

HONECK, R. P., & KIBLER, C. (1985). Representation in cognitive psychological theories of figurative language. In W. Paprotte & R. Dirven (Eds.), *The ubiquity of metaphor* (pp. 381–423). Philadelphia: Benjamins.

HONECK, R. P., KIBLER, C., & SUGAR, J. (1985). The conceptual base view of categorization. *Journal of Psycholinguistic Research, 14,* 155–172.

HONECK, R. P., SUGAR, J., & KIBLER, C. (1982). Stories, categories, and figurative meaning. *Poetics, 11,* 127–144.

HONECK, R. P., VOEGTLE, K., DORFMUELLER, M., & HOFFMAN, R. (1980). Proverbs, meaning, and group structure. In R. P. Honeck & R. R. Hoffman (Eds.), *Cognition and figurative language* (pp. 127–162). Hillsdale, NJ: Erlbaum.

LARKIN, J. H. (1985). Understanding, problem representations, and skill in physics. In S. F. Chipman, J. W. Segal, & R. Glaser (Eds.), *Thinking and learning skills: Vol 2. Research and open questions* (pp. 141–160). Hillsdale, NJ: Erlbaum.

LESGOLD, A. (1984). Acquiring expertise. In J. R. Anderson & S. M. Kosslyn (Eds.), *Tutorials in learning and memory* (pp. 31–60). New York: W. H. Freeman.

McDERMOTT, J., & LARKIN, J. H. (1978). Re-representing textbook physics problems. *Proceedings of the Second National Conference of the Canadian Society for Computational Studies of Intelligence.* Toronto, ON, Canada: University of Toronto Press.

MEANS, M. L., & VOSS, J. F. (1985). Star wars: A developmental study of expert and novice knowledge structures. *Journal of Memory & Language, 24,* 746–757.

MURPHY, G. L., & MEDIN, D. (1985). The role of theories in conceptual coherence. *Psychological Review, 92,* 289–316.

OSHERSON, D. N., & SMITH, E. E. (1981). On the adequacy of prototype theory as a theory of concepts. *Cognition, 9,* 35–58.

PATEL, V. L., & GROEN, G. J. (1986). Knowledge based solution strategies in medical reasoning. *Cognitive Science, 10,* 91–116.

ROSCH, E. H. (1978). Principles of categorization. In E. Rosch & B. B. Lloyd (Eds.), *Cognition and categorization.* Hillsdale, NJ: Erlbaum.

ROSCH, E. H., MERVIS, C. B., GRAY, W., JOHNSON, D. M., & BOYES-BRAEM, P. (1976). Basic objects in natural categories. *Cognitive Psychology, 8,* 382–439.

SMITH, E. E., & MEDIN, D. L. (1981). *Categories and concepts.* Cambridge, MA: Harvard University Press.

VOSS, J. F., TYLER, S. W., & YENGO, L. A. (in press). Individual differences in the solving of social science problems. In R. F. Dillon & R. R. Schmeck (Eds.), *Individual differences in cognition.* New York: Academic Press.

VOSS, J. F., VESONDER, G. T., & SPILICH, G. J. (1980). Generation and recall by high-knowledge and low-knowledge individuals. *Journal of Verbal Learning & Verbal Behavior, 19,* 651–667.

16

Richard E. Mayer

Human Nonadversary Problem Solving

The purpose of this chapter is to examine briefly the nature of human nonadversary problem solving. A related purpose is to determine how an information-processing model of problem solving—inspired by and implemented on computers—can serve as the basis for a theory of human problem solving. The chapter consists of three parts: an introduction, which defines key terms and concepts in human nonadversary problem solving; a body, which explores six major characteristics of human nonadversary problem solving; and a conclusion, which summarizes the implications for a theory of human problem solving.

1. INTRODUCTION

1.1. Definitions

What is a problem? A problem solver has a problem when a situation is in one state, the problem solver wants the situation to be in a different state, and the problem solver does not know an obvious way to eliminate obstacles between the two states. In short, a problem consists of three components; the given state, the goal state, and obstacles that block movement from the given to the goal state.

An important implication of this definition is that a problem always exists relative to the problem solver. Another way to make this point is to say that the same situation may be a problem for one person but not for another person. For example, 3 + 5 = ___ is likely not to be a problem for an adult who has a memorized answer; i.e., the adult has no obstacles between the givens and the goal. In contrast, 3 + 5 = ___ is likely to be a problem for a young child who has not yet memorized the number facts; the child may use a strategy for deriving the answer, such as reasoning that "I can take 1 from the 5 and give it to the 3. Then, 4 plus 4 is 8."

A distinction can be made between well-defined and ill-defined problems. A well-defined problem has a clearly specified given state, goal state, and operators that may be applied to problem states. For example, solving an algebra equation such as $X + 2 = 4(X - 2)$ is a well-defined problem for most adults since they can clearly specify the given state (i.e., the equation), the goal state (e.g., $X = \_\_\_$), and the legal operators (i.e., adding the same number to both sides, adding the unknown to the both sides, etc.). An ill-defined problem lacks a clear specification of one or more of the given state, the goal state, or the operators. For example, writing a chapter on problem solving can be an ill-defined problem because the goal state and the legal operators are not easy to specify.

Another important distinction can be made between routine and nonroutine problems. Routine problems are familiar problems that, although not eliciting an automatic memorized answer, can be solved by applying a well-known procedure. Although the problem solver does not immediately know the answer to a routine problem, the problem solver does know how to arrive at an answer. For example, the problem 888 × 888 is a routine problem for most adults. In contrast, nonroutine problems are unfamiliar problems for which the problem solver does not have a well-known solution procedure and must generate a novel procedure. For example, suppose you were given a full glass of water and asked to pour out half of the water; if you have never solved a problem like this before, this is a nonroutine problem. (One solution procedure is to tilt the glass until the water line forms a diagonal going from one corner of the top to the opposite corner of the bottom).

The Gestalt psychologists (Duncker, 1945; Katona, 1940; Wertheimer, 1959) have pointed out that routine problems require "reproductive thinking"—applying already known solution procedures to the initial problem state—while nonroutine problems require "productive thinking"—generating a creative or novel procedure.

These authors argue that school tasks tend to emphasize routine problems rather than nonroutine problems, i.e., mechanical thinking rather than creative thinking. This chapter focuses on nonroutine problems, and to some extent on ill-defined nonroutine problems.

What is problem solving? Problem solving is cognitive processing that is directed toward solving a problem. In short, the definition of problem solving consists of three components: (1) Problem solving is cognitive in that it occurs internally in the mind or cognitive system, (2) problem solving is a process in that operators are applied to knowledge in memory, (3) problem solving is directed in that the cognitive activity has a goal (Mayer, 1983).

This definition is broad enough to include many cognitive activities that involve conscious cognitive control, including aspects of learning and remembering, or language comprehension and production. For example, if you were asked to summarize the foregoing paragraph, that would be an act of problem solving. Problem solving is also involved in many nondirect retrieval tasks, such as naming all the states that border Texas. In contrast, many cognitive activities that involve automatic processing or undirected thinking are excluded by this definition. For example, decoding of printed words into sounds is an automatic cognitive process for most adults and hence cannot be considered problem solving. Daydreaming is not problem solving because it does not have a goal (although some scientists have introspected that great insights have come through daydreaming).

This definition of problem solving involves three main theoretical entities: symbols, operators, and control. Symbols are used to represent the initial and goal states of the problem, operators are applied to the various states of the problem to generate new states, and control refers to metacognitive processes such as planning and monitoring a solution procedure.

1.2. Types of Problems

A major distinction [is that] between adversary and nonadversary problems. Adversary problems involve two or more players who compete against one another in a game, such as chess or checkers. Nonadversary problems, such as solving a puzzle or finding a cure for a disease, do not involve competition against opposing players in a game. Orthogonal to the foregoing distinctions between well-defined versus ill-defined problems and routine versus nonroutine problems, the universe of possible nonadversary problems can be broken into several categories: transformation problems, arrangement problems, induction problems, deduction problems, divergent problems.

In transformation problems, an initial state is given, and the problem solver must determine the proper sequence of operators to apply in order to transform the given state through a series of intervening states into the goal state. An example is the Tower of Hanoi problem: Given three pegs (peg A, peg B, and peg C) with a large, medium, and small disk on peg A (with the large on the bottom and the small on top), the goal is to have the three disks on peg C (with the large on the bottom and the small on top), by moving only one disk at a time and never placing a larger disk on top of a smaller disk or moving a larger disk that has a smaller disk on top of it. Algebra equations and water jar problems are other examples.

In arrangement problems, all the elements of the problem are given and the problem solver must determine how to organize the givens in order to satisfy the goal. An example is a matchstick problem (Katona, 1940): Given nine matchsticks, make four triangles. Anagrams and cryptarithmetic are other examples.

In induction problems, a series of instances is given and the problem solver must induce a rule or pattern that describes the structure of the problem. An example is an oddity problem in which you must choose the item that does not belong (Kittel, 1957); *gone start go stop come.* Other examples include series completion and analogy problems.

In deduction problems, premises are given and the problem solver must apply the appropriate rules (e.g., logic) to draw a conclusion. An example is Wason's (1966) card-turning problem: Given four cards with A, D, 4, and 7, respectively on one side, which ones would

Table 1 _____

A Model of Problem Solving

PROBLEM PRESENTATION
—(apply representational processes)→
PROBLEM REPRESENTATION
—(apply solution processes)→
PROBLEM SOLUTION

---

you turn over to test the premise "If a card has a vowel on one side, then it has a number on the other side"? Other examples include categorical, linear, and conditional syllogisms.

In divergent problems, the problem solver is given some situation and asked to generate as many possible solutions as possible. An example is the brick problem: List all the possible uses for a brick. Other examples include listing all possible hypotheses for "who done it" in a mystery story.

1.3. Analysis of Problem Solving

Problem solving can be analyzed into two major phases: representation and solution. Representation involves moving from a statement or presentation of the problem in the world to an internal encoding of the problem in memory. More specifically, representation involves mentally encoding the given state, goal state, and legal operators for a problem. Solution involves filling in the gap between the given and goal states. More specifically, solution involves devising and carrying out a plan for operating on the representation of the problem.

Table 1 summarizes a straightforward analysis of the problem-solving process that could serve as a framework for both human and machine problem solving. The capitalized words represent states and the arrows represent transitions between states. First, the problem-as-presented is converted into some cognitive representation, by applying representational processes to the presented problem. The input to the representational process could be a statement of the problem in words; the output could be a representation of the given state, the goal state, and all legal operators for producing intermediate states. Second, the solution procedures are applied to the cognitive representation, eventually yielding the problem solution.

The representation and solution processes may be analyzed, respectively, as building a problem space and using procedures for searching for a path through the problem space (Newell & Simon, 1972). The input to the solution process is a cognitive description of the problem (including the given state, goal state, intermediate states, legal operators) and the output is a search path (i.e., application of a series of operators) between the given and goal states. The search through the problem space (i.e., the connections among the given, goal, and all intervening states) is controlled by a set of procedures, such as a means–ends analysis strategy.

Can a straightforward information-processing model be applied to human nonadversary problem solving? To answer this question, consider the following problem:

Construct four equilateral triangles using six toothpicks.

According to our model, the first step is to convert the words of the problem into some cognitive representation such as that summarized in the following:

Given: Six sticks on tabletop
Goal: Four equilateral triangles
Operators: Moving sticks around on tabletop

The next step is to apply operators that will convert the given state into the goal state. For example, one frequent attempt is to use four sticks to make a square and then lay the other two sticks as diagonals. Unfortunately, this is an unacceptable solution because the four triangles created by these moves are not equilateral. After spending 5 to 10 minutes on the problem, many problem solvers give up. A correct solution requires that the problem solver use three dimensions rather than just two—that is, the problem solver must change his representation of the problem givens and

allowable operators. For example, you can construct a pyramid with one equilateral triangle as a base and three equilateral triangles as sides.

This example points out several challenges to (or constraints on) the straightforward model of problem solving presented in Table 1. First, humans often distort the problem to be consistent with their expectations. For example, a problem solver may encode the term *equilateral triangle* as *triangle*, since most puzzle problems involve general shapes such as square, circle, triangle. Thus, the process of comprehending each of the propositions in the problem-as-presented can involve distorting the problem. Second, humans focus on inappropriate aspects of the problem. For example, a problem solver may make the assumption that the problem must be solved in two-dimensional space rather than in three dimensions. This approach to the problem puts blinders on the problem solver's search for solution. Third, the problem representation changes during problem solving. As the problem solver sees that the problem-as-represented is difficult to solve, the problem solver can change the representation to allow for more kinds of operators, such as moving the sticks in three dimensions or breaking the sticks. Fourth, the problem solver may apply procedures rigidly. For example, if the problem solver has just solved a series of geometry puzzle problems that each involve constructing diagonals, the problem solver is likely to apply a similar procedure in this problem. Fifth, problem solving involves insight, intuition, and creativity. In this problem, some problem solvers may report having "aha" experiences in which the pieces of the problem fit together. Sixth, the control of the problem-solving process is influenced by the problem solver's beliefs about problem solving. A problem solver who believes that all problems are solved within 5 minutes will give up if he or she has not solved the problem within 5 minutes. As you can see, the first three observations focus mainly on representation and the last three focus mainly on solution processes.

The straightforward analysis of problem solving appears to require some modifications in light of these six observations and corresponding research findings. To the extent that findings contradict the straightforward information-processing model, they constitute challenges to applying the model to human problem solving. Similarly, when Gilhooly (1982) compared a simple information-processing model with data from a number of studies on thinking, he concluded that while useful up to a point, it could not cover all the data, and would require replacement by a more elaborate model. The next section examines these six challenges to the model of problem solving summarized in Table 1.

2. CONSTRAINTS ON A MODEL OF HUMAN NONADVERSARY PROBLEM SOLVING

2.1. Humans Systematically Distort the Problem to be Consistent With Prior Knowledge

When a person is verbally presented with a problem, the first step may be to translate the words of the problem into some internal cognitive representation. The process of going from words to mental representation involves more than straightforward decoding of the words; it also involves using one's prior knowledge. One kind of prior knowledge is knowledge of problem types or what Mayer (1982, 1987) has called "schematic knowledge."

For example, Riley, Greeno, and Heller (1982) asked elementary school children to listen to an arithmetic word problem and then repeat it. Errors in immediate recall may be used to diagnose possible encoding errors. For example, one problem was:

Joe has three marbles.
Tom has five more marbles than Joe.
How many marbles does Tom have?

One of the most common errors in recall was to change a sentence that asserted a relation into a sentence that assigned a value to a variable. For example, when this happened, the second sentence would be recalled as "Tom has five marbles."

Corresponding results have been obtained in adults. Mayer (1982) read a series of algebra story problems to adults and asked them to recall them from memory. For example, one problem was as follows:

A river steamer travels 36 miles downstream in the same time that it travels 24 miles upstream. The steamer's engines drive in still water at a rate of 12 miles per hour more than the rate of the current. Find the rate of the current.

The most common error in recall was to change relational sentences into assignment sentences. When this happened in the river steamer problem, the second sentence was remembered as "The steamer goes 12 miles per hour in still water."

These kinds of results suggest that humans use schemas for representing sentences in story problems. Apparently, some people do not have as effective schemas for relational sentences as for assignment sentences. Thus, a relation is occasionally encoded as an assignment.

Similarly, humans may have a limited set of schemas for problem types. For example, Riley et al. (1982) identified three types of arithmetic word problems: cause/change problems (such as "Joe has 3 marbles. Tom gives him 5 more marbles. How many marbles does Joe have now?"), combination problems (such as "Joe has 3 marbles. Tom has 5 marbles. How many do they have altogether?"), and comparison problems (such as "Joe has 3 marbles. Tom has 5 more marbles than Joe. How many marbles does Tom have?"). Although all three problem types require the same kinds of arithmetic computation, young children found combination and comparison problems to be more difficult than cause/change. Results suggested a developmental trend in which students begin by interpreting each problem as a cause/change problem, and eventually learn to discriminate among problem types.

Mayer (1982) and Hinsley, Hayes, and Simon (1977) obtained similar results with older problem solvers. For example, Mayer (1982) found that when students erred in recalling a problem, they tended to change it from an uncommon version to a more typical version of the problem. Hinsley et al. presented an ambiguous problem (about cars driving along intersecting roads) that could be interpreted as a distance-rate-time problem or a triangle problem; when subjects made mistakes they tended to misread information in a problem in a way that was consistent with their schema. For example, one subject who interpreted the problem as a "triangle problem" misread "4 minutes" as "4 miles" and assumed this was the length of a leg of the triangle.

In summary, problem solvers use their prior knowledge—such as schematic knowledge—to guide their interpretation of the presented problem. This process can result in distortions that change the problem to be more consistent with the problem solver's prior knowledge. Distortions in the representational process can lead to the problem solver's working on a problem that is different from the one that was actually presented.

2.2. Humans Focus on Inappropriate Aspects of the Problem

When a problem is presented in words, a problem solver may represent the givens, goals, and operators in a way that is consistent with the problem statement but which limits the process of problem solution. The problem solver, for example, may place limits on the problem-solving operators that were not part of the problem statement or may define the goal or given state in a narrower way than is necessary.

For example, consider the bird problem presented by Posner (1973, pp. 150–151):

Two train stations are 50 miles apart. At 2 P.M. one Saturday afternoon two trains start toward each other, one from each station, Just as the trains pull out of the stations, a bird springs into the air in front of the first train and flies ahead to the front of the second train. When the bird reaches the second train it turns back and flies toward the first train. The bird continues to do this until the trains meet. If both trains travel at the rate of 25 miles per hour and the bird flies at 100 miles per hour, how many miles will the bird have flown before the trains meet?

The problem solver may represent the goal of the problem as determining the sum of the distances that the bird flies on each trip between the trains. In contrast, the problem solver may represent the goal of the problem as determining the amount of time the bird flies and then converting that to a measure of miles flown. The former representation leads to much difficulty, while the latter makes the problem simple.

As another example, consider the old monk problem presented by Hayes (1978, p. 178):

Once there was a monk who lived in a monastery at the foot of a mountain. Every year the monk made a pilgrimage to the top of the mountain to fast and pray. He would start out on the mountain path at 6 A.M., climbing and resting as the spirit struck him, but making sure that he reached the shrine at exactly 6 o'clock that evening. He then prayed and fasted all night. At exactly 6 A.M. the next day, he began to descend the mountain path, resting here and there along the way, but making sure that he reached his monastery again by 6 P.M. of that day.

Given this information, your job is to prove or disprove the following assertion: Every time the monk makes his pilgrimage there is always some point on the mountain path, perhaps different on each trip, that the monk passes at the same time when he is climbing up as when he is climbing down.

One way to represent this problem is to think of the monk climbing up from 6 A.M. to 6 P.M. on one day and climbing down from 6 A.M. to 6 P.M. on the next day. In contrast, you could think of the problem as one monk climbing up and one climbing down on the same day, both beginning at 6 A.M. and ending at 6 P.M. Although the former representation leads to great difficulty, the latter makes clear that the ascending and descending paths must cross at some time during the day.

The wording of a problem can affect a problem solver's tendency to represent the problem in a useful way. For example, Maier and Burke (1967) found that most subjects missed the following problem:

A man bought a horse for $60 and sold it for $70. Then he bought it back again for $80 and sold it for $90. How much did he make in the horse business?

In contrast, all subjects correctly answered the problem when it was worded as follows:

> A man bought a white horse for $60 and sold it for $70. Then he bought a black horse for $80 and sold it for $90. How much money did he make in the horse business?

As you can see, when subjects are encouraged to represent the problem as two separate transactions, they perform better than when they represent it as a series of three transactions on the same horse.

Finally, consider the nine-dot problem, in which you are given nine dots arranged as below:

Your job is to draw four straight lines, without lifting your pencil from the paper, so that each dot is touched by one of the lines.

Adams (1974) suggests that problem solvers represent this problem in a way that creates "conceptual blocks." For example, some problem solvers represent the problem as saying that the lines cannot go outside the square, i.e., they create a self-imposed boundary or limit on acceptable solutions. In contrast, the correct answer requires drawing lines that extend beyond the boundaries of the square. In an important series of experiments summarized by Weisberg (1986), simply telling problem solvers to go outside the square did not make the problem trivially easy. Thus, helping students not to focus on inappropriate aspects of the problem does not ensure that they will immediately solve the problem.

In summary, the initial representation that a problem solver creates can limit the subsequent search process. Thus, initial representation is not a trivial or automatic process, but rather a crucial step that can affect the solution process. There may be several forms for representing the givens, goals, and operators; each may be consistent with the problem statement, but some may limit the ensuing search process.

2.3. Humans Change the Problem Representation During Problem Solving

Once a problem has been translated from words into some internal representation, the problem representation does not necessarily remain static during the ensuing problem solution process. As the search process progresses, the problem solver may reformulate the original representation of the problem. Thus, representation and solution are interactive processes that are influenced by one another.

Duncker's (1945) tumor problem provides a classic example of how problem solving requires successive reformulations of the problem. Consider the following problem:

> Given a human being with an inoperable stomach tumor, and rays that destroy organic tissue at sufficient intensity, by what procedure can one free him of the tumor by these rays and at the same time avoid destroying the healthy tissue that surrounds it?

Duncker (1945) presents the thinking-aloud record (or protocol) of a subject who is solving the tumor problem, which is presented in abbreviated form below:

1. Send rays through the esophagus.
2. Desensitize the healthy tissue by means of chemical injection.
3. Expose the tumor by operating.
4. One ought to decrease the intensity of the rays on their way; for example— would this work?—turn the rays on at full strength only after the tumor has been reached.
5. One should swallow something inorganic (which would allow passage of the rays) to protect the healthy stomach walls.
6. Either the rays must enter the body or the tumor must come out. Perhaps one could alter the location of the tumor— but how? Through pressure? No.
7. Introduce a cannula.
8. Move the tumor toward the exterior.
9. The intensity ought to be variable.
10. Adaptation of healthy tissue by previous weak application of the rays.
11. I see no more than two possibilities: either to protect the body or to make the rays harmless.

12. Somehow divert . . . diffuse rays . . . disperse . . . stop! Send a broad and weak bundle of rays through a lens in such a way that the tumor lies at the focal point and thus receives intense radiation.

In this example, Duncker notes that the subject continually changes how he represents the givens and goals of the problem. The subject seems to deal with general or functional representations of the goal before moving on to specific solutions. For example, the subject deals with general goals, such as "avoid contact between rays and healthy tissue," which suggest more specific goals, such as "displace tumor toward surface," which suggest specific solutions, such as "use pressure." The subject seems to move from one general representation to another, including "avoid contact between rays and healthy tissue," "desensitize healthy tissue," and "lower intensity of the rays on their way through the healthy tissue." It is through reformulating this general representation of the goal that the subject comes to represent the goal as "give weak intensity in the periphery and concentrate in the tumor," which leads to the specific solution of "use lens."

According to Duncker, problem solving does not involve applying solution procedures to one's specific representation of the problem. Instead, the problem representation is continually changing, moving from general descriptions of the goal and givens to more specific descriptions. The process of problem solution is not a phase of problem solving that follows neatly after the problem has been represented; instead, problem solution is tied to the process of successively reformulating the problem representation.

2.4. Humans Apply Procedures Rigidly and Inappropriately

Once a person has acquired a set of well-practiced procedures, these can be applied to many problems. However, well-learned procedures can be misapplied, i.e, used in situations where they are not appropriate or where they should be modified. Rigidity in problem solving occurs when the problem solver applies well-practiced but inappropriate procedures.

A classic example of rigidity in problem solving comes from the Luchins (1942) water jar problems. Suppose that you are given three empty jars of various sizes and an unlimited supply of water; your job is to use these jars to produce a certain amount of water. For example, if you are given empty jars of 21, 127, and 3 units each and asked to produce 100 units of water, you could fill the 127-jar and scoop out 21 and 3 and 3. If you were given 14, 163, and 25 and asked to produce 99, you could fill the 163 and scoop out 14 and 25 and 25. If you were given 18, 43, and 10 and asked to get 5 you could fill the 43 and scoop out 18 and 10 and 10. If you were given 9, 42, and 6 and asked to get 21, you could fill the 42 and scoop out 9 and 6 and 6. If you were given 20 and 59 and 4, and asked to get 31, you could fill the 59 and scoop out 20 and then 4 and 4. Now, suppose that the next problem is to get 20 units of water using jars of size 23, 49, and 3. Luchins found that most students used the procedure, fill the 49 and subtract 23 and 3 and 3. In contrast, a simpler solution is to fill the 23 and scoop out 3—a procedure used by most students who do not receive the previous five problems. These results suggest that past use of a procedure (such as the $b - a - 2c$ procedure for the water jar problems) can blind the problem solver to more efficient, but less frequently used, procedures (such as $a - c$ for the sixth problem).

Another example of rigid application of procedures occurs when students use the keyword approach to solving arithmetic word problems (Briars & Larkin, 1984; Mayer, 1987). In the keyword approach, children add the numbers in a problem when it contains an expression such as "altogether" and subtract the smaller from the larger number in a problem when it contains a word such as "difference." For example, consider the following problem:

John has 5 marbles. Susan has 3 more marbles than John. How many do they have all together?

A child using the keyword approach would carry out the procedure, 5 plus 3 equals 8. As you can see, blind application of procedures that worked previously in similar situations can lead to errors on new problems.

In summary, automaticity of problem-solving procedures can lead to rigidity in the problem solution process. Although a problem solver may know how to apply a given operator, the problem solver may not know the conditions under which it is or is not appropriate to apply the operator. Humans may tend to select procedures that are familiar, well practiced, or just used in similar problems—even when such procedures are not appropriate.

2.5. Humans Are Intuitive and Insightful and Creative

In some cases, when a problem solver is presented with a novel problem, the problem solver must generate a creative solution. A novel (or nonroutine) problem is one that the problem solver has never seen before, and a creative solution is an action that the problem solver has never used before. Where does a creative solution come from? According to behaviorist theories of problem solving, the problem solver generalizes from a similar problem or engages in random solution attempts (Weisberg, 1986). According to Gestalt theories of problem solving, the problem solver must have insight into the problem, i.e., see how the parts of the problem fit together in new ways (Katona, 1940; Kohler, 1925; Wertheimer, 1959). Thus, for behaviorist theories the same processes are involved in solving routine and nonroutine problems, while for Gestalt theories, nonroutine (or creative) problem solving involves qualitatively different thinking than routine problem solving.

As an example of the role of insight, consider Wertheimer's (1959) parallelogram problem: Given a parallelogram of height h and base b, find the area. If you have already learned the formula for parallelograms, area = height × base, then this problem simply requires a blind application of the rule—what Wertheimer calls "reproductive thinking." In contrast, if you know how to find the area of a rectangle but you do not know how to find the area of a parallelogram, then this is a novel problem for you and requires a creative (insightful) solution. One insight is to see that the triangle on one side of the parallelogram can be cut off and placed on the other side, producing a rectangle with sides b and h. Since you know how to find the area of a rectangle, the problem is all but solved. Here, the problem solver has insight into the structure of parallelograms; that is, the problem solver sees the relationship between parallelograms and rectangles. Van Hiele (1986) argues that this kind of problem solving is based on intuitive thinking.

As another example, consider Polya's (1965, p. 2) pyramid problem:

Find the volume F of the frustrum of a right pyramid with square base, given the altitude h of the frustrum, the length a of a side of its upper base, and the length b of its lower base.

If you do not know the formula for finding the volume of the frustrum of a right pyramid, then this is a novel problem that requires a creative solution. Polya assumes, however, that you do know the formula for finding the volume of a pyramid. One insight is seeing that you could create the full pyramid by adding a smaller pyramid to the top of the frustrum; then, to get the volume of frustrum you could subtract the volume of the smaller pyramid from the volume of the full pyramid.

In summary, these examples point to role that insight plays in creative problem solving. Unfortunately, the Gestalt psychologists and even contemporary Gestalt-inspired theorists (Van Hiele, 1986) do not offer clear definitions of insight. However, these observations give some rationale for supposing that qualitatively different solution processes may be involved in routine versus nonroutine problems. For example, in a recent review, Weisberg (1986) offered a reasonable compromise between a "genius" view—which holds that creative problem solving is a mysterious and unanalyzable process—and the "behaviorist" view—which holds that the same processes are involved in routine and nonroutine problem solving; the compromise is that while routine and nonroutine problem solving may be different from one another, both can be studied and analyzed scientifically.

2.6. Humans Let Their Beliefs Guide Their Approach to Problem Solving

Finally, the sixth observation concerns the role of what Schoenfeld (1985a, b) calls "control" of the problem solution process. Humans decide which problems are the ones they should try to solve, which procedures to use, whether the procedures are working or need to be replaced, whether the problem is worth continued attention, etc. One kind of knowledge that affects the control of problem solving is the belief system of the problem solver. Beliefs about problem solving include ideas about what are reasonable ways to solve problems, when it is appropriate to stop working on a problem, etc.

Consider the following problem from Schoenfeld (1983, 1985a, b):

> You are given two intersecting straight lines and a point *P* on one of them. . . . Show how to construct, with straightedge and compass, a circle that is tangent to both lines and that has the point *P* as its point of tangency to one of them.

In Schoenfeld's study, no students ever derived a solution to the problem using mathematical proof. Instead, all students used trial-and-error construction; when they were asked why a particular construction works, they responded, "It just does."

Schoenfeld concluded that students believe "proof is worthless for discovery" and thus do not think of using proof even though they are capable of doing so. Schoenfeld (1985b, p. 372) lists three beliefs that many of his students seemed to possess:

> Belief 1: Formal mathematics has little or nothing to do with real thinking or problem solving. Corollary: Ignore it when you need to solve problems.
>
> Belief 2: Mathematics problems are always solved in less than 10 minutes, if they are solved at all. Corollary: Give up after 10 minutes.
>
> Belief 3: Only geniuses are capable of discovering or creating mathematics. Corollaries: If

you forget something . . . you won't be able to derive it on your own. Accept procedures at face value, and don't try to understand why they work.

Some other widely held beliefs of mathematical problem solvers (Silver, 1985) are the following: There is always one correct way to solve any mathematical problem; mathematics is not applicable to solving real-world problems; mathematics problems can be solved using only a few basic operations and can always be solved in only a few minutes.

As an example of how specific beliefs affect problem solving, consider the taxicab problem (Kahneman & Tversky, 1973; Shaughnessy, 1985; Tversky & Kahneman, 1980):

> A cab was involved in a hit-and-run accident at night. Two cab companies, the Green and the Blue, operate in the city . . . 85% of the cabs are Green and 15% are Blue. A witness identified the cab as a Blue cab. The court tested his ability to identify cabs . . . the witness made correct identifications in 80% of the cases and erred in 20% of the cases. What is the probability that the cab involved in the accident was Blue rather than Green?

Shaughnessy (1985, p. 404) summarizes a study in which some students say that the probability is 100% that a Blue cab was involved in the accident. One subject "just believed it was a Blue cab"; another subject said, "Oh, the witness was right. It was a Blue cab." These subjects simply do not seem to believe in the concept of probability; for them, events either happen or don't happen.

In summary, the problem solver's beliefs about problem solving can affect the process of problem solution. The persistence of the problem solver, the problem solver's selection of solution procedures, and even the problem solver's decision to approach a certain problem are influenced by the problem solver's beliefs. This observation points out that problem solving involves more than purely cognitive events.

3. CONCLUSION

The foregoing examples have provided some challenges to the straightforward picture of problem solving suggested by the information-processing model. More specifically, these examples have called into question four implicit premises of the information-processing model summarized in Table 1: atomization, componentialization, mechanization, and concretization.

The first premise concerns the atomization of problem-solving elements. In the information-processing approach, the problem is represented as a given state, a goal state, and a set of operators that can produce intermediate states. The atoms in this analysis of the problem are states and actions for transforming states. These can be clearly specified for well-defined problems. However, our examples show that determining the atoms for ill-defined problems is often the crucial part of problem solving rather than the starting point. Further, consistent with the "mental chemistry" theory, the atoms may change as they are combined during the problem-solving processes.

The second premise concerns componentialization of problem-solving processes. In the information-processing approach, problems are first translated into internal representations; then, operators are sequentially applied to create a series of new problem states. However, our examples show that representation and solution are interactive processes; i.e., the problem representation is continually reformulated during the process of problem solution.

The third premise concerns the mechanization of problem solution processes. In the information-processing approach, a problem-solving strategy such as means–ends analysis is used to guide the solution process. This is an algorithm that requires no insight, no invention, no intuition. Yet our examples show that many problems require general strategies that are much less algorithmic and more intuitive than means–ends analysis.

The fourth premise concerns the concretization of problem-solving states. In the information-processing approach, each concrete action results in movement from one concrete state to another. However, our examples have shown that thinking sometimes occurs at a general or a functional level rather than at the level of specific problem states. Problem solvers may sometimes find a functional solution before hitting upon a specific course of action.

Each of these four implicit premises underlying the information-processing approach must be carefully examined in light of our current understanding of human problem solving. It would be convenient if we could use the same framework to describe human and machine problem solving; for example, it would be convenient if an information-processing model inspired by, and implemented on, machines could also be applied to human problem solving. However, this chapter has shown some of the constraints that need to be considered before a unified theory of human and machine problem solving can be created.

ACKNOWLEDGMENT. Preparation of this chapter was supported by Grant MDR-8470248 from the National Science Foundation.

REFERENCES

Adams, J. L. (1974). *Conceptual blockbusting.* New York: Freeman.

Briars, D. J., & Larkin, J. H. (1984). An integrated model of skill in solving elementary word problems. *Cognition and Instruction, 1,* 245–296.

Duncker, K. (1945). On problem solving. *Psychological Monographs, 58*(5, Whole No. 270).

Gilhooly, K. J. (1982). *Thinking: Directed, undirected, and creative.* London: Academic Press.

Hayes, J. R. (1978). *Cognitive psychology: Thinking and creating.* Homewood, IL: Dorsey Press.

Hinsley, D., Hayes, J. R., & Simon, H. A. (1977). From words to equations. In P. Carpenter & M. Just (Eds.), *Cognitive processes in comprehension.* Hillsdale, NJ: Erlbaum.

Kahneman, D., & Tversky, A. (1973). On the psychology of prediction. *Psychological Review, 80,* 237–251.

Katona, G. (1940). *Organizing and memorizing.* New York: Columbia University Press.

Kittel, J. E. (1957). An experimental study of the effect of external direction during learning on transfer and retention of principles. *Journal of Educational Psychology, 48* 391–405.

Kohler, W. (1925). *The mentality of apes.* New York: Harcourt, Brace & World.

Luchins, A. S. (1942). Mechanization in problem solving. *Psychological Monographs, 54*(6, Whole No. 248).

Maier, N. R. F., & Burke, R. J. (1967). Response availability as a factor in problem-solving performance of males and females. *Journal of Personality and Social Psychology, 5,* 304–310.

Mayer, R. E. (1982). Memory for algebra story problems. *Journal of Educational Psychology, 74,* 199–216.

Mayer, R. E. (1983). *Thinking, problem solving, cognition.* New York: Freeman.

Mayer, R. E. (1987). Teachable aspects of problem solving. In D. Berger, K. Pezdek, & W. Banks (Eds.), *Applications of cognitive psychology.* Hillsdale, NJ: Erlbaum.

Newell, A., & Simon, H. A. (1972). *Human problem solving.* Englewood Cliffs, NJ: Prentice-Hall.

Poyla, G. (1965). *Mathematical discovery* (Vol. 2), New York: Wiley.

Posner, M. I. (1973). *Cognition.* Glenview, IL: Scott, Foresman.

Riley, M. S., Greeno, J. G., & Heller, J. I. (1982). Development of children's problem-solving ability in arithmetic. In H. Ginsberg (Ed.), *The development of mathematical thinking.* New York: Academic Press.

Schoenfeld, A. H. (1983). Beyond the purely cognitive: Belief systems, social cognitions, and metacognitions as driving forces in intellectual performance. *Cognitive Science, 7,* 329–363.

Schoenfeld, A. H. (1985a). Metacognitive and epistomological issues in mathematical understanding. In E. A. Silver (Ed.), *Teaching and learning mathematical problem solving: Multiple research perspectives.* Hillsdale, NJ: Erlbaum.

Schoenfeld, A. H. (1985b). *Mathematical problem solving.* Orlando, FL: Academic Press.

Shaughnessy, J. M. (1985). Problem-solving derailers: The influence of misconceptions on problem-solving performance. In E. A. Silver (Ed.), *Teaching and learning mathematical problem solving: Multiple research perspectives.* Hillsdale, NJ: Erlbaum.

Silver, E. A. (1985). Research on teaching mathematical problem solving: Some underrepresented themes and needed directions. In E. A. Silver (Ed.), *Teaching and learning mathematical problem solving: Multiple research perspectives.* Hillsdale, NJ: Erlbaum.

Tversky, A., & Kahneman, D. (1980). Causal schemata in judgment under uncertainty. In M. Fishbein (Ed.), *Progress in social psychology.* Hillsdale, NJ: Erlbaum.

Van Hiele, P. M. (1986). *Structure and insight.* Orlando, FL: Academic Press.

Wason, P. C. (1966). Reasoning. In B. M. Foss (Ed.), *New horizons in psychology.* Harmondsworth, UK: Penguin.

Weisberg, R. (1986). *Creativity: Genius and other myths.* New York: Freeman.

Wertheimer, M. (1959). *Productive thinking.* New York: Harper & Row.

17

John H. Flavell

Young Children's Understanding of Thinking and Consciousness

A developmental psychologist shows a 5-year-old a candy box and asks her what is in it. "Candy," says the child. When she then opens up the box, however, she discovers to her surprise that it actually contains crayons rather than candy. What will a naive child who has not opened the box think is in it, the experimenter now inquires. "Candy!" says the child, grinning at the trick. The researcher repeats the procedure with a 3-year-old. The response to the first question is the expected "candy," but the response to the second is surprising: "crayons." Even more surprising, the child also says he himself had initially thought crayons would be in the box. Unlike the 5-year-old, the 3-year-old shows no evidence of understanding that either he or other people could hold a belief that is false.

Findings such as this stud a new and exciting area of cognitive-developmental research concerning the ontogenesis of our knowledge and beliefs about the mental world—our folk psychology or naive theory of mind. More than was true of earlier metacognitive and social-cognitive approaches to the same general problem, this new approach probes children's developing conceptions of the most basic components of the mind, such as beliefs and desires, and children's knowledge of how these components affect and are affected by perceptual inputs and behavioral outputs. In just a few short years, this fast-growing area has spawned scores of research articles and a number of book- and monograph-length treatments.[1]

DEVELOPMENTAL HIGHLIGHTS

During infancy, children come to view people very differently from other objects. They see people as *compliant agents*, that is, as kindred creatures who move under their own power (agency) and are responsive to the infants' requests and other communications (compliance). Infants also acquire some sense of intentionality, recognizing that people's behavior, unlike that of objects, makes reference to or is "about" something other than itself. Children demonstrate some capacity for empathy by the end of infancy, suggesting that by this point they have begun to construe people as experiencers as well as agents.

During the early preschool years, children acquire the basic distinction between mental and physical events. For example, they can distinguish between an imagined dog and a real dog. They show a beginning understanding of percepts, knowledge, desires, emotions, and their interrelations. Thus, they know that another person viewing from a different position may not be able to see an object that they presently see, and for that reason might not know it is there. Also, they recognize that people are likely to feel sad or happy depending on whether their desires are fulfilled. Young preschoolers also develop pretense skills, and the ability to interpret as pretense the make-believe of other people.

Later in the preschool period, children seem to acquire a rudimentary mental-representational conception of the mind. That is, they begin to sense that people form and act upon mental representations of reality, representations that may not portray reality correctly. This newly acquired conception makes it possible for them to understand false beliefs, as in the foregoing candy-crayons task. Similarly, it enables them to think of deceptive or illusory objects and situations as appearing or seeming to be one thing to a perceiver while simultaneously really being something different. For example, older preschoolers readily understand that a straight object viewed through a distorting lens looks bent (i.e., is perceptually represented as being bent) but is really straight.

Subsequent to the preschool years, children further elaborate their understanding of people's minds as mental-representational devices. For example, they increasingly realize that how people represent what they perceive will be influenced by the nature and quality of the perceptual information they receive and their prior knowledge and experience. In addition, school-age children endow themselves and other people with enduring personality traits, come to understand second- as well as first-order beliefs (i.e., beliefs about beliefs), and show numerous metacognitive acquisitions, such as knowledge about memory and memory strategies.

THINKING

Most of the research done in this area thus far has focused on children's understanding of mental states, such as beliefs, desires, knowledge, emotions, and intentions. In contrast, there has been little investigation of children's knowledge about mental *activities*, that is, mental things that one could be said to do rather than have.[2] The paradigmatic mental activity is that of *thinking*, defined here very broadly as attending to, thinking of, or being conscious of anything. In a recent series of studies,[3] my colleagues and I assessed preschoolers' understanding of thinking by testing their ability to distinguish thinking of something from seeing it, acting on it, talking about it, and knowing it—four activities or states that often co-occur with thinking and that young children might therefore confuse with thinking. Some distinctive characteristics of thinking become evident when we contrast it with these four. First, in contrast to knowing something, thinking of or about something tends to be an episodic, on-and-off activity rather than a continuous, enduring state. Second, unlike physical action and talking (aloud), thinking is covert. Third, unlike seeing and other perceptual activities, thinking can and often does proceed in the absence of any relevant sensory input.

Our studies revealed that young children (3 to 4 years of age) know at least enough about thinking to be able to distinguish it from seeing, talking, acting, and knowing under some circumstances. One of the studies showed that even young 3-year-olds could accept and apparently understand that a person could be thinking of one thing while looking at or physically acting on something else. In another study, they gave evidence of believing that a person whose eyes and ears were covered could nevertheless think about both present and absent objects. In a third study, one experimenter showed another experimenter (and the subject) a trick box that appeared to be empty when first opened but had money in it when reopened and asked the second experimenter how the money got in there. The second experimenter said, "That's a hard question. Hmm. Give me a minute." She then turned away from the box and looked stereotypically pensive, much in the manner of Rodin's *The Thinker*. The 3- and 4-year-old subjects were asked, "What is she *doing* right now?" Interestingly, almost all the 4-year-olds said "thinking," even though that word had not previously been mentioned in the testing session. Although only a few of the 3-year-olds gave this answer, they did show some understanding subsequently. That is, on further trials of this kind, they usually replied in the affirmative when asked if the second experimenter was thinking about the problem stimulus, but in the negative when asked if she was seeing it, talking about it, or touching it. Similarly, in an unpublished study by Rosenkrantz,[4] almost all of a sample of 3-year-olds identified the more pensive looking of two people engaged in a drawing task as the one who was "thinking."[5] Our finding that children as young as 36 months of age are capable under some circumstances of viewing thinking as different from talking goes strongly counter to Piaget's claim that even children as old as 6 or 7 years of age often construe thinking as synonymous with speech.[6] Finally, the results of three other studies in this series suggest that most 4-year-olds do not treat "thinking about" and "knowing about" as synonymous. Rather, they seem quite willing to say—often correctly, but not always—that a person does not know something but is currently thinking about it, or does know it but is not currently thinking about it.

STREAM OF CONSCIOUSNESS

Of course, there is more to learn about thinking, broadly defined, than that it is an internal activity distinguishable from perceiving, acting, talking, and knowing. One of its most central and interesting characteristics is its tendency to flow incessantly in a conscious person—the continuous "stream of consciousness" about which William James[7] and many other people have written. I have just cited evidence that preschoolers will usually infer that a person is thinking when the visible evidence for this activity is clear and strong, as when the person has just been given a problem to solve and looks stereotypically reflective. Would they also infer a continuous stream of mental content or activity when there is no perceptual input or behavioral output to suggest it, for example, when a person is just sitting quietly, with nothing to do or look at? My colleagues and I recently conducted three studies to find out.[8]

In the first study, children (of 3, 4, and 6 to 7 years) and adults were trained and tested as follows. One experimenter (call her Mary) said that last night while she was deeply asleep and not dreaming, her mind was "empty of thoughts and ideas," and pointed to an empty "thought bubble" to represent her empty mind. However, she said that on her way to school this morning, she had had some thoughts and ideas, and after describing them, she pointed to a thought bubble containing three asterisks to illustrate this nonempty state of her mind. Then, at the other experimenter's request, Mary went across the room "to wait for a few minutes." She sat quietly in a chair with her back to the subject and facing a blank wall. The other experimenter then said to the subject: "Mary is just sitting there waiting, isn't she? How about her mind right now? Is she having some thoughts and ideas, or is her mind empty of thoughts and ideas? Point to the picture [thought bubble] that shows how her mind is while she is waiting there." There were two such Waiting trials in the testing session, given in alternation with a Looking trial (Mary looking at a picture) and a Problem-Solving trial (Mary trying to figure something out). We reasoned that subjects who believed in an ever-present stream of consciousness would opt for the thought bubble with the three asterisks on the Waiting trials as well as on the other two trials. We found a striking increase with age in the tendency to show this pattern of attribution. For example, the percentages of subjects attributing some thoughts and ideas on both Waiting trials were 5% for 3-year-olds, 20% for 4-year-olds, 55% for 6- to 7-year-olds, and 95% for adults. In contrast, the age increases for the Looking and Problem-Solving trials were much less marked, with 65% or more of the subjects in even the youngest groups attributing ideation on these trials.

Studies 2 and 3 used only 4-year-olds as subjects. In Study 2, we strongly emphasized that "thoughts and ideas" should include idle, undirected ones as well as directed ones. Nevertheless, the mean percentage of correct Waiting trials was similar to that found in Study 1 for this age group. In addition, 62% of the children said that if she tried, the second experimenter would be able to keep her mind "completely empty of all thoughts and ideas" for 3 min (a period of time with which subjects had been familiarized just previously). Similarly, in Study 3, 4-year-olds tended to say that the mind of a waiting person was "not doing anything" rather than "doing something." This was true when the waiting individual was the child subject as well as when it was the experimenter.

Consistent with this last result, in a series of current studies, we are repeatedly finding that 5-year-olds are inclined to deny that they had been having any thoughts just previously, even though experiences we had given them just previously ensured that they must have been thinking. In contrast, children of 7 to 8 years are proving to be much better introspectors.

CONCLUDING SPECULATIONS

Our studies suggest that, although they know something about thinking, preschoolers are not aware of the continuous, nonstop nature of mental activity. There are at least three reasons why this awareness might develop relatively late. First, as was the case in our Waiting trials, there is often no visible evidence to suggest that other people are thinking, because no problem has just been presented to them and

they show no pensive facial expressions or behaviors. Second, adults probably find few reasons to call children's attention to the ceaseless flow of mental content, and there is no single common term for it (in English, at least) for the adults to use or the children to learn. Finally, our data and common observation suggest that preschoolers are relatively lacking in the disposition or ability to reflect on the contents of their own consciousness.

How might children come to discover the stream of consciousness? One possibility is that they first notice it during those relatively rare periods when they are awake but not engaged perceptually or motorically with the external world, such as perhaps just prior to falling asleep or just after waking up. Some of the trains of thought that occur at such times might have two properties that would facilitate this awareness. On the one hand, these thoughts may be charged with negative affect and therefore impossible not to notice (e.g., worries about monsters). On the other hand, they may persist as salient mental content despite the child's fervent wish that they go away. More generally, persistent worries and other abiding preoccupations may be among the first examples of the stream of consciousness that children notice.

In conclusion, our results suggest that young children's conception of themselves and other people as mental creatures may be very different from that of older children and adults, despite their considerable knowledge about the mental world. Adults and older children tend to assume that mental activity is essentially continuous in time, with *something*—one thing or another—going on all the time in a waking mind. Young children, in contrast, may view mental activity more as an on-and-off, episodic affair. They may assume that the mind is active only when it has some job to do—when there is some stimulus to notice or some problem to solve. When the mind has nothing to do, they may assume that it does nothing, much as our bodies do nothing when we are physically inactive. For decades, psychologists have asked what mental content young children will attribute to other people—for example, whether children will egocentrically misattribute their own perspectives to others. Our data suggest that the question should sometimes be whether children are likely to attribute to others any mental content at all, egocentric or otherwise.

ACKNOWLEDGMENTS

The author acknowledges the valuable assistance of Frances Green and Eleanor Flavell in conducting this research and the support of Grant MH-40687 from the National Institute of Mental Health.

NOTES

1. See. e.g., L. J. Moses and M. J. Chandler, Traveler's Guide to children's theories of mind, *Psychological Inquiry, 3,* 286–301 (1992); J. Perner, *Understanding the Representational Mind* (MIT Press, Cambridge, MA, 1991); H. M. Wellman, *The Child's Theory of Mind* (MIT Press, Cambridge, MA, 1990).

2. This *do–have* distinction is owed to R. D'Andrade, A folk model of the mind, in *Cultural Models in Language and Thought,* D. Holland and N. Quinn, Eds. (Cambridge University Press, New York, 1987). For other work on children's understanding of mental activity, see the research by Wellman and colleagues cited in J. D. Woolley and H. M. Wellman, *Origin and truth: Young children's understanding of the relation between mental states and the physical world,* unpublished manuscript, University of Texas at Austin (1992).

3. J. H. Flavell, F. L. Green, and E. R. Flavell, *Young children's knowledge about thinking,* unpublished manuscript, Stanford University, Stanford, CA (1992).

4. S. L. Rosenkrantz, *Children's recognition of the facial expressions associated with cognitive states,* unpublished manuscript, Stanford University, Stanford, CA (1991).

5. For results similar to those of Rosenkrantz, see S. Baron-Cohen and P. Cross, Reading the eyes: Evidence for the role of perception in the development of a theory of mind, *Mind and Language, 7,* 172–186 (1992).

6. J. Piaget, *The Child's Conception of the World* (Routledge and Kegan Paul, London, 1929).

7. W. James, *The Principles of Psychology,* Vol. 1 (Henry Holt, New York, 1890).

8. J. H. Flavell, F. L. Green, and E. R. Flavell, Children's understanding of the stream of consciousness, *Child Development* (in press).

18

Daniel M. Wegner
and David J. Schneider

Mental Control: The War of the Ghosts in the Machine

Sometimes it feels as though we can control our minds. We catch ourselves looking out the window when we should be paying attention to someone talking, for example, and we purposefully return our attention to the conversation. Or we reset our minds away from the bothersome thought of an upcoming dental appointment to focus on anything we can find that make us less nervous. Control attempts such as these can meet with success, leaving us feeling the masters of our consciousness. Yet at other times we drift back to gaze out the window or to think again of the dentist's chair, and we are left to wonder whether mental control is real—and, if it is, how we might exercise it effectively.

THE NATURE OF MENTAL CONTROL

One way to approach this problem is to assume that mental control is a real phenomenon, ask people to exercise it, and see what happens. Some noteworthy regularities in the effects of mental control become evident on following this line of inquiry. This chapter is about experiments we have conducted in which people are asked to control their minds while they are describing the course of their thoughts. We begin by describing the course of our own thoughts.

A "Tumbling-Ground for Whimsies"

Mental control is connected to two of the most important controversial concepts in psychology—consciousness and the will. Even William James, a champion of the study of things mental, warned that consciousness has the potential to make psychology no more than a "tumbling-ground for whimsies" (1890, Vol. 1, p. 163). Psychology since James has echoed his concern. Although the idea of altogether abolishing consciousness from psychology only held sway at the peak of behaviorism, even after a cognitive revolution there remains a preference for the study of mind through its processes rather than its conscious content. The will, in turn, is relegated to the status of illusion by many—among them Gilbert Ryle, who called it the "ghost in the machine" (1949, p. 15). The question, then, of whether the will can operate upon consciousness is doubly troubling.

James held that we exert our wills by "effort of attention" (1890, Vol. 2, p. 562). He voiced the useful intuition that we do one thing as opposed to another by steering our consciousness. *How* we do this, however, is unclear. We appear to attend to one thing as opposed to another by—well, by just doing so. James's account only indicates that the willful movement of consciousness from one object to another feels like work, and that this movement can be contrasted with those cases in which our attention is drawn, seemingly without our effort, by forces beyond our will. Mental control is, in this light, one of the irreducible elements of conscious experience. This irreducibility is one of the puzzling aspects of mental control that has left those inclined to deal with this issue talking of ghosts and whimsies.

It is possible to study the operation of mental control in a useful way, however, without any further insight into this puzzle. One need only assume that there is a cognitive process responsible for activating and deactivating attentional mechanisms according to priorities that are reflected in conscious thoughts. A scientific understanding of this process does not require that we be able to see into it as we do it, any more than a science of movement requires that we have insight into the enervation of our muscles as we walk like a chicken. It is time to set aside the dissection of the conscious experience of willing, and study instead the observable circumstances and consequences of this experience.

There is one other feature of mental control that has given it a reputation as a phantom of the ganglia. Mental efforts sometimes fail, and we do not know enough about mental control to understand why this happens. Sometimes the right idea will not come, despite furrowed brows, squinted eyes, and all the deliberate concentration one can muster. This may not at first seem strange, because efforts of all sorts frequently fail. But we find it surprising because whereas the effort to make a thought appear on command sometimes does not work, seemingly similar physical efforts rarely fail in the physically healthy. It is odd to say that "I couldn't get it out of my mind" or "I couldn't concentrate on the idea," but it seems most peculiar to say that "I couldn't make my finger move."

Even mental control that is initially successful can subsequently falter. Unlike physical effort, which, once initiated typically suffers few indigenous interferences (i.e., other than from physical restraint), our thoughts seem remarkably capricious. On good days our thoughts are as precise as a hawk gathering small rodents, but more often our thoughts seem like fluttery butterflies that not only fail to stay put for long but are subject to the winds of competing thought. Try as we may, we cannot concentrate on reading a novel or solving an equation when there are interesting distractions nearby. Or we may struggle to make particular thoughts go away in the midst of a sleepless night, only to have them return all too soon. And it is something of a universal tragedy that when we attempt to reject thoughts of hot fudge sundaes from our minds while dieting, we must usually watch as they then march through our imaginations again and again.

The Aims of Mental Control

There are two general goals to which we aspire in controlling our minds: having something in mind, and not having it in mind. Psychology gives us many terms for each. Having something in mind is "thinking," "attending," "retrieving," "perceiving," "encoding," and so on; not having something in mind is "forgetting," "denying," "repressing," "avoiding," "filtering," and so forth. The activities in which we engage when we consciously attempt to achieve one of these states are most generally called "concentration" and "suppression," respectively. Although there are other potential goals for mental control—one, perhaps, for each mental operation people can perform—it is clear that these are most fundamental. If we could not concentrate or suppress, it seems there would be little else we could do to our minds.

Normally, when we are thinking of one thing, we are not thinking of something else. Cognitive psychologists have often held that this dual function of the process of attending suggests the operation of two subprocesses, one that brings items to attention and one that filters out everything else (e.g., Broadbent, 1958). The central idea here is that *both* processes must be operating at all times in order to keep one thing in our conscious attention. If we assume that mental control processes are simply willful versions of such automatic processes, then we can suggest that concentration and suppression are typically associated. In concentrating on X, we suppress not-X; by the same token, in suppressing X, we concentrate on not-X.

By this logic, the two processes are always simultaneous. The reason we have different names for them and experience them as distinct is that we try to do one at a time (and the other follows). So, for instance, we may try to concentrate on writing a book chapter (and suppress thoughts of other things, such as going swimming). Alternatively, we may try to suppress a thought, say, of smoking a cigarette (and concentrate on other things, such as eating). In either case, we are primarily aware of intending only one of the processes, but we nevertheless must use the other process as well in order to fulfill our intention. This is true because both processes are versions of the "effort of attention" described by James, and we cannot move attention toward something

without at the same time moving it away from something else.

The simultaneity of concentration and suppression suggests that there are two distinguishable forms of each process. First, there are primary and auxiliary forms of concentration; primary concentration is attending to something because we want to do so, whereas auxiliary concentration is attending to something because we wish to suppress attention to something else. In a similar vein, there are primary and auxiliary forms of suppression. Primary suppression is keeping attention away from something because we want to do so, whereas auxiliary suppression is keeping attention away as a means of concentrating on something else. Primary concentration is thus accompanied by an auxiliary suppression (as when one avoids thinking about the noise down the hall in order to study). And primary suppression brings with it an auxiliary concentration (as when one tries not to think of a broken romance by focusing on a television program.)

Our studies of mental control have centered on the case of primary suppression with auxiliary concentration. This is the form of mental control that people appear most anxious to have, in large part because lapses of suppression announce themselves intrusively. We know quite clearly when an unwanted thought returns to consciousness. In a sense, our plan to suppress marks the thought as something of which we must be wary, and its return is thus heralded by an immediate reorientation to the suppression problem. By contrast, when we merely try to concentrate, it is quite possible to lose sight of the plan and mentally drift away, for minutes or perhaps even days. The only sign that we have failed to concentrate occurs if we happen in our mental meandering to stumble across the concentration target. And even then, the concentration target and our earlier failure do not seem to burst into our minds with nearly the force of a returning unwanted thought.

The reason for examining suppression rather than concentration, in short, is not too far removed from the sheer love of sport. When people concentrate, the purpose of mental control is to maintain a line of thought. In a sense, one part of the mind is cheering on another. But when people suppress, the purpose of mental control is to challenge a line of thought. One part of the mind is set to defeat another. Skirmishes can break out on many mental fields of battle, and the most placid, unsuspecting states of mind can be ambushed from the blue by unwanted thoughts. Thought suppression is thus an occasion for mental conflict, a true war of the ghosts in the machine.

THE CASE OF THOUGHT SUPPRESSION

The fact that we sometimes suppress thoughts because they are painful is no surprise either to introspective laypeople or to readers of Freud. Sometimes mental pain seems as unbearable as its physical counterpart, and one does not have to be a committed hedonist to recognize that painful stimuli are typically avoided. Freud, of course, built much of his theory around such episodes. Although our work has not been much oriented toward Freudian ideas, he offered many masterful insights not only about the unconscious but the conscious part of mental life. We begin by considering his approach, and then turn to the basic problems of why people suppress, how they do it, what effect their efforts have, and how they might do it most competently.

Freud and Forgetting

Unfortunately, Freud was often most vague at the point where he should have been most precise, and it is hard to extract a consistent theory about the mental life from his work. This is especially true in the case of his accounts of suppression and repression. For example, it is commonly assumed that Freud made a sharp distinction between conscious "suppression" and unconscious "repression." In fact, he continuously and throughout his career used the terms interchangeably; furthermore, he never stated explicitly that repression referred only to pushing conscious material

into the unconscious (cf. Erdelyi & Goldberg, 1979).

Freud preferred a broad definition of repression: "[T]he essence of repression lies simply in the function of rejecting and keeping something out of consciousness" (1915/1957, p. 105). It is certainly true that many (indeed, most) of the examples he used invoke a stronger and more popular sense of the term, involving the unconscious, but it is also true that he was generally perfectly explicit that removing cathexis (roughly, attention, in this context) from an idea was a sufficient condition for repression, defined as above. As far as we know, the closest he ever came to distinguishing between suppression and repression came in a long footnote in Chapter 7 of *The Interpretation of Dreams:* "For instance, I have omitted to state whether I attribute different meanings to the words 'suppressed' and 'repressed.' It should have been clear, however, that the latter lays more stress than the former upon the fact of attachment to the unconscious" (Freud, 1900/1953, Vol. 5, p. 606).

Psychoanalysts have now focused for many years on the notion of unconscious repression to the exclusion of simple suppression. Although Freud himself can surely be faulted for promoting this particular line of orthodoxy in psychoanalytic theorizing, his primary concern was in how we keep former ideas from recurring. This activity could involve suppression alone, and certainly need not depend on either unconscious motivation or memory erasure, the central features of classical repression. Each of these features of the concept of repression has served in its own way as a theoretical albatross.

The dogma of unconscious motivation, for example, requires that research on repression must typically arrive at the scene after the fact. We cannot know beforehand exactly what unconscious motive might be energized, nor when that motive might act, nor which particular conscious thought it might choose as a repression target; these things are all deeply unconscious. So, according to psychoanalysis, we must typically wait until after a repression has happened and then bring in the research crew to sift the ashes. For this reason, repression has seldom been approached as a cognitive process, and the research in this area has typically settled instead on the far weaker tactic of isolating individuals who tend to repress, and examining their other personality characteristics. This circuitous avenue of inquiry has met with some success (see, e.g., Davis, 1987), but of course cannot clarify the repression process itself.

Classical repression theory does make the strong prediction that memory can be erased, however, so much research has focused on this claim. It is in this domain that the Freudian notion of repression has received its most stunning disconfirmations. Holmes (1974) reviewed a long list of studies of repression and found no clear evidence for the occurrence of forgetting motivated by ego threat. Erdelyi (1985) sympathetically reviewed a series of his own and others' studies of hypermnesia (the retrieval of more information from memory than was retrievable at an earlier point), and concluded that no fully convincing demonstration had yet been made. Although there are many clinical cases of amnesia (e.g., Breznitz, 1983; Rapaport, 1959), and a variety of indications that physical illness or injury can render memory inaccessible (e.g., Yarnell & Lynch, 1973), there is little indication that the widespread and frequent memory losses Freud envisioned are at all so common in daily life. Studies of hypnotic amnesia (see Kihlstrom, 1983) and directed forgetting (e.g., Geiselman, Bjork, & Fishman, 1983) show instead that certain memory processes under voluntary control (e.g., the avoidance of rehearsal at encoding) may on occasion contribute to the occurrence of motivated forgetting.

What all this means is that the topic of thought suppression per se is relatively neglected and misunderstood. Consciously keeping a thought from consciousness is the task of suppression, and we know comparatively little about how such an activity proceeds. Do people control their minds, not by forgetting, but by failing to access thoughts that are nonetheless accessible in memory? Such "selective inattention" could perform many of the tasks that psychoanalysts have counted on unconscious repression to accomplish. Indeed, several theorists have argued that inattention is all we need to avoid painful affect (e.g., Klinger, 1982). One need not forget a thought forever, and also forget the forgetting, merely to remove the thought from one's focus of attention. All that is required is thinking of something else, and continuing to do so.

Why Do We Suppress?

There are many possible answers to the question of why a thought might be unwanted. Freud suggested several answers, but offered no unified picture of why people suppress. His most general theme was that those instinctually driven ideas that fail the censor's and/or superego's tests of acceptability will be suppressed. In Freud's earlier writing, he stressed the unacceptability of ideas as a direct motive for repression, whereas in his later work he was more inclined to stress the anxiety aroused by the ideas as the motive force behind repression. In any event, he never suggested (as did many of his followers) that suppression exists only for "dirty" thoughts. Indeed, in his work on dreams and his subsequent theoretical work, he often referred to pain in the broadest possible sense as a motive for repression.

A broad desire to avoid unpleasantness does not account fully, however, for a number of instances in which people tend to engage in suppression. It is possible to refine this global motive into at least three distinct categories (Wegner, 1988, 1989). One general class of such instances involves efforts at *self-control*. When people diet, try to quit smoking, attempt to get more exercise, try to stop using drugs, want to avoid alcohol, resolve to watch less television, or even attempt to break off a destructive or unhappy relationship, they usually find that they desire to suppress thoughts of the unwanted activity as well. Any straightforward definition of "pleasantness" would not class thoughts of food, alcohol, drugs, and the like as unpleasant, especially to the person who is feeling deprived; for this reason, it seems useful to suggest that instances of self-control can make thoughts *unwanted*, even though they may not be strictly unpleasant.

A dedicated psychoanalyst might note that the agonies of self-control are consistent in some respects with the struggles Freud envisioned between id and superego. We would concur with this, but expand this characterization to speak of self-control as a clash between habitual, automatic processes spawned by a history of appetitive contact with an entity, and enlightened, controlled processes attempting to redirect behavior. Mental control, in this analysis, is the first step toward any sort of self-control. One must avoid thinking of the addictive object in order to stop the instigation of the addictive behavior. The only way to bypass the exercise of mental control in these circumstances is to act precipitously to prevent oneself from ever performing the unwanted behavior—padlocking the refrigerator in the case of food, perhaps, or avoiding alcohol by moving to Saudi Arabia.

A second source of suppression occurs in the need for *secrecy*. There is nothing that can instigate suppression faster than the threat that something normally private might be made public. The prototypical situation occurs when one encounters a person from whom a secret must be kept. With the person present, it is deeply tempting to blurt out the secret whenever it comes to mind—or at least one worries that this will happen. Thus, one makes a special point of suppressing the secret thought whenever the relevant person is around. The range of relevant people differs for different secrets, of course, and at the extreme one may find oneself suppressing a thought whenever anyone at all is present or even imagined.

This cause of suppression is strongly social in origin, forged in large part by the schism that inevitably develops between our private thoughts and our public lives. Self-deception is, in this sense, the child of social deception. We admire someone from a distance, for example, and because we fear our sentiments will not be reciprocated, we keep quiet about our feelings. We must hold this back each time we are in the person's presence, and we become a dithering caricature of ourselves as we work so hard to be normal. Alternatively, there may be some occurrence in our childhood that we have never troubled to tell anyone about. It

may not even be particularly traumatic (in the Freudian sense), but the secrecy alone is enough to make us try not to think of it when we encounter potential audiences (Pennebaker, 1988). Other instances occur when we harbor discriminatory opinions of someone and work extra hard at suppressing our usual disparaging thoughts to keep from appearing prejudiced when the person is around to notice (see Fiske, Chapter 8, this volume). The source of our secrets, in sum, can be concern about any social, moral, or personal blunder, but the most socially unacceptable secrets tend to spawn the greatest suppression.

The third wellspring of suppression can best be called a motive to find *mental peace*. Quite simply, we sometimes observe that we are thinking something too often for our liking. A dream is repeated several nights in a row: we notice we keep toying with a lock of our hair; the unnamed pain in our chest reappears each time we feel stressed; or the same worry about our family's safety comes up over and over. The mere repetition of a thought may be sufficient to suggest to us the need for mental control, and we try not to think of it. Such thoughts are not necessarily abhorrent because of any special unpleasantness, although they can be; rather, we hope to suppress them because we have decided we are thinking them too often. The decision that a thought occurs "too often" will often be based, of course, in some unwanted emotional reaction that the thought engenders. This motive thus can encompass a wide range of what Freud imagined as the beginnings of suppression or repression—all those thoughts that are too disturbing to think because they produce negative affect. For many such thoughts, even one occurrence is too many, and in search of mental peace we put them aside as soon as we can.

These sources of suppression—self-control, secrecy, and mental peace—are not mutually exclusive. Many cases of keeping secrets, for example, can be cast as instances of self-control as well, and the pursuit of mental peace may be the conscious desire that arises during mental control attempts originally set in motion by self-control or secrecy. Partitioning the sources of mental control in this way is not meant to provide an exhaustive system of independent motivational categories. Indeed, these three sources of the urge to suppress could well be seen as subservient to some more general motive, such as esteem maintenance, control, or the like. This partition is useful as a way of highlighting the principal everyday circumstances in which mental control is engaged: when we are dissatisfied with ourselves, when we hide things from others, and when we are not at peace in our minds.

How Do We Suppress?

The strategies people use to suppress unwanted thoughts can be described as either direct or indirect. A direct strategy, as noted earlier, is primary suppression through auxiliary concentration—actively trying to think of something else. The indirect strategies are many; they include such devices as using alcohol, engaging in strenuous physical activity, or performing some palliative action that makes the unwanted thought less intrusive (e.g., coming back home to check whether the stove was really left on). When suppression is auxiliary to the attempt at primary concentration, we may also call the suppression attempt indirect. Many forms of psychotherapy can also be classed as indirect forms of suppression, in that attempts at problem-solving, emotional expression, cognitive restructuring, and the like are commonly addressed toward the elimination of unwanted thoughts. Only "thought stopping" (Wolpe & Lazarus, 1966) verges on a direct therapeutic approach. With this technique, the client is taught to call out "stop" whenever an unwanted thought occurs in a therapeutic session, and is encouraged to continue this procedure covertly outside the session.

When people are asked to describe their own strategies for coping with everyday obsessions and worries, the most frequently mentioned tactic is the perfectly direct one—simple self-distraction (Rachman & de Silva, 1978). Respondents say they try to think about something else. People who report worrying too much appear to point to this tactic as well. They blame their worry on a personal inability to distract themselves, claiming that for them, worry subsides only in the presence of attention-demanding environmental events (Borkovec, Robinson, Pruzinsky, & DePree, 1983). The accuracy of self-reports of the relative usage of different tactics is debatable, however, because certain tactics may simply be more evident to the self-reporter than others, independent of their actual usage. Suffice it to say that in everyday life, the suppression of thoughts by direct mental control happens enough that people notice it.

In the laboratory, this tactic is easily observed as well. Subjects in our initial study of thought suppression were asked to spend a 5-minute period verbalizing the stream of their thoughts for tape recording (Wegner, Schneider, Carter, & White, 1987, Experiment 1). They were prompted to think aloud, verbalizing every thought, feeling, or image that came to mind, and were assured that the recordings would be completely confidential. The subjects were then asked to continue their reporting, but some were now to follow an additional instruction: "In the next 5 minutes, please verbalize your thoughts as you did before, with one exception. This time, try not to think of a white bear. Every time you say 'white bear' or have 'white bear' come to mind, though, please ring the bell on the table before you."

Subjects given this instruction typically began by describing their plan to suppress: "Okay, then, I'll think about the light switch instead," or "I guess I'll talk about my sister's operation." As a rule, this auxiliary concentration succeeded for some time, as the subject talked on about the chosen replacement for "white bear." But overall, the self-distraction tactic was not very successful: Subjects rang the bell a mean of 6.1 times in 5 minutes and mentioned a white bear a mean of 1.6 times in the period as well. The degree of thinking about a white bear did decrease over the experimental session, however, such that by the final minute of the period most subjects no longer reported more than one occurrence (mention or bell ring).

We made another observation in this study about how people suppress, and though it did not seem important at the time, it has turned out to be a crucial one. Most of the time, people carried out their suppression by concentrating in turn on each of a wide variety of different items; this seemed to be a kind of *unfocused self-distraction,* a wandering of thought to one item after another, seemingly in search of something that might be truly interesting. The flip side of this approach, then, was a tactic of *focused self-distraction,* always turning to one thing as a distracter whenever the unwanted thought intruded. This second sort of distraction is the only thing that psychologists encourage people to do in research on how distraction can dull pain, emotion, and the like (see McCaul & Malott, 1984), so no one has ever really considered the unfocused variety before—despite its apparently greater popularity. As it turned out, the subsequent effects of thought suppression are highly dependent on the difference between the focused and unfocused strategies.

With What Effect Do We Suppress?

The white-bear study was arranged to examine also what happens to thinking when the need for suppression is over. The subjects who were asked to suppress in the experiment were asked in a final time period to continue their stream-of-consciousness reports, this time with the instruction to think of a white bear. These subjects showed a level of thinking about a white bear (15.7 bells and 14.4 mentions) significantly greater than that shown by subjects in a comparison group who were asked from the start (immediately after the practice period) to think about a white bear (11.8 bells and 11.5 mentions). In short, the mere act of avoiding a thought for 5 minutes made subjects oddly inclined to signal a relative outpouring of the thought when thinking about it was allowed. We found not only that the absolute level of thinking of a white bear was greater in this group, but also that there was an accelerating tendency to think of a white bear over time. That is, whereas thinking about a white bear in all the other conditions of the experiment declined over the 5-minute session, in those subjects expressing after suppression, the level of thinking continued to increase.

This pattern suggests a "rebound" effect—an increase in preoccupation with a thought that was formerly suppressed. Much of our work on thought suppression has been prompted by the many parallels between this effect and a wide array of familiar phenomena in psychology. Certainly, Freud (1914/1958) was among the first to point out that an attempt to deny or repress a thought might lead to a subsequent obsession (conscious or unconscious) with that thought. But other observers have remarked on many kindred effects: The suppression of grief following a loss appears to hamper coping and amplify the later grieving that is exhibited (Lindemann, 1944); the suppression of thoughts about a surgery prior to its occurrence foreshadows great anxiety and distress afterwards (Janis, 1958); the suppression of thoughts about eating may be one of the features of dieting that leads to later relapse and binge eating (Polivy & Herman, 1985); the suppression of thoughts about early traumatic occurrences can portend later physical illness and psychological distress (Pennebaker, 1985: Silver, Boon, & Stones, 1983); the failure to express emotions can lead to subsequent emotional problems (Rachman, 1980). In short, the rebound effect in the white-bear study reminded us of many things, and we wondered whether it might provide a laboratory setting within which these phenomena might be explored.

The first step in such exploration must be the development of a theoretical understanding of the phenomenon. Why is it that suppression yields a later rebound of preoccupation? At this point, the distinction we observed between focused and unfocused self-distraction again becomes relevant. If someone spends the entire suppression period in unfocused self-distraction, it is likely that the person will think about many things, both in the laboratory setting and outside it. Each of these things will be concentrated on for a short time, usually as a replacement for a white-bear thought. All these topics will then become linked to a white bear in the person's mind by virtue of their single common quality—they are *not white bears.* Many different distractors, in short, become associated with the unwanted thought. It makes sense, then, that when these former distractors are encountered once more (say, in the later period when expression is invited), they serve as reminders of the earlier unwanted thought. The rebound may stem, then, from the special way in which people enlist their ongoing thoughts to help distract them from the thought they are trying to suppress.

We have tested this idea in several ways. In our first follow-up on the white-bear study (Wegner, Schneider, Carter, & White, 1987, Experiment 2), we tested this explanation by replicating the original experiment with one exception: Some of the subjects in the group who were asked to suppress white-bear thoughts were given a brief instruction to engage in *focused* self-distraction. They were told after the suppression instruction, "Also, if you do happen to think of a white bear, please try to think of a red Volkswagen instead." This group, when later given the chance to express thoughts of a white bear, did so at a significantly reduced level. Unlike the subjects in this study who were allowed to go their own way (and who typically used the unfocused, "think-about-anything" method), these individuals experienced a noteworthy drop in the rebound of the unwanted thought.

One lesson to be gleaned from this study is that wild-eyed ranging about for distractors is not a good method for thought suppression. True, this may be all that seems possible in the face of a particularly daunting unwanted thought. But it is more likely that one will defeat the rebound effect by choosing one special distractor and turning to it whenever the unwanted thought comes to mind. This tactic presumably prevents all the other things one might think about—whether they arise in memory or are instigated by observation of one's surroundings—from becoming cues to the unwanted thought. The focused distractor becomes the primary cue to that thought, and because it is not especially salient during the later expression period, there is no strong cuing of the unwanted thought to yield a rebound of preoccupation.

We find that in talking to people about this experiment, several have reported using their own versions of focused self-distraction. Often,

the single distracter that is chosen in these cases is a religious one—thoughts of God, engaging in prayer, and so on. Others report doing arithmetic in their heads. In any case, we would predict that the single focused distractor might become a fairly strong reminder of the unwanted thought if suppression went on long enough, and thus could itself become unwanted (unless it were somehow absolved of its distressing tone by virtue of pairing with other, more positive experiences). We did not test these kinds of conjectures in the red-Volkswagen study, but they do suggest an interesting line of inquiry.

A different set of derivations from the observation of unfocused self-distraction was tested, however, in subsequent research (Wegner, Schneider, McMahon, & Knutson, 1989). This research examined the hypothesis that thought suppression in a particular context tends to "spoil" that context for the person; it makes that context an unusually strong reminder of the unwanted thought. This notion follows from the idea that when people engage in unfocused self-distraction, they pick many of the different distracters they will use from their current surroundings. These surroundings, later on, can become reminders of the unwanted thought and so may serve to cue the rebound of preoccupation when expression is allowed.

This research called for some subjects to complete the usual sequence of thought suppression followed by expression (or the comparison sequence of expression followed by suppression) in one context—a laboratory room in which a set of slides on a single theme was being shown. Subjects saw either a slide show of classroom scenes, or one of household appliances. Other subjects participated with different slide shows appearing during the initial and later periods of the experiment. We expected that subjects in this latter group who suppressed in the context of one slide show and then expressed in the context of another would show little of the rebound effect, and this is what happened. The degree to which the participants expressed the thought following suppression in a different context was reliably less than the amount of expression following suppression in a constant context. Therefore, the rebound effect was most pronounced when people distracted themselves by thinking about their surroundings, and then thought of the surroundings again when they were allowed to consider the formerly suppressed thought.

The implications of these findings are quite practical. The results suggest, for example, that residential treatment facilities for addictions, alcoholism, overeating, and the like may have a common benefit. Getting away from home during treatment may help, all by itself. Because people suppress thoughts of their forbidden behaviors in the strange surroundings of the facility, they may come to associate many of the features of the facility with their particular self-control problem. When they leave, however, these reminders are left behind, the rebound of preoccupation is disrupted, and there would seem to be a much greater likelihood of long-term success for the treatment. When we are bothered by unwanted thoughts at home or at work, though, it is tempting to suppress them right there. This strategy is likely to fail, for when we try to divest ourselves of a thought in a place, we seem in a sense to leave it there—only to find it again when we return.

Our work on suppression to date indicates, in sum, that people do not do it very well. The question that begins this section ("With what effect do we suppress?") must be met at this time with a disappointing reply: Apparently, we suppress with only temporary and incomplete success. Although our research subjects have been able to reduce their thinking about an innocuous item, a white bear, to relatively low levels in a short time, they nonetheless are not able simply to shut off the thought at will. And once the thought is suppressed, an invitation to return to it appears to have the ironic effect of prompting renewed preoccupation that proceeds at a level beyond what might have occurred had suppression never been started. This effect, too, can be overcome under certain circumstances, but it seems that people's natural proclivities (to use unfocused self-distraction and to stay in the same surroundings) work against them to make the task of long-term suppression most difficult. The effects of

thought suppression, it seems, are not usually what we want them to be.

How Might We Suppress More Effectively?

Inevitably, the discussion of thought suppression comes around to home remedies: What should people do when they have unwanted thought? This is one of the great problems of our field, one of the main reasons why clinical psychology and psychotherapy were invented. It should be obvious that our research program is not yet mature enough even to have spawned clinical research, let alone to have yielded solid suggestions for psychotherapy or self-help. With this caveat out of the bag, we feel a bit better about offering our preliminary and untested nostrums.

Our simplest advice would be to avoid suppression, to stop stopping. The work we have conducted and the research by others we have reviewed seems to identify suppression as a strategy that can produce consequences every bit as discomfiting as the unwanted thoughts toward which it is directed. At the extreme, it may be that thought suppression can be the cause rather than the cure of unwanted thoughts, serving over time and in the right circumstances to produce "synthetic obsessions" that can be as painful as those derived from traumas (Wegner, 1988, 1989). Often people use thought suppression to deal with unwanted thoughts when a better strategy would be to work on the unwanted realities that those thoughts represent. We are not recommending that all suppression is nonsense, for there are some junctures at which it seems the only proper solution. When on the brink of a tall building one gets the urge to throw oneself off, it is surely best to suppress the thought. But we do believe that thought suppression is often a mental Band-Aid, a stopgap solution that can create its own problems.

If one must suppress, there are better and worse ways to do it. The research to this point suggests that suppression is likely to be more successful in the long run if we use a limited range of distracters—things we can focus on repeatedly, rather than sorting recklessly through every other thought that might be available. And in this enterprise, it may be best, too, if to do our suppression today, we get away from home or away from the environs we will have to inhabit later. There is the real possibility that the suppressed thoughts will be cued by the very context in which we suppressed them, climaxing our struggle to suppress with a very disappointing conclusion.

That's it. We hesitate to offer more advice at this point, because we believe there are enough unanswered questions that to offer advice now would be premature. We cannot be certain, after all, that white-bear-type studies capture the same processes that occur when people in everyday life attempt to suppress thoughts. The white-bear experiment adds the artificial requirement that people must report their thoughts aloud, for example, and it deals with thoughts that are not nearly as emotional as the ones people usually attempt to suppress.

Work on these things is currently underway. In one study (Chandler & Wegner, 1987), evidence of a rebound effect was found even when people were not asked to ring bells or report white-bear thoughts. It was arranged instead for them to talk freely "off the top of their heads" about any or all of five different topics written on a page before them. They did this during the usual white-bear experiment design: One group was asked first not to think of a white bear, then to think of it; another group did thinking first and then not thinking. The topics had been scaled ahead of time for their relevance to "white bear" ("iceberg" being very relevant, for example, and "gym shorts" being much less relevant). What we found was that subjects assigned to think of a white bear after suppression, as compared to those assigned to think about it from the outset, talked more about white-bear-relevant thoughts and less about thoughts irrelevant to white bears. So, even without the artificial thought-reporting requirement, an effect very much like the rebound effect was observed.

And in another recent set of experiments, the question of how people suppress more involving and emotional thoughts has been under scrutiny. Wenzlaff, Wegner, and Roper (1988) looked at how depressed and nondepressed people handle unwanted thoughts. Mildly depressed college students (as determined by the short form of the Beck Depression Inventory; Beck & Beck, 1972) and their nondepressed counterparts were asked to read a page-long story and imagine themselves in the starring role of either a very positive incident (e.g., finding a missing child) or a very negative one (e.g., being in a serious car accident). They were then asked to write their ongoing thoughts on three blank pages, and were paced through the pages to allow 3 minutes for each. In a column down the right side of each page, they were to make a check mark each time the thought of the story they had read came to mind.

Some subjects were put up to the task of suppression; they were asked not to think of the story, if they could. Others were not given any special instruction, and were merely told to describe whatever was on their minds. When we counted the marks subjects made, and also their written mentions of the target thought, we found that depressed subjects had a particularly difficult time suppressing negative thoughts. Nondepressed subjects were generally able to suppress both positive and negative thoughts, and depressed subjects did a fine job of suppressing positive thoughts. But when the depressed people tried to suppress a negative thought, they succeeded at first, only to experience a later resurgence of negative thinking. By the third page of writing, their reporting of the negative thought was back up to the same level as that of depressed subjects who had not even tried to suppress.

Further analyses of this study, and further experiments, have explored how this unusual resurgence takes place. What seems to happen is that depressed people distract themselves from negative thoughts by using *other negative thoughts*. These then serve as strong reminders of the thought that was first unwanted, and so return the depressed persons to the initial problem in short order. Nondepressed people, in turn, use positive distracters to get away from negative thoughts, and so leave the whole arena of negative thinking behind. This suggests again that the nature of the self-distraction strategy people use can be very important in determining how successful their thought suppression will be. So, if there is one last piece of advice we can sneak in, it is to look on the bright side. Positive self-distraction may be a generally useful technique whenever we have negative unwanted thoughts—even if we are not depressed at the time, but particularly if we are.

CONCLUSIONS

We should tie up at least one loose end before we draw the chapter to a close. We should explain the allusion to F. C. Bartlett that occurs in the odd mix of metaphors in the chapter subtitle. His story of the "War of the Ghosts" (1932) was used in his classic research on how people transform information in their minds. Although the story itself is not strictly relevant to our concerns, his general approach to psychology is right on target. One of the ideas that Bartlett championed was the role of motivation and affect in cognition, and that is a basic issue in this chapter.

Mental control must be counted as a central form of motivated cognition. Although motivation may affect our thoughts of many things, coloring our views of others and ourselves (see, e.g., Sorrentino & Higgins, 1986), its influence on thought is seldom held in such sharp relief as when we are motivated to control our thoughts directly. Mental control requires conscious motivation, and its success and failure can often appear in our conscious thoughts as well. So, although certain purists in both the cognitive and motivational camps of psychology would prefer not to use both explanatory networks at the same time in any domain of study, in the case of mental control this is simply impossible. Mental control is just too clear a case of motivated thought for either the motivation or the thinking to be ignored.

Our studies of thought suppression reveal that people engage in sensible activities when they are asked to suppress a thought in the laboratory. They try to think of other things, and over time they often can succeed. But thought suppression has ironic and troubling

effects as well, in that the suppressed thought can return, sometimes to be more absorbing than it was at the start. It is therefore evident that motivated thinking may not have the clear-cut success we sometimes find with motivated physical activities. When we want to brush our teeth or hop on one foot, we can usually do so; when we want to control our minds, we may find that nothing works as it should. A war of the ghosts in the machine, it seems, may leave us with defeated spirits.

ACKNOWLEDGMENTS

We thank Toni Wegner, James Pennebaker, and the editors for helpful comments on an earlier draft.

REFERENCES

Bartlett, F. C. (1932). *Remembering.* Cambridge, England: Cambridge University Press.

Beck, A., & Beck, R. (1972). Screening depressed patients in family practice: A rapid technique, *Postgraduate Medicine, 52,* 81–85.

Borkovec, T. D., Robinson, E., Pruzinsky, T., & DePree, J. A. (1983). Preliminary exploration of worry: Some characteristics and processes. *Behaviour Research and Therapy, 21,* 9–16.

Breznitz, S. (Ed.). (1983). *The denial of stress.* New York: International Universities Press.

Broadbent, D. (1958). *Perception and communication.* Oxford: Pergamon Press.

Chandler, G., & Wegner, D. M. (1987). *The effect of thought suppression on preoccupation with associated thoughts.* Unpublished manuscript, Trinity University.

Davis, P. J. (1987). Repression and the inaccessibility of affective memories. *Journal of Personality and Social Psychology, 53,* 585–593.

Erdelyi, M. H. (1985). *Psychoanalysis: Freud's cognitive psychology.* San Francisco: W. H. Freeman.

Erdelyi, M. H., & Goldberg, B. (1979). Let's not sweep repression under the rug: Toward a cognitive psychology of repression. In J. F. Kihlstrom & F. J. Evans (Eds.), *Functional disorders of memory* (pp. 355–402). Hillsdale, NJ: Erlbaum.

Freud, S. (1953). The interpretation of dreams. In J. Strachey (Ed.), *The standard edition of the complete psychological works of Sigmund Freud* (Vol. 4, pp. 1–338; Vol. 5, pp. 339–627). London: Hogarth Press. (Original work published 1900)

Freud, S. (1957). Repression. In J. Strachey (Ed.), *The standard edition of the complete psychological works of Sigmund Freud* (Vol. 14, pp. 146–158). London: Hogarth Press. (Original work published 1915)

Freud, S. (1958). Remembering, repeating, and working-through. In J. Strachey (Ed.), *The standard edition of the complete psychological works of Sigmund Freud* (Vol. 12, pp. 145–150). London: Hogarth Press. (Original work published 1914)

Geiselman, R. E., Bjork, R. A., & Fishman, D. L. (1983). Disrupted retrieval in directed forgetting: A link with posthypnotic amnesia. *Journal of Experimental Psychology: General, 112,* 58–72.

Holmes, D. S. (1974). Investigation of repression: Differential recall of material experimentally or naturally associated with ego threat. *Psychological Bulletin, 81,* 632–653.

James, W. (1890). *The principles of psychology* (2 vols.). New York: Holt.

Janis, I. (1958). *Psychological stress.* New York: Wiley.

Kihlstrom, J. F. (1983). Instructed forgetting: Hypnotic and nonhypnotic. *Journal of Experimental Psychology: General, 112,* 73–79.

Klinger, E. (1982). On the self-management of mood, affect, and attention. In P. Karoly & F. H. Kanfer (Eds.), *Self-management and behavior change* (pp. 129–164). New York: Pergamon Press.

Lindemann, E. (1944). Symptomatology and management of acute grief. *American Journal of Psychiatry, 101,* 141–148.

McCaul, K. D., & Malott, J. M. (1984). Distraction and coping with pain. *Psychological Bulletin, 95,* 516–533.

Pennebaker, J. W. (1985). Inhibition and cognition: Toward an understanding of trauma and disease. *Canadian Psychology, 26,* 82–95.

Pennebaker, J. W. (1988). Confiding traumatic experiences and health. In S. Fisher & J. Reason (Eds.), *Handbook of life stress, cognition, and health* (pp. 669–682). Chichester, England: Wiley.

Polivy, J., & Herman, C. P. (1985). Dieting and binging: A causal analysis. *American Psychologist, 40,* 193–201.

Rachman, S. (1980). Emotional processing. *Behaviour Research and Therapy, 18,* 51–60.

Rachman, S., & de Silva, P. (1978). Abnormal and normal obsessions. *Behaviour Research and Therapy, 16,* 233–248.

Rapaport, D. (1959). *Emotions and memory.* New York: International Universities Press.

Ryle, G. (1949). *The concept of mind.* London: Hutchinson.

Silver, R. L., Boon, C., & Stones, M. H. (1983). Searching for meaning in misfortune: Making sense of incest, *Journal of Social Issues, 39,* 81–102.

Sorrentino, R. M., & Higgins, E. T. (Eds.). (1986). *Handbook of motivation and cognition: Foundations of social behavior.* New York: Guilford Press.

Wegner, D. M. (1988). Stress and mental control. In S. Fisher & J. Reason (Eds.), *Handbook of life stress, cognition, and health* (pp. 683–697). Chichester, England: Wiley.

Wegner, D. M. (1989). *White bears and other unwanted thoughts.* New York: Viking Press.

Wegner, D. M., Schneider, D. J., Carter, S., III, & White, L. (1987). Paradoxical consequences of thought suppression. *Journal of Personality and Social Psychology, 53,* 1–9.

Wegner, D. M., Schneider, D. J., McMahon, S., & Knutson, B. (1989). *Taking worry out of context: The enhancement of thought suppression effectiveness in new surroundings.* Manuscript submitted for publication.

Wenzlaff, R., Wegner, D. M., & Roper, D. (1988). Depression and mental control: The resurgence of unwanted negative thoughts. *Journal of Personality and Social Psychology, 55,* 882–892.

Wolpe, J., & Lazarus, A. A. (1966). *Behavior therapy techniques.* New York: Pergamon.

Yarnell, P. R., & Lynch, S. (1973). The "ding": Amnesic states in football trauma. *Neurology, 23,* 196–197.

PART • FOUR

LANGUAGE

George A. Miller

❖

Beryl Lieff Benderly

❖

George Lakoff

❖

Dianne Horgan

Language

The study of language is an interdisciplinary endeavor. The fields of anthropology, computer science, linguistics, philosophy, and psychology have all made important contributions to our understanding of language. In this section, George A. Miller, a psychologist, Beryl Lieff Benderly, a journalist and author, George Lakoff, a linguist, and Dianne Horgan, a psychologist, provide samples of the work currently being done on language.

Psychologists have a long-standing interest in language. In the late nineteenth and early twentieth centuries, Wilhelm Wundt (1832–1920), who founded the first psychology laboratory in 1879, wrote extensively about language, and language was the centerpiece of his *Völkerpsychologie*, or "ethnic psychology." Wundt's approach to language eventually fell out of favor, however, and when language was later taken up by early proponents of behaviorism, it was treated as a peripheral phenomenon and reduced to the study of the movements of the larynx. Subsequent behaviorists did attempt to treat word meaning, but they successively reduced it to reference and then to conditioning. In the 1950s when information theory appeared on the psychology scene, the concept of redundancy was extracted from it and applied to language. Redundancy in this context means old information, and language is "old" on a number of levels, including the phonological (sound structure), the syntactic, the semantic, and the pragmatic. That is, by virtue of knowing a language, people are able to predict that, given that certain speech sounds, grammatical structures, or meanings have occurred, then certain other speech sounds, grammatical structures, or meanings are likely to follow. The predicted elements are old by virtue of being predictable. And for normal adults, language is 50 percent to 60 percent redundant. Studies in the 1950s established that redundancy enormously facilitates the perception, learning, and memory of language. However, these studies did not force a change in the then-fashionable behavioristic view of language, which was that language is a set of stimulus-response bonds of various strengths.

THE CHALLENGE TO THE BEHAVIORIST VIEW CAME FROM NOAM CHOMSKY, who proposed that language is a highly structured system, hierarchically (instead of horizontally) arranged, and rule based. Chomsky focused on generative rules, rules that allow people to produce a potentially infinite set of sentences, and this on the basis of a small, finite set of rules. Later, in the 1960s, he argued that language has a "surface structure" and a "deep structure." His evidence was intuitive—different sentences can arrange words differently but mean the same thing; the same sentence can have different and distinct meanings; and different sentences can be similar on a surface (phrase) level but different on a semantic level. The idea that language is structured, creative, and related on different and abstract levels, and all this by virtue of abstract rules, was anathema to behaviorists.

One implication of behavioristic theory is that well-learned language consists of a highly probable string of words. However, Chomsky and George Miller demonstrated in the early 1960s that grammaticality is unrelated to the sequential probability of words. Chomsky's famous sentence—"Colorless green ideas sleep furiously"—made the point. The sequential probability from one word to the next is very low, but the sentence seems grammatical.

Finally, in 1959 Chomsky wrote a review of B. F. Skinner's book *Verbal Behavior* (1957). In strong terms, Chomsky argued that a purely behavioral approach to language was not going to work. In general, Chomsky felt that Skinner's stimulus-response-reinforcement approach vastly underestimated the complexity of language—its structuredness, creativity, levels, etc. This review proved to be influential and contributed to the ascendancy of the newer information-processing view.

CHOMSKY'S THEORY AND APPROACH MADE LANguage a central focus in cognitive psychology; nevertheless, it became clear by the late 1960s that, as right as Chomsky's theory was about some things, it had its limitations. In particular, the theory neglected the relationships among language, mind, and culture (factors Wundt had wanted to relate), and it failed to consider the pragmatic aspects of language, most obviously its role in communication. That is, the theory seemed to posit an independent, biologically given module that somehow resisted interaction with other mental structures and with the purposes and interests of the lan-

guage user. However, psychologists want to know how language is used to reason, remember, solve problems, control behavior, and communicate with other people. Chomsky's theory shed no light on these questions.

IN "THE PLACE OF LANGUAGE IN A SCIENTIFIC Psychology," George A. Miller discusses the history and future of the psychological study of language. His discussion is framed in terms of five questions, all of which might be viewed as an implicit tribute to Chomsky. First, how does language fit into general theories of cognition? Miller finds that many theorists have acknowledged the importance of language, but few have pursued it in any detail, with the exception of Wundt, Bühler, and some behaviorists. The second question, which asks if linguistics is a branch of cognitive psychology, is answered in the affirmative. Chomsky took this position, but his perspective was somewhat unique. Third, the innateness of language, which is virtually unquestioned, at least with respect to obvious factors such as articulatory structures, cerebral asymmetry, and the like. There is good evidence that much of phonology and syntax are strongly constrained by biology. The fourth question involves the language-communication relationship. Miller argues that the mental representation and communication systems have combined to create a unique capacity for language, that is, for relating speech sounds and meanings, for conveying information, and for using language to communicate indirectly. As for the last question—what lies ahead—Miller answers by saying that if he were a young psycholinguist, he would learn as much as he could about biology and computers.

THE INNATENESS QUESTION SURFACES AGAIN IN THE article by Beryl Lieff Benderly, "The Great Ape Debate: Can Gorillas and Chimps Use Language or Not?" If apes can learn a language, then there would seem to be less force to claims that language is unique to humans. Benderly reviews the history of the attempts to teach apes to communicate in a human language, from the difficult and unsuccessful attempts to teach apes to speak, to the much more successful attempts to teach apes to use sign language. Washoe, Koko, and numerous other apes have succeeded in learning signs, and they apparently use them creatively. But is this a true demonstration of language use?

In her article, Benderly focuses on the criticisms of this research. Critics have suggested the following: The apes were not taught American Sign Language but a simple variant of it, a kind of pidgin sign language; the apes were just imitating and were incapable of signing appropriately on their own; the apes never learned syntax, the rules for putting the signs together in some ordered way; and the experimenters unconsciously signaled the apes to respond in certain ways (the so-called Clever Hans effect). Targets of these criticisms have responded by noting that critics have overlooked the details of their research and that proper tests have in fact been conducted. Finally, researchers who have worked with apes say that what lies at the heart of such criticisms of their efforts are deep philosophical differences over the nature of language. Regardless of the future of this debate, Benderly's quote from Allen Gardner will continue to be appropriate: "Whether the graybeards of linguistics call it language is not interesting. It's what the chimps do that's interesting."

"A FIGURE OF THOUGHT," BY GEORGE LAKOFF, IS quite a change of pace from the Miller and Benderly articles. Lakoff presents metaphor as a distinctive style of thought, a basic way in which people deal with abstract concepts. Lakoff states that metaphor has traditionally been studied as a figure of speech, a device for beautifying and enriching language. But his observations on metaphor show it to be a figure of thought—a systematic mapping of ideas from one meaning domain to another. Lakoff begins by describing "love as a journey," the metaphor that first revealed to him

the idea that metaphors are not individual links between two unlike domains but families of such links. Linguistic metaphors such as "we're at a crossroads" or "we may have to go our separate ways" belong to the same central conceptual metaphor. Lakoff states that the existence of such families, their apparent use in reasoning about love, and the ease of understanding new members are evidence for the existence of conceptual metaphors. This way of viewing language is a long way from Chomsky's emphasis on syntax rather than on the conceptual value of language to an individual.

LANGUAGE IS AN INSTRUMENT PAR EXCELLENCE FOR thought. And one form of thought is humor. Life without humor is unthinkable for most people. Humor has both a cognitive and emotional value. It relieves tension, expresses sentiments, makes unbearable situations more bearable, and so on. But what do we know about it? Humor can be expressed in verbal and nonverbal ways, and it can be simple or complex. How does it begin in children when they start to play with language?

In Dianne Horgan's "Learning to Tell Jokes: A Case Study of Metalinguistic Abilities," language is approached from a functional/communication standpoint. Horgan studied the spontaneous humor production of one child from age 16 months to age 48 months. Her basic premise was that humor production parallels cognitive growth, in particular the child's growing metalinguistic sense that language is an object or tool to be used for other purposes. Horgan organizes the child's humor into what she considers to be four stages and speculates that the child saw language as a game and that the game served important social functions for the child. This perspective is quite removed from the original Chomsky-inspired emphasis on structural aspects of language as derived from biology.

19

George A. Miller

The Place of Language in a Scientific Psychology

Abstract: *One of the psychologists' great methodological difficulties is how they can make the events they wish to study publicly observable, countable, measurable. It is significant to note that the device most often used for conversion from private to public is language. Thus speech is a crucial problem for psychology. None of their other activities gives the same sort of insight into another person as does their language. Since people spend so many of their waking hours generating and responding to words, and since speech is such a typically human mode of adjustment, no general theory of psychology will be adequate if it does not take account of language.*

The abstract of this paper is a slightly revised version of a paragraph published in 1951 (Miller, 1951, p. 3). Only two changes were required in order to bring the original passage up to date. One was to substitute "language" everywhere that "verbal behavior" occurred in the original version. And, since women also talk, the other change was to correct my generic use of "he" and "man" to "they" and "people." Interesting stories could be told about the need for both of those revisions, but that is not my concern here. My concern today is the same as it was in 1951: I still believe that "no general theory of psychology will be adequate if it does not take account of language."

No new data are reported here; we already know far more about language than we understand. Here I am concerned with the larger question of where the topic of language fits in our general theories of human cognition.

You may feel that the importance of language is already sufficiently obvious and that contemporary psychological theories do now take adequate account of it, in which case you will see little reason to repeat this truism over and over. But I have observed over the years that there is a tendency for even the best scientific psychologists to lose sight of large issues in their devotion to particular methodologies, their pursuit of the null hypothesis, and their rigorous efforts to reduce anything that seems interesting to something else that is not. An occasional reminder of the larger reasons why we flash those stimuli and measure those reaction times is sometimes useful.

IS LANGUAGE IMPORTANT?

Is language really important for psychology? The range of answers that famous psychologists have given to that question is remarkable. A small sampling should illustrate what I mean.

First, there are those who assume that language is important and tried to do something about it. If we go back to the beginning of experimental psychology, it is clear that Wundt understood the importance of language. Wundt, you will recall, believed that higher mental processes cannot be analyzed experimentally; he believed that the only way to understand complex psychological processes is by analysis of their cultural products—which puts the study of language in a central role. The first two books of Wundt's *Völkerpsychologie* (1900–1909) introduced his theory of language, which then served as a basis for the eight additional books that followed. But it was published shortly before World War I, when anti-German feelings ran high in the United States. It is unfortunate that the *Völkerpsychologie* was little read outside of Germany; some students of Wundt's writings (Blumenthal, 1970) claim that he anticipated important developments in linguistic theory, ideas that lay neglected until Chomsky redefined the science of linguistics in the 1950s.

Bühler inherited Wundt's mantle as the leading linguistic psychologist. Bühler objected to many of Wundt's ideas about linguistic structure and placed much more emphasis on how language is used, but he agree with Wundt concerning the importance of language for psychology. Bühler wanted to collaborate with linguists. In his important *Sprachtheorie* (1934) he commented that "if the constantly

evoked mutual assistance of psychology and linguistics is to bear fruit, specialists on both sides must dare to intervene in the others' conceptions." (Taken from a translation of Chapter 7 of *Sprachtheorie* in Jarvella and Klein [1982, p. 17].) And for a while that happened. But Bühler's work in Vienna was interrupted in 1938 by political events, and his *Sprachtheorie* was never translated into English. Although interest in the psychology of language remained alive in Europe, events took a different course in America.

A second attitude toward language was suspicion and distrust. For example, James, while wearing his psychological hat, listed language as a major source of error in psychology. In the *Principles* he complained that "language was originally made by men who were not psychologists" (James, 1890/1981, vol. 1, p. 193), with the result that it is difficult to distinguish between the thought of a thing and the thing itself. James also blamed the discreteness of words for the common failure to recognize that the stream of thought flows continuously.

A third point of view was that language is important, but that it can be explained in terms of something simpler. Watson pioneered this theoretical territory. In *Behaviorism* he proposed that all thinking is a matter of *"language habits*—habits which when exercised implicitly behind the closed doors of the lips we call *thinking.*" Having reduced thinking to language, he next reduced language to talking: "Language as we ordinarily understand it, in spite of its complexities, is in the beginning a very simple type of behavior" (Watson, 1924, p. 225). He then went on to describe, stage by stage, how children acquire their language habits.

This view of language, as a complicated kind of vocal behavior not basically different from other kinds of behavior, was adopted by many great American psychologists. Tolman, for example, while admitting that speech distinguishes human beings from other animals, still claimed to find nothing extraordinary or unique about it: "Speech accomplishes the same sort of result that other behaviors would, only more expeditiously" (Tolman, 1932, p. 236). On Tolman's view, it is not speech, but human intelligence—the amazing human ability to learn and to adapt—that is so extraordinary and unique.

Twenty-five years later Skinner would not even admit that speech distinguishes human beings from other animals. Skinner felt that early humans, before the appearance of spoken languages, were not very different from modern humans: "What was lacking was not any special capacity for speech but certain environmental circumstances" (Skinner, 1957, p. 461). When the environmental circumstances became favorable, humans began reinforcing one another's vocal behavior. Given appropriate environmental circumstances, apes should do the same. Although Skinner's attempts to explain language in terms of his theories of reinforcement were developed at far greater length than Tolman's, the two agreed basically that human language is not unique.

A fourth stance was to deny that humans enjoy any special apparatus for speaking. For example, in 1891 the young neurologist Freud devoted a monograph to discrediting claims that there are special centers for speech and language in the human brain: "We have rejected the assumptions that the speech apparatus consists of distinct centres separated by functionless areas . . . the speech area is a continuous cortical region within which the associations and transmissions underlying the speech functions are taking place" (Freud, 1891/1953, p. 62). Freud recognized that these associations and transmissions are enormously complex, but he believed that the speech area is located where it is, not because human beings inherit some unique neurological organization to support language, but simply because this area is where projections from the optic, auditory, and motor nerves overlap and associations can be formed. Why the corresponding areas in the brains of other primates do not also support language was not a question that he raised.

Finally, a fifth position was the most popular: Admit that language is important and then ignore it. The early Gestalt psychologists may have had this attitude, although they mention language so seldom that it is hard to tell. Koffka once wrote that "an ultimate explana-

tion of the problems of thought and imagination will not be possible without a theory of language and other symbolic functions. But we shall exclude the study of language from our treatise" (Koffka, 1935, p. 422). This exclusion was necessary, Koffka explained, because language is so complicated. But, whatever the reason, language did not play an important role in Gestalt theory—which may, after all, have been wiser than trying to reduce it to something simpler.

A better historian could probably find still other opinions about the place of language in a scientific psychology, but this sample should suffice to show that early psychologists held mixed views about it. But the attitude favored by most of our founding fathers was one of simple neglect. Other mental processes were given higher priority and language was left to the professional linguists.

IS LINGUISTICS A BRANCH OF COGNITIVE PSYCHOLOGY?

Perhaps one reason that many early psychologists held this view was that the conception of language available to them at the time was not yet ready for psychological consumption. Scientific linguistics emerged during the 19th century as the study of sound changes in the evolution of Indo-European languages, an undertaking that relied on the existence of ancient written documents. Around the turn of the century the tools developed for those studies were borrowed by cultural anthropologists and used to study exotic languages having no previous body of written literature. In the hands of anthropologists, the linguistic theories of the day served largely as a guide for drawing generalizations based on transcribed samples of speech. They carefully sorted and classified these transcriptions the same way archaeologists sort and classify pots or tools.

Not until the 1950s was there a scientific alternative to the anthropological approach. In 1957 Chomsky argued that language, properly conceived, is not a collection of literary texts that have been preserved or a corpus of utterances that some anthropologist has transcribed. A language is something that people know, something that children learn and adults use. Any particular corpus can contain only a small sample of the infinite variety of sentences that a native speaker could produce and understand. Linguistics is not the study of recorded instances. For Chomsky, the subject matter of linguistics is the *competence* of language users, not their performance. Performances—overt acts of speaking—are merely the evidence from which competence can be inferred.

Describing abilities is, of course, a responsibility of psychology, so Chomsky's redefinition had the effect of making linguistics a branch of cognitive psychology. As he himself once put it: "The theory of language is simply that part of human psychology that is concerned with one particular 'mental organ,' human language" (Chomsky, 1975, p. 36). A person who speaks a language has mastered a highly complex system of knowledge, which raises three basic questions:

1. What is this system of knowledge?
2. How does it arise?
3. How is it used?

These are classical questions, as basic to human psychology as to linguistics, and Chomsky's answers to them have been widely influential.

What Is a Language?

Chomsky pointed out that a native speaker's knowledge of his language must have a generative character. Since there is no rule limiting the length of grammatical sentences, there must be an indefinitely large number of sentences that native speakers could produce and understand. It is inconceivable that this set of grammatical sentences could be mastered by memorizing them, one at a time. Some kind of generative system must lie at the heart of linguistic competence. Chomsky implied that careful analysis of that generative system could reveal much about the cognitive architecture of the human information processing system.

How Does Language Arise?

But how could such a generative system be acquired? The sample of speech that a child is exposed to is finite and every child is exposed to a different sample, yet everyone in the same language community acquires the same generative system. To Chomsky, these facts meant that certain aspects of language are innate and specific to our species. The knowledge system develops as children learn to shape their innate and universal grammar to the local requirements of the particular language community into which they happen to have been born.

How Is Language Used?

Chomsky assumed that the knowledge system that native speakers have mastered is used both to produce and to understand grammatical sentences in that language. That is to say, knowledge of the language enables native speakers to relate phonological strings to semantic interpretations—to relate sound and meaning. And he emphasized that sentence production is highly creative—it is not under direct control by environmental stimuli, but can serve any purposes a speaker happens to have at the moment. (Note that Chomsky did not attempt to enumerate the purposes a speaker might have for using language. Chomsky's interest in the use of linguistic knowledge ends with the assignment of semantic interpretations to phonological strings.)

Chomsky's ideas had a broad impact, on both linguists and cognitive psychologists. How to characterize the knowledge system of a person who speaks a natural language became a central problem for linguists. The collection of empirical data about language acquisition was given a theoretical focus. And psycholinguistic studies of language comprehension flourished.

Beginning in the 1950s, therefore, one important change that cognitive psychologists introduced—one among many—was to move language into a central place in the study of human cognition. In part this move was necessary in order to justify the detailed analyses of verbal protocols that became increasingly fashionable (Ericsson & Simon, 1984). But a deeper reason was a growing realization that the capacity for human language really is extraordinary and unique. Today many cognitive psychologists agree that language is a central problem for our science. But what is meant when we say that today is not what I had in mind in 1951; today our reasons for saying it are much more persuasive.

In 1951 I argued for the importance of language by considering its role in the study of perception, learning, thinking, and the other standard chapter headings of introductory psychology (Miller, 1951). In fact, I thought of that 1951 book as an introductory text in which all of the examples were taken from studies of speech and language. In repeating the argument here I want to take a different approach.

I have, rather arbitrarily, selected two issues for discussion, one that has received more attention than it deserves during the past thirty years, and another that, until very recently, has received less. The first is "the innateness question": what does it mean to say that language is innate? This question is distinguished by the heat that it has generated, but I think it is worth discussing because it establishes that we cannot deal with such issues in the absence of a sophisticated theory of linguistic knowledge. The second question has forced itself to the attention of psychologists as the importance of situational contexts has become increasingly apparent. My way of considering situational influences on linguistic communication is to ask: What is the relation between language and communication?

IS LANGUAGE AN INNATE CAPACITY?

Some of the heat over the claims of innateness was generated because many psychologists had been raised with a healthy distrust of nativism. To assume that some complicated pattern of behavior is innate without exhaustively eliminating alternative hypotheses has all the advantages of theft over honest toil. Talk of the innateness of language triggered some deep prejudices. But claims that the capacity to learn

human language is innate now have many persuasive arguments in their favor:

1. The acquisition of language unfolds in much the same way in all normal children;
2. Language is species-specific—even the most isolated human groups have language, yet extremely intelligent apes do not;
3. The basic design features of human languages are universal; and
4. Specialized neurological structures devoted to the production and perception of speech have been identified.

More than twenty years ago Eric Lenneberg (1967) wrote a forceful summary of this evidence, and the major claims he made then have not been successfully refuted.

Given the weight of evidence, even skeptics have begun shifting their position: instead of simply denying that the capacity for language is innate, they now demand a more precise characterization of what the claim of innateness entails.

The claim is different for different components of language. Anyone who has studied a foreign language knows that there are three kinds of things to be learned: pronunciation, grammar, and vocabulary, corresponding respectively to the phonological, syntactic, and lexical components of language.

The Phonological Component

As far as I know, no one has ever seriously challenged the assumption that the ability to make and recognize the sounds of natural language is innate and species-specific. The nature of those sounds depends intimately on the neurophysiological structure of the speech organs, and that structure is a part of our genetic inheritance. Learning to use that structure for linguistic purposes is largely a matter of learning which subset your own language happens to have selected from the finite set of possible articulatory coordinations. There is much still to be learned about the subject, but the existence of innate constraints on the phonological component can hardly be doubted.

The Lexical Component

The lexical component of language stands at the opposite extreme. The knowledge of words and their meanings is learned. No serious scientist would claim that vocabulary is innate. The nature and organization of the lexical component has been my special interest in recent years and I have many stories I could tell about it, but none of them could be used to argue for innateness. Except, perhaps, in the ultimate sense that the ability to learn is itself innate.

The Syntactic Component

The major battle over innateness has centered on the syntactic component: is syntax more like the lexical or the phonological component? It resembles phonology to the extent that a relatively limited variety of rules can characterize all known languages, but it differs from phonology in that no obvious anatomical or neurophysiological basis for those universal features is known.

Those who argue for innateness generally do so by producing examples of linguistic properties that could not reasonably be supposed to have been learned. Probably the simplest example of such an argument is one used by Chomsky (1975, pp. 30–35). In English there is a consistent relation between certain declarative and interrogative sentences:

The door is locked.	Is the door * locked?
It was blowing away.	Was it * blowing away?
You can come in.	Can you * come in?

and so on. After observing this correspondence, a young child learning English might be expected to induce some such hypothesis as the following:

A. *To form a yes-no question, take the first "is" (or other helping verb like it, "was," "can," etc.) and move it to the front of the sentence.*

Hypothesis A is simple, it works well, and a child could find a great deal of evidence to support it. But it is wrong, as the following application of the hypothesis shows:

The door that is closed is locked.	Is the door that * closed is locked?

A much better hypothesis would be:

B. *To form a yes-no question, analyze the declarative sentence into phrases, then take the first "is" (or other helping verb like it, "was," "can," etc.) that follows the first noun phrase and move it to the front of the sentence.*

Hypothesis B is more complicated than A, but it gives the correct result for the sentence about the locked door. First, analysis of the declarative sentence shows that the first noun phrase is "the door that is closed," so rule B looks for the first "is" following this noun phrase:

The door that is closed is locked.	Is the door that is closed * locked?

Hypothesis B is said to be *structure-dependent*. That is to say, a child cannot adopt hypothesis B unless he or she is able to analyze sentences into phrases. The structure-independent hypothesis A does not require parsing and therefore seems far simpler and more probable than hypothesis B.

What does this have to do with the innateness of syntax? The empirical fact is that children learning English unerringly adopt the more complicated hypothesis B. The very first time they encounter a sentence as complex as the one about the locked door, they have no hesitation in adopting the structure-dependent hypothesis. How could they know to do that? It is extremely unlikely that anyone teaches them hypothesis B. The plausible answer, according to Chomsky, is that some part of the child's innate linguistic competence is a general principle that all rules of syntax must be structure-dependent. "The principle of structure-dependence is not learned, but forms part of the conditions for language learning" (Chomsky, 1975, p. 33).

Anyone who takes such arguments seriously should also take seriously the search for innate neurological mechanisms corresponding to the unlearned principles. In the case of structure dependence, one can at least speculate about what to look for. If syntactic structure is to be consistent with the structure of the underlying mental representation, then the linguistic principle of structure-dependence might reflect a need to respect representational structure. But such speculations lead immediately into a pit of controversy—what is the relation between linguistic and nonlinguistic mental representations? I am not interested in defending some particular position in this debate. I am simply pointing out that such questions are near the heartland of cognitive psychology.

The nature of representational systems is a topic of central importance to psychology. So the fact that language is intimately involved in representational systems argues that language is also a topic of central importance to psychology.

HOW ARE LANGUAGE AND COMMUNICATION RELATED?

Whatever the exact relation between language and representational systems, it does not exist in a vacuum. People have a reason for relating them. Which brings me to the second issue that I wanted to discuss.

Human language is the happy result of bringing together two systems that all higher organisms must have: a representational system and a communication system. (The opinions expressed here resulted from reading Sperber and Wilson, 1986.) A representational system is necessary if an organism is going to move around purposefully in its environment; a communication system is necessary if an organism is going to interact with others of its own kind. Presumably, some of the historical disagreements over the importance of language for our understanding of human cognition arose because different protagonists identified language with different parts of this combination. It is certainly true that human beings are not the only animals capable of a complex representational intelligence, nor are they the only animals that communicate. But human beings do seem to be the only animals in which a single system serves both of these functions.

There is no sense in which one could say that it is necessary for the representational and the communicative systems to be combined. Many animals are able to form representations of objects and events around them and can also communicate well enough to reproduce and

raise their young, yet are totally lacking anything as complicated as human language. It is simply an evolutionary peculiarity of human beings that these two important systems have combined to create a unique capacity for language. In order to convey a sense of the improbability of any such a development, Sperber and Wilson (1986) liken it to an elephant's trunk:

> The originality of the human species is precisely to have found this curious additional use for something which many other species also possess, as the originality of elephants is to have found that they can use their noses for the curious additional purpose of picking things up. In both cases, the result has been that something widely found in other species has undergone remarkable adaptation and development because of the new uses it has been put to. However, it is as strange for humans to conclude that the essential purpose of language is for communication as it would be for elephants to conclude that the essential purpose of noses is for picking things up. (pp. 173–174)

Nothing is known about how it happened that the representational and the communicative systems were combined, but, however it occurred, it was an important step in human evolution and so is worth some discussion, however speculative. Presumably it could not have occurred in an organism that had not already evolved a highly elaborate representational system, with a rich assortment of operations that could be performed on those representations. One critical step in this evolutionary innovation must have been the development of an ability to form structured representations of long, complicated vocalizations and to map those linguistic representations onto nonlinguistic representations of people, objects, and events. That is to say, a critical step was the evolution of an enriched representational system that could map back and forth between sounds and meanings. The structure of this elaborate system for encoding and decoding provides linguists with the subject matter for syntactic analysis.

Another critical step must have been the development of an ability to use this elaborate system for communication. A reasonable speculation would be that human language would only have evolved in a species that was already actively communicating—that had a need to communicate and could take immediate advantage of improvements in its communicative system. Otherwise, a capacity to map meanings into sounds would have offered little selective advantage, yet we know that the survival value of human language must have been very great. It is somewhat ironic that the need for this second evolutionary step is easily overlooked because the value of language for communicating is now so blindingly obvious. But much more is involved than most people realize. Underestimating the distance between a semantically interpreted sentence and a successful human communication has frustrated many attempts to turn computers into conversational partners.

Communication requires much more than the accurate transmission of a coded message. The source must have considerable information about the recipient and the recipient must attribute certain intentions to the source: in particular, the recipient must recognize that the source was intending to communicate. For many animals, the recognition of communicative intentions is instinctive: when an animal bares its fangs, for example, the foe recognizes that it intends to attack. But for human communication, the range of possible intentions is broad, the amount of information required to select appropriate intentions for the large set of possible intentions can be unpredictably large, and attributing the wrong intention to a speaker is far more likely.

The subtleties of human communication sound forbiddingly abstract when we try to characterize them formally, but no one has difficulty understanding them in everyday examples. So consider an example. Suppose that Henry hears Sally say, "David drinks." And suppose that Henry hears this clearly, knows who David is, knows the meaning of the verb *drink*, can parse the sentence correctly, and knows the conditions under which the sentence would be true—in short, suppose that Henry has no difficulty constructing a literal semantic interpretation for this sentence. Henry will still not understand what representa-

tion Sally intended to communicate. Was she speaking to Henry or simply thinking out loud? Is it a reminder to pick up something for David to drink, or a warning that David has a drinking problem, or a prediction that David will provide a drink if asked? Henry's choice among several possible interpretations will depend on the context of Sally's utterance. That is to say, Henry will have constructed some representation of the communicative episode in which he and Sally are participating; the effect of the utterance on Henry will depend both on his semantic interpretation of Sally's sentence and on his representation of their situation.

It is not an inconsequential fact that Sally and Henry are both human beings with a common evolutionary history, and so have an intuitive understanding of one another's representational systems. The more they know about each other's representational systems, the more relevant and efficient their communications can be. That is to say, Sally must have some knowledge of what Henry knows in order to estimate whether Henry can understand what she intends that her sentence should communicate.

Computers handle languages with great facility. Indeed, our appreciation of what a strange system human language is owes much to our understanding of the variety of artificial languages that can be used to program computers. We are even able to program computers to assign reasonable semantic interpretations to many grammatical sentences. But we have not yet been able to endow computers with anything like the complex communicative systems that people deal with so easily.

One of the important consequences of taking language seriously is that cognitive psychologists are now rediscovering the complexity of communication.

WHAT LIES AHEAD?

In 1962 I said that "one of the best ways to study the human mind is by studying the verbal systems that it uses" (Miller, 1962, p. 762). I had been saying that for several years, but in 1962 I went on to claim that such a program was not only important, but was possible. "In the years ahead," I concluded, "I hope we will see an increasing flow of new and exciting research." That hope has now been fulfilled. Today, the psychology of language is generally accepted as a central topic in cognitive psychology.

Will psycholinguistics continue its vigorous growth? I feel confident in predicting that language will continue to be important for theories of human psychology, but the fact that a problem is important does not guarantee that anyone will solve it. A good problem is one that lies just on the horizon of our ignorance—not so far off as to be out of sight, but not so close that it is obvious. I believe that there are some good problems that can feed the continued growth of the field; I thought I would close these remarks with some opinions about where those problems are.

Let me approach it this way. If I were a young man, trained in cognitive psychology and interested in language, what would I prepare myself to work on? My response to this question is clear and immediate: I would try to learn everything I could about biology and about computers. A psychologist who masters either one of these fields will be uniquely prepared for the future; a psychologist who mastered them both, in addition to psychology, would be a scientific superman.

Psychology in general has important relations to both of these fields, and the psychology of language is no exception. At the interface of psychology and biology there are two attractive ways to go. On the one hand, molecular biology is revealing the secrets of heredity, which promises to explain what we really mean when we speak of the innateness of language. But the second important focus in the life sciences is neurobiology, where the connections to psychology seem much more obvious and significant progress is much more likely to be realized within another lifetime.

The important question is to decide what problems should be solved first. Neuroscientists are making extraordinary progress in unravelling the processes that go on inside neurons and at synapses between neurons; understanding the biochemical basis for memory—for some kinds of memory, at least—seems only a few years away. By common consent, this part of science is being built from the bottom up, presumably on the assumption that the function of the nervous system will become clear as soon as all of its molecules have been identified. In my opinion, this situation creates a remarkable opportunity for psychologists interested in the brain as an information processing system. For example, new techniques for mapping and imaging the brain are becoming available, and each one opens a new window through which to observe how this remarkable organ stores representations and operates on them. At present our best evidence about this representational system is derived from speech, but a combination of speech and dynamic brain imaging should be far more informative.

At the interface with computer science, my choice of a goal is easier. From the very beginning of the computer age it has been a popular dream to have computers that people can talk to. One outcome of the attempts to realize that dream has been the discovery of how much more complicated it is than anyone ever imagined. Language is so obvious and natural for human beings that we all too easily take it for granted. The unexpected difficulties that have arisen should persuade any thoughtful psychologist that shallow explanations will never suffice.

It may turn out, somewhere in the future, that someone will be able to give a principled account of why such a program of research must fail—why computers of the kind available to us today could never be made to combine representational and communicative functions the way human beings do. I doubt that that will occur, but even if it were true, I would still want to prepare myself to undertake the work required to enable computers to comprehend language. Even if the program of research were to fail—and that is not at all certain—attempts to carry it out would still be enormously instructive. If it succeeded, of course, the practical implications for society would rival those of the invention of movable type. But even if it failed, an understanding of why it failed would surely carry important implications about the nature of the human mind.

In my secret heart, of course, I do not see these two projects as unrelated, but rather as two sides of single effort to understand the psychological bases of human language. I believe that the best opportunity for constructing and testing theories adequate to the intricacy of the brain and the complexity of human mental life is through the construction of computer simulations. To be trained to contribute to both of these lines of research, to understand both, and to help to bring them together—that would be a career for anyone to envy.

REFERENCES

Blumenthal, A. L. (1970). *Language and psychology: Historical aspects of psycholinguistics.* New York: Wiley.

Bühler, K. (1934). *Sprachtheorie: Die Darstellungsfunktion der Sprache.* Jena, Germany: Fischer.

Chomsky, N. (1957). *Syntactic structures.* The Hague: Mouton.

Chomsky, N. (1975). *Reflections on language.* New York: Pantheon.

Ericsson, K. A., & Simon, H. A. (1984). *Protocol analysis.* Cambridge, MA: MIT Press.

Freud, S. (1953). *On aphasia: A critical study.* (E. Stengel, Trans.). New York: International Universities Press. (Original work published 1891)

James, W. (1981). *The principles of psychology.* (Vols. 1–2). Cambridge, MA: Harvard University Press. (Original work published 1890).

Jarvella, R. J., & Klein, W. (1982). *Speech, place, and action: Studies in deixis and related topics:* New York: Wiley.

Koffka, K. (1935). *Principles of gestalt psychology.* New York: Harcourt Brace.

Lenneberg, E. H. (1967). *Biological foundations of language.* New York: Wiley.

Miller, G. A. (1951). *Language and communication.* New York: McGraw-Hill.

Miller, G. A. (1962). Some psychological studies of grammar. *American Psychologist, 17,* 748–762.

Skinner, B. F. (1957). *Verbal behavior.* New York: Appleton-Century-Crofts.

Sperber, D., & Wilson, D. (1986). *Relevance: Communication and cognition.* Oxford: Blackwell.

Tolman, E. C. (1932). *Purposive behavior in animals and men.* New York: Century.

Watson, J. B. (1924). *Behaviorism.* New York: Norton.

Wundt, W. (1900–1909). *Völkerpsychologie: Eine Untersuchung der Entwicklungsgesetze von Sprache, Mythus und Sitte.* (Vols. 1–10). Leipzig: Engelmann.

Based on an address to the First Annual Convention of the American Psychological Society held in Alexandria, Virginia, June 10, 1989.

20

Beryl Lieff Benderly

The Great Ape Debate: Can Gorillas and Chimps Use Language or Not?

In 1969 social scientists received astounding news. Two University of Nevada psychologists, Beatrice and R. Allen Gardner, claimed to have taught Washoe, a chimpanzee, to communicate in a human language. If true, this achievement knocked the foundation out from under many scientists' understanding of man's place in the universe.

In a number of disciplines that study the human species, it had been believed that homo sapiens, and only homo sapiens, has language. Indeed, whole edifices of thought had been raised upon this assumption. Some physical anthropologists saw language as the crucial selective advantage responsible for the explosive development of the human brain. The great linguist Noam Chomsky had asserted that linguistic ability is not only unique to but innate in our species, a genetically transmitted feature of a distinctively human cognition. And yet the Gardners had the unassailable proof, in the small, hairy form of Washoe, that we are not the only linguistic creatures on earth. Or so it seemed.

Earlier attempts to teach chimpanzees to talk had failed. The most successful pongid conversationalist had learned to articulate only three or four words, and those, as one writer put it, "with a heavy chimpanzee accent." For centuries mynas and other birds had been trained to repeat sentences. But the primate researchers were not interested in having animals merely parrot human utterances; they wanted to see if apes could use language as people do, flexibly, appropriately, and in novel circumstances. Reasoning that the chimps' failure lay not in their intellect—they are among the most intelligent and humanlike animals—but in their inadequate vocal equipment, the

Gardners decided to teach an ape a human language communicated by the hands. Specifically, they would attempt to raise Washoe to use American Sign Language (ASL), the gestural language of North American deaf people. They would provide Washoe with a homelike atmosphere, not because they saw her as a child but because they had no firm idea of how language was acquired and thought that the total immersion method that works for humans might work for chimpanzees as well.

In the next decade, scientific journals, the popular press, and the television screen seemed full of signing apes. Roger Fouts of the University of Oklahoma reported on several, and Francine Patterson of Stanford made a similar claim for a gorilla named Koko. Sarah, a chimpanzee trained by David Premack, now of the University of Pennsylvania, communicated with her trainers in an artificial language "written" in colored plastic shapes, and Lana, protégée of Duane Rumbaugh of Georgia State University and the Yerkes Regional Primate Research Center of Emory University in Atlanta, did so in Yerkish, a computer language. The animals appeared able to answer questions, follow instructions, and make requests and observations.

Recently, however, a number of scientists have begun to question this early work. Books and articles attacking the original researchers' methodologies, training techniques, reporting practices, conceptualizations, and even their motives have become more numerous every month. The widely publicized failure of a Columbia University team headed by Herbert Terrace to teach language to a chimpanzee called Nim—short for Neam Chimpsky—has attracted the attention of the popular press to the growing controversy. Prominent among the critics are Duane and Sue Savage-Rumbaugh of the Lana project, who now raise serious methodological and philosophical questions about their own earlier conclusions.

But several of those who claimed success stand staunchly by their guns. The Gardners, Fouts, and Patterson maintain that their early reports were accurate and will, in time, be recognized as such by all fair-minded students of the question. They further believe that their

work has been misinterpreted, misunderstood, even misrepresented by their detractors.

Perhaps the simplest conceptual point at issue is what language the apes were exposed to in the first place. All those who reported attempts to train apes to sign—the Gardners, Fouts, Patterson, and Terrace—stated that they used ASL. But, as Terrace's former students Mark Seidenberg and Laura Petitto argue, the evidence on this point is cloudy at best.

Used by perhaps 500,000 American deaf people, ASL is a language in its own right, totally unrelated to English. Unlike spoken languages, with structures built on distinctions among sounds or groups of sounds, ASL is structured on distinctions among motions of the hands and upper body. Each correctly executed sign contains four elements: two properly formed hands, oriented to one another at the proper angle, carrying out a proper motion, at the proper point on the head or body. A change in any of these elements can change the meaning of the sign, just as a change in a single element—vibration of the vocal chords—will change the spoken word "tin" into "din." Fluent users of ASL arrange signs according to grammatical principles quite unlike those of English. Because ASL is rarely, if ever, taught formally, and because linguists have only partially codified its syntax and semantics, very few hearing people not born to deaf parents ever attain mastery. None of the ape researchers had a high degree of fluency when they began, although some have grown more skillful over the years.

Nonetheless, it appears that the apes were not taught ASL, but rather a number of vocabulary items taken from ASL but arranged approximately according to English word order. In other words, they were taught one or another form of pidgin sign English.

Pidgins are a common enough linguistic phenomenon. The various forms of pidgin English that serve as *lingua franca* on some Pacific Islands, for example, consist of genuine English words but cannot be considered versions of English. Their vocabularies and their manners of combining words and marking grammatical functions violate the canons of English.

Similarly, the hybrid forms of English-based sign language are not the invention of ape researchers. For many years such systems have served as *lingua franca* between hearing and deaf people. Other artificially created sign systems that express English grammatical markers also are being used with some deaf children. Pidgins usually lack many of the resources of the separate languages that influence them.

In the case of pidgin sign English, for example, the system lacks the grammatical markers both of English, which depend mainly on sound differences, word order, and suffixes, and of ASL, which depend mainly on modulations of sign forms in space. This rather impoverished form is really not a language, but a manual code for English; among human beings, at least, using it assumes that both parties to a conversation know some English and are providing at least some English grammatical markers in their heads. As hearing signers become more proficient, however, there is some tendency to edge toward ASL-like usage, and English word order may not always be observed. Thus, if the apes were taught this kind of sign language—and the evidence indicates that, regardless of their trainers' claims, they were—then it is difficult to know what, if any, grammar they could have learned.

But even if the apes have not learned a specific language used by a real human community, does this mean that they have not learned language? Is the speech of Tonto or Man Friday less linguistic for being stilted English? Here the debate goes beyond data and becomes a matter of definition. Whether or not pongid communications fall inside or outside the boundary of human language behavior depends entirely on where that boundary is.

Until 11 years ago this question hardly mattered; no one attempted to differentiate human linguistic abilities from those of other primates because it was generally assumed that other primates had none. Since then, no commonly accepted definition has emerged, and the question has become extremely vexing. Several ape researchers compared their protégés' efforts to the early stages of child language, prompting a subsidiary debate over the features of early language and the processes of its acquisition.

Can a definition of language include the often unintelligible talk of small children, or must it be limited to the well-formed utterances of adults?

Scientists generally include childish stabs at speech (or signing) in the category of language, on the assumption that any normal child will eventually grow into a normally linguistic adult. The early, imperfect attempts of childhood are seen merely as steps toward that goal. In the case of apes, however, there is no such assumption. Critics have insisted that ape utterances must be included or excluded from the realm of language solely on their own merits. Some researchers argue that this applies a higher standard to the apes than to ourselves.

Certain critics, Terrace prominent among them, insist that grammar is the hallmark of language. Terrace acknowledges that Nim and other apes acquired sizable vocabularies of signs. But Nim, Terrace argues, did not use a grammar to generate sentences; he merely combined signs in imitation of combinations previously signed by his teachers. Others have countered that the conditions of Nim's training may have precluded a fair chance to learn any grammar. He had 60 different teachers in four years, nearly all of them hearing people, and thus was exposed to many inexpert and inconsistent versions of signing. Nor does everyone accept sign order in two- or three-sign utterances as a valid measure of grammaticalness. In ASL, sign order in short utterances has little or no grammatical significance.

Others reject Terrace's standard as either too inclusive or not inclusive enough. Premack claimed linguistic ability for Sarah because she mastered the syntactical principles of a simple system using plastic tokens of different shapes and colors. She learned to associate various tokens with actions, objects, or properties—a blue triangle stood for "apple," for instance—and to arrange them in ordered strings that, according to David and Ann James Premack, contain grammarlike, hierarchical relations among the elements. She correctly interpreted the command "Sarah insert apple pail banana dish" to mean that the apple went in the pail and the banana in the dish, not that the apple, pail, and banana all went into the dish. But, says William Stokoe of Gallaudet College, a leading researcher in the structure of sign language, "When language is reduced to that level, then to me it isn't language."

Does language have to resemble human interaction rather than mimic symbolic logic? Fouts rejects grammar as the only defining characteristic; the important feature, he says, is communication. For him, what stands out is not only that apes use signs grammatically but that they use them flexibly, combining them into new utterances never seen before but appropriate to the circumstances. There are many famous and highly controversial examples of apparently original ape coinages. On first seeing a swan, Washoe signed "water bird." When Lucy tasted watermelon and Koko tasted stale sweet rolls, they signed, respectively, "drink fruit" and "cookie rock." Lucy called a radish "cry hurt food." A feverish, diarrheic Washoe, when asked "What wrong with you?", signed "hurt" over her belly.

But did Washoe really mean by "water bird" a bird who inhabits the water, or did she merely respond to the simultaneous presence of water and a bird? Was this utterance in fact original or merely accidental? Did she ever combine "water" and "bird" with other signs, to produce, for example, such nonsensical combinations as "water shoe," "water food," "water banana," or "water tickle"? Critics charge that the Gardners have not presented a sufficiently large sample of Washoe's utterances to permit such judgments. The Gardners believe that their critics have not studied with sufficient care the data on a number of apes they have laid out in a long series of papers.

Some scientists dismiss the entire search for a universal definition of language as fruitless. "Everyone knows what languages are," Stokoe says, "but no one knows what 'language' is." Allen Gardner remarks, "Whether the graybeards of linguistics call it language is not interesting. It's what the chimps do that's interesting."

What the apes are doing is a crucial, philosophical question. We might almost phrase it, "What do they know and when do they know it?" Do they indeed mean or understand what

they are signing, and if so, how can we know? An American diplomat newly arrived in South America once watched as his 10-year-old son Tommy, who knew no Spanish, played soccer with some neighborhood boys. Tommy spotted a hole in the opposing line. "*Aquí, Aquí!*" he shouted, and a teammate kicked the ball to him. Later, while complimenting Tommy on picking up the language so quickly, the father asked what *aquí* meant.

"I don't know, Dad," Tommy said, "but it sure gets me the ball in a hurry."

Tommy, in short, had not learned Spanish at all. He had merely learned a way of manipulating the Spanish-saturated world that his playmates inhabit. They know that *aquí* means "here." He knows nothing of the sort, but he has learned that it will produce a certain response. Is this all that the apes have learned to do, or have they truly entered into the cognitive world of human users of language? A central difficulty of this debate is that psychology has yet to agree on a means of knowing, a means, in other words, of telling comprehension from mere conditioning. In Tommy's case we can ask; in Washoe's we cannot. Critics argue that all the apes' reported behavior can be explained more simply than that some animals use language with understanding.

In supporting so radical an assertion as "apes have language," the critics insist the burden of proof, and a very onerous burden they believe it to be, lies on those who advance the claim rather than on those who would disprove it. For Terrace, the Rumbaughs, and Thomas Sebeok and Donna Jean Umiker-Sebeok of Indiana University, the fact that apes appear to use language does not constitute proof. The animals may have learned nothing more than an association between an object, action, or context and a certain gesture. They may have learned that signing is highly valued, indeed required, by their trainers. It is people who gloss the apes' actions, these critics point out, people who assign human definitions that may be loaded with meaning. For example, when Lana pushes buttons to produce an utterance like "Please machine give Lana drink," can it be reasonably argued, her trainers ask, that what she meant by pressing the button glossed as "please" is what human beings understand by that word? Can it be said that she intended to be polite, or just that she knew that she got no food without pushing that button?

The Gardners are critical of comparing the vocabulary usage of immature chimpanzees to that of fluent adults. They emphasize the developmental nature of vocabulary growth and communicative abilities, and maintain that such pongid skills resemble those of a very young human child.

The trap of anthropomorphism—ascribing human traits to nonhumans—lies open for all who interpret animal behavior, and many critics believe that the ape researchers have fallen right in. The Sebeoks suggest that ape language could be nothing more than an extreme case of the Clever Hans phenomenon, well-known from elementary textbooks in psychology. Clever Hans was a horse who confounded turn-of-the-century Germany by solving any mathematical problem put to him, so long as the answer was a number. Panels of scientists, both friendly and hostile, examined him, but always he showed the flabbergasting ability to tap his foot the right number of times. Not until closely monitored experiments were undertaken did the truth emerge. Hans had not learned mathematics but human body language. He read unconscious cues from the people around him, and saw from their stance, their hands, their eyes, their breathing, when to stop tapping.

Could it be that the trainers are cuing the apes rather than conversing with them? Terrace and associates subjected several hours of video tapes of Nim and his teachers to close scrutiny and report that they found a great deal of cuing, probably unconscious. Indeed, Terrace writes, until this analysis, he was convinced that Nim truly could converse. Terrace also believes that he sees a good deal of cuing in the films of the Gardners and Washoe, and that, like Nim, Washoe only initiated signing for rewards not otherwise obtainable. The Gardners, however, based on work by Stokoe, dispute the validity of frame-by-frame analysis of signing. Sign conversations among humans are full of overlapping signs because vision can tolerate simultaneous signals far better than

hearing can. What Terrace sees as cuing, the Gardners believe is participation in discourse, an important source of data on language acquisition. Terrace's claim that the chimps signed only for rewards is false, according to the Gardners. "The film contains two long scenes in which Washoe is signing to herself, signing 'in' and 'out' as she places toys inside a hat, signing 'That red' of a red boot she is wearing." Patterson claims that the very act of filming may upset the ape or teacher or both to the point that the animal's signing suffers.

The debate will make no progress, the Sebeoks suggest, until the psychologists, linguists, and anthropologists step back and let animal training experts see what is going on. In their view, the whole thing might be a deception; not a conscious hoax, they hasten to make clear, but something even more disturbing, a systematic self-deception by well-meaning but methodologically confused scientists.

But the Gardners, Fouts, and Patterson insist that something very language-like is going on. The skirmishing over what to call it, they fear, takes attention from the phenomenon itself. Their years of experience tell them that something profoundly important happens between certain people and certain apes—that apes can and often do use signs to communicate. According to Fouts, for example, chimps can refer to objects or events not present—one of the critics' key requirements for symbolism, and a widely accepted criterion of language. In an experiment with Nim's brother Ally, several objects were hidden in various locations in a partitioned test room while Ally looked on. Ally was then questioned in another area of the room by an experimenter unaware of the locations of the concealed objects. The chimp responded correctly 161 times out of 240 trials, using the preposition-location relationship, such as "Ball under box" to the question "Where ball?"

Terrace's failure to train Nim, Fouts claims, proves nothing except the inadequacy of Terrace's training methods. While living at the Oklahoma Primate Center, after the Columbia project ended, Nim is said to have signed very well, without the interruptions and repetitions that troubled Terrace.

The basic disagreement is philosophical. It has to do with man's relationship to the other primates. Fouts insists that those suggesting that apes can master elements of human language are not the ones making radical claims; those who deny the possibility are doing so. Science knows very little about the limits of apes in the wild, Allen Gardner points out. Nor does it know much about how apes use signs among themselves. Washoe, now a matron of 15, has taught several signs to her foster son Loulis. Fouts and his assistants are careful to use only five signs in Loulis' presence, but the young chimp has a vocabulary larger than that. Washoe has been seen indicating an object and repeatedly making the sign for it, like a teacher in a classroom, and even forming her charge's hand into the proper shape, just as the Gardners did for her.

The assumption that only humans have language may be nothing more than that—a groundless belief, according to Fouts, supported by evidence far less sound than that in the disputed ape studies.

Human language, to his mind, is only one of a range of communication forms developed by animal species, at least some of which we share with our evolutionary second or third cousins, the apes. In our present state of knowledge, we know enough neither about them nor about ourselves to make categorical statements. The only correct assumption, Fouts argues, is that we may resemble them in important ways; in short, that "evolution is correct" and applies to homo sapiens as well.

But even if further disputation and research show that "linguistic" apes are nothing more than shrewd and subtle manipulators of human beings, this alone gives us a glimpse into far more interesting and challenging minds than previously imagined.

21

George Lakoff

A Figure of Thought

For two millennia we were taught a dogma that was largely unquestioned and came to be viewed as definitional. Metaphor was called a figure of *speech*. As such, it was taken to be a matter of special language: poetic or persuasive language. As a matter of *language*, rather than *thought*, it was viewed as dispensable. If you have something to say, you could presumably say it straightforwardly without metaphor; if you chose metaphor it was for some poetic or rhetorical purpose, perhaps for elegance or economy, but not for plain speech and ordinary thought. Metaphor was seen as contrasting with ordinary, everyday literal language, language that could be straightforwardly true or false, that could fit the world directly or not.

Teaching Berkeley undergraduates forces one to question traditional values—even if those values have stood for two thousand years. In 1978, I taught a small undergraduate seminar (there were five students) in which metaphor was one of a number of topics. I had received a prepublication copy of the Ortony (1979) collection on *Metaphor and Thought*, and we were discussing the chapters in the volume. One day one of the students came in too upset to function. She announced that she had a metaphor problem, and asked the small assembled group for help. Her boyfriend had just told her that their relationship "had hit a dead-end street."

It being Berkeley in the 1970s, the class came to the rescue. The metaphor makes sense, we soon figured out, only if you're traveling toward some destination, and only if love is viewed as a form of travel. If you happen onto a dead-end street when you're traveling toward a destination, then you can't keep going the way you've been going. You have to turn back. "What I really want," the woman said, "is for us to go into another dimension."

There is nothing like a disappointing love affair for calling a philosophy of long standing into question. Metaphor, in the traditional view, was supposed to be a matter of speech, not thought. Yet here was not just a way of talking about love as a journey, but a way of thinking about it in that way and of reasoning on the basis of the metaphor. In our culture, there is a full-blown love-as-journey metaphor that is used for comprehending and reasoning about certain aspects of love relationships, especially those having to do with duration, closeness, difficulties, and common purpose.

English is full of expressions that reflect the conceptualization of love as a journey. Some are necessarily about love; others can be understood that way:

> Look *how far we've come*. It's been *a long, bumpy road*. We can't turn back now. We're at *a crossroads*. We may have to *go our separate ways*. We're *spinning our wheels*. The relationship isn't *going anywhere*. The marriage is *on the rocks*.

These are ordinary, everyday expressions. There is nothing extraordinary about them. They are not poetic, nor are they used for rhetorical effect. The most important ones are those such as "Look how far we've come," which aren't necessarily about love, but can be so understood. Examples like this show that what is involved is not just conventional language, but a conventional mode of thought. They reflect a way of thinking about love:

> The lovers are travelers on a journey together, with common goals. The relationship is their vehicle, and it allows them to pursue those common goals together. The journey isn't easy. There are impediments, and there are places (crossroads) where a decision has to be made about which direction to go in and whether to keep traveling together.

The mode of travel can be of various types: car ("long bumpy road," "spinning our wheels"), train ("off the track"), boat ("on the rocks," "foundering"), or plane ("just taking off," "bailing out").

The metaphor involves understanding one domain of experience, love, in terms of a very different domain of experience, journeys. The metaphor can be understood as a mapping (in the mathematical sense) from a source domain (in this case, journeys) to a target domain (in this case, love). The mapping is tightly structured. There are ontological correspondences, according to which entities in the domain of love (e.g., the lovers, their common goals, their difficulties, the love relationship, etc.) correspond systematically to entities in the domain of a journey (the travelers, the vehicle, destinations, etc.):

> The lovers correspond to travelers.
> The love relationship corresponds to the vehicle.
> The state of being in the relationship corresponds to the physical closeness of being in the vehicle.
> The lovers' common goals correspond to their common destinations on the journey.
> Difficulties correspond to impediments to travel.

The mapping includes epistemic correspondences in which knowledge about journeys is mapped onto knowledge about love. Such correspondences permit us to reason about love with the knowledge we use to reason about journeys. Let us take an example:

Two travelers are traveling somewhere in a vehicle and it hits some impediment and gets stuck. If they do nothing, they will not reach their destinations. There are a limited number of alternatives for action: (a) They can try to get the vehicle moving again, either by fixing it or getting it past the impediment that stopped it; (b) they can remain in the stuck vehicle and give up on getting to their destinations in it; and (c) they can abandon the vehicle. The alternative of remaining in the stuck vehicle takes the least effort but does not satisfy the desire to reach their destination.

The ontological correspondences map this scenario (sometimes called a *knowledge structure* in the cognitive sciences) onto a corresponding love scenario, in which the corresponding alternatives for action are seen. Here is the corresponding love scenario that results from applying the ontological correspondences to this knowledge structure.

Two people are in love and pursuing their common goals in a love relationship. They encounter some difficulty in the relationship that, if nothing is done, will keep them from pursuing their goals. Their alternatives for action are: (a) They can try to do something so that the relationship will once more allow them to pursue their goals; (b) they can leave the relationship as it is and give up on pursuing their goals; and (c) they can abandon the relationship. The alternative of remaining in the relationship takes the least effort but does not satisfy goals external to the relationship.

What constitutes the love-as-journey metaphor theme is not any particular word or expression. It is the ontological and epistemic mapping across conceptual domains, from the source domain of journeys to the target domain of love. The metaphor is not just a matter of language, but of thought and reason. The language is a reflection of the mapping. The mapping is conventional, one of our conventional ways of understanding love.

If metaphors were just linguistic expressions, we would expect different linguistic expressions to be different metaphors. Thus, "We've hit a dead-end street" would constitute one metaphor. "We can't turn back now" would constitute another, quite different metaphor. "Their marriage is on the rocks" would involve a still different metaphor. And so on for dozens of examples. Yet we don't seem to have dozens of different metaphors here. We have one metaphor, in which love is conceptualized as a journey. It is a unified way of conceptualizing love metaphorically that is realized in many different linguistic expressions.

Another way to put the question is this: How can a speaker of English know that a relatively neutral journey sentence such as "Look how far we've come" can be about love (as well as about other activities that are conceptualized as journeys)? A grammar of English and an English dictionary would be of no use. None of the individual words would be listed in an English lexicon as being about love. Not "look" or "far" or "come" (in the sense used here). What we need to know is that we live in a culture in which love is conceptualized as a journey.

But where is this knowledge localized? It is not part of the grammar or lexicon of English, nor is it part of any general concept of metaphor. Rather, it must be part of our conceptual system—part of the way we understand what love is. There is a single metaphor, and it is conceptual in nature: Love is understood as a

journey. As a result, many expressions about journeys of the appropriate sort—"dead-end street," "crossroads,"—can be understood as being about love.

What is particularly interesting is that new and imaginative extensions of the mapping can be understood instantly, given the ontological correspondences and other knowledge about journeys. Take the song lyric, "We're going riding in the fast lane on the freeway of love." The traveling knowledge called upon is this: When you drive in the fast lane, you go a long way in a short time and it can be exciting and dangerous. The danger may be to the vehicle (the relationship may not last) or the passengers (the lovers may be hurt, emotionally). The excitement of the love journey is sexual. Our understanding of the song lyric depends upon the pre-existing metaphorical correspondences of the love-as-journey metaphor. The song lyric is instantly comprehensible because those metaphorical correspondences are already part of our conceptual system. An understanding of novel metaphor, in most cases, will depend on the understanding of conventional metaphors.

The love-as-journey metaphor was the example that first convinced me that metaphor was not a figure of speech, but a mode of thought, defined by a systematic mapping from a source to a target domain. What convinced me were the three characteristics of metaphor that I have just discussed: (a) the systematicity in the linguistic correspondences, (b) the use of metaphor to govern reasoning and behavior based on that reasoning, and (c) the possibility for understanding novel extensions in terms of the conventional correspondences.

One of the virtues of a new theory is that new and interesting issues and puzzles arise that previously could not even be formulated. In the theory that Johnson and I have proposed (Lakoff & Johnson, 1980), the following are among the new questions that arise: What determines the details of the ontological correspondences? In a system of conventional metaphors, how are the metaphors related to one another? Are some metaphors possible only because other metaphors are already in the system? Does social knowledge play a role in characterizing metaphors?

At present, the theory is so new that relatively few metaphors have been analyzed in sufficient detail to provide answers to such questions. To understand what answers to such questions might be like, let us speculate as to how the love-as-journey metaphor might be viewed as a product of other metaphors. What needs to be shown is how a collection of other metaphors plus certain bits of folk knowledge combine to determine the ontological correspondences of the love-as-journey metaphor theme.

Suppose we begin with the purposes-as-destinations metaphor, which we refer to as M1: The source domain is space; the target domain is intention. Ontological correspondences include:

A purpose corresponds to a destination.
Achievement of the purpose corresponds to movement to the destination.
A difficulty corresponds to an impediment to movement (e.g., getting stuck, going up a hill, encountering a barrier).
Maintaining the purpose corresponds to keeping the destination in sight.

Examples include:

We've still got *a long way to go*. We're *almost there*. Our goal is *in sight*. We've *reached our goal*. There's *nothing in our way*. It's been *uphill all the way*. Don't *look back* now.

Now consider the most basic version of the life-as-journey metaphor (M2): The source domain is journey; the target domain is life. Ontological correspondences include:

Birth corresponds to the beginning of the journey.
Death corresponds to the end of the journey.

Now let us put M1 and M2 together with three pieces of folk knowledge, namely:

K1: People want to achieve many purposes in their lives.
K2: Achieving purposes in life may be difficult and take a long time.
K3: A journey involves traveling a long way through a number of intermediate destinations.

What results is a complex metaphor of life as a long, difficult, purposeful journey. Let us call this metaphor M3, where M3 = M1 + M2 + K1 + K2 + K3. Here is the structure of M3: The source domain is journey; the target domain is life. Ontological correspondences include:

Birth corresponds to beginning of journey.
Death corresponds to end of journey.
Purposes correspond to intermediate destinations.
Achieving a purpose corresponds to reaching an intermediate destination.
Difficulties correspond to impediments to movement.

Epistemic correspondences include:

K1: People want to achieve many purposes in their lives (this corresponds to):
K1': People want to reach many intermediate destinations on their journeys.
K2: Achieving purposes in life may involve encountering difficulties and may take a long time (this corresponds to):
K2': Reaching destinations on a journey may involve encountering impediments and may take a long time.

This metaphor, when filled out beyond this skeletal characterization, would account for why we speak of people as being "aimless" or "having direction in their lives," why we can understand people as "making progress," why important achievements that mark that progress are called "milestones," and why people can view things as "standing in their way."

The love-as-journey metaphor is intimately related to the metaphor of life as a purposeful journey. A long-term love relationship is understood as a journey through life together with the love relationship as vehicle. But let us be somewhat more specific. Consider the folk belief:

K4: People in a long-term love relationship adopt a commitment to each other's major goals; as a result, their major goals are shared goals and they pool their resources to achieve them. The love relationship thus facilitates achieving those goals.

Metaphorically, this puts people in long-term love relationships on the same journey, since common goals correspond to common destinations.

To see why the love relationship is understood as the vehicle in the love-as-journey metaphor, let us look at a very basic metaphor whose source domain is physical space and whose target domain is interpersonal relationships:

M4: Intimacy corresponds to closeness.
Lack of intimacy corresponds to distance.

Examples include:

We used to be very *close*, but we've drifted *apart* over the years. We're pretty *distant* these days.

A second basic metaphor is:

M5: An interpersonal relationship corresponds to a container.
The people in the relationship correspond to the contents of the container.

Examples include:

We *got into* the relationship without thinking. It's a difficult relationship to *get out of.* I'm thinking of *leaving* the relationship.

A third basic metaphor is:

M6: An interpersonal relationship is a constructed object.

Examples include:

It took us a long time to *build* that relationship. We have a *solid* relationship. Their relationship is very *fragile* and it may *fall apart.* We need to *patch up* our relationship.

Suppose we add these metaphors to the ones discussed above and consider a few pieces of folk knowledge about vehicles and love relationships:

K5: A vehicle is a container.
K6: A vehicle is a constructed object.
K7: People in a vehicle are physically close.
K8: People in a love relationship are intimate.
K9: People in the same vehicle are on the same journey.
K10: A vehicle facilitates a journey.

Putting all this together, we can now compare our knowledge about vehicles to our metaphorical knowledge about love relationships:

A vehicle is a constructed object, which is a container with people in it who are close and are on the same journey, and which facilitates the journey.
A love relationship is a constructed object, which is a container with people in it who are close and are on the same journey, and which facilitates the journey.

Thus, the properties that characterize the vehicle on a journey are metaphorical properties that characterize the love relationship in the love-as-journey metaphor.

The love-as-journey metaphor is anything but a fanciful, random, idiosyncratic way of understanding love relationships. It is instead a part of the fabric of our culture. Every aspect of the love-as-journey metaphor is motivated by other metaphors in our conceptual system and by various pieces of folk knowledge and belief. The rest of our conceptual system provides all the conceptual resources that are needed to view love as a journey of the kind I have already discussed.

But there is a big difference between, on the one hand, having all the equipment and supplies and skills to build a house and, on the other hand, actually doing the building. The rest of our conceptual system provides all of the equipment needed for a love-as-journey metaphor; in addition to this, the metaphor actually has to be put together as a conceptual unit. It has to be conventionalized. This is one of the major differences between a deductive system in formal logic and a human conceptual system. In a formal deductive system, all the consequences that can be drawn are drawn. This is not necessarily true in a human conceptual system. Everything necessary for a conventional metaphorical mapping may be present, but that does mean that the mapping will be conventionalized and become part of our normal automatic way of understanding experience.

How do we know that the love-as-journey metaphor has actually become an existing conceptual unit of its own? The prima facie evidence is the existence of conventional expressions—idioms, fixed formulas, and clichés that are based on it. Evidence in this case are expressions about love relationships such as "on the rocks," "off the track," "this relationship isn't going anywhere," and clichéd expressions that turn up over and over in the wedding speeches of ministers such as "As you travel together on the journey of life." Conventional expressions express conventional ideas. If the expressions exist as a conventional part of the language, then the ideas that they express exist in the conventional conceptual system on which the language is based.

There is a big difference between having a metaphorical mapping exist as a unit in your conceptual system and putting together the same metaphor fresh the first time. Any concept that is part of the conventional conceptual system is used automatically, unconsciously, and effortlessly; that goes for metaphorical concepts (e.g., the concept of love as a journey) as well as for nonmetaphorical concepts. A metaphorical mapping made up anew is going to be used consciously and with effort.

But do all competent speakers of a language have the same conventionalized metaphors? And how do we know, for any given individuals, whether the love-as-journey metaphor is conventionalized *for them*? The analytic methods devised by Johnson and myself (Lakoff & Johnson, 1980) are not sufficient to answer such questions. All our methods permit is an analysis of conventional metaphors in the conceptual system underlying the speech of an *idealized* native speaker. Quinn's techniques of discourse analysis can show, in some cases, which metaphors a particular speaker is using in everyday reasoning (see Holland & Quinn, in press). But Quinn's techniques, though extremely elegant, are difficult to apply and are not universally applicable. Like syntactic analysis, metaphorical analysis is not very good at studying individual variation, and works best for idealized speakers.

Incidentally, it is to be expected that speakers would vary as to whether a given metaphor has been conventionalized or not. Take, for example, the woman who first brought up the dead-end street example. Why didn't she understand her boyfriend instantly? Why did she need help? The reason is that she did not normally think about love that way. And she didn't want to.

When Johnson and I wrote *Metaphors We Live By* (Lakoff & Johnson, 1980), we were confronted with a terminological question: Should we adapt the term *metaphor* to describe mappings such as those described above, given that the term had not been used that way in the past? It made sense etymologically, since such mappings across conceptual domains consti-

tute a "carrying across." But that was not our primary reason.

The study of metaphor is defined by a subject matter. For example, the song lyric given above—"We're going riding in the fast lane on the freeway of love"—is the kind of novel, poetic expression that constituted the subject matter of the traditional theory. The job of the traditional theory was to account for its subject matter—novel metaphor used poetically and rhetorically. That is, its job was to explain how we understand such expressions and to show what general principles are involved. Johnson and I maintain that the theory we have outlined, when appropriately filled out, will indeed account for the poetic use of metaphor, and will do it via conceptual mappings of the sort we have described.

But the new theory we have put forth accounts for more than the data that the old theory was supposed to account for. In the process, we have discovered structure in ordinary, everyday language that was not previously known to be there, and we believe that the same principles cover both the new phenomena and the old. In fact, we claim that most poetic metaphors (the old phenomena) can be understood only given an account of already existing conventional metaphorical correspondences (the new phenomena).

It is inevitable that when theories change, word meanings change with them. Motion meant something very different to Aristotle than it does to us. Aristotle took illness and growth as instances of motion, and proposed general laws of motion to cover all cases. Energy did not mean the same thing to Newton as to Einstein. It would have been meaningless to Newton to speak of measuring the mass of particles in terms of energy, as particle physicists do now. In Newtonian physics, mass and energy were different kinds of things; in Einsteinian physics, they are not.

Similarly, the claim that metaphors are to be accounted for by a mapping from one conceptual domain to another results in a radical meaning change. *Metaphor* no longer means what it did before. In the theory that Johnson and I (Lakoff & Johnson, 1980) have proposed, metaphor refers primarily to a principle by which one concept is understood in terms of another. When we use metaphor to refer to a linguistic expression, we mean an expression that is an instance of such a conceptual principle. Sometimes we use the terms *conceptual metaphor* and *linguistic metaphor* to mark the distinction. Of course, we would use the term *metaphor* for the same linguistic expressions that the term was originally used for, though in contexts where a confusion might arise, we have taken to calling such expressions linguistic metaphors to distinguish them from the corresponding conceptual principles.

Within the traditional theory of metaphor, it would make no sense to speak of there being a love-as-a-journey metaphor that is conceptual in nature, nor would it make sense to speak of expressions used to speak of love (e.g., "dead-end street," "crossroads," "on the rocks," etc.) as instances of a metaphorical conception of love. In the traditional view, each expression would be a different metaphor, because metaphors can only be linguistic, not conceptual, in nature. The traditional theory is so different from the theory we are putting forth that the analysis suggested above of the love-as-journey metaphor would not make any sense within the traditional theory and could not even be discussed sensibly within that theory.

What is important to bear in mind is that the term *metaphor* as it was traditionally used in theoretical discussions, was defined relative to a theory. That theory went virtually unquestioned for two thousand years. Because the theory was not even noticed as being a theory, the definition of metaphor relative to that theory was taken as the correct definition of metaphor. But metaphor also referred to a certain range of phenomena, phenomena that we are trying to provide an adequate theory of. We have kept *metaphor* because we are trying to provide an adequate theory of the phenomena that the term has always referred to. Einstein, after all, did not abandon the term *energy* when he discovered that energy was not distinct from mass.

The change in the meaning of terminology that necessarily accompanies theory change can be extremely disturbing to those who were brought up with the old theory. One of the old terms whose meaning is changed under the new theory is *literal*; another is *dead metaphor*. The old meanings of these terms were theory-dependent. There is no way to change the theory as we have and keep the old meanings of these terms. I will discuss the reasons why in future columns.

REFERENCES

Holland, D., & Quinn, N. (Eds.). (in press). *Cultural models in language and thought*. Cambridge, England: Cambridge University Press.

Lakoff, G., & Johnson, M. (1980). *Metaphors we live by*. Chicago: University of Chicago Press.

Ortony, A. (Ed.). (1979). *Metaphor and thought*. Cambridge, England: Cambridge University Press.

22

Dianne Horgan

Learning to Tell Jokes: A Case Study of Metalinguistic Abilities

Most of the recent literature on children's humour looks at school-age children's responses to humorous stimuli, emphasizing the role of cognition. Much less is known about very early humour, particularly spontaneous jokes and their linguistic structure. When linguistic aspects of humour are discussed, it is usually with respect to fairly sophisticated elements such as ambiguity. This note will examine earlier spontaneous jokes (between ages 1;4 and 4;0) and will analyse them in terms of the metalinguistic abilities they represent.

The Piagetian-cognitive perspective provides a framework from which to view these data. Towards the end of the sensorimotor period children begin symbolic play. According to Schultz (1976), humour and symbolic play are closely related in the beginning, but become more differentiated as the child develops. In symbolic play, a child reproduces a motor schema outside of its normal context. That is, a child begins to be able to pretend. Children at this age pretend to be reading, sleeping, eating, putting on make-up, etc. Symbolic play can be viewed as self-constructed incongruity. Support for the relationship between symbolic play and humour comes from the fact that symbolic play is almost always accompanied by laughter: the child thinks it is funny to pretend to sleep, eat, put on make-up. McGhee (1979) describes what happens after the development of make-believe play. McGhee's stages are reflections of cognitive development and correspond to Piaget's descriptions of cognitive acquisitions. Stage 1 consists of incongruous actions towards objects, such as Piaget's child pretending a leaf was a telephone. Stage 2 consists of incongruous labelling of objects and events, such as calling a hand a foot. The absence of action towards the object characterizes the increase in cognitive ability. Stage 1 and 2 jokes are seen mostly during the pre-school years. Stage 3 may start around 3 years. This stage involves conceptual incongruity, which entails violating one or more aspects of a concept. McGhee describes examples of word play during this stage. Children's humour first approaches adult humour in Stage 4 with an appreciation of ambiguity. This begins around age 7 with attainment of concrete operations, and is the stage most systematically studied. Children now can understand riddles. Research such as McGhee and Fowles & Glanz (1977) clearly demonstrates the relationship of humour to both cognition and metalinguistic abilities at this stage.

Relatively little is known about metalinguisic knowledge before age 7. Gleitman, Gleitman & Shipley (1972) presented evidence that some children as young as two displayed metalinguistic knowledge. By metalinguistic knowledge we mean the capacity to view language as an object. Many of the examples of metalinguistic abilities cited by Gleitman *et al.* are also early attempts at humour. In one such example the experimenter is trying to elicit a correction of a deviant sentence. She says *Allison, mailbox fill!* Allison, demonstrating a sense of humour as well as sophisticated metalinguistic knowledge, replies *We don't have any mailbox fills here.* Allison demonstrates her abstract knowledge of compound nouns. Gleitman *et al.* do not suggest that such metalinguistic ability is present in all 2-year-olds and are reluctant to speculate on its origins. But they go on to discuss the precocious metalinguistic abilities of one 7-year-old who, in their words, 'had had a good deal of exposure to language games'. Slobin (1978) has written about the precocious metalinguistic abilities of his daughter, and speculates that exposure to foreign languages may have focused her attention on relevant aspects of language. She, too, was exposed to language games. Many of Slobin's metalinguistic examples appear to be attempts at jokes.

This paper will present some longitudinal data from another somewhat atypical child. Kelly, the first-born daughter of a philosopher and a psycholinguist was also exposed to language games from an early age. As part of a

longitudinal study of her language development, I have collected a number of her spontaneous jokes. Most of these are closely related to her developing language skills and demonstrate early metalinguistic abilities. They offer additional insights into very early humour and its relationship to developing metalinguistic skills. We will look at Kelly's jokes in the context of her overall language system and see what they tell us about her knowledge of language. I have categorized her jokes into four types. Although they emerged in a sequential order, the earlier types continued. Thus her development consisted of adding additional types of jokes and producing increasingly complex versions of old types.

VIOLATIONS OF SEMANTIC CATEGORIES

These included examples from McGhee's stages 1, 2 and 3. At 1;4, when Kelly had a vocabulary of less than 20 words, she learned the word *shoe*. Several days later, she put her foot through the armhole of a nightgown, saying *Shoe*, accompanied by shrieks of laughter. Later that day, she put her foot into a tennis ball can, saying *Shoe* and laughing. It is hard for me to believe that this is a case of overgeneralizing the word *shoe* based on its function. She was telling a joke. It was as though she was saying 'Look, a shoe is something you put on your foot; a nightgown is NOT something you usually put on your foot, but I did!' She had violated the semantic category—shoes can be boots, sandals and other perceptually distinct items, but there are things that can be put on feet that are NOT shoes. As soon as she could put two words together, she formed similar jokes by violating semantic restrictions—*Bed cry* would be accompanied by laughter. Throughout her development, the acquisition of a new word would stimulate a joke attempt of this type. When she was 1;11 I told her I was proud of her. She correctly surmised that only people are proud of you. She used a joke to 'show off' (and to test) her new knowledge: *Daddy's proud of you. Grandma's proud of you. Uncle David's proud of you. Hamburger* NOT *proud of you. Ha, ha.* Of course, sometimes her analyses were incorrect and her jokes failed. After asking me why men could not wear dresses and contemplating my response about customs, she concluded that customs were something only men had. *Daddy has a custom. Uncle David has a custom. Mommy has a custom! Ha, ha, mommies can't have customs! The clock has a custom! Ha, ha, clocks can't have customs!*

This sort of joke-telling is a very effective strategy for a language learner: you hear a new word, make a hypothesis about the semantic restrictions, and test your hypothesis by violating those restrictions. Thus, Kelly learned from our responses that she had correctly analysed *proud*, but had incorrectly analysed *custom*.

PHONETIC PATTERN GAMES

These are characteristic of McGhee's stage 3. This general category of jokes consisted of phonetic pattern games. At 1;8, she said *Cow go moo. Mommy go mamoo. Daddy go dadoo. Ha ha.* These jokes, like the violations of semantic categories, became more sophisticated as she got older. For example, at 3;3 she began starting the last syllable of every content word with a [t] and stressing that syllable: *banana* became *banaTA*, *dinner* became *dinTER*, *strawberry* became *strawberTEE*, *Kelley* became *KelTEE*, *Mommy* became *MomTEE*, etc. Her special way of talking was always accompanied by much giggling.

CHANGING ESTABLISHED PATTERNS

These are more complex types of McGhee's stage 3 jokes. This third general kind of joke involved changing established patterns. Thus at 2;3 we heard that *Little Bo People had lost her steeple* and that *Rudolph the red-nosed reindeer, you'll go down and get a hamburger.* At 2;3 she invented the following rhyme:

Five socks. Pick up stocks.
Seven ox. Close the gox.
Nine tens. Start agains.

At 2;9, the following song occurred:

K: Mommy, listen. Somebody come and play with me (*a Sesame Street song*).
Somebody come and play with I.

M: Oh, that's silly. It's supposed to be 'me'.
K: Somebody come and play with I—van! Ha, ha.
Somebody come and play with pee.
Somebody come and play with Pee—ter! Ha, ha.
Somebody come and play with cheese.
Somebody come and play with Cheez—Whiz! Ha, ha.

At 2;4, she was fascinated with Dr Seuss's *There's a Wocket in my Pocket*, and tried to do her own versions:

M: (*trying to have a serious conversation*): Mommy has a baby in her tummy.
K: Yeah, and a wocket in her pocket!
M: No, really, there's a baby in there.
K: Mommy's got a deer in her ear, too!

RIDDLE-LIKE QUESTIONS

Early jokes in this category are characteristic of McGhee's stage 3. We can see the transition to stage 4 in this group of jokes. At 2;6, Kelly began making up her own riddles. As far as I know she had never heard an actual riddle—it is not a joke form used by her parents and she did not play with older children or watch TV. We did, however, frequently ask stylized questions that were structurally similar: *How does a cow/frog/cat/horse/etc. go?* or *What's daddy's name?* She became very adept at these. Even *What's Kelly's Daddy's brother's name?* would only cause a momentary delay. At 2;6 she initiated similar riddle-like games:

K: What does Jennifer have named Sheila?
D: I dunno. What does Jennifer have named Sheila?
K: A doggie named Sheila. What does Mary have named Alice?
D: I dunno. What does Mary have named Alice?
K: Does she have a pussycat named Alice?
D: Does she have a pussycat named Alice?
K: Yeah.

Slightly later, riddles that were further removed from the *What's the name* game appeared:

K: How do aspirins make?
M: Huh?
K: How do aspirins make?
M: I dunno, how do aspirins make?
K: They make you feel better.

and

> K: What did Mommy woke?
> D: I dunno. What did Mommy woke?
> K: Up.

By 2;7, these riddle-like jokes had evolved even further; now like the distorted *Somebody come and play* song, Kelly deliberately set up a linguistically misleading context.

> K: Do we kick Mary?
> M: No, we don't kick Mary!
> K: Do we kick Jennifer?
> M: No, we don't kick Jennifer!
> K: Do we kick the swimming pool?
> M: No, we don't kick the swimming pool!
> K: We kick IN the swimming pool. Ha, ha!

Another such example came at 3;0:

> K: Mommy, do you love me?
> M: Yes.
> K: Do you love me TO HIT YOU? Ha, ha!

What can we conclude from these examples? We see a developmental progression for the appearance of different types of jokes. Each kind of joke seems to reflect increased cognitive complexity. The jokes in each stage exhibit the same kinds of cognitive skills described by McGhee. The metalinguistic knowledge represented by each can be summarized as follows.

I. *Violations of semantic categories.* The child must realize that certain words can be applied to a CLASS of objects. That is, the child must be able to recognize categories such as animate versus inanimate in order to be able to violate the restrictions purposefully.

II. *Phonetic pattern games.* To be able to alter the phonetics of a word to make a rhyme or to fit a more general rule demands that the child see the words as arbitrary symbols for the objects and not as essential properties of the objects. The child must, in some rudimentary sense, appreciate the arbitrariness of words.

III. *Changing an established pattern.* This is a more sophisticated version of II. In II, the child is tinkering at the phonetic level. In III, the child is altering the pattern by changing words. In order for these jokes to work, the child has to choose a related word (e.g. *peep/people; sheep/steeple*), then fit it into the proper place, preserving the syntax and something of the semantics. So the move from II to III would involve acquiring the ability to change item *x* to *y* where both *x* and *y* make sense, over and above the ability to change *x* to *y* where *y* is objectively recognizable as a permutation of *x*. This requires a broader range of linguistic knowledge than does changing the phonetic patterns of words.

IV. *Riddle-like questions.* Here the child sees the joke as having a set structure. Thus, Kelly told many jokes that started with the same structure: *How do* NOUN VERB? According to Piaget, symbolic play develops into stylized games with rules. The development of humour may follow a similar course. Kelly's early riddles followed a 'formula' or a rule. She had to match her joke to the riddle format. Thus, at this point, Kelly's jokes not only revealed metalinguistic ability, but also metajoke ability.

How do these results fit with the various theories of humour? They certainly support the cognitive-perceptual model of humour; all the jokes deal with incongruity or ambiguity, reflect Kelly's increasing cognitive capacity, and fit McGhee's stages. We also have support for Freud's progression from mere 'nonsense', or unresolvable incongruity, to jokes with meaning. Some jokes after 2;4 had motives reflecting conflict over sex, aggression, or siblings, but certainly not all of Kelly's jokes (and not the earliest jokes) resulted in any reduction of tension or anxiety. In none of the situations in which jokes occurred was Kelly in a state of noticeable anxiety.

Perhaps the most interesting questions raised by this study revolve around the reasons for Kelly telling jokes. One is certainly cognitive development; also, some jokes were motivated by sexual and aggressive drives. But what makes some children tell jokes and others not? We have hinted at a few possible factors. Kelly was exposed to and reinforced for language games. Her metalinguistic knowledge was advanced. Her symbolic play was unusually imaginative and elaborate. Fowles & Glanz (1977) suggest three factors that are involved in humour: (1) cognitive ability, (2) familiarity with jokes, and (3) attention to language. The latter they consider a talent. Kelly had these factors as well. Brodzinsky (1975) found that reflective, as opposed to impulsive children develop a sense of humour earlier. Kelly is a reflective child. Two other aspects of her personality appear related: she has a high tolerance for degraded stimuli and she focuses attention on patterns.

Kelly's tolerance for degraded stimuli has been striking throughout her development. While most children expect the signifier (the inappropriate object which is to undergo the make-believe action) and the signified (the normal object which would normally undergo the real action) to share some perceptual features, Kelly would accept almost any object to stand for another. For example, at 2;8 she was looking for an umbrella for her play. She settled, quite happily, on a little plastic 'G'. At this age, I observed Kelly playing with several children of about the same age. I invariably found I could easily infer the theme of the other children's play from their props. With Kelly it was much harder. For example, Kelly and another child were playing with a toy stove, pots and pans. The other child was realistically 'cooking'. I was unable to figure out what Kelly was doing. She responded to my queries with *It's not really a stove, but actually it's a computational stove and potty chair.* Kelly's tolerance for degraded stimuli may be related to her willingness to 'degrade' or alter established patterns.

The other aspect of Kelly's general cognitive and linguistic style that seems to be related to her humour development was her unusual attention to patterns and the social context of language. In the child language literature (i.e. Nelson 1973, Bloom, Lightbown & Hood 1975, Horgan 1980) we find two general approaches to language. They have been given different labels by different researchers, but one type of child—the 'referential'—seems to concentrate on the semantic content of the message and the individual words, while the other type—the 'expressive'—concentrates more on the personal-social context and the patterns of language—the 'gestalts'. Kelly was an expressive type. She, like other expressive speakers, saw language, not as a system to refer to objects, but more as a social game. In all her behaviour, Kelly was a seeker of patterns. It was important to her that breakfast consist of Wheat Chex on top of Cheerios and not the other way around. At 1;4 we took her to Churchill Downs. She quickly extracted the pattern of the social ritual: when in a crowd of people, stand up and yell 'Go!'. That is exactly what Kelly did whenever she was in a crowd for months thereafter. Her obvious attention to patterns and to the social context was no doubt a contributing factor in her development of jokes. In her jokes she first attended to the pattern, then altered it in some way while preserving the rhyme or the cadence. She saw jokes as a form of social exchange. Questions for Kelly were rarely a means of seeking information, but more often were a means of initiating social interaction. Her riddle-like questions are an excellent example of this.

Kelly was very sensitive to the form of language as evidenced by her frequent 'corrections' of our speech:

M: You're a good cook.
K: Sorry. I'm a good cooker!

and

M: I need to cut your hair.
K: Hairs! Sorry!

At 3;2 a neighbour told me she was having a friend for dinner. Kelly 'corrected' her by pointing out that you can't eat friends. Kelly was also aware of multiple meanings for the same phonetic sequence, when she observed *There are two jeans: Jessica's mommy named Jean and jeans to wear.*

All of these factors no doubt contributed in some way to Kelly's spontaneous joking. Future research needs to examine such types of individual variation and their relationship to humour. So far most research has concentrated more on what makes children laugh than on what makes some children comedians.

REFERENCES

Bloom, L., Lightbown, P. & Hood, L. (1975). Structure and variation in child language. *Monogr. Soc.Res.Ch.Devel.* **160.**

Brodzinsky, D. M. (1975). The role of conceptual tempo and stimulus characteristics in children's humor development. *DevPsych* **II**. 843–50.

Fowles, L. & Glanz, M. E. (1977). Competence and talent in verbal riddle comprehension. *JChLang* **4**. 433–52.

Gleitman, L. R., Gleitman, H. & Shipley, E. (1972). The emergence of the child as grammarian. *Cognition* **I**. 137–63.

Horgan, D. (1980). Nouns: love 'em or leave 'em. *Annals of the New York Academy of Sciences*, **345**, 5–26.

McGhee, P. (1979). *Humor: its origin and development*. San Francisco: Freeman.

Nelson, K. (1973). Structure and strategy in learning to talk. *Monogr.Soc.Res.Ch.Devel.* **149**.

Shultz, T. (1976). A cognitive-developmental analysis of humor. In A. J. Chapman & H. C. Foot (eds), *Humor and laughter: theory, research, and applications*. New York: Wiley.

Slobin, D. (1978). A case study of early language awareness. In A. Sinclair, R. J. Jarvella & W. J. M. Levelt (eds), *The child's conception of language*. Berlin: Springer-Verlag.

PART · FIVE

APPLICATIONS

Alan Baddeley

❖

Judith H. Langlois and Lori A. Roggman

❖

Ronald P. Fisher and R. Edward Geiselman

❖

Dean Delis, John Fleer, and Nancy H. Kerr

❖

Paul W. Foos, Benjamin Algaze,
and George Kallas

❖

Matthew D. Smith and Craig J. Chamberlin

❖

Paul Rozin, Susan Poritsky, and Raina Sotsky

❖

National Research Council

❖

Diane F. Halpern

Applications

Psychologists have always had an interest in practical applications, and that certainly has been the case in the United States and Great Britain, where a pragmatic spirit has permeated the psychological enterprise from its very beginnings in the late nineteenth century. Even during the heyday of behaviorism, the so-called great white rat era, many behaviorists had an intense interest in practical matters, including such concerns as how to raise children, how to deal with emotional problems, and how to lead a happy and productive life. John B. Watson and B. F. Skinner, considered to be the founders of behaviorism, wrote copiously about the uses of behavioral principles in everyday life. Their interest in everyday life may seem ironic to some because behaviorism is generally viewed as taking a removed approach to the study of human beings, preoccupied as it was (and is) with finding a set of laboratory-inspired principles to explain behavior.

THIS TENSION BETWEEN PURE RESEARCH AND PRACTICAL APPLICATION HAS A parallel in cognitive psychology. Wilhelm Wundt, famous for having founded modern experimental psychology in 1879, is now generally considered to have been a cognitive psychologist. His *content psychology* focused on conscious processes, including attention, perception, decision-making (voluntary or "will" processes), language, and more social psychological phenomena as well. However, whether he was pursuing his laboratory work or his *Völkerpsychologie* (folk or cultural psychology), Wundt's interests were decidedly theoretical and oriented toward basic research. This pattern was repeated by the early cognitivists of the 1950s and 1960s, since, almost exclusively, their activities focused on shaking off the conceptualizations of behaviorism and on exploring the theoretical and empirical consequences of the new ideas of information theory, the computer metaphor, and Noam Chomsky's linguistics. (See the selection by Howard H. Kendler in Part 1 for a fuller discussion of the development of cognitive psychology.)

By the middle 1970s attitudes seem to have changed in cognitive psychology. The scope of cognitive psychology was broadened by the development of an alliance of sorts between cognitive psychology and other areas of psychology, such as social, personality, clinical, and developmental psychology, and by the realization that cognitive psychology could help clarify issues in a wide range of applied settings. Thus, some cognitivists set about studying the relevance of psychology to law, mathematics, music, psychotherapy, and medicine, as well as everyday life—memory slips, planning, procrastination, and so on. In the 1980s, although the majority of cognitive psychologists were primarily engaged in basic research in academic settings, there was a headlong rush to explore the practical world. New journals catering to applied topics were developed. Edited volumes on application proliferated. And research articles on topics that straddle the boundary between pure research and application (e.g., expertise) were published in mainstream journals. Cognitivists seemed to have taken the position that everyday life is a rich, valid source of ideas as well as a testing ground for more laboratory-grounded theoretical notions.

THE ARTICLES IN THIS SECTION REPRESENT A SAMPLE of current work in applied cognitive psychology. The first article, Alan Baddeley's "The Cognitive Psychology of Everyday Life," sets the tone for the section. As Baddeley puts it, "We must constantly be prepared to attempt to generalize our models to the outside world of everyday life." He then describes some of his own research adventures, including his tests on the manual dexterity of divers some 100 feet below the Mediterranean sea, the effects of alcohol on the mood, word recall, reasoning, and fine motor control of some members of the London Hospital's Diving Group, and an examination of absentmindedness in real-life situations. This is a typically interesting and humorous account by Baddeley.

One of the dilemmas of basic research is that in order to gain more control over the phenomenon being studied, and this in the service of allowing better inferences about cause and effect, inputs and outputs are often simplified. In research on memory, this means that manageable verbal stimuli are used, and that precise, codable, measurable behaviors are sought from subjects. The problem, of course, is that methodological simplification may lessen the ability to generalize the results to more complex real-life situations (although many would argue that the right kind of simplification may create an opportunity for a cornucopia of generalization).

THE THREE PAPERS ON MEMORY IN THIS SECTION indicate that the dilemma just alluded to may be overstated. In these cases—memory for eyewitness situations and music, and judgments of facial beauty—it turns out that principles stemming from laboratory research can profitably be applied from one domain to another, or from inside the laboratory to outside the laboratory.

In the first of these papers, "Attractive Faces Are Only Average," Judith H. Langlois and Lori A. Roggman take a cue from experimental work on prototypes and apply it to the question of facial beauty. Is facial beauty culture bound, or are more universal principles involved? Evolution theory implies that people should prefer average faces because they presumably represent less harmful genes. Experimental work in cognition has consistently shown that people represent some events in terms of prototypes and that people experience prototypes, or average events, as familiar even though they have never actually perceived a prototype. Langlois and Roggman reasoned, therefore, that attractive faces could well be prototypical faces. In their experiment they generated computer (digitized) composite faces that incorporated from 2 to as many as 32 individual faces. Ratings of the faces' attractiveness did indeed indicate that the composites (the prototypes) were more attractive than the individual faces and that the more individual faces there were in the composite, the more attractive it was rated. The generally simpler stimuli that have been used in laboratory experiments on prototypes can therefore be generalized to some extent to the more complex human face.

Ronald P. Fisher and R. Edward Geiselman attack the problem of helping people to remember crime-related events in their article "Enhancing Eyewitness Memory With the Cognitive Interview." Eyewitness testimony for such events is notoriously poor, yet the legal system and juries seem to place great faith in such testimony. Cognizant of this dilemma, Fisher and Geiselman used some basic principles of memory to construct a technique they believed would improve eyewitness testimony. Specifically, they relied upon the encoding specificity principle (the more similar the recall cues are to the cues in the original learning situation, the better the recall), the use of multiple recall cues, multiple perspectives for recall, forward and backward recall, and the training of subjects in the use of specific mnemonic techniques. They showed subjects a simulated crime and had law enforcement personnel test their recall two days later using one of three techniques: a standard police interview, an interview with hypnosis, and their specially constructed cognitive interview. The results indicated superior recall with the hypnosis interview and the cognitive interview. Moreover, the latter was the technique of choice, since it was less time-consuming, required less training, and probably reduced the effect of potentially misleading questions, which was a factor in the hypnosis situation.

MUSIC COGNITION IS ANOTHER TOPIC THAT HAS become increasingly popular in the last 10 years or so. What could be more applied? Music is deeply embedded in every culture. It is a source of emotional satisfaction to just about everyone—for some, a necessity of life. Still, music is structurally complex, and therefore difficult to work with, and it often requires knowledge of music notation, which most cognitive scientists do not have. Nevertheless, on a theoretical level, some thinkers believe that music and language share some deep cognitive principles. This idea is pursued by Dean Delis, John Fleer, and Nancy H. Kerr in "Memory for Music." Research on language has indicated that people remember the underlying meaning or significance of linguistic messages, whereas surface-level information, such as the particular words and their order, is quickly lost. Moreover, if the linguistic material is ambiguous, in that it does not easily activate known schemata, the material may not be comprehended or recalled well. However, when appropriate schemata are activated by means of appropriate titles or other cues, then performance improves greatly. Understanding is in any case an active, constructive process. Delis et al. reasoned, therefore, that music might be remembered better if subjects were asked to construct mental images for some musical passages and that concrete titles (as opposed to abstract titles) would facilitate this process. This is indeed what they found, as the concrete titles condition led to higher vividness ratings and better recognition. Thus, similar principles may apply to memory for language as for music.

ASIDE FROM MUSIC COGNITION, THERE IS THE OLD but difficult topic of the relationship between cognition and emotion. Cognitive psychologists are aware that emotion cannot be excluded, and there has been a recent upsurge of research in the area. One example is the paper by Paul W. Foos, Benjamin Algaze, and George Kallas, "Effects of Cognitive Interference on Biofeedback Learning." Evidence suggests that biofeedback training can help some people with certain kinds of psychophysiological disorders. But when this training works, how does it work? Through experimentation Foos et al. compared the *reinforcement view* of biofeedback, in which the auditory/visual feedback the individual gets in training serves to reinforce the individual's desired response, and the *cognitive view*, in which the feedback is used to select the mental strategies (images, language, rehearsal, etc.) that are most effective for the individual. The authors reasoned that if the cognitive view is correct, then any task that would interfere with these mental strategies should reduce biofeedback learning, whereas by the reinforcement view, such a task should have no effect.

Foos et al. had experimental subjects try to learn to change their hand temperatures while checking words for the letter E (a simple task), doing some mental addition (a harder task), or doing neither task. The results indicated that the mental addition task interfered with the subjects' ability to raise their hand temperatures, thereby supporting the cognitive view.

The authors advise biofeedback trainers to get their clients to clear their minds and relax and perhaps to teach their clients to use particular mental strategies.

THE TOPIC OF PERCEPTUAL-MOTOR SKILLS IS RARELY treated in texts on cognition. Perhaps this is because motor skills just seem to "happen," often rather quickly and effortlessly. This seeming ease of execution may mask the cognitive background for the act, however. Good athletes tend to make complicated motor acts look easy. How do they do it? Is it just practice? Or is something more involved, such as planning, reasoning, and cunning? To what extent are motor skills subject to influence by "top-down" or knowledge-based processes?

Theorists such as Paul Fitts have argued that motor skills seem to evolve through three phases: a cognitive or fact phase in which the goals of a motor sequence are learned; an associative or procedural phase in which responses are mapped to particular cues in an ultimately automatized way; and a final phase in which motor procedures are guided in an efficient way by the environment. Expertise confers a freeing-up of working memory capacity and a consequent ability to attend more closely to task-relevant cues.

This point is nicely illustrated in Matthew D. Smith and Craig J. Chamberlin's article "Effect of Adding Cognitively Demanding Tasks on Soccer Skill Performance." In soccer, as in most sports, the athlete must manage multiple sources of information. Smith and Chamberlin used a dual-task methodology to assess the effect of secondary tasks on the running speed (the primary task) of female soccer players with different levels of expertise. The players first ran through a short slalom course, then ran the course while dribbling a soccer ball (with their feet), and finally dribbled through the course while identifying geometric shapes on a screen at the end of the course. The results indicated that the novice, intermediate, and expert players all ran about the same speed when no secondary task was required but that each addition of such a task reduced running speed. The more expert the player, however,

the less her speed was reduced by these tasks. The authors argue that, as in this case, even an expert's performance can suffer if the secondary tasks "functionally interfere," that is, if they use up the same resources or require the same movements as the primary tasks (such as in running and dribbling in soccer).

WHAT COULD BE MORE CENTRAL TO THE FUNCTIONing of a modern technological society than reading? Yet in the United States, an estimated 15 to 20 percent of the adult population is functionally illiterate. They cannot read road signs, follow directions on a recipe, or understand documents pertaining to crucial aspects of their lives. They are incapable of becoming knowledgeable about a myriad of everyday facts and events as reported in newspapers and magazines, and they are removed from important ideas about science and the state of the world. To some extent this deficiency is compensated for by television, but watching television also seems to detract from time that could be spent reading. For many inhabitants of the United States, the printed word is not part of their culture, and the reasons why are as varied as they are numerous. Reading skills are absent or deficient in adults and children for economic, political, sociological, psychological, and neurophysiological reasons.

The problems that some children have in reading is highlighted by Paul Rozin, Susan Poritsky, and Raina Sotsky in "American Children With Reading Problems Can Easily Learn to Read English Represented by Chinese Characters." These investigators selected nine children in the second grade in an inner-city school who were poor readers. The investigators tutored them in reading English and in learning the English equivalent of 30 Chinese characters (e.g., different characters represented "mother," "and," and "fish"). Such characters are related in a nearly one-to-one relationship to words or ideas. The results indicated that there was a significant improvement in reading the Chinese characters but not in reading English. The authors suggest that this could be due to the students' increased motivation to learn the characters or to the ideographic nature of the characters. As a practical consequence, they suggest that poor readers might be given more wholistic units to learn, such as syllables, as a means of making the transition to the alphabetically based English orthography (writing system).

BILLIONS OF DOLLARS ARE SPENT EACH YEAR ON advertising, and, of course, anything with the socioeconomic punch that advertising has draws a lot of attention. Mostly, people seem to be more concerned with advertising's potential for harm rather than with its potential benefit. In his satiric 1932 novel *Brave New World*, Aldous Huxley (1894–1963) warned of the use of persuasion for mass mind control. In the 1950s, sociologists who examined advertising and mass media wrote extensively about "hidden persuaders." In more recent years, some social critics have become concerned about the supposed existence of subliminal messages in movies, audiotapes, billboards, and even company logos that they claim promote evil or satanic or sexually deviant practices.

This sounds like just the kind of situation that cognitivists could shed some light on. The article "Subliminal Self-Help," by the National Research Council, does just that. Self-help audio- and videotapes are big business in this country, often involving high-tech methods such as speech compression. People buy the tapes in order to help them stop smoking, lose weight, gain more confidence, become more optimistic, and even become better bowlers. But do the tapes work? Or, more precisely, do the subliminal messages work?

The article begins with an attempt to provide a workable definition of subliminal perception. To wit, it can be defined in terms of the relationships between the stimuli presented to people, their claims about whether or not they perceived the stimuli, and whether or not the stimuli had a reliable effect on their performance. For example, suppose that a color word (e.g., blue) is very briefly presented to someone but that the individual claims that he or she did not see the word. Suppose further that presentation of the color word had no effect on the individual's ability to accurately and quickly name an actual color stimulus (e.g., blue). Add another result to this, namely that the color word is presented for a longer time, the individual claims to have seen it, and, indeed, performance in naming the actual color is quite good. But, now, what if the color word is presented for an intermediate period of time, the individual claims not to have seen it, and yet performance in naming the color is quite good? That is, the individual's claim in this latter situation belies her or his color-naming performance.

This set of results would strongly suggest that subliminal perception is real. But it is not a matter of people having a special, subconscious stimulus-detecting mechanism. Rather, it is a pattern of relationships between stimuli, people's claims about the stimuli, and the empirically observed effects of the stimuli. Moreover, this line of reasoning requires that in order to validly claim that subliminal perception has occurred, some minimal level of stimulation must be present. Interestingly, investigation of some self-help tapes reveals that this condition is not met because even the best technology cannot detect a stimulus and, for that matter, people cannot discriminate between those occasions in which a stimulus is there and when it is not.

If subliminal perception is not responsible for public claims of the effectiveness of these tapes, what is? The National Research Council theorizes that people's commitment to improvement (as evidenced by their buying the tapes), their desire to justify their efforts in using them, and their expectations of benefit all play a role in fostering these claims. The council concludes that "there is neither theoretical foundation nor experimental evidence to support claims that subliminal self-help audiotapes enhance human performance."

THE FINAL PAPER, BY DIANE F. HALPERN, "Analogies as a Critical Thinking Skill," is a good wrap-up for this section because Halpern explores both the theoretical and practical aspects of analogy. Her analysis is carried out in the context of the current interest on the part of educators and education policymakers in critical thinking. This is an educational movement that emphasizes that students should know more than "just the facts"; they should instead explore the implications of the facts, relate the facts to other facts, question the source of the facts, and so on. The question is whether or not students can be taught how to go beyond the facts. Halpern reviews evidence that suggests that they can. She also presents evidence from her own research that shows that material is better understood and remembered when students are given an analogy for verbal material. Whether or not students will continue to use potentially helpful learning and comprehension techniques beyond the classroom or laboratory is another question.

23

Alan Baddeley

The Cognitive Psychology of Everyday Life

Over the last 40 years, experimental psychology has concentrated almost exclusively on studying behaviour in the laboratory. While laboratory-based research is likely to retain its importance, it is essential that the theories and concepts developed in this way be exposed to the more bracing conditions found outside the laboratory. Examples of the value of such research are given from the area of stress where work on alcohol and driver performance are discussed, and from studies of everyday memory, illustrated by work on saturation advertising and on absent-mindedness. Developments so far have been primarily in the area of cognitive psychology, but it is suggested that a willingness to move outside the laboratory is likely to be even more fruitful in studying the problems of conative and orectic psychology, the study of the will and the emotions.

I would like to begin by thanking the Society for the honour of inviting me to help it commemorate C. S. Myers. Unlike some of my distinguished predecessors, I cannot claim to have known Myers, although I have reason to be grateful for his efforts in founding both the Psychological Laboratory at Cambridge and the *British Journal of Psychology*. He was, it appears, a man of broad interests, his work ranging from studies of the sensory and perceptual characteristics of primitive peoples, through more conventional laboratory-based psychology to personnel selection and industrial psychology. I like to think therefore that he would be sympathetic to both the topic of my lecture and the longer-term conclusions I hope to draw from it.

The development of psychology over the last 100 years has differed from its development over the previous 1000 in one major respect. There has been a consistent tendency to attempt to explore and understand the human mind by studying it under conditions that are much more controlled than those obtaining in everyday life. As a result of this, I think that despite the breast-beating and complaints of lack of progress that have been fashionable over the last few years, we do know substantially more than was known 100 years ago. It is true however that very often our knowledge is confined to problems that are easy to investigate rather than problems that are important, and we need to be constantly on our guard against creating a psychology that is limited to the psychological laboratory. To take a concrete example, some of the mathematical models of learning developed in the 1960s provided an extremely elegant account of the subject's performance. Unfortunately, these accounts were based on the highly artificial task of learning to associate single letters with digits, and proved quite unsuitable for generalizing beyond this rather limited task. I would like to present the simple argument that if we are to avoid a preoccupation with pseudo-problems then we must constantly be prepared to attempt to generalize our models to the outside world of everyday life, and to feed back into the laboratory the problems and insights that a study of the everyday world provides. The plea for what Brunswik would term 'ecological validity' is not a new one, and is unlikely to arouse very much controversy. Where the difficulty lies is in achieving the blend of rigour and realism that is necessary if one is to carry out useful work outside the laboratory. I do not think that there are any simple general answers, but I think there are a number of characteristic problems. I would like to illustrate these by talking mainly about the work in this area carried out by my colleagues and myself, not because I regard it as in any way exemplary, but simply as a convenient way of talking about the important, if often prosaic, difficulties that arise in this intriguing but difficult area.

My first venture outside the laboratory occurred in the early 1960s when as an amateur scuba diver I became interested in the possibility of mixing business and pleasure and conducting a study on nitrogen narcosis, the drunkenness that occurs when divers breathe air at depth (Baddeley, 1966a). Virtually all research carried out up to that time had been done in dry pressure chambers where the effect of depth would be simulated by raising the pressure of the atmosphere within the chamber to that equivalent to the relevant depth of sea water. Work carried out by the US Navy indicated that divers showed a small but significant impairment in manual dexterity under dry conditions at a pressure of air equivalent to 100 feet of sea water. I decided to take advantage of a Cambridge University diving expedition to Cyprus to test this under open sea conditions. I used a very simple test of manual dexterity which involved moving 16 nuts and bolts from 16 holes at one end of a brass plate, to the 16 holes at the other, the subject performing this while seated on a canvas chair at the bottom of the ocean. I found the effects of testing the subject at 100 feet rather than 10 feet to be substantially greater than one would have expected from the US dry pressure results. I was subsequently able to confirm this by running further subjects in a pressure chamber and finding the small decrement predicted by the US study. Generalizing from the laboratory to the outside world in this case would clearly have given rise to an unduly optimistic view of the subject's ability to cope with nitrogen narcosis, at least under anxiety-provoking open sea conditions.

Although this was my introduction to both the problems and rewards of experimenting outside the laboratory, one would be stretching a point to describe performance at 100 feet below the surface of the Mediterranean as an example of 'everyday life', for most of us at least. In order to give some flavour of the more detailed aspects of this type of work I would like to describe a small unpublished study carried out more recently on the effects of alcohol.

There has over the years been an enormous number of experiments on the effect of alcohol on performance. For the most part these have been quite rightly concerned with plotting dose response curves, and as such have needed to impose very constrained conditions on the subject and his alcohol intake. Such rigorously controlled conditions are of course very different from the situation in which alcohol is usually imbibed. Most studies require the subject to drink either alcohol or a placebo mixture on an empty stomach, and test him individually in a laboratory. The situation in real life is typically very different. Subjects may well have eaten before starting to drink, they drink what and when they choose and they frequently do so in a sociable group. The question arose as to whether, under these more realistic conditions, one would pick up reliable effects of alcohol on performance. A colleague who had worked extensively on alcohol felt that it was unlikely, but since an opportunity had cropped up to carry out such a test it seemed worth trying, if only to develop experience in group testing under extreme conditions.

A group of 14 members of the London Hospitals Diving Group were tested on two occasions during their Easter diver training session. During this the club rented accommodation in Cornwall and dived during the day and indulged in a certain amount of social drinking in the evening. All subjects were given a practice on one evening, and were then randomly assigned to one of two equal groups. One group was tested on a second evening after returning from the pub, while the second was tested at a similar time after a sober evening. The performance of the two groups was then assessed by taking each subject's practice score and expressing his test score as a percentage of this. This minimizes the effect of individual differences, and allows a relatively sensitive comparison between the two groups. All subjects first completed a questionnaire on drinking habits, and then the following tests.

(1) *Mood adjective check list.* This comprises a series of 16 scales each represented by a 10 cm line with a word at each end (e.g. alert–drowsy, tense–relaxed). Subjects were required to place a check mark at a point on the line representing their current state of mind (Herbert *et al.*, 1976).

(2) *Free recall.* Subjects attempted to recall lists of 16 unrelated words. The words were read out at a 2 s rate, and 30 s were allowed for recall in any order the subject wished. On each session four such lists were presented.

(3) *Verbal reasoning.* This required subjects to verify a number of sentences of varying degrees of syntactic complexity. Each sentence described the order of occurrence of two letters, A and B and was followed by the pair AB or BA and ranged in complexity from simple actives (e.g. A follows B–BA) to negative passives (e.g. A is not preceded by B–BA) (Baddeley, 1968). Subjects worked on this test for 3 min.

(4) *Semantic processing.* This task is based on studies of semantic memory in which subjects are required to verify some statement about the outside world (e.g. *Canaries have wings*, or *Canaries have gills*). There has in recent years been a great deal of interest in the process of accessing information in semantic memory, and although this has rarely been studied under stress conditions, the ability to utilize stored information is clearly of considerable practical importance. The task was adapted by Baddeley & Thomson (unpublished) for use as a stress test by creating a large number of sentences. These were typed on sheets of paper and subjects proceeded to tick the ones they regarded as correct and place a cross by the ones they judged wrong, working as rapidly as they could for 3 min.

Control subjects were induced to refrain from drinking, while experimental subjects had a normal supper and drank socially at the pub, choosing their own beverage and paying for it in the normal way. All subjects were paid an honorarium for taking part, but most of them in fact donated this to the diving club. Subjects reported drinking during the evening the equivalent of 5.4 pints of beer on average (range 3–7 pints). It was not possible to obtain accurate readings of blood alcohol level, but a rough indication of blood alcohol level was obtained using the alcometer, a device which is regarded as suitable for preliminary screening but not for accurate determination of blood alcohol levels. This indicated levels ranging

Table 1

The Influence of Alcohol on Mean Percentage Correct in Free Recall

	Run 1 (practice)	Run 2 (test)	Run 2—Run 1
Control	38.1	36.1	− 2.0
Alcohol	45.3	29.6	− 15.7

from 0.05 to 0.20 per cent with a mean of about 0.10 per cent, indicating that most subjects were around or above the legal limit of 0.08 per cent.

We found a marked change in reported mood, with the alcohol group rating themselves as less alert, and more 'feeble', 'muzzy', 'clumsy', 'mentally slow', 'dreamy' and 'incompetent'. There was however no substantial difference in their level of tranquillity as expressed by such adjectives as 'calm', 'contented', 'tranquil', 'relaxed', and 'happy'.

The mean number of words recalled out of 16 under the various conditions is shown in Table 1. The performance of the two groups was compared by testing the hypothesis that the improvement from the initial practice trial to Run 1 would be significantly greater in the control condition than it would in the case of those subjects who were given alcohol on Run 2, since in their case any beneficial effects of practice would be offset by the detrimental effect of alcohol. In the case of free recall, comparison between the two groups using a Mann–Whitney U test indicated significantly poorer performance in the alcohol group in their overall performance ($U = 2.5$, $P < 0.01$). Using the technique proposed by Tulving & Colotta (1970) we separated out the primary and secondary memory components. When these were compared, there remained a highly significant difference between the groups in secondary memory performance ($U = 5.0$, $P < 0.01$) while the difference in the primary mem-

ory or recency component was of borderline significance ($U = 13$, $0.05 < P < 0.1$).

The results of the semantic processing test are shown in Table 2. These were again analysed using the Mann–Whitney U test to compare the groups, and showed a highly significant effect of alcohol, with no overlap between the two groups ($U = 0$, $P < 0.001$). There was no difference in error rate between the two conditions.

Table 3 shows performance on the grammatical reasoning test. This showed no reliable tendency for alcohol to decrease speed ($U = 18$, $P > 0.05$). An additional measure of motor skill was provided by measuring the ticks made by the subjects in response to the semantic processing and verbal reasoning tests. As has been reported elsewhere (Wing & Baddeley, 1978) these became significantly larger and more variable in size in the alcohol group.

It is clear then that our experiment detected significant effects of alcohol, despite the rather uncontrolled environmental conditions in which it was run. To what extent however are the effects detected consistent with what one might expect from the laboratory-based literature? The deficit in long-term memory performance is one which has been very frequently documented (e.g. Weingartner et al., 1976). The somewhat equivocal result in the case of the primary memory component of free recall is also in line with the somewhat equivocal literature on this topic, with some reports

Table 2

The Influence of Alcohol on Speed of Semantic Processing as Measured by Mean Number of Sentences Verified in 3 Min

	Run 1 (practice)	Run 2 (test)	Run 2—Run 1
Control	102.9 (1.25)	121.7 (1.40)	18.8 (0.15)
Alcohol	108.4 (1.31)	100.7 (1.56)	− 7.7 (0.25)

Note. Mean percentage errors shown in parentheses.

Table 3 _____

The Influence of Alcohol on Grammatical Reasoning

	Run 1 (practice)	Run 2 (test)	Run 2— Run 1
Control	37.9 (8.0)	43.3 (6.2)	5.4 (− 1.8)
Alcohol	31.0 (7.6)	33.3 (7.9)	2.3 (0.3)

Note. Mean number of items completed in 3 min; mean percentage errors shown in parentheses.

failing to observe an effect of alcohol on recency (Jones & Jones, 1977) while others do report some impairment of the primary memory component (Rundell & Williams, 1977). The discrepancy probably stems from the susceptibility of the recency effect to the particular strategy the subject adopts, with alcohol possibly influencing the subject's choice of strategy, or consistency in using a particular adopted strategy. Our semantic processing effect is to the best of my knowledge a new finding, since I know of no other study which attempts to examine the effect of alcohol on access to semantic memory. On the assumption that a great many activities in a real-life situation would be likely to depend on access to long-term memory, if replicated this could be a finding of some practical importance. The absence of a decrement in performance on verbal reasoning on the grammatical reasoning test came as something of a surprise, since this task is known to be sensitive to the effect of nitrogen narcosis, which subjectively at least resembles those of alcohol. The absence of an effect does however appear to be genuine since a later and independent study by Strong (personal communication) also found no effect of alcohol on this test. Finally, the sensitivity of motor skill to effects of alcohol has been well established previously, the main contribution of our measure of tick size being to show that it is possible to detect the decrement without recourse to complex equipment, or indeed a separate test since the motor skill measure

comes as a bonus in measuring the subject's reasoning and semantic processing performance.

Merely citing results gives the impression that this was very much like the standard laboratory experiment. It was not, although the ways in which it differed tend to be those which are not typically reported in journal articles. The experiment had originally been planned as a design involving practice followed by two experimental sessions, with half the subjects drunk the first night and sober the second, and half the reverse. This raised a number of problems, not least being that of persuading each subject to remain sober on the appropriate evening. This was further complicated by the fact that testing occurred after closing time, which meant that the control group not only had to remain sober but also had to remain awake after a hard day's diving until 11 p.m. in the evening. It had the additional drawback that the experimenter had to remain abstemious on all three occasions. The design was further complicated by the fact that people arrived in Cornwall at different times and stayed for different periods, making the original three tests impossible to achieve for several subjects and hence forcing us to fall back on the simpler two test separate groups design.

The actual process of testing was also fraught with problems. It had for example been intended to measure body sway using a simple device involving a post with pulleys mounted on the top. Under the very crowded living conditions, the post was stored in the kitchen and was used by someone to dry out damp teacloths with the result that the pulley corroded, making it unusable. Further difficulties arose in the case of the technician in charge of the alcometer who, when acting as a subject, failed to return from the pub. This was both worrying and awkward, since she was the only person who knew where the alcometer was stored. Eventually she reappeared, having spent the intervening period in a disco where further alcohol was available. Meanwhile the rest of the group were woken up and breathalized, while she completed the test. Her overall performance was not substantially different from that of the rest of the drunken group other than on mood ratings, where the realization of the worry and disruption she had caused moved her substantially away from the comparative euphoria shown by the remaining subjects.

The difficulties and incidents involved in testing drunken medical students in a group are probably more numerous than one normally finds in experiments in the field, but not different in kind. Our results indicated that one can carry out the sort of tests used in the laboratory even under these rather unpromising circumstances, and that clear decrements are observed, despite the lack of control over the dosage conditions. In interpreting these results however it is perhaps worth pointing out the importance of the attitude of the subjects. In particular, the atmosphere of the cottage livingroom in which the experiment was carried out changed dramatically once testing began from that of a party or bar room to one of an examination room, with each subject intent on the task in hand. This was both a strength and weakness of the study. It was a strength since without that degree of cooperation and motivation, it would have been impossible to collect adequate data. It was a weakness because we were testing the limits of what the subject could do over a relatively short period of time, not what he would have achieved had he not been so intent on attempting to resist any impairment from the alcohol.

This point is made very nicely in an unpublished study by Ivan Brown. In one experiment subjects drove through Cambridge while performing a secondary task under two conditions, when sober and after drinking a single glass of sherry, which was offered as a New Year social gesture rather than presented as part of the experiment. There was significant decrement on the secondary task and a reliable decrease in driving speed. On a subsequent experiment, when one or two glasses of sherry were presented to the subject as a special part of the experiment, speed of driving was unaffected, although there still was a tendency for

the alcohol conditions to impair the secondary task.

Clearly there are ethical limits to the extent to which one can manipulate factors such as alcohol intake without the subject being aware of the purpose of the experiment. Since his awareness is likely to influence his behaviour, it is important to supplement experimental investigation with more naturalistic studies. A good example of the strengths and weaknesses of this type of approach comes from a recent study by Brewer & Sandow (1980). For a period of a year, a research team comprising a psychologist, an engineer and a medical officer attended a sample of all accidents occurring in Adelaide. They obtained blood alcohol samples, and the psychologist interviewed those involved in the accident with a view to identifying the nature of any pre-accident manoeuvres. This was followed within one or two weeks of the accident by a more detailed interview which further explored the possibility that the driver might have been engaged in some secondary activity immediately preceding the accident. A total of 403 drivers were interviewed in this way, of which 305 provided full information. Brewer & Sandow observed a reliable tendency ($X^2 = 9.56$, d.f. = 1, $P < 0.01$, one-tailed) for those cases in which alcohol was involved for subjects to have been indulging in a second task such as reaching for cigarettes at the time of the accident. Such a result is interesting and broadly consistent with the previously observed sensitivity of dual task performance to the effects of alcohol (e.g. Hamilton & Copeman, 1970). However, as the authors point out, their results could be criticized as showing possible bias effects in the interviewer's expectations, or for that matter it may be that the subjects who were drunk at the time of their accident were more likely to attribute it to some secondary factor than to a straightforward error of judgement. Such possibilities obviously have to be borne in mind in interpreting the data, but it is not easy to see how they could have been avoided. In short, studies based on naturalistic observation are liable to be very expensive and time consuming as this obviously was, and to provide data which are open to more than one interpretation. This does not mean that such observations are not important, but does imply that both observational and experimental approaches have their limitations, and that an adequate understanding of phenomena in the real world will require us to use both.

It could be argued that most of the examples I have given so far have consisted merely of carrying out a laboratory-type experiment under slightly more naturalistic conditions. I have therefore selected as my next example an instance where one uses a 'natural' experiment to throw light on a number of issues which have previously been studied largely in the laboratory. The instance in question is an experiment by Debra Bekerian and myself on the recent attempt by the BBC to familiarize the public with the new radio wavelengths adopted following an international agreement (Bekerian & Baddeley, 1980). As you may recall, the BBC went in for an intensive saturation advertising campaign which involved announcements every few minutes on all radio channels, often accompanied by complex jingles and backed up by newspaper and television advertisements. After several weeks of this irritating repetition, it occurred to us that we ourselves were still completely uncertain as to what the new wavelengths were, and Debra Bekerian and I therefore decided that we would try to evaluate the campaign.

We prepared a simple questionnaire which we gave to members of our subject panel. This asked which programmes they listened to and how long per day. They were asked if they knew of any impending change in broadcasting, and if so what and when the change was to be. They were then questioned specifically about radio wavelengths, being asked to indicate what the current wavelengths of the various channels were, and what the new wavelengths were to be. In addition to inviting them to give a numerical response if they could, a spatial representation of a radio dial was presented in each case and they were invited to mark the location of each channel. They were then invited to perform a similar function for current radio wavelengths. Some 50 subjects were tested after

approximately eight weeks' exposure to the campaign; they reported having listened to the radio for an average of 2.5 hours per day. If, as the BBC estimated, their announcements were made at a rate of about 10 per hour this means that our subjects had on the whole been exposed to the information on well over 1000 occasions by radio alone. How much had they learnt?

We found that only nine of our 50 subjects were even prepared to hazard a guess as to the numerical frequency of the new wavelengths and we therefore combined numerical and graphic responses. One can broadly categorize such responses as accurate (within 5 MHz VHF or 50 kHz Medium Wave, of the correct tuning), inaccurate, (a deviation of more than 5 MHz or 50 kHz cycles), an accuracy which is not substantially different from what one might obtain by responding at random, or no response. For even the best-known channel, Radio 2, only 32 per cent were within reasonable range of an adequate response, while accuracy for most channels was 10 per cent or less. The overwhelming response for all wavelengths was 'don't know'. This could be contrasted with the fact that all our subjects knew that the change was to take place, and 84 per cent knew the exact date of the change.

Why was the campaign so conspicuously unsuccessful? A number of theoretical possibilities are suggested by the laboratory literature. Several studies, including those by Tulving (1966) and Craik & Watkins (1973) have suggested that mere repetition of verbal materials does not increase long-term retention. For long-term learning to occur, some form of additional semantic coding (Baddeley, 1966b) or deeper or more elaborate coding (Craik & Tulving, 1975) are said to be necessary. Against this however there are claims that rote repetition may enhance learning, particularly when instead of words, relatively meaningless materials such as nonsense syllables (or radio wavelengths?) are used (Mechanic, 1964).

A second possibility is that subjects simply became so bored with the whole campaign that they failed to attend to the information presented. Experiments in which subjects are required to process one of two spoken messages and ignore the second suggest that little or nothing is retained of the unattended message (e.g. Glucksberg & Cowan, 1970). However, such messages have usually been presented in competition with other spoken messages to which the subject was attending; it is not at all clear that a similar failure to remember would have occurred in the absence of the need to attend to a competing message.

A third possible hint comes from a very similar phenomenon observed by Morton (1967) who took advantage of the fact that all telephones at that time had dials marked for both digits and letters (telephone codes then used both). He simply required a total of 151 subjects to write out the letters associated with each of the digits 0–9. He found that none of his subjects was accurate. Nickerson & Adams (1979) have recently shown a similar lack of learning when American subjects were tested on their retention of the detailed characteristics of a 1 cent piece. Once again performance was extremely poor. Presumably in the case of both the telephone and the 1 cent piece subjects simply do not need to retain more than a fraction of the detailed information present. In the case of the telephone he could always search for the letter and need never operate entirely from memory. In the case of the coin, he merely needs to be able to discriminate between a 1 cent piece and coins of other denominations or coins of other countries. Could this be the reason for the poor performance of our subjects?

One clear indication that it probably was came from the analysis of their ability to report the 'old' wavelengths. This proved to be virtually as bad as the new. Since our subjects were presumably able to tune in and listen to the radio several times a day it seems clear that at some level they did possess the necessary wavelength information, but that it was not expressible numerically or on the particular visual scale we had presented to them. It seems most likely that they were using some form of visual guidance, either from the markings of the stations on the dial, or possibly from some idiosyncratic features of their own radios such

as a particular scratch or knob position. Fortunately the BBC had, in addition to their extensive advertising campaign, posted a series of adhesive labels to each household, so that the problem of tuning could be solved by finding the new wavelength location and sticking on a label.

We are naturally concerned that our estimate of the effectiveness of the campaign might have done it far less than justice. We therefore used a follow-up questionnaire which was given to some subjects two to three weeks after the changeover. Of those questioned, 70 per cent indicated that they had indeed had difficulty with the transition. A total of 10 per cent reported that they had made special efforts to learn the new wavelengths, but they seemed to be no more successful in reproducing them than subjects who reported no such attempt. By far the most successful strategy seems to have been to wait for the change and then hunt for the station and attach the stickers.

What can one learn from such a study? From a purely technical point of view, it suggests that one can occasionally carry out experiments under conditions which would be extremely difficult to set up experimentally. There must be very few experimenters who would be prepared to present their subjects with over 1000 presentations of such material, and even fewer subjects who would willingly tolerate it. The results are consistent with a number of laboratory phenomena, but it is probably true to say that although the BBC could have been warned of the potential snags, the detailed results could not have been predicted with any degree of conviction. As such they bear on our theoretical understanding of human memory, although not allowing precise theoretical conclusions, they do have a bearing on the robustness of certain laboratory phenomena. From a practical point of view, they suggest that an experimental psychologist with some knowledge of the memory literature could probably have produced something rather more effective for considerably less than the half a million pounds the campaign cost.

So far the examples I have chosen have comprised relatively traditional problems looked at in a real-life rather than a laboratory context. The final area I would like to consider however is one in which the problem would be very familiar to the man in the street, but appears to have been largely neglected by the experimental psychologist, namely that of remembering to do something, or its converse, absent-mindedness. The study of memory has traditionally concentrated on our ability to retain information, and subsequently reproduce it when cued by the experimenter. In everyday life however one common memory problem is that of cueing oneself to perform an action at a particular time. Indeed, one could argue that this is the major problem of forgetting in everyday life, since remembering information can normally be ensured by simply writing it down as in the case of a shopping list, whereas remembering at the right time is much harder to guarantee. Questionnaire studies of memory indicate that this is reported by subjects as a memory problem, but such studies unfortunately tend not to throw much light on the underlying mechanism. Further investigation calls for more objective observation: how this can be achieved is a problem that has concerned Arnold Wilkins, John Harris and myself over recent years.

Arnold Wilkins and I began by attempting to produce a situation in which a subject's ability to remember to perform a particular action at a particular time could be monitored objectively. We began by asking members of our subject panel to take away postcards and post them back to us on specified days. We expected to observe that the longer the delay the lower the probability of the card being returned. It turned out that our subjects were very conscientious and obeyed the instruction with the utmost accuracy over even the longest interval used. An independent study carried out in the United States in which patients attending a clinic were required to return cards did in fact obtain exactly the sort of 'forgetting' that we had been hoping to observe (Levy & Claravall, 1977). While it is reassuring to have such loyal and conscientious subjects there are times when one might hope for lower levels of motivation!

Our second attempt (Wilkins & Baddeley, 1978) required our subjects to perform a rather more demanding routine than merely responding once. We used a device that was invented by Arnold Wilkins to simulate the task of taking pills at regular intervals. The device comprised a light-box containing a digital watch with a light-emitting diode display. Over the watch was placed a film cassette. Depressing a button on the outside of the box illuminated the watch. The subject's task was to press the button exposing the film and recording the time four times a day at 8.30 a.m., 1.00 p.m., 5.30 p.m. and 10.00 p.m. each day for seven days. The subjects were instructed that if they forgot to push the button at the target time they should push it as soon as they remembered. If they did not remember before the next response was due, then this should be noted on a label attached to the device. We were interested in whether ability to perform this memory task accurately was related in any way to performance of more conventional memory tasks, and for that reason we chose two groups of subjects; one comprised 16 subjects who had been found to perform particularly well on a task involving the free recall of 16 disyllabic words (mean score 49 per cent recall), while a second group of 15 subjects were selected as performing particularly poorly on free recall (mean per cent correct 31 per cent). Both groups were members of the APU subject panel, and were mainly housewives.

Results suggested that subjects were able to perform the button pressing task reasonably accurately, with responses peaking at, or just before the target time, but showing a relatively long tail of late responses extending up to about two hours after the target interval. There was an average of only about one omission per subject over the whole seven days, with no difference between the two groups. In terms of temporal accuracy however a reliable difference did occur; those subjects who had good memories as measured by their free recall performance were significantly *less* accurate than those with poor memories. It seems reasonably clear that capacity for remembering *when* to do something is not the same as capacity for remembering lists of words.

We were encouraged to have found a task which did show some potentially interesting patterns of error but nevertheless were dissatisfied at the relatively small amount of data one obtained over a period of as long as a week. The experiment was administratively somewhat complex to organize, and the rate of data collection slow because of the limited number of testing devices available. It therefore seemed advisable to attempt to produce a more intensive way of accumulating data on the issue of remembering to do something at a specific time. Arnold Wilkins and John Harris finally came up with a technique which appears to be quite promising.

The task in this case is more similar to that of boiling an egg while performing some absorbing second task such as watching television than to that of remembering to take pills. More specifically, subjects are invited to come to the laboratory and watch a film. While watching it they are told that they will from time to time need to respond by holding up a card. The time when the response should be made is given on each of the series of cards. The subject's watch is always removed however, so that the only way she can be certain of gauging the time is to look at a clock which is placed behind her. A video camera is located in front of the subject so that it is possible to check first of all whenever she looks behind her to see the time, secondly at what time she holds up her card. This method has the advantage of not only requiring an externally verifiable response at a specified time, but also allows the subject's clock observations to be monitored. It is hoped that these additional data will allow the formulation and testing of much more specific models of the underlying process of remembering when to perform a particular action. Preliminary results are encouraging. They suggest that a subject's 'observing responses' tend to show a scalloping increase as the crucial interval approaches. Operant conditioners will no doubt see similarities with the behaviour of

pigeons and rats on fixed interval schedules, while vigilance theorists might notice some similarities to the observing response behaviour observed by Holland many years ago in vigilance tasks. Whether the similarities will prove theoretically fruitful however still remains to be seen.

I would like to close on a final study of absent-mindedness which is distinguished both by its neatness and by the fact that it was carried out not by research psychologists, but by sixth form pupils taking A-level psychology. As such, it illustrates very neatly the point that in this area extremely interesting and worthwhile results can be obtained without the need for either complex equipment or sophisticated theorising.

The study in question was carried out by the Bexhill Sixth Form College and submitted to the BBC TV series 'Young Scientist of the Year' (Wakeford *et al.*, 1980). The study began by asking a total of 326 14–18-year-old pupils to record instances of absent-mindedness over a four-week period. The number of instances ranged from zero to more than 10. They comprised primarily what Reason (1977) would term slips of action, typical examples being to answer the telephone giving full address rather than just a telephone number, going into the butcher's and asking for a toilet roll or attempting to put on tights while still wearing slippers. Occurrence of reported incidents showed a clear pattern throughout the day with peaks between 7.00 and 9.00 a.m., 12.00 and 2.00 p.m., and 4.00 and 7.00 p.m. It is suggested that these times tend to be associated with routine activities, and that the slips of action often occur when trying to perform a routine activity at the same time as some other process. This in turn suggests the hypothesis that subjects who are particularly liable to make such errors of absent-mindedness may have difficulty in performing two tasks at the same time.

The sixth-formers tested this by selecting two extreme groups. One of these comprised 20 subjects who reported no absent-minded events, while the other comprised 20 subjects reporting more than eight incidents of absent-mindedness. They tested memory span in both groups, and had them perform two further tasks, counting backwards in threes from a specified number, and mirror drawing. This required the subject to trace round a star, monitoring his performance through an angled mirror. Results of the various tasks are shown in Table 4 from which it is clear that when performed alone, the two groups showed no trace of difference on any of the three tasks. When subjects were required to count backwards while performing the mirror drawing task, clear differences did appear with the subjects who reported many absent-minded incidents finding it significantly more difficult to combine the two tasks than those who reported no such incidents. If this result proves readily replicable it will clearly have considerable implications for an understanding of slips of action and absent-mindedness. (Alas, attempts to replicate it have so far been quite unsuccessful.)

I suggested in my introduction that I regard the study of everyday life as a rather important new development in cognitive psychology. Nevertheless the examples I have given have all been rather ordinary, none of them producing results that would startle the men in the street, or that are likely to overthrow major theories. Why then do I regard this trend as important?

I think that it is important because it represents a return to fundamentals; an acceptance of the need to relate theory to problems outside the laboratory. In this respect it would probably be much more familiar and congenial to C. S. Myers than would the psychology of the 1950s or 1960s. In the 1950s, in North America particularly, there was an emphasis on the need for experimental rigour and control. In my own field of memory this tended to be associated with the dustbowl empiricist approach of traditional verbal learning. Perhaps even more characteristic of this period was the preoccupation with learning in animals where it was felt that much greater degrees of experimental control were possible. At this period, everyday life was considered far too messy to

Table 4 _____

Single and Dual Task Performance of Absent-Minded and Non-Absent-Minded Subjects (data from Wakeford *et al.*, 1980)

	Single task	Dual task	Decrement
Non-absent-minded			
Digit span	7.51	—	—
Mirror drawing (time)	57.7	61.9	4.2
Backward counting (items)	28.2	27.0	1.2
Absent-minded			
Digit span	7.5	—	—
Mirror drawing (time)	52.3	71.8	19.5
Backward counting (items)	31.0	22.9	7.1

merit the serious consideration of the psychologist.

The 1960s saw the beginnings of a revolt against this preoccupation with experimental control, but this tended to take the form of a range of new theoretical approaches, each operating as if it had a monopoly of the 'truth'. Whether the particular version of the 'truth' was based on Piaget, Skinner, Chomsky or artificial intelligence, its disciples were interested in the real world, if at all, primarily as a means of illustrating the 'truth' to the uninitiated. Everyday problems were interesting only in as far as they could be incorporated within the intellectual empire of the theorist in question. The 1970s have seen a considerable reduction in the Messianic fervour that characterized the theorizing of the 1960s, accompanied by a growing conviction that solving applied problems may actually be a respectable occupation for a psychologist. The reduction in the intensity of belief in theoretical positions has made it much more acceptable to tackle problems which do not have obvious theoretical answers, and the reduction in theoretical arrogance is beginning to allow much more cross-fertilization between different disciplines within psychology.

I think that the concept of cognitive psychology has proved particularly useful here. The label 'cognitive psychology' tends to have overtones which go considerably beyond the literal meaning of studying the intellect. It has come in recent years to imply a more relaxed theoretical and methodological stance than was typical in the 1950s and 1960s, but at the same time one which is concerned at producing empirically testable models. Cognitive psychology has often been associated with information-processing concepts, but it is by no means confined to such an approach. A psycholinguist concerned with grammar, a Piagetian concerned with child development or a functionalist concerned with concept formation might well all regard themselves as cognitive psychologists while strongly denying the use of information-processing concepts.

Under the broad umbrella of cognitive psychology there are signs that the gap between experimental psychology and clinical, educational and social psychology is at last showing signs of closing. In the clinical area, the clearest examples are probably in neuropsychology where there is a growing interest in the relationship of normal function to its breakdown in the brain-damaged, with theories of normal function being applied to the study of amnesia, dyslexia and aphasia. Less well developed, but in the long term equally promising are the attempts to apply cognitive psychology to the understanding of depression and to the use of imagery techniques in behaviour modification. In the case of social psychology, links are beginning to grow between the cognitive psychology of knowledge structures and theories of attitude development, while techniques devised for the study of memory for prose are beginning to throw light on individual attitudes. In the area of educational psychology, there is a great increase in the attempt to apply cognitive psychology to the understanding of such tasks as reading, spelling and arithmetic. Serious attempts are also being made to provide a systematic analysis of individual differences in cognitive capacity which may subsequently provide a much more satisfactory basis for psychometrics than the methodologically sophisticated but theoretically

somewhat sterile approach which has dominated psychometrics over the last half century.

A concern with problems of everyday life not only tends to break down barriers within psychology but also increases contacts outside the discipline. Obvious examples include the developing relationship between cognitive psychology and forensic problems. These range from studies of eyewitness identification of faces and events to the evaluation of probabilistic evidence in a real-life context. The contribution of psychology to medicine is also growing, being by no means confined to the traditional problems of clinical psychology. Ley's (1978) work on doctor–patient communication is a particularly good example of the application of laboratory techniques to an important real-life problem, while the evaluation of programmes of rehabilitation or therapy is a difficult problem in which the skills of the cognitive psychologist seem likely to play an increasingly useful role. The growth of environmental psychology represents yet another instance of the techniques of the cognitive psychologist being applied to a range of important practical problems outside the traditional scope of the psychologist.

The term 'cognitive psychology' formed one part of a tripartite division of psychology suggested, I believe, by McDougall, the other two components being *conative* psychology (the psychology of the will), and *orectic* psychology (the psychology of the emotions). While cognitive psychology is now very extensively studied, the will and the emotions are still sadly neglected. I suspect that one major reason for this is that the intellect can be studied relatively easily in the laboratory whereas the experimental study of the will and the emotions, while equally important, is much more difficult to carry out in the laboratory.

If we are to develop an adequate understanding of man, however, the will and the emotions will have to be studied, and I myself believe they should be studied objectively and not left exclusively to the novelist or the phenomenologist. It is in this area that the psychology of everyday life may eventually yield the greatest rewards. I look forward then to the development of techniques for working outside the laboratory which may subsequently allow us to go beyond cognitive psychology to a conative and orectic psychology of everyday life.

ACKNOWLEDGEMENTS

I am grateful to the Bexhill Sixth Form College for permission to use their results and to Dr Arnold Wilkins and Dr John Harris for much useful discussion.

REFERENCES

BADDELEY, A. D. (1966a). Influence of depth on the manual dexterity of free divers: A comparison between open sea and pressure chamber testing. *Journal of Applied Psychology,* **50,** 81–85.

BADDELEY, A. D. (1966b). The influence of acoustic and semantic similarity on long-term memory for word sequences. *Quarterly Journal of Experimental Psychology,* **18,** 302–309.

BADDELEY, A. D. (1968). A three-minute reasoning test based on grammatical transformation. *Psychonomic Science,* **10,** 341–342.

BEKERIAN, D. A. & BADDELEY, A. D. (1980). Saturation advertising and the repetition effect. *Journal of Verbal Learning and Verbal Behavior,* **19,** 17–25.

BREWER, N. & SANDOW, B. (1980). Alcohol effects on driver performance under conditions of divided attention. *Ergonomics* **23,** 185–190.

CRAIK, F. I. M. & TULVING, E. (1975). Depth of processing and the retention of words in episodic memory. *Journal of Experimental Psychology: General,* **104,** 268–294.

CRAIK, F. I. M. & WATKINS, M. J. (1973). The role of rehearsal in short-term memory. *Journal of Verbal Learning and Verbal Behavior,* **12,** 599–607.

GLUCKSBERG, S. & COWEN, G. N., Jr. (1970). Memory for nonattended auditory material. *Cognitive Psychology,* **1,** 149–156.

HAMILTON, P. & COPEMAN, A. (1970). The effect of alcohol and noise on components of a tracking and monitoring task. *British Journal of Psychology,* **61,** 149–156.

HERBERT, M., JOHNS, M. W. & DORE, C. (1976). Factor analysis of analogue scales measuring subjective feelings before and after sleep. *British Journal of Medical Psychology,* **49,** 373–379.

JONES, B. M. & JONES, M. K. (1977). Alcohol and memory impairment in male and female social drinkers. In I. M. Birnbaum & E. S. Parker (eds), *Alcohol and Human Memory.* Hillsdale, NJ: Lawrence Erlbaum.

LEVY, R. & CLARAVALL, V. (1977). Differential effects of a phone reminder on appointment keeping for patients with long and short between-visit intervals. *Medical Care,* **15,** 435–438.

LEY, P. (1978). Memory for medical information. In M. M. Gruneberg, P. E. Morris & R. N. Sykes (eds), *Practical Aspects of Memory.* London: Academic Press.

MECHANIC, A. (1964). The responses involved in the rote learning of verbal materials. *Journal of Verbal Learning and Verbal Behavior,* **3,** 30–36.

MORTON, J. (1967). A singular lack of incidental learning. *Nature,* **215,** 203–204.

NICKERSON, R. S. & ADAMS, M. J. (1979). Memory for a common object. *Cognitive Psychology,* **11,** 287–307.

REASON, J. (1977). Skill and error in everyday life. In M. J. A. Howe (ed.), *Adult Learning.* London: Wiley.

RUNDELL, O. H. & WILLIAMS, H. L. (1977). Effects of alcohol on organizational aspects of human memory. In F. A. Seixas (ed.), *Currents in Alcoholism,* vol. 2. New York: Grune & Stratton.

TULVING, E. (1966). Subjective organisation and effects of repetition in multi-trial free-recall learning. *Journal of Verbal Learning and Verbal Behavior,* **5,** 193–197.

TULVING, E. & COLOTTA, V. A. (1970). Free recall of trilingual lists. *Cognitive Psychology,* **1,** 86–98.

WAKEFORD, F., CLEMENTS, K., VINER, J. & WHAY, J. (1980). An investigation into the incidence and causes of absent minded behaviour. BBC TV's Young Scientist of the Year Competition.

WEINGARTNER, H., ADEFRIS, W., EICH, J. E. & MURPHY, D. L. (1976). Encoding-imagery specificity in alcohol state-dependent learning. *Journal of Experimental Psychology: Human Learning and Memory,* **2**, 83–87.

WILKINS, A. J. & BADDELEY, A. D. (1978). Remembering to recall in everyday life: An approach to absent mindedness. In M. M. Gruneberg, P. E. Morris & R. N. Sykes (eds), *Practical Aspects of Memory.* London: Academic Press.

WING, A. M. & BADDELEY, A. D. (1978). A simple measure of handwriting as an index of stress. *Bulletin of The Psychonomic Society,* **11**, 245–246.

The fourteenth Annual Myers Lecture given on 28 March, 1980 at the University of Aberdeen.

24

Judith H. Langlois and Lori A. Roggman

Attractive Faces Are Only Average

Abstract: *Scientists and philosophers have searched for centuries for a parsimonious answer to the question of what constitutes beauty. We approached this problem from both an evolutionary and information-processing rationale and predicted that faces representing the average value of the population would be consistently judged as attractive. To evaluate this hypothesis, we digitized samples of male and female faces, mathematically averaged them, and had adults judge the attractiveness of both the individual faces and the computer-generated composite images. Both male (three samples) and female (three samples) composite faces were judged as more attractive than almost all the individual faces comprising the composites. A strong linear trend also revealed that the composite faces became more attractive as more faces were entered. These data showing that attractive faces are only average are consistent with evolutionary pressures that favor characteristics close to the mean of the population and with cognitive processes that favor prototypical category members.*

What makes a face beautiful? The answer to this question has eluded scientists[1] and philosophers even though interest in the question has continued for centuries. Research in social and developmental psychology, even without a conceptual definition of beauty or a specification of its stimulus dimensions, has nevertheless produced some of the most robust and widely replicated findings in the social and behavioral sciences: Both children and adults respond more positively to attractive rather than unattractive individuals (see reviews by Berscheid & Walster, 1974; Langlois, 1986; Sorell & Nowak, 1981).

Until recently, most researchers interested in attractiveness effects have avoided investigating the stimulus dimensions of beauty, both

From Judith H. Langlois and Lori A. Roggman, "Attractive Faces Are Only Average," *Psychological Science*, vol. 1, no. 2 (March 1990), pp. 115–121. Copyright © 1990 by The American Psychological Society. Reprinted by permission of Cambridge University Press.

because of the intractable nature of the problem and because of several well-entrenched assumptions about standards of beauty and preferences for attractiveness. For example, it has been assumed, at least since the publication of Darwin's *Descent of Man* (1871), that standards of beauty are culturally specific and that attempts to determine universal or underlying dimensions of beauty are futile. It has also been widely held that standards of attractiveness are only gradually learned by children through exposure to the media and culture in which they live.

Both these assumptions, however, have been challenged by new data. First, a number of recent cross-cultural investigations have demonstrated surprisingly high (e.g., 66–.93) interrater reliabilities in judgments of attractiveness (e.g., Bernstein, Lin, & McClellan, 1982; Cunningham, 1986; Johnson, Dannenbring, Anderson, & Villa, 1983; Maret, 1983; Maret & Harling, 1985; Richardson, Goodman, Hastorf, & Dornbusch, 1961; Thakerar & Iwawaki, 1979; Weisfeld, Weisfeld, & Callaghan, 1984). The cross-cultural data suggest that ethnically diverse faces possess both distinct and similar structural features; these features seem to be perceived as attractive regardless of the racial and cultural background of the perceiver.

Second, a number of recent studies of infants have demonstrated that when infants 3 to 6 months of age are shown pictures of adult-judged attractive and unattractive faces, they prefer attractive ones (Langlois, Roggman, Casey, Ritter, Rieser-Danner, & Jenkins, 1987; Langlois, Roggman, & Rieser-Danner, in press; Samuels & Ewy, 1985; Shapiro, Eppler, Haith, & Reis, 1987). Thus, even before any substantial exposure to cultural standards of beauty, young infants display behaviors that seem to be rudimentary versions of the judgments and preferences for attractive faces so prevalent in older children and adults.

Taken together, the cross-cultural and infant data suggest that there may be universal stimulus dimensions of faces that infants, older children, and adults cross-culturally view as attractive. The ability to detect these stimulus dimensions may be innate or acquired much earlier than previously believed. Such findings thus compel a more intensified search for answers to the old question of what defines a beautiful face.

THE LENGTH OF NOSES

Most recent attempts to define beauty have taken a feature-measurement approach (Cunningham, 1986; Hildebrandt & Fitzgerald, 1979; Lucker, 1981). While some progress has been made in identifying facial measurements that predict attractiveness ratings, the findings have been contradictory both within and between studies (Cunningham, 1986; Farkas, Munro, & Kolar, 1987). Even if consistent results were to be obtained, the feature-measurement approach would not provide a parsimonious answer to the question of what makes a face attractive. Thousands of measurements of the face are possible (Farkas, 1981), although research so far has employed only a few of the many possible facial measurements. Furthermore, even if we could accurately and reliably predict attractiveness judgments from feature measurements, we would still not know why the combination of certain measurements are perceived as attractive by infants, children, and adults.

Parsimony, Biology, and Cognition

A more parsimonious solution to defining beauty and explaining why certain facial configurations are perceived as attractive is suggested by two distinct fields of inquiry, evolutionary biology and cognitive psychology. Darwin's theory of natural selection (1859), or at least modern day versions of it,[2] suggests that average values of many population features should be preferred to extreme values. In the most ubiquitous form of natural selection, normalizing or stabilizing selection, evolutionary pressures operate against the extremes of the population, relative to those close to the mean (Barash, 1982; Dobzhansky, 1970). Thus, individuals with characteristics (especially some morphological features) that are close to the mean for the population should be less likely to carry harmful genetic mutations and, therefore, should be more preferred by conspecifics (Bumpas, 1899; Schmalhausen, 1949; Symons, 1979). The robust preference shown for attractive individuals has been puzzling in light of this evolutionary fact, given that more attractive individuals are at the extreme rather than in the middle of the distribution of attractiveness ratings.

Results from a second domain of investigation, cognitive and developmental psychology, also converge on the suggestion that the average value of faces should be preferred. It is well known that even young infants are capable of forming concepts and of abstracting prototypes from individual exemplars of a category (Cohen & Younger, 1983; Quinn & Eimas, 1986). A prototype can be defined as the central representation of a category, as possessing the average or mean value of the attributes of that category and as representing the averaged members of the class (Reed, 1972; Rosch, 1978; Rosch, Mervis, Gray, Johnson, & Boyes-Braem, 1976; Rosch, Simpson, & Miller, 1976). After seeing several exemplars from a category, both infants and adults respond to an averaged representation of those exemplars as if it were familiar; that is, they show evidence of forming mental prototypes, and they rely on such abstracted prototypes to recognize new instances of the category (Quinn & Eimas, 1986: Rosch, 1978; Strauss, 1979).

For example, using schematic faces, Strauss demonstrated that even young infants recognized facial prototypes made from the averaged values of previously viewed facial features rather than from the most frequently viewed features. Infants responded to a prototype or averaged face as highly familiar even though they had never seen it before. Others have also shown that infants will average features from various kinds of visual stimuli to form prototypes (Bomba & Siqueland, 1983; Younger, 1985; Younger & Gotlieb, 1988).

Thus, evidence exists demonstrating that the average value of members of a class of objects is often prototypical, that infants are capable of forming prototypes by averaging features, and that infants assign prototypes special status by recognizing prototypical category members

even when they have not seen them before. To the extent that a face is a good example or prototype and is thus easily recognized as a face, infants may show more interest in it than a less prototypical face. These facts imply an explanation for studies showing that infants prefer attractive faces: Perhaps an attractive face is attractive simply because it is prototypical.

If attractive faces are attractive because they represent a prototype or an average of a face, then a prototype created by averaging several faces would be expected to be attractive. Such an attractive "average" face would be consistent with both evolutionary and cognitive theory and would help explain why young infants and adults from diverse cultures prefer attractive faces. Considerable progress may be made in both defining facial beauty and in understanding the broad preferences for a beautiful face if it can be shown that faces representing the average value of the population are judged as attractive.

COMPUTER FACES

To evaluate whether the "average" face is more attractive than the individual faces used to create them, we digitized individual faces, averaged them, and had adults rate the physical attractiveness both of the individual faces and the averaged composite images. We predicted that these average faces would be attractive, that this effect would generalize across different sets of both composite faces and raters, and that composite faces would be more attractive than the mean level of attractiveness of the individual faces used to create them.

To test these hypotheses, we photographed male and female undergraduate students from a standard distance in a full-front view of the face and neck. Background and lighting were identical across subjects. Subjects were asked to pose with a "pleasant but neutral, closed mouth expression." Clothing was draped with a solid light-colored cloth to eliminate all variation in appearance. Subjects wearing glasses or earrings were asked to remove them. Males with facial hair were not included in the population of faces.

The population of facial photographs included a pool of 336 males (including 26 Hispanics and 21 Asians) and a pool of 214 females (including 24 Hispanics and 18 Asians). From each pool, a sample of 96 faces was randomly selected without replacement and randomly divided into three sets of 32 faces from which three composites were created. No face was included in more than one composite set.

Each face was digitized by scanning the photograph with a video lens interfaced with a computer. Using a zoom lens and "joystick" markers, faces were adjusted for size and position by matching the location of the eye pupils and the middle of the lip line across all faces. A 512 × 512 matrix of numeric gray values then represented each facial image. By arithmetically averaging those matrices, a series of achromatic composite facial images was created. For each set, composites were created at five levels of averaging: two faces, four faces, eight faces, sixteen faces, and thirty-two faces.

These composites were then contrast enhanced to clarify the image. Initially, each image was "smoothed," meaning that each pixel in the matrix was adjusted to the average value of the pixels immediately surrounding it so that any double edges creat[ed] by averaging were minimized. "Extra" edges occasionally remained in the composites with eight or fewer faces and were removed from the image. Subsequently, the gray value difference between each pixel and its surrounding area was doubled so that the resulting smoothed edges were sharpened. Contrast was also enhanced by increasing the range of gray values, similarly to the way the contrast adjustment on a standard television affects the image. The individual faces were smoothed and contrast enhanced in the same manner as the composites to create photographically similar images. The composite and individual faces were then photographed by a matrix camera with direct input from the computer screen.

Each set of individual faces and its corresponding composites were rated for physical attractiveness by a minimum of 65 (range = 65–80) males and females enrolled in under-

graduate psychology classes. Three hundred raters participated; some raters evaluated more than one set of faces. The slides of the individual and composite faces from each set were projected in random order and were shown for 10 seconds each. Raters scored each facial image on a 1 to 5 scale ranging from 1 = very unattractive to 5 = very attractive. The raters were told that the photographs were taken from a television screen, to ignore any reduction of photographic quality caused by the TV image, and to judge only the physical attractiveness of faces.

Reliability of the attractiveness ratings was assessed separately for each set of images using coefficient alpha and ranged from .90 to .98. Separate estimates of reliability for male and female raters ranged from .90 for one group of 23 male raters to .98 for one group of 46 female raters. Only three raters from the total of 300 were eliminated from the data set because of low inter-rater correlations with the rest of the raters.

Composite Faces

For each facial image, all ratings were averaged to produce a mean attractiveness score. Table 1 shows the means and standard deviations for each set of individual faces and for each level of the composites. The mean attractiveness scores of the 32- and 16-face male and female composite faces are one standard deviation or more above the mean for the individual male and female faces. Differences in attractiveness scores among levels of the composites were evaluated using analysis of variance (ANOVA) with sex and level of composite as factors. A significant effect for the number of faces entered into the composite was obtained, $F(4, 25) = 3.16$, $p = .03$, but there were no significant effects for sex or for the interaction between sex and composite level. The main effect for composite level was followed up by a test of linearity, which revealed a strong linear effect of increasing attractiveness as more faces were entered into the composite, $F(1, 25) = 10.43$, $p = .004$.

Individual vs. Composite Faces

The individual faces were compared to the composites in three ways for each sex. First, individual faces were compared to the composites using an analysis of variance with a single factor with six levels: the individual face level and each of the five levels of composites (2, 4, 8, 16, 32). This overall test was followed by planned comparisons between the composites at each level of averaging and the individual faces that were averaged into the composite: 32 faces from each of the three sets ($n = 96$) were compared to the three 32-face composites; 16 faces from each of the three sets ($n = 48$) were compared to the three 16-face composites, and so on. Two sample t tests with separate variance estimates were used for these planned comparisons because of differences in the variance and sample size between the individual faces and the composites. Finally, within rater, paired t tests were used to compare raters' judgments of the 32-face composites with their ratings of all the individual faces.

Table 1

Attractiveness Ratings for Individual and Composite Faces

	n	Mean	SD
Male Faces			
Individual Faces			
Set 1	32	2.60	.53
Set 2	32	2.51	.54
Set 3	32	2.42	.48
Sets 1–3	96	2.51	.52
Composite Faces			
2-face level	3	2.34	.12
4-face level	3	2.45	.61
8-face level	3	2.75	.57
16-face level	3	3.31	.17
32-face level	3	3.27	.08
Female Faces			
Individual Faces			
Set 1	32	2.38	.67
Set 2	32	2.48	.63
Set 3	32	2.42	.66
Sets 1–3	96	2.43	.64
Composite Faces			
2-face level	3	2.87	.49
4-face level	3	2.84	.77
8-face level	3	3.03	.34
16-face level	3	3.06	.18
32-face level	3	3.25	.07

Male Faces

The attractiveness scores of the 96 individual male faces ranged from 1.8 to 3.8 with a mean of 2.51 ($SD = .52$) The ANOVA comparing images of individual male faces with 2-, 4-, 8-, 16-, and 32-face images revealed a significant effect of the number of faces, $F(5, 93) = 2.90, p = .017$. The planned comparisons showed that the 32- and 16-face composites were rated as significantly more attractive than their corresponding individual male faces ($t = 10.60, p = .001$; $t = 7.24, p = .001$, for the 32- and 16-face composites, respectively). The composites made of eight or fewer faces, however, did not differ significantly from their individual faces.

The within-rater analyses revealed that of the 96 individual male faces, only three were judged as significantly more attractive than their corresponding composite, about what would be expected by chance. By comparison, 80 of the individual male faces were rated as significantly less attractive than the composite.

Female Faces

The attractiveness scores of the 96 individual female faces ranged from 1.20 to 4.05, with a mean of 2.43 ($SD = .64$), similar to the mean of the males. The results for the analyses of the female faces were similar to the results for the male faces. There was a significant overall effect of the number of faces in each image revealed by the ANOVA, $F(5, 93) = 2.38, p = .043$. The planned comparisons showed that the 32- and 16-face composites were rated as significantly more attractive than their corresponding individual female faces, but that the other composites did not differ significantly from their individual faces ($t = 10.46, p = .001$; $t = 4.83, p = .005$, for the 32- and 16-face composites, respectively).

Again, the raters' attractiveness judgments for each individual female face were compared to their ratings of the 32-face composites. Of the 96 individual female faces, only 4 were rated as significantly more attractive than the composites, whereas 75 were judged as significantly less attractive.

DISCUSSION

Galton's Meat-Eaters

In the 1800s, a number of articles and commentaries were published on composite portraits created by Galton and Stoddard in which they superimposed photographic exposures of faces (Galton, 1878; 1883; Stoddard, 1886; 1887). The apparent purpose of these composite portraits was to create graphic representations of types of faces. Galton enjoyed creating composites of criminals, meat-eaters, vegetarians, and tuberculosis patients. Stoddard created composites of the 1883, 1884, and 1886 senior classes of Smith College and of members of the National Academy of Sciences. Although both Galton and Stoddard noted that the composites were "better looking" than their individual components because "the special villainous irregularities in the latter have disappeared" (Galton, 1878, p. 135), their observations were not pursued systematically until now. The data provided here offer empirical evidence that composite faces, at least those of a group of predominantly Caucasian males and females, are indeed attractive and are rated as more attractive than are the individual faces comprising the composite.

Mathematical Averages

The computerized technique of mathematically averaging faces provides several advantages over the photographic method of Galton and Stoddard. First, the images are precisely averaged rather than superimposed by hand based on only roughly equivalent units of time exposure. Second, our technique allowed us to standardize lighting and contrast and to perform precise image enhancement procedures on all of the faces equivalently. Finally, the random selection procedure ensured that faces were included in the composite in an unbiased

fashion. Thus, some of the composites were begun with an unattractive face, some with an attractive face; some composites had more unattractive than attractive faces, others had the reverse. The mean attractiveness ratings of the 16- and 32-face composites indicated that the attractiveness of the individual faces in these composites was not an important determinant of the attractiveness of the composite. As Stoddard (1887) discovered, neither was the order in which the faces were entered and averaged.[3]

Despite the technical advantages of a computerized technique over the timed multiple-exposure photography of the last century, we do not presume to have simulated the human mind. Our digitized images, even at 262,144 pixels per image, do not approach the quality of an image of a face viewed live, and our technique only approximates the averaging process that is assumed to occur when humans form mental prototypes. Nevertheless, by using image-processing techniques and by collecting objective and reliable ratings of attractiveness, we have empirically demonstrated that average faces are perceived as attractive. We replicated this finding in two populations, male and female young adults, and in three separate samples from each population using several analytic approaches. Our results demonstrating this robust effect confirm the subjective impressions of those who, in the last century, have viewed composite faces and commented on their striking attractiveness. At the same time, our results will surprise contemporary researchers who have not considered an attractive face to be average.

The attractiveness scores of the composites indicated that faces attain both average values and high attractiveness ratings when 8 to 16 faces are combined into a composite image. Likewise, the variability of the attractiveness ratings of the 16- and 32-face composites was lower than that for most of the other composites and those of all of the individual faces. These statistical findings are mirrored by observation: Inspection of the composites reveals that the 16- and 32-face composites look very similar to each other, both within and between same-sex composite sets. That this similarity should hold between composite sets is especially interesting given that no individual face appeared in more than one set. Thus, the averaging procedure, in addition to producing attractive faces, also seems to produce a typical face. Other research is consistent with this finding: Faces rated as more attractive are also rated as more typical and less unusual; in turn, faces rated as attractive and typical are rated as more similar to each other than to other faces (Light, Hollander, & Kayra-Stuart, 1981).

The typicalness and "averageness" of attractive faces helps to explain why they are preferred. Faces may be preferred by infants and adults alike if they are perceived as prototypes of a face; that is, as more *facelike*. Unattractive faces, because of their minor distortions (e.g., malocclusions, etc.), may be perceived as less facelike or as less typical of human faces. In the study presented here, although we have not shown that attractive faces are perceived as prototypes, we have demonstrated that prototype faces are perceived as attractive. Conceptually, averaging the gray values of digitized images of faces creates a prototype by definition (Reed, 1972; Rosch, Simpson, & Miller, 1976; Wittgenstein, 1953). Methodologically, averaging matrices of pixels to create prototypes from exemplars is the inverse of procedures used in previous research to create category exemplars from prototypes, such as random distortions of prototype dot patterns (Bomba & Siqueland, 1983; Posner & Keele, 1968). This method of creating a prototype by averaging facial images is also similar to creating a schematic prototype by averaging facial features (Strauss, 1979).

Infants may prefer attractive or prototypical faces because prototypes are easier to classify as a face. Faces are such an important class of visual stimuli for humans, and the perception of faceness in infancy is a critical part of the development of social responsiveness. If humans have evolved to respond to facial configurations for the purpose of extracting relevant social information (e.g., McArthur & Baron, 1983), both infants and adults may respond most strongly to the most facelike or prototypic stimuli in the environment. Because of the importance of the information conveyed by faces for social interaction, humans should therefore have built-in or early developing preferences for them.

Beauty Detectors

The ability of both infants and adults to abstract a prototype by averaging features will not come as a surprise to some biologically oriented theorists. Symons (1979), for example, has proposed an innate mechanism that detects the population mean of anatomical features. In the case of faces, this proposed "beauty-detecting" mechanism averages observed faces; selection pressures are assumed to favor built-in preferences for these average faces over preferences for faces more distant from the mean. Perhaps because of the difficulty of shifting perspectives from ratings of attractiveness to the dimension of faces themselves, however, the field of study concerned with facial attractiveness and its effects on social relations and social behavior has failed to pursue Symons' proposal until now.

Although the nomenclature of the evolutionary and cognitive perspectives is quite different, these perspectives offer more similarity than difference in the predictions made for prototypic or averaged faces and the tendency of infants and adults from diverse cultures to notice and prefer them. The data provided here do not, however, allow us to choose between evolutionary theory, which suggests that preferences for attractive faces are innate, and cognitive theory, which suggests that preferences for attractive faces are acquired early in life through exposure to category exemplars.[4] Indeed, it may be that the mechanism by which such preferences would become built-in is an inevitable outcome of the categorical abstraction of social stimuli. In any case, both the evolutionary and cognitive developmental perspectives bring coherence to the cross-cultural and infant data when the metric of average faceness rather than attractiveness ratings is designated for study.

In their seminal review of physical attractiveness effects, Berscheid and Walster (1974) concluded that there was no answer to the question of what constitutes beauty. Nor could Berscheid and Walster discern a foreseeable answer to this question. The data provided here suggest that attractive faces are those that represent the central tendency or the averaged members of the category of faces. Such a definition of attractiveness is parsimonious and fits with both evolutionary and cognitive theory. Certain limitations, however, should be noted in these data. Our composites were created by averaging the faces of young, university students from the southwest. Although it is quite unlikely that the faces of these undergraduates differ in any meaningful way from those in other geographical areas of the United States, generality should be ensured by making composites of faces from different geographical locations. Composites of faces from other cultures should also be evaluated. Although a composite of 32 Asian faces will surely look different than that of a Caucasian composite face, we would predict that such an Asian composite face would, nevertheless, be judged as very attractive by both Asian and non-Asian raters.

We also acknowledge that a sample of movie stars might be rated as more attractive than our composites. It may be the case that although averageness is a necessary and critical element of attractiveness, other elements may also be important in influencing judgments of attractiveness. However, whether the digitized versions of faces of movie stars are more attractive in some absolute sense or are merely rated as more attractive because of their exposure and familiarity to raters (e.g., Harrison, 1969; Zajonc, 1968) is unclear and will need to be resolved by future research. Finally, we make no claim that our analysis applies to aesthetics in general; although average faces may be quite attractive, average (i.e., composited) art is not at all likely to be attractive and, in fact, hardly seems to be a useful construct.

We end by noting that the topic of physical attractiveness and its effects on social behaviors and relationships has been described as "undemocratic" (Aronson, 1969). Social scientists may be less disturbed by studying the effects of attractiveness knowing that attractive faces, in fact, are only average.

ACKNOWLEDGMENTS

This work was supported by grants from the National Science Foundation (BNS-8513843) and the National Institute of Child Health and Human Development (HD-21332) to Judith H. Langlois.

We thank Lisa Musselman and the Advanced Graphics Laboratory at the University of Texas for assistance in creating the composite images. This paper profited from discussions with and comments from many people, especially Arnold Buss, David Buss, Leslie Cohen, Donald Foss, Joseph Horn, Kevin Miller, Deborah Tharinger, Del Thiessen, and the reviewers of *Psychological Science*.

NOTES

1. The first psychologist to experimentally study beauty was probably Fechner in 1876 (Osborne, 1953).
2. Darwin himself did not believe there were either common cross-cultural preferences for beauty or common underlying dimensions of beauty.
3. We did not systematically test variations of order. However that the attractiveness of the composites is unrelated to the attractiveness of the faces entered at the beginning of the averaging process is obvious from the nearly identical attractiveness ratings and appearance of the 32-face composites within each gender, compared to the wide range of attractiveness of the first four faces entered into each composite set and from the four-face composites.
4. The ability to categorize is the innate component from this perspective (Cohen, 1988). Unfortunately, the innate versus early acquired distinction cannot be investigated in infants at birth because of the immature status of the visual system (Banks & Salapatek, 1983).

REFERENCES

Aronson, E. (1969). Some antecedents of interpersonal attraction. In W. J. Arnold & D. Levine (Eds.), *Nebraska symposium on motivation* (pp. 143–177). Lincoln: University of Nebraska Press.

Banks, M. S., & Salapatek, P. (1983). Infant visual perception. In P. H. Mussen, M. M. Haith, & J. J. Campos (Eds.), *Handbook of child psychology: Vol. 2, Infancy and developmental psychobiology* (pp. 435–571). New York: Wiley.

Barash, D. P. (1982). *Sociobiology and behavior*. New York: Elsevier North Holland.

Bernstein, I. H., Lin, T., & McClellan, P. (1982). Cross- vs. within-racial judgments of attractiveness. *Perception & Psychophysics, 32*, 495–503.

Berscheid, E., & Walster, E. (1974). Physical attractiveness. In L. Berkowitz (Ed.), *Advances in experimental social psychology* (pp. 157–215). New York: Academic Press.

Bomba, P. C., & Siqueland, E. R. (1983). The nature and structure of infant form categories, *Journal of Experimental Child Psychology, 35*, 294–328.

Bumpas, H. C. (1899). The elimination of the unfit as illustrated by the introduced sparrow. *Biology lectures in marine biology at Woods Hole, Massachusetts, 11*, 209–226.

Cohen, L. B. (1988). An information-processing approach to infant cognitive development. In L. Weiskrantz (Ed.), *Thought without language* (pp. 211–228). New York: Oxford.

Cohen, L. B., & Younger, B. A. (1983). Perceptual categorization in the infant. In E. K. Scholnik (Ed.), *New trends in conceptual representation: Challenges in Piaget's theory?* (pp. 197–220). Hillsdale, NJ: Erlbaum.

Cunningham, M. R. (1986). Measuring the physical in physical attractiveness: Quasiexperiments on the sociobiology of female facial beauty. *Journal of Social and Personality Psychology, 50*, 925–935.

Darwin, C. (1859). *On the origin of species by means of natural selection, or the preservation of favoured races in the struggle for life*. London: Watts & Co.

Darwin, C. (1871). *The descent of man and selection in relation to sex*. London: John Murray.

Dobzhansky, T. (1970). *Genetics of the evolutionary process*. New York: Columbia University Press.

Farkas, L. G. (1981). *Anthropometry of the head and face in medicine*. New York: Elsevier North Holland.

Farkas, L. G., Munro, I. R., & Kolar, J. C. (1987). Linear proportions in above- and below-average women's faces. In L. G. Farkas & I. R. Munro (Eds.), *Anthropometric facial proportions in medicine* (pp. 119–129). Springfield, IL: Charles C. Thomas.

Galton, F. (1878). Composite portraits. *Journal of the Anthropological Institute of Great Britain & Ireland, 8*, 132–142.

Galton, F. (1883). *Inquiries into human faculty and its development*. New York: Macmillan.

Harrison, A. A. (1969). Exposure and popularity. *Journal of Personality, 37*, 359–367.

Hildebrandt, K. A., & Fitzgerald, H. E. (1979). Facial feature determinants of perceived infant attractiveness. *Infant Behavior and Development, 2*, 229–329.

Johnson, R. W., Dannenbring, G. L., Anderson, N. R., & Villa, R. E. (1983). How different cultural and geographic groups perceive the attractiveness of active and inactive feminists. *The Journal of Social Psychology, 119*, 111–117.

Langlois, J. H. (1986). From the eye of the beholder to behavioral reality: The development of social behaviors and social relations as a function of physical attractiveness. In C. P. Herman, M. P. Zanna, & E. T. Higgins (Eds.), *Physical appearance, stigma, and social behavior: The Ontario symposium* (pp. 23–51). Hillsdale, NJ: Erlbaum.

Langlois, J. H., Roggman, L. A., Casey, R. J., Ritter, J. M., Rieser-Danner, L. A., & Jenkins, V. Y. (1987). Infant preferences for attractive faces: Rudiments of a stereotype? *Developmental Psychology, 23*, 363–369.

Langlois, J. H., Roggman, L. A., & Rieser-Danner, L. A. (in press). Infants' differential social responses to attractive and unattractive faces. *Developmental Psychology*.

Light, L. L., Hollander, S., & Kayra-Stuart, F. (1981). Why attractive people are harder to remember, *Personality and Social Psychology Bulletin, 7*, 269–276.

Lucker, G. W. (1981). Esthetics and a quantitative analysis of facial appearance. In G. W. Lucker, K. A. Ribbens, & J. A. McNamara (Eds.), *Psychological aspects of facial form*. Ann Arbor, MI: The Center for Growth and Development, University of Michigan.

Maret, S. M. (1983). Attractiveness ratings of photographs of Blacks by Cruzans and Americans. *The Journal of Psychology, 115*, 113–116.

Maret, S. M., & Harling, G. A. (1985). Cross cultural perceptions of physical attractiveness: Ratings of photos of whites by Cruzans and Americans. *Perceptual Motor Skills, 60*, 163–166.

McArthur, L. A., & Baron, R. M. (1983). Toward an ecological theory of social perception, *Psychological Review, 90*, 215–238.

Osborne, H. (1953), *Theory of beauty: An introduction to aesthetics*. New York: Philosophical Library.

Posner, M. I., & Keele, S. W. (1968). On the genesis of abstract ideas. *Journal of Experimental Psychology, 77*, 353–363.

Quinn, P. C., & Eimas, P. D. (1986). On categorization in early infancy. *Merrill-Palmer Quarterly, 32*, 331–363.

Reed, S. K. (1972). Pattern recognition and categorization. *Cognitive Psychology, 3*, 382–407.

Richardson, S. A., Goodman, N., Hastorf, A. H., & Dornbusch, S. M. (1961). Cultural uniformity in reaction to physical disabilities. *American Sociological Review, 26*, 241–247.

Rosch, E. (1978). Principles of categorization. In E. Rosch & B. B. Lloyd (Eds.), *Cognition and categorization* (pp. 27–47). Hillsdale, NJ: Erlbaum.

Rosch, E., Mervis, C. B., Gray, W. D., Johnson, D. M., & Boyes-Braem, P. (1976). Basic objects in natural categories. *Cognitive Psychology, 8,* 382–439.

Rosch, E., Simpson, C., & Miller, R. S. (1976). Structural bases of typicality effects. *Journal of Experimental Psychology: Human Perception and Performance, 2,* 491–502.

Samuels, C. A., & Ewy, R. (1985). Aesthetic perception of faces during infancy, *British Journal of Developmental Psychology, 3,* 221–228.

Schmalhausen, I. I. (1949). *Factors of evolution: The theory of stabilizing selection.* Philadelphia: Blakiston.

Shapiro, B. A., Eppler, M., Haith, M. M., & Reis, H. (1987, April). *An event analysis of facial attractiveness and expressiveness.* Paper presented at the meeting of the Society for Research in Child Development. Baltimore, MD.

Sorell, G. T., & Nowak, C. A. (1981). The role of physical attractiveness as a contributor to individual development. In R. M. Lerner & N. A. Busch-Rossnagel (Eds.), *Individuals as producers of their development: A life-span perspective* (pp. 389–446). New York: Academic Press.

Stoddard, J. T. (1886). Composite portraiture. *Science, 8*(182), 89–91.

Stoddard, J. T. (1887). Composite photography. *Century, 33,* 750–757.

Strauss, M. S. (1979). Abstraction of prototypical information by adults and 10-month-old infants. *Journal of Experimental Psychology: Human Learning and Memory, 5,* 618–632.

Symons, D. (1979). *The evolution of human sexuality.* New York: Oxford University Press.

Thakerar, J. N., & Iwawaki, S. (1979). Cross-cultural comparisons in interpersonal attraction of females toward males. *Journal of Social Psychology, 108,* 121–122.

Weisfeld, G. E., Weisfeld, C. C., & Callaghan, J. W. (1984). Peer and self perceptions in Hopi and Afro-American third- and sixth-graders. *Ethos, 12,* 64–83.

Wittgenstein, L. (1953). *Philosophical investigations.* New York: Macmillan.

Younger, B. A. (1985). The segregation of items into categories by ten-month-old infants. *Child Development, 56,* 1574–1583.

Younger, B., & Gotlieb, S. (1988). Development of categorization skills: Changes in the nature or structure of infant form categories? *Developmental Psychology, 24,* 611–619.

Zajonc, R. B. (1968). Attitudinal effects of mere exposure, *Journal of Personality and Social Psychology Monograph Supplements, 9,* 1–27.

25

**Ronald P. Fisher
and R. Edward Geiselman**

Enhancing Eyewitness Memory
With the Cognitive Interview

Abstract: *Basic principles of cognition were incorporated into an interactive interview format to try to enhance the recall of eyewitnesses to crime. Subjects observed a filmed simulation of a crime and were interviewed by experienced law enforcement agents two days later. Across several studies, the Cognitive Interview was found to elicit between 25–35% more correct information than did a standard police interview, without generating any more incorrect information. The Cognitive Interview is easily learned by novice and experienced interviewers and should be useful in a variety of investigative interviews.*

A major determinant of whether or not a criminal case is solved is the completeness and accuracy of the eyewitness account. Nevertheless, eyewitness reports are known to be incomplete and unreliable (e.g., Loftus, 1979). To compound the problem, law enforcement agents receive little formal training in effective methods to interview co-operative eyewitnesses (Harris, 1973). As a result, police interviews are guided more by common sense than by scientific principles of memory retrieval. Fisher, Geiselman, and Raymond (1987) found that the typical police interview begins with an open-ended question, requesting the respondent to recall as much as possible about the event. Somewhere in the middle of the respondent's narration, there followed a sequence of direct, short-answer questions about specific, relevant details of the event. When the respondent indicated that he or she could not recall, little assistance was provided by the inter-viewer to facilitate the respondent's memory. While no formal study has been undertaken to characterize the "standard" police interview, it is likely that such a common sense approach typifies many investigative interviews. Unfortunately, common sense is not always the best navigator, especially when the course is as complex as the human mind. The purpose of the present study, therefore, was to develop scientifically based interview methods to enhance the accuracy of eyewitness reports and to test these methods empirically in a controlled, yet ecologically valid, laboratory setting.

During the past twenty years, there has been a growing interest among experimental psychologists in the area of eyewitness testimony. In general, the focus of this interest has been to demonstrate the fallibility of eyewitness memory. Unfortunately, we have contributed very little on the positive side, developing techniques to assist the beleaguered witness. At first glance, it might appear that psychologists would have contributed extensively to this endeavor, since we have developed a wide variety of memory-enhancing techniques. Virtually all of these mnemonics, however, are applicable only at the encoding phase, during the crime, when victims are least likely to strategically control learning operations. Our primary goal, then, was to develop a set of retrieval mnemonics, which could be used during the post-event interview, when memory is more likely to be under strategic control.

One dramatic technique for eyewitness memory enhancement is hypnosis. Hypnosis has been reported to be useful in criminal cases especially when trauma to the witness is involved. Enhanced memory under hypnosis also obtains in some controlled laboratory experiments. On the whole, though, the evidence about memory under hypnosis is mixed. Many studies find no memory enhancement with hypnosis (see Smith, 1983, for a review). Of greater practical consequence, hypnosis may distort the memory process (see Orne, Soskis, Dinges, & Orne, 1984). As a result of the inconsistency in the empirical literature, and as a general safeguard against the potential problems encountered with memory under hypnosis, several United States states have placed restrictions on the admissibility of hypnosis

recall in a court of law—although, note the recent Supreme Court decision reversing this ruling.

In order to develop an alternative memory-enhancing technique, free from the legal constraints of hypnosis, we sought to apply generally accepted principles of memory, as found by cognitive psychologists in controlled, laboratory studies. The theoretical underpinnings of the Cognitive Interview are based on two such principles. First, the effectiveness of a retrieval cue is related to the number of features it shares with the encoded event (Flexser & Tulving, 1978). Second, there may be several retrieval paths to the encoded event, so that information not accessible with one retrieval cue may be accessible with a different cue (Tulving, 1974).

Based on these two principles, we developed a memory-retrieval procedure for eyewitnesses called the Cognitive Interview that consists of four general retrieval mnemonics. Of these, two attempt to increase the feature overlap between encoding and retrieval contexts (a) mentally reinstating the environmental and personal context that existed at the time of the crime, and (b) reporting everything, regardless of the perceived importance of the information. The other two mnemonics encourage the use of many retrieval paths: (c) recounting the events in a variety of temporal orders (e.g., both forward and backward) and (d) reporting the events from a variety of perspectives (e.g., from that of the witness and also from that of a prominent character). These four principles are explained to the respondent before the interviewer asks the initial open-ended question requesting a narration of the crime scene. In addition, several specific mnemonics, geared to elicit specific details, are described. These include mnemonics for recalling names, physical appearance, numbers, speech characteristics, and conversation. Generally, these mnemonics are based on eliciting partial information when the complete form is inaccessible. For example, if respondents cannot think of a particular name, they are encouraged to think of the length of the name, number of syllables, frequency, ethnicity, etc.

EXPERIMENTAL TESTS

Since a primary goal of our research plan was to test the Cognitive Interview under ecologically valid conditions, the events to be remembered were simulated violent crimes, as depicted on Los Angeles Police Department training films and the interviews were conducted face-to-face by experienced law enforcement investigators. In the first major study (Geiselman, Fisher, MacKinnon, & Holland, 1985), we compared the Cognitive Interview with two interview procedures that have been used by police, the hypnosis interview and the standard police interview. Eighty-nine U.C.L.A. volunteer students viewed a 4-minute film of a violent crime and were interviewed 48 hours later in one of three methods: Standard, Hypnosis, and Cognitive. In the Standard condition, the interviewers were told to conduct the interview in the same fashion as they would a typical real-world interview. In the Hypnosis condition, the interviewers were instructed first to conduct a hypnosis induction and then to proceed with their standard interview. In the Cognitive condition, the interviewers were told to present the Cognitive Interview instructions first to the witness and then proceed with the interview. In all, over 120 hours of recorded interviews were generated for analysis. The results show that significantly more correct statements were elicited by the Cognitive (41.15) and Hypnosis (38.00) interviews than by the Standard interview (29.40). $F (2, 77) = 5.27$, $p < .01$. The Cognitive and Hypnosis interviews were not reliably different from one another. Since the number of correctly recalled events could be raised spuriously by simply lowering the witness's threshold for saying anything, correct or incorrect, we also examined the number of incorrect statements. There were no reliable differences in error rates across the three conditions, $F (2, 77) = 1.99$, $p > .14$. The superiority of the Cognitive and Hypnosis interviews held even when the results were scored only for the 20 facts with the greatest investigative value (e.g., suspect description). In a follow-up study of nonstudent witnesses, perhaps a more representative sam-

ple of the real world, the results replicated the earlier findings (Geiselman, Fisher, MacKinnon, & Holland, 1986).

Although the Cognitive and Hypnosis procedures were equally effective, the Cognitive Interview can be learned and applied with considerably less training than hypnosis. In addition, it took significantly less time to instruct the respondent in the general cognitive techniques than to perform a hypnosis induction. Thus, the Cognitive Interview is more efficient than hypnosis. Since one criticism of hypnosis is that it may heighten the suggestibility of the respondent to information embedded within a leading question, we next examined the effects of leading questions with the Cognitive Interview (Geiselman, Fisher, Cohen, Holland, & Surtes, 1986). Following a staged event, in which a classroom was interrupted, student witnesses were questioned about the event. Embedded within one of the initial questions, however, was a leading statement. For example, in the original event, one of two classroom intruders was carrying a blue backpack. The leading question was: "Was the guy with the green backpack nervous?" At the end of the interview, the witnesses were asked, "What color was the backpack?" The students who were questioned using the Cognitive Interview were less likely to change the color of the backpack from blue to green than were students who were questioned using the standard interview. Thus, unlike the effects of hypnosis, which enhances respondent's suggestibility to leading questions, the Cognitive Interview appears to reduce the biasing effects of leading questions.

NEW DEVELOPMENTS

Following several hours of interviewing respondents, analyzing experimental interview protocols, and perusing actual tape recorded police interviews, two sources of improving the Cognitive Interview became apparent. First, there were characteristic differences between effective and ineffective interviewers. To improve the Cognitive Interview, then, we modeled good and poor interviewers, to build in those attributes of good interviewers and to delete those faults characteristic of poor interviewers. One typical difference, e.g., is that effective interviewers asked more open-ended questions, whereas ineffective interviewers asked more direct, short-answer questions. We also noticed that, in many of the field interviews, the sequence of questions seemed unplanned and generally unrelated to the mental activities of the respondent. Furthermore, it appeared that this haphazard question order frequently created a barrier, which obstructed memory. To overcome some of this interviewer-induced forgetting, we developed further guidelines about the sequential order of the interview. This last development of the Cognitive Interview is too detailed to describe here, but let us summarize the major point. In essence, the interviewer's goal is to infer the respondent's mental representation of the event, and then structure the interview so as to be compatible with that representation.

In a recently completed study (Fisher, Geiselman, Raymond, Jurkevich, & Warhaftig, 1987), we compared the revised version of the Cognitive Interview with the simpler version used in the earlier studies. Student volunteers were trained to conduct eyewitness interviews either according to the original Cognitive Interview or the revised version. We followed the same general experimental technique as mentioned before: Volunteer eyewitnesses viewed a film of a violent crime and then returned to be interviewed 48 hours later. When the original Cognitive Interview technique was used, approximately the same number of correct responses (39.56) were generated as in earlier studies, which simply testifies to the reliability of the experimental method. With the revised version, the number of correct responses increased dramatically, by 46% (57.50). $F (1, 14) = 7.60$, $p < .02$. This was not caused simply by eliciting more responses, as the number of incorrect responses was almost identical for the two techniques. Rather, it reflects a more efficient method to search through memory.

It is always hazardous to compare the results across different experiments, but one of the more impressive findings is that in the most recent study, the three interviewers were high school and undergraduate students with no prior training in eyewitness interviewing. In the earlier studies, the interviewers were law enforcement personnel with several years of practice using hypnosis and interviewing eyewitnesses. Nevertheless, under comparable experimental conditions, the novice students, using the revised version of the Cognitive Interview, elicited considerably more correct information than did the experienced law enforcement interviewers conducting either a typical police interview or a hypnosis interview.

The revised version requires considerably more time to learn—a few hours—than does the original Cognitive Interview and demands more practice to reach proficiency. In addition, the interviewer must be more mentally active during the interview, as he or she must be sensitive to the respondent's output, and make instantaneous decisions about the course of the interview. Nevertheless, the demonstrated superiority of the revised technique seems to more than warrant the extra expense of learning time and effort.

PRACTICAL CONSIDERATIONS

It is not at all clear how much information may be stored in a witness's memory of a crime. It is clear, however, that the amount actually recalled will depend heavily on the interview method. Furthermore, it is apparent that the common-sense approach to interviewing, as used by experienced, but untrained, law enforcement agents is not nearly as efficient as scientifically developed methods based on controlled laboratory studies. Finally, it should be noted that the theoretical basis for the Cognitive Interview is grounded in principles of memory, in general, not specifically eyewitness memory for details of crime. We might expect, therefore, that the Cognitive Interview, or a modified version of it, could be used to improve any type of investigative interview that depended on accuracy and extent of the respondent's memory.

REFERENCES

Fisher, R. P., Geiselman, R. E., & Raymond, D. S. (1987) 'Critical analysis of police interview techniques.' *Journal of Police Science and Administration*, in press.

Fisher, R. P., Geiselman, R. E., Raymond, D. S., Jurkevich, L. M., & Warhaftig, M. L. (1987) 'Enhancing enhanced eyewitness memory: Refining the cognitive interview.' *Journal of Police Science and Administration*, in press.

Flexser, A. & Tulving, E. (1978) 'Retrieval independence in recognition and recall.' *Psychological Review*, 85, 153–171.

Geiselman, R. E., Fisher, R. P., MacKinnon, D. P., & Holland, H. L. (1985) 'Eyewitness memory enhancement in the police interview: Cognitive retrieval mnemonics versus hypnosis.' *Journal of Applied Psychology*, 70, 401–412.

Geiselman, R. E., Fisher, R. P., MacKinnon, D. P., & Holland, H. L. (1986) 'Enhancement of eyewitness memory with the cognitive interview.' *American Journal of Psychology*, 99, 385–401.

Harris, R. (1973) *The police academy*. New York, Wiley & Sons.

Loftus, E. F. (1979) *Eyewitness testimony*. Cambridge, MA: Harvard University Press.

Orne, M. T., Soskis, D. A., Dinges, D. F., & Orne, E. C. (1984) 'Hypnotically induced testimony.' In G. L. Wells & E. F. Loftus (Eds.) *Eyewitness testimony: Psychological perspectives*. New York: Cambridge University Press.

Smith, M. (1983) 'Hypnotic memory enhancement of witnesses: Does it work?' *Psychological Bulletin*, 94, 387–407.

Tulving, E. (1974) 'Cue-dependent forgetting.' *American Scientist*, 76, 559–573.

26

Dean Delis, John Fleer, and Nancy H. Kerr

Memory for Music

Subjects created imaginal interpretations of classical music passages in accordance with themes which were either concrete and comprehensible or abstract and difficult to comprehend. Recognition memory for the musical passages was found to be superior in the former condition. The results support the hypothesis that meaningful interpretation of stimulus material is a major determinant of memory accuracy. The implications of the results for comparisons of music and language are also discussed.

The present experiment is concerned with the effect of people's meaningful interpretations of musical passages on their subsequent memory for them. Meyer (1967) has distinguished between two types of meaning in music, calling the melodic properties of a passage the "embodied meaning" and the images and ideas that a passage may evoke the "designative meaning." Meyer has noted that the structural characteristics of "embodied meaning" of a musical passage affect an individual's memory for the music, and recent research supports his observation (Dowling, 1973; Dowling & Fujitani, 1971; Dowling & Hollombe, 1977; White, 1960). Thus, just as one tends to remember familiar and well-organized visual (Goldstein & Chance, 1971) and linguistic (Miller & Selfridge, 1950) patterns, one also has better memory for musical passages which have coherent "embodied meaning." The current study was designed to determine whether the "designative meaning" of a musical passage also affects memory for the music itself.

The possibility that designative meaning may affect memory for music follows directly from recent research which indicates that the meaningful interpretation of a stimulus material is an important determinant of memory accuracy. For example, both Bransford and Johnson (1972) and Bransford and McCarrell (1974) tested recall for linguistic materials and found that memory for sentences was enhanced when the subject had been provided with a meaningful context for the sentences. Wiseman and Neisser (1974) used ambiguous pictures as stimuli in a recognition experiment and found that subjects had better memory for those pictures perceived as faces than for those perceived as meaningless patterns of black and white. Bower, Karlin, and Dueck (1975) found that recall of potentially meaningless pictures (droodles) was improved when subjects were given a verbal interpretation which gave the pictures a meaning. All of these studies share the same general experimental procedure: (1) subjects are presented with stimulus materials which are difficult to "understand"; (2) a record is kept of which of the stimulus materials are meaningfully interpreted by the subjects; and (3) the subjects are given a memory test for the material. The studies all have shown that memory for a stimulus is superior when the subjects "understand its underlying meaning," supporting the hypothesis that memory performance is not a function of the surface characteristics of the stimulus alone (the medium), but that the subjects' understanding of the meaning of the stimulus (the message) is an important determinant of memory for the material.

Since music can be thought of as having both a surface string of notes and an underlying designative meaning, musical stimuli can be used in an experiment on memory analogous to the experiments described above. However, there is one important difference between the symbolic properties of music and those of language and pictures. Unlike words and pictures, musical notes do not act as socially agreed upon referents to objects and events in the physical world, and thus there is no guarantee that one person's designative interpretation of a musical passage will be similar to another's. Early research (Downey, 1897) demonstrated that, although emotional reactions to music may be similar across individuals, the images, thoughts, and ideas which

listeners associate to a particular passage are generally very different. Thus, while in previous research employing linguistic and visual stimuli the material had an inherent deep meaning which could be "discovered" by the subjects, in an experiment employing musical stimuli the subjects' task would be to *create* their own designative interpretations. This suggests the hypothesis that subjects can improve their memory for musical passages by creating richer, more elaborate designative interpretations of the passages.

In order to test the hypothesis, the following experimental procedure was developed. Subjects were asked to make designative interpretations of musical passages by constructing visual images while listening to them. Imagery was chosen as the vehicle for making designative interpretations because it has been found that music readily lends itself to the evocation of visual images (Seashore, 1967), and because visual imaging has been found to be a powerful strategy in general for enhancing memory for linguistic material (Paivio, 1969). The subjects' designative interpretations of the musical passages were manipulated by presenting the same musical passages with several different titles, half of the titles referring to objects, scenes, or events which had been rated as highly "concrete" and "comprehensible," the other half, as "abstract" and "difficult to comprehend." By instructing subjects to try to imagine, as they listened to the music, those things to which the title of a particular passage referred, it was possible to test whether the easy-to-comprehend titles would encourage richer designative interpretations of the music than the difficult-to-comprehend titles, and if so, whether subsequent memory for the music would be enhanced.

METHOD

Subjects
The subjects were 36 students (9 females, 27 males) from introductory psychology courses at the University of Wyoming, who volun-

teered for the experiment to receive extra class credit. They were run in individual sessions.

Procedure and Materials

The subjects were individually presented with six 1-min passages of classical music. The passages were taken from a selection of 20 19th and 20th century symphonic pieces, all of which were full orchestral works. In order to minimize the possibility that some subjects might be familiar with particular works of music, thus giving them an advantage on the memory test, the 20 symphonic pieces were played to an independent group of psychology undergraduates (n = 32) who were asked to rate each passage on a scale ranging from "1" (very familiar) to "7" (never heard before). The six passages which received the lowest "familiarity" ratings were chosen for the experiment (Bartok's *Divertimento for Orchestra*, second movement; Berlioz's *Symphonie Fantastique*, first movement; Mahler's *Symphony No. 2*, first movement; Prokofiev's *Love for Three Oranges*, part five; Nielson's *The Inextinguishables*, first movement; and Debussy's *Prelude to the Afternoon of a Faun*, first movement. The mean "familiarity" rating was 5.49).

At the start of the experiment, a sheet listing six titles was placed before the subject, who was told that the titles were the composers' thematic interpretations of the music. Three of the titles had been rated independently by a group of psychology undergraduates (n = 33) as highly concrete and easy to comprehend, and three had been rated as abstract and difficult to comprehend (concrete titles: *Ocean Voyage*, *Peasants in the Field*, and *Winter Forest*; abstract titles: *Refuge in Truth*, *Philosophical Questions*, and *Rebirth of Justice*). The six titles were ordered randomly on six different sheets with the constraint that each title be paired equally with all six passages of music; the sheets were assigned randomly to the 36 subjects with the constraint that each title sheet be presented to six subjects. In this way, the same passage of music was paired equally with all six titles, with six subjects imaging to each music-title combination.

Before listening to a passage, the subjects were instructed to: read the title of that pas-

sage; listen to the passage and mentally visualize those things to which the title referred that possibly could be related to the sounds of the music; after hearing each passage, describe their images into a tape recorder; and rate their images for each passage in terms of how vivid they were, on the average. (Sheehan's 1967 adaptation of Bett's vividness of imagery scale was used.) The subjects were asked to describe their images of the passages as a check to be sure that they had understood the instructions. The vividness of imagery scale was used as the measure of the richness of the subjects' designative interpretations of the passages.

After the images to all six passages were described and rated, subjects were given an incidental recognition test, which consisted of 24 5-sec passages. Twelve of the 5-sec passages were taken from the test passages used in the imaging phase of the experiment (two 5-sec passages from each 1-min passage), and 12 were taken from other classical music sources (from symphonic pieces which also received low familiarity ratings: Sibelius' *Symphony No. 1*, first movement; Beethoven's *Symphony No. 3*, second movement; Stravinsky's *Firebird*, first movement; Lalo's *Symphonie Espagnole*, fourth movement; Thompson's *Louisiana Suite*, pastoral; Rachmaninoff's *Symphony No. 3*, first movement. The mean "familiarity" rating of these passages was 5.04). The subjects were told to write "yes" if they recognized the 5-sec passage as taken from the six passages they had just heard, and "no" if they did not recognize the test passage. In addition, they were asked to rate their confidence in all of their answers using a 5-point scale, with "1" indicating very little confidence and "5" indicating high confidence. The unexpected recognition test was used to avoid the possibility that subjects might use strategies of remembering other than imaginal elaboration.

Apparatus

The six 1-min and 24 5-sec passages were played from a Teac tape recorder, Model A-2340. Subjects listened to the passages through Telex headphones, Model ST-20.

RESULTS

Vividness Ratings

Vividness ratings ranged from "1" (very vivid) to "7" (no image). A 6 (passages) by 2 (concrete vs. abstract title) within-subjects factorial design was used. Table 1 shows the mean vividness ratings for the concrete and abstract title conditions. Differences assessed using a within-subjects analysis of variance showed that images were rated significantly more vivid when associated with the passages that had been given concrete titles than when associated with those given abstract titles [$F(1,35) = 13.198$, $p < .005$]; there were no other significant effects. This finding supports the hypothesis that concrete titles lead to richer, more elaborate, designative interpretations of the music.

Recognition Scores

Only the recognition test responses associated with the 12 5-sec passages taken from the original passages were analyzed for effect of title on passage recognition, since the 12 "new" distractor items were paired with neither a concrete nor an abstract title. A "yes" response to one of the original passages was therefore a hit, and a "no" response was a miss. Each recognition response was combined with its accompanying confidence rating (1-5) and assigned a numerical value from 1 to 10, 1-5 corresponding to incorrect responses, 6-10 to correct responses, and the deviation from 5 or 6 to the degree of confidence. Thus, a "yes" response with a confidence rating of 5 was assigned a value of "10," the *most correct* possible score, since the confidence rating indicates that the subject claimed not to be guessing; a "no" response with a confidence rating of 5 was assigned a "1," the *most incorrect* possible score, since the confidence rating indicates that the subject was not unsure of the response. A "yes" response with a confidence rating of 4 was assigned a "9"; a "no" response with a confidence of 4 was assigned a "2"; etc. Thus, the closer the confidence rating of a response

Table 1

Mean Vividness Ratings and Recognition Scores for Musical Passages When Assigned Easy- or Difficult-to-Comprehend Titles

Titles	Vividness Ratings*	Recognition Scores**
Easy to Comprehend	2.92	6.77
Difficult to Comprehend	4.68	5.79

* Lower numbers indicate more vivid imagery.
** Higher numbers indicate better recognition memory.

approached 1, the more the subject was objectively/subjectively wrong.

The dependent measure is patterned after the method used in previous studies (Bransford, Barclay, & Franks, 1972; Bransford & Franks, 1971) to assess recognition memory in a completely within-subjects design. We employed a scale from 1 to 10, instead of a scale from −5 to +5 as had been used previously, to avoid artificial inflation of the difference due to the gap at the zero value between positive and negative scores.

Since the recognition test contained two 5-sec passages from each of the six original passages, each subject gave two responses in each treatment condition. The design was thus a 6 (passages) by 2 (concrete vs. abstract title) by 2 (recognition responses) within-subjects factorial. Table 1 shows the mean recognition scores for the concrete and abstract title conditions. A within-subjects, repeated measures analysis of variance revealed significantly better recognition when passages were given concrete rather than abstract titles [$F(1,35) = 11.87$, $p < .005$]. There was also a significant passage effect [$F(5,35) = 6.02$, $p < .01$]; however, there were no significant interaction effects, indicating that recognition scores were not inflated due to specific title-passage combinations. These results support the hypothesis that interpreting a musical passage in accordance with easy-to-comprehend themes improves memory for the passage.

Since the observed effects of passage title are based on entirely within-subjects comparisons, there is no reason to believe that subjects' overall guessing strategies affected the two kinds of material differently. Nevertheless, the possibility that response biases existed was tested by analyzing the responses to the distractor items using a system similar to that used for the experimental items. A "no" response to a distractor item was a correct rejection, and a "yes" response was a false alarm. A "no" response with a confidence rating of 5 was assigned a recognition score of "10," the *most correct* possible rejection of a distractor item; a "yes" response with a confidence rating of 5 was assigned a "1," the *most incorrect* possible false alarm. The recognition scores for distractor items thus ranged from 1 to 10, 1-5 corresponding to false alarms, 6-10 to correct rejections, and the deviation from 5 or 6 to the degree of confidence. The mean recognition score for distractor items was "6.1." That this value is greater than "5" indicates that the subjects did not have a general response bias to report "yes."

DISCUSSION

As Bower et al. (1975) have noted, experiments which show the importance of "understanding" the meaning of linguistic and pictorial material for memory accuracy are "intuitively obvious," their significance being to demonstrate weaknesses in theoretical orientations which address only the surface characteristics of the stimuli to be remembered. The present experiment addresses a question, however, whose answer is less obvious. Since the relationship between the surface string of notes and designative meaning in music is arbitrary, it is not readily apparent that "real world" interpretations would affect memory for music. Intuitively, it would seem that only the structural properties—the "embodied" meaning—would need to be addressed. However, the present study indicates that interpreting patterns of notes into comprehensible themes serves to impart organization upon the notes in much the same way that discovering "faces" in patterns of black and white (Wiseman & Neisser, 1974) serves to organize the patterns for more fluent assimilation into existing cognitive schemata. Presumably, subjects who are able to provide a coherent perceptual interpretation of a musical passage on its initial presentation are reminded of that interpretation on subsequent exposure and are able to report recognition of the music.

The present study also has implications for researchers and theorists interested in drawing analogies between language and music. Previous research has suggested that encoding strategies for music and language may be similar, but the empirical basis has been limited to evidence that stimulus characteristics, such as rhythmic grouping and rate of presentation, are systematically related to subjects' responses to both musical and verbal stimuli (Dowling, 1973). The current study extends previous findings by demonstrating that the processing strategies and skills that subjects use in a given experimental task may affect encoding of and memory for music as well as for verbal materials. Thus, just as a subject's memory for a verbal passage may be affected by the referential interpretation assigned by the experimenter of supplied by the subject (Bransford & McCarrell, 1974), memory for a musical passage may be similarly affected. The finding also provides an empirical base for the distinction between "embodied" and "designative" meaning in music by showing a significant and independent effect of "designative meaning" as a determinant of memory.

REFERENCES

Bower, G. H., Karlin, M. B., & Dueck, A. Comprehension and memory for pictures. *Memory & Cognition*, 1975, **3**, 216–220.

Bransford, J. D., Barclay, J. R., & Franks, J. J. Sentence memory: A constructive versus interpretive approach. *Cognitive Psychology*, 1972, **3**, 193–209.

Bransford, J. D., & Franks, J. J. The abstraction of linguistic ideas. *Cognitive Psychology*, 1971, **2**, 331–350.

Bransford, J. D., & Johnson, M. K. Contextual prerequisites for understanding: Some investigations of comprehension and recall. *Journal of Verbal Learning and Verbal Behavior*, 1972, **11**, 717–726.

Bransford, J. D., & McCarrell, N. S. A sketch of a cognitive approach to comprehension: Some thoughts about understanding what it means to comprehend. In W. B. Weimer & D. S. Palermo (Eds.), *Cognition and the symbolic processes.* Hillsdale, N.J.: Erlbaum, 1974.

DOWLING, W. J. Rhythmic groups and subjective chunks in memory for melody. *Perception & Psychophysics,* 1973, **14**, 37–40.

DOWLING, W. J., & FUJITANI, D. S. Contour, interval, and pitch recognition in memory for melodies. *Journal of the Acoustical Society of America,* 1971, **49**, 524–531.

DOWLING, W. J., & HOLLOMBE, A. W. The perception of melodies distorted by splitting into several octaves: Effects of increasing proximity and melodic contour. *Perception & Psychophysics,* 1977, **21**, 60–64.

DOWNEY, J. E. A musical experiment. *American Journal of Psychology,* 1897, **9**, 63–69.

GOLDSTEIN, A. G., & CHANCE, J. E. Recognition of complex visual stimuli. *Perception & Psychophysics,* 1971, **9**, 237–241.

MEYER, L. B. *Music, the arts, and ideas.* Chicago: University of Chicago Press, 1967.

MILLER, G. A., & SELFRIDGE, J. A. Verbal context and the recall of meaningful material. *American Journal of Psychology,* 1950, **63**, 176–187.

PAIVIO, A. Mental imagery in associative learning and memory. *Psychological Review,* 1969, **76**, 241–263.

SEASHORE, C. E. *Psychology of music.* New York: Dover, 1967.

SHEEHAN, P. W. A shortened form of Betts' questionnaire upon mental imagery. *Journal of Clinical Psychology,* 1967, **23**, 386–389.

WHITE, B. Recognition of distorted melodies. *American Journal of Psychology,* 1960, **73**, 100–107.

WISEMAN, S., & NEISSER, U. Perceptual organization as a determinant of visual recognition memory. *American Journal of Psychology,* 1974, **4**, 675–681.

We would like to thank Sandy Wiseman and David Foulkes for their helpful comments on an earlier draft, and Hugh McGinley for his assistance with statistical analysis.

27

Paul W. Foos, Benjamin Algaze, and George Kallas

Effects of Cognitive Interference on Biofeedback Learning

Students learned to raise the skin temperature of their hands while perform-ing no other task or one of two other tasks simultaneously. Other tasks involved checking to see whether a presented word contained the letter E or mentally adding two two-digit numbers. Only mental addition interfered with biofeedback learning. These results support a cognitive information-processing view of biofeedback learning and not a traditional reinforcement view. Suggestions are made for trainers and learners.

In biofeedback training, an individual who is given information about bodily changes (e.g., in muscle tension, skin temperature, heart rate) attempts to modify those changes. People are generally quite successful at learning how to do this, and biofeedback has become a valuable tool in the treatment of many psychosomatic disorders (Green & Green, 1977; Wentworth-Rohr, 1984). There are, however, conflicting views on how biofeedback works and on what the best approach in training might be. These views are briefly described below and tested in two simple experiments.

The *reinforcement* view is based on a behavioral analysis of biofeed-back training. Quite simply, the reason that individuals are able to gain some control over bodily changes is that they are reinforced for doing so. For example, the response of increasing blood flow to the hands to produce warmer hands is reinforced by the visual and/or auditory signal that indicates success; success is reinforcing. Because the response has been reinforced, it will tend to be repeated. The individual need only be aware of a response-reinforcement contingency. In training, it is thus important to provide a strong and appropriate reinforcement and to use techniques (e.g., a variable ratio schedule) that will maintain the learned response in the future.

The *cognitive* view is based on an information-processing analysis of biofeedback training. In learning how to warm the hands, the individual tries a number of different mental strategies, such as rehearsing a phrase (e.g., "warmer hands") or focusing on an image (e.g., of hands on a warm stove). Rather than serve as a reinforcer, the visual and/or auditory signal provides information that enables the learner to select the most effective mental strategy. Considerable cognitive effort is required. In training, it is thus important to suggest different strategies that others have found effective.

In the following experiments, all participants were trained to alter the skin temperature of their hands. Such training has been shown to be an effective treatment for headache (see, e.g., Blanchard, Andrasick, Evans, Neff, & Appelbaum, 1985). In the first experiment, some participants raised their hand temperatures while others lowered their hand temperatures; in the second experiment, all participants tried both tasks.

So that the reinforcement and cognitive views could be compared, participants in each experiment were asked to learn while also performing another task and while not performing another task. These other tasks demanded different levels of processing (see Craik & Lockhart, 1972) and, thus, different amounts of cognitive effort. For example, one task involved determining whether or not a presented word contained the letter E, a task that requires very little cognitive effort. The other task, which involved the mental addition of two two-digit numbers, required much more cognitive effort. If biofeedback learning also requires considerable cognitive effort, mental addition should interfere with this learning to a much greater extent than would checking words for the letter E. If biofeedback learning occurs through reinforcement, with little (or no) cognitive effort, neither task should produce much interference.

METHOD

Participants

The subjects in both experiments were undergraduate students at Florida International University who participated to fulfill a course requirement and/or to earn extra credit. In the first experiment, 5 randomly assigned students learned to raise hand temperature while another 5 tried to lower hand temperature. In the second experiment, 14 participants tried to raise and lower their hand temperatures.

Materials

For the E checking task, all words were high-frequency (Kučera & Francis, 1967) and were printed on index cards for presentation. For the mental addition task, two randomly selected two-digit numbers were printed on each index card, separated by a plus sign.

Apparatus

All participants learned to alter hand temperature by using the Cyborg Biolab 21 System and received visual (i.e., a moving bar on a television monitor) and auditory (i.e., a tone that changed pitch) feedback. A thermal probe was taped to the forefinger of the nondominant hand, which rested in the participant's lap during training.

Procedure

In both experiments, all participants tried to alter hand temperature under three different conditions. On a third of the 5-min trials, they altered temperature and performed no other task. On another third, they altered temperature while also checking presented words for the letter E and responded verbally (i.e., "yes" or "no"). On another third, they altered temperature while performing mental addition and responded verbally.

Table 1

Mean Temperature Change for Each Condition in Each Experiment

	Experiment	
Additional Task	1	2
None	1.08	.79
E Checking	1.79	.95
Addition	.16	−.12

Note—Means are reported in degrees Fahrenheit. Only means for temperature raising are shown.

The order in which these three learning sessions were presented was incompletely counterbalanced across three blocks of trials for all participants in the first experiment, producing a total of nine trials (i.e., three for each condition, which occurred once in each of three blocks). In the second experiment, all received the same incomplete counterbalancing across blocks for nine trials followed by a second nine trials. Half received nine trials of raising temperature first followed by nine of lowering temperature; the other half received nine of lowering followed by nine of raising. In both experiments, baseline temperatures were recorded before each trial. Data consisted of the change from baseline recorded on each trial.

RESULTS AND DISCUSSION

Table 1 shows the mean temperature change from baseline for temperature raising under all conditions for both experiments. Participants were unable to significantly lower their temperatures from baseline in any of the conditions in either experiment.

In the first experiment, participants were able to significantly raise their hand temperatures except when performing mental addition [$F(1,16) = 4.39$, $p < .05$]. This finding was replicated in the second experiment [$F(1,234) = 5.16$, $p < .05$]. These results support the cognitive information-processing view of biofeedback learning. When cognitive effort is directed to another demanding task, such as mental addition, no biofeedback learning takes place.

These results have two important implications for biofeedback trainers and learners. First, one must be able to devote cognitive effort to biofeedback and not elsewhere if learning is to occur. Thus, the learning environment should be free of distractions to aid the learner in focusing on the learning task. The learner should try to clear her/his mind from other activities while learning to perform. In many cases, this may require the trainer to thoroughly relax the learner before beginning training.

Second, successful mental strategies should be suggested to the learner, because this may speed the learning process. Trainers should make themselves aware of the strategies that other clients have used successfully. In the present experiments, participants reported success with a number of imagery strategies such as picturing hands over a fire or in an oven. One very successful participant said that she imagined pushing the blood into her hands to make them warm. Such strategies may be good starting places for new learners.

REFERENCES

BLANCHARD, E. B., ANDRASICK, F., EVANS, D. D., NEFF, D. F., & APPELBAUM, K. A. (1985). *Individual predictors of self-regulating treatment outcome in tension headache.* Paper presented at the annual meeting of the Biofeedback Society of America, New Orleans.

CRAIK, F. I. M., & LOCKHART, R. S. (1972). Levels of processing: A framework for memory research. *Journal of Verbal Learning & Verbal Behavior, 11,* 671–684.

GREEN, E., & GREEN, A. (1977). *Beyond biofeedback.* New York: Dell Publishing.

KUČERA, H., & FRANCIS, W. N. (1967). *Computational analysis of present-day American English.* Providence, RI: Brown University Press.

WENTWORTH-ROHR, I. (1984). *Symptom reduction through clinical biofeedback.* New York: Human Sciences Press.

28

Matthew D. Smith
and Craig J. Chamberlin

Effect of Adding Cognitively Demanding Tasks on Soccer Skill Performance

Summary.—*The effect of adding cognitively demanding elements to the performance of a real-world motor task in which functional interference among the elements in performance existed was investigated across level of expertise. The primary task involved running as quickly as possible through a 15.25-m slalom course. Two secondary tasks were used, dribbling of a soccer ball and identification of geometric shapes projected on a screen located at the end of the slalom course. 4 novice, 5 intermediate, and 5 expert female soccer players served as subjects and performed three trials each of three experimental conditions: running through the slalom course, running through the slalom course while dribbling a soccer ball, and running through the slalom course while dribbling a soccer ball and identifying geometric shapes. Analysis of variance using a 3 (experimental condition) × 3 (level of expertise) design gave significant main effects and a significant interaction. The latter indicated that, although the addition of cognitively demanding elements caused a decrement in performance, the amount of decrement decreased as level of expertise increased. It was concluded that structural interference between elements of performance decreased the positive effect of automation of one element on dual task performance.*

Most sport skills entail concurrent processing of information from a variety of sources and the performance of more than one skill at a time. This particularly true of invasion games such as basketball, soccer, ice hockey, and rugby. Normally, an athlete performing in these games is required to locomote about the environment while manipulating an object and processing information for the purpose of strategic decision-making. Given the cognitive demands of only one of the performance requirements, it can be considered a feat of substantial proportion when we observe a skilled athlete processing multiple inputs of information and performing multiple tasks with minimal performance decrement on any one of the tasks.

Considerable research effort has been expended investigating the mechanisms that underlie an individual's capacity to perform multiple tasks simultaneously. The majority of studies have made use of the dual-task paradigm, wherein a subject is required to respond to more than one stimulus with more than one response, have employed laboratory tasks, and have developed minimal levels of expertise (e.g., Kantowitz & Knight, 1976; Wrisberg & Shea, 1978). A notable exception to this study is another by Leavitt (1979). In this experiment, the author investigated the capabilities of ice hockey players to perform simultaneous multiple tasks across different levels of skill. The primary task that the subjects performed was skating as rapidly as possible through a slalom course of pylons set on the ice, a typical drill incorporated into real-world ice-hockey practice sessions. Two secondary tasks were used— identifying geometric shapes projected onto a screen set at the end of the ice arena and stickhandling a puck. Subjects were measured for the time taken to complete the slalom course under conditions of the primary task alone or in combination with one or both of the secondary tasks.

The results of this study indicated that progressively adding the secondary tasks to the primary task had little effect on the performance of experienced ice hockey players but adversely affected the performance of novice players. This finding appeared to support a model which hypothesizes a decrease in attentional demands as learning progresses, such as that proposed by Fitts and Posner (1967), leading to an automation of elements of the total performance.

The potential for functional interference between the primary and secondary tasks in Leavitt's (1979) study is quite small. The two motor tasks employed (skating and stickhan-

dling) are performed with different limbs. However, in a number of sport skills, functional interference is a problem that must be faced by the performer. For example, the analog of Leavitt's (1979) ice hockey task in soccer would be running while manipulating the ball and observing patterns of action as the basis for further decision-making. In this situation, running and ball manipulation must be accomplished by the same limb. The problem investigated here, then, was whether a similar pattern of results to Leavitt's (1979) study would be found when functional interference between the primary and secondary tasks was introduced. A reasonable prediction would be that a different pattern of results would be observed, since the act of manipulating a ball with the foot while running could be considered a qualitatively different action to running alone. Therefore, automation of the running action would not affect dribbling a soccer ball to the same extent as automation of the skating action would affect stickhandling a puck.

METHOD

Subjects

Fourteen female soccer players served as subjects and were grouped according to soccer playing experience (novice, $n = 4$, age in years, $M = 13.3$, $SD = 1.0$, playing experience = 15 40-min. physical education class lessons; intermediate, $n = 5$, age in years, $M = 11.8$, $SD = 1.1$, M playing experience = 7 seasons; expert, $n = 5$, age in years, $M = 19.0$, $SD = 1.0$, M playing experience = 24.8 seasons; note that 2 seasons are played per year). All subjects volunteered to participate and informed consent was obtained prior to testing.

Apparatus and Task

The primary task required of subjects was to run as rapidly as possible through a slalom course that consisted of six standard traffic cones set 3.05 m apart on a gymnasium floor.

The first secondary task was to dribble a soccer ball and the second secondary task was to identify geometric shapes projected onto a screen at the end of the slalom course.

The arrangement of cones resulted in a total distance from start to finish of 15.25 m. A Kodak Ektagraphic slide projector was set 3.96 m from the last cone in the slalom course on a table that was 68.6 cm in height. A 1.22 m² projection screen was placed 3.96 m from the slide projector. Six slides were loaded into the slide projector. Each slide had two vertical columns of black and white geometric shapes with six or seven randomly ordered shapes in each column. The shapes used were triangles, squares, rectangles, diamonds, and circles, and were either filled or unfilled. When projected on the screen the over-all dimension of the slide was 91.44 cm × 60.96 cm. All timing was done with a Sportline Econosport stopwatch.

Procedure

Each subject ran through the slalom course three times for each of three experimental conditions. The first condition consisted of running through the course as quickly as possible (Condition R). The second condition consisted of running through the course as quickly as possible while dribbling a soccer ball (Condition RD). The third condition consisted of running through the course as quickly as possible while dribbling a soccer ball and identifying geometric shapes (Condition RDS). Each group of subjects were tested during a single testing session. After an adequate warm-up, one subject would perform the three trials of one condition consecutively, followed by each other subject performing their trials of the same condition. This procedure was repeated for the other two conditions. Since trials were kept to a minimum to prevent a learning effect, and fatigue was not a factor, it was deemed unnecessary to counterbalance for an order effect within groups.

Before each trial, the subjects were given a "ready, go" command. Prior to the trials on the condition RDS, the subjects were shown one of the geometric shape slides on the screen. They

Table 1 _____

Means and Standard Deviations for Movement Time Data by Level of Expertise and Experimental Condition

Level of Expertise		Condition		
		Run	Dribble	Run, Dribble, Shape
Novice	M	3.81	9.00	13.06
	SD	0.24	1.44	2.77
Intermediate	M	3.69	7.94	9.16
	SD	0.17	1.26	0.93
Expert	M	3.27	5.93	7.59
	SD	0.21	0.27	0.62

were instructed to shout out the names of the shapes and to preface the naming with "black" if the shape was filled. The subjects performed the naming function in a top to bottom fashion, beginning with the left column and then proceeding to the right column. As the "ready, go" command was given, the experimenter changed the slide projected on the screen. If an error in the running and dribbling performance occurred, that trial was repeated by the subject.

RESULTS

The dependent variables measured were movement time (MT, time from go command until completion of the slalom course) and, for the Condition RDS, number of shapes identified. For MT, the median score of the three trials under each condition was considered representative of a subject's performance. Means and standard deviations for the median data were calculated for each group under each condition (see Table 1). Similarly, the means of the median scores for the number of shapes identified during the RDS condition were also calculated for each group.

Movement Times

Analysis was accomplished using a 3 × 3 (condition × level of experience) analysis of variance with Newman-Keuls follow-up tests for significant effects. Level of significance was established at $p = .05$. Significant main effects for condition ($F_{2,33} = 114.12$, $p < .01$) and level of experience ($F_{2,33} = 25.49$, $p < .01$) and a significant interaction of condition by level of experience ($F_{4,33} = 6.54$, $p < .01$) were found.

Inspection of Figure 1 would indicate that the significant interaction was due to the addition of cognitively demanding elements having the least effect on the expert group and the greatest effect on the novice group. The follow-up Newman-Keuls analyses indicated that there was no difference among the groups during the Run condition. However, all groups were significantly different from each other on the Run-dribble condition, while the novice group was significantly slower than the other two groups at completing the Run-dribble-shapes condition. Within each group, adding cognitively demanding tasks resulted in a significant slowing of performance for all possible comparisons except between the second and third conditions for the intermediate group.

Shape Identification

Analysis of the shape identification data was accomplished using a one-way analysis of variance. There were no significant differences among the three groups in terms of the number of shapes correctly identified while performing under the Run-dribble-shape condition.

DISCUSSION

In this study, the effect of progressively adding cognitively demanding elements to the performance of the primary task of running through a slalom course was examined across three levels of expertise. The intent was to provide a replication of Leavitt's (1979) study, but using a task which introduced some functional interference among the elements of task performance. The addition of cognitively demanding elements had a detrimental effect on the performance of the primary task across all levels of expertise, but the magnitude of this detrimental effect decreased as level of expertise increased.

Figure 1

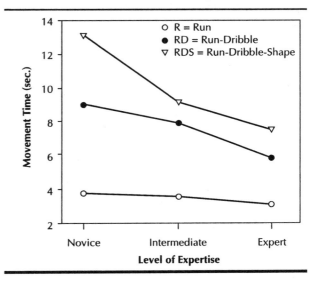

Time to Complete the Slalom Course by Experimental Condition Across Level of Expertise

The results are roughly congruent with those of Leavitt (1979), but there are some interesting differences. Significant is the finding that being required to perform additional elements, such as manipulating a soccer ball and identifying geometric patterns, did decrease performance within the most expert group. In Leavitt's (1979) study, the expert group was able to maintain their performance across all experimental conditions. Two possible reasons can be hypothesized to explain this apparent discrepancy.

First, the level of expertise of the expert group in this study may have been less than that in Leavitt's (1979) study. In our study, female college soccer players from an NCAA Division II program served as subjects for the expert group. In Leavitt's study, collegiate male ice hockey players from major sport universities (roughly congruent to NCAA Division I institutions) in Canada served as subjects for the expert group. An argument can be made for Leavitt's subjects representing a more elite level of performance than the present subjects.

Second, given the functional interference in performance, the dual task of running and dribbling a soccer ball is qualitatively different from the dual task of skating and stickhandling. In ice hockey, each element of performance is relatively independent of the other. Therefore, automation of a singular element, such as skating, would increase attentional capacity available for the performance of other elements, such as stickhandling and decision-making. Minimal disruption of the skating skill should occur when additional performance elements are required. In soccer, running must be modified when manipulation of the ball is required because there is functional interference between the tasks. Automation of the running action would not have a similar effect in soccer as automation of skating in ice hockey since the act of running while dribbling a soccer ball could be considered a singular skill. The need, then, is to automate the action of running while manipulating the ball as a whole skill.

The previous conclusion, that the effectiveness of automatizing an element of performance is dependent on the independence the element maintains, is very similar to the conclusion that has been drawn from work done on whole-part learning. In that research, increasing the relative independence of a part results in greater effectiveness of using a part learning procedure (e.g., Newell, Carlton, Fisher, & Rutter, 1989; for a more detailed discussion of whole-part learning, see Chamberlin & Lee, in press).

The results of this study and the attentional research completed to date suggest that teachers should not ask novices to perform simultaneous tasks either from the same or different perceptual classes. Also, teachers should first provide some automation in the base element of a task before adding additional elements, although the need is to identify what constitutes the base element. However, these conclusions are tempered by the need for additional research which makes use of real-world tasks. In particular, studies which involve the confound of functional dependence versus independence of the elements of performance should be undertaken.

REFERENCES

Chamberlin, C. J., & Lee, T. D. (in press) Arranging practice conditions and designing instruction. In R. N. Singer, M. Murphey, & L. K. Tennant (Eds.), *Handbook on research in sport psychology.* New York: Macmillan.

Fitts, P. M., & Posner, M. I. (1967) *Human performance.* Belmont, CA: Brooks/Cole.

Kantowitz, B. H., & Knight, J. L. (1976) Testing tapping timesharing: II. Auditory secondary task. *Acta Psychologica, 40,* 343–362.

Leavitt, J. (1979) Cognitive demands of skating and stick handling in ice hockey. *Canadian Journal of Applied Sport Sciences, 4,* 46–55.

Newell, K. M., Carlton, M. J., Fisher, A. T., & Rutter, B. G. (1989) Whole-part training strategies for learning the response dynamics of microprocessor driven simulators. *Acta Psychologica, 71,* 197–210.

Wrisberg, C. A., & Shea, C. H. (1978) Shifts in attention demands and motor program utilization during motor learning. *Journal of Motor Behavior, 10,* 149–158.

29

Paul Rozin, Susan Poritsky, and Raina Sotsky

American Children With Reading Problems Can Easily Learn to Read English Represented by Chinese Characters

Abstract: *With 2.5 to 5.5 hours of tutoring, eight second-grade inner-city school children with clear reading disability were taught to read English material written as 30 different Chinese characters. This accomplishment eliminates certain general interpretations of dyslexia, for example, as a visual-auditory memory deficit. The success of this program can be attributed to the novelty of the Chinese orthography and to the fact that Chinese characters map into speech at the level of words rather than of phonemes. It is proposed that much reading disability can be accounted for in terms of the highly abstract nature of the phoneme (the critical unit of speech in alphabetic systems) and that an intermediate unit, such as the syllable, might well be used to introduce reading.*

American urban school systems are experiencing great difficulties in teaching reading. In many major cities, average reading performance is a few grades behind national norms; many children never learn to read adequately. This enormous problem undoubtedly has many causes (1) including (i) our failure to understand the reading process and thus to design a most effective method for teaching it; (ii) difficulty in motivating and engaging children, particularly those in inner-city schools, in activities related to reading; (iii) the possibility that some perceptual (2) or cognitive abilities necessary for reading are not well or equally developed in all 6-year-olds; and (iv) dialect differences between teachers (or texts) and students (3).

From Paul Rozin, Susan Poritsky, and Raina Sotsky, "American Children With Reading Problems Can Easily Learn to Read English Represented by Chinese Characters," *Science,* vol. 171 (March 26, 1971). Copyright © 1971 by The American Association for the Advancement of Science. Reprinted by permission.

In attempts to teach second graders with reading backwardness in a Philadelphia inner-city school, one of us (P.R.), in collaboration with H. Savin, found two characteristic problems. One was clearly motivational: the children had had difficulty in the past with reading and seemed to be deliberately and actively uninvolved in reading or anything that they considered to be reading. The children's interest was easy to engage, but not in reading. Second, the children seemed to have particular difficulty in giving phonological interpretations in response to visually presented letters; that is, they could not, at least overtly, recognize such letters as representing components of their own or others' speech. Thus, they had difficulty (i) in identifying words by initial or final sounds and (ii) in combining a sequence of letters into a known English word (what is often called "blending"). Many of the children did not know all the alphabetic symbol-sound correspondences, which was surprising since they seemed to have excellent memories and could be taught arbitrary new symbols rather quickly.

If we assume that this "phonetic mapping" inability and inadequate motivation are two fundamental causes of reading disability in this inner-city population, then it should be possible to teach such children to read a simplified version of the Chinese logographic system, with interpretation into English. Such material would obviously be new to the children and thus might provide adequate motivation. The phonetic mapping inability would also be circumvented, because Chinese characters map into language at the morphemic (word) level rather than at the phonemic level. We emphasize that the purpose of this experiment was not to devise a new curriculum for reading but to highlight specific problem areas for future research and enrichment programs.

Nine black children in the second semester of the second grade in an inner-city Philadelphia school were randomly selected from the class list of one second-grade homeroom class (4), with the restriction that no child have a reading level higher than level 3 (middle first grade) according to the system in use in the Philadelphia school system (5). The nine children selected were individually tested for reading skills by the experimenters. The basic criterion for acceptance in the experiment was that the child be unable to read a series of six simple consonant-vowel-consonant trigrams (PIP, ZIF, WAT, LAG, REN, GUB) and be unable to read reliably a set of rhyming words (CAT, FAT, MAT, SAT) after being given the pronunciation for AT. Eight of the nine children were unable to handle this material adequately. They were usually unable to guess even the initial sound of the unfamiliar trigrams. The child who showed some competence at these tasks was not continued in the experiment.

Tutoring sessions were held in supply closets or small rooms with minimum furnishings. Individual sessions lasting from 20 minutes to 1 hour were held during the afternoon school hours approximately two to three times a week. The tutoring took place from March through June 1970 and involved a total of 14 to 25 sessions, or 8 to 14 hours per child (see Table 1). Each child dealt with only one of the three experimenters throughout the entire period, and tutoring was always on a one-to-one basis.

The tutoring sessions were informal; an initial session or two was devoted to getting to know the child and gauging his reading ability. A tutoring session was generally made up of four components:

1) Gaining rapport. A small portion of the time was spent in talking informally with the child or in playing games with him.

2) Tutoring in normal English reading. This consisted of practicing letter-sound relationships, "blending" sounds, and reading primer and preprimer material. It occupied about one-third of the total tutoring time.

3) Intelligence testing. The Wechsler Intelligence Scale for Children was administered to each child during the course of the experiment. No more than three subtests were given in any one session.

4) Chinese tutoring. The material to be taught consisted of 30 Chinese characters. They were read directly in their actual English translation. Chinese was never spoken. The symbols were read from left to right in the customary pattern of English orthography. The characters were selected primarily for their

Table 1

Summary of Results

Subjects		Tutoring		Stage II		Final sentences		Mother-car story			IQ	Reading level (5)	
Sex	Age (years: months)	Total (hours: minutes)	Chinese (hours: minutes)	Time (minutes: seconds)	Errors (No.)	Time (minutes: seconds)	Errors (No.)	Time (minutes: seconds)	Errors (No.)	Compre-hension		Before	After
M	7:11	10:03	4:28	0:36	1	2:08	6	2:42	5	1/3	83	1	2
M	7: 9	14:10	4:42	0:54	0	1:43	0	2:07	6	1.5/3	85	2	2
M	7:11	11:00	5:24	1:15	0		4	0:56	4	3/3	80	2	3
F	7:11	10:42	5:00	1:05	0		4	1:06	3	1/3	82	3	3
M	8: 0	11:51	4:06	0:34	2	1:50	6		4	2/3	96	2	3
M	8: 8	8:30	3:30	0:40	0		2	1:00	0	2/3	80	2	3
M	8: 2	8:26	2:35	1:00	0	1:00	1	1:30	1	3/3	96	2	2
F	7: 5	9:10	2:36	0:50	2		1	2:40	0	3/3	107	3	4

The test for stage II contained a total of 21 characters (12 different characters). The final test sentences contained 40 items. The mother-car story (9) contained 40 items. The IQ is the score on the Wechsler Intelligence Scale for Children.

ability to fit together to form a wide variety of English sentences (Figure 1). The sentences used could be read and understood by a native Chinese (6). An additional criterion was the avoidance of characters of great visual complexity or high similarity to already selected symbols.

The set of actual characters selected, with their English equivalents, is presented in Figure 1. For convenience in instruction, the set was divided into six subsets, to be presented in sequence. The subsets were planned to allow formation of many English sentences from the very beginning.

For the first unit, symbols of minimum visual complexity were selected from the full set of 30. At the beginning of the experiment these symbols (Xerox copies from an introductory Chinese reader) were pasted on 1-inch (2.54-cm) squares of cardboard and were arranged in different sequences. In later stages, pages with written material (similar to the test page in Figure 2) were also used (7). The children were introduced to a few symbols at a time, were given a few rote-memorization trials, and were then presented with a sequence of characters that could be translated into simple English sentences. They were encouraged to make up sentences of their own. In the tutoring

sessions, the children were corrected when they misread a word, unless they offered a word that was semantically equivalent, such as little instead of small. Since the Chinese orthography maps directly into the meaningful units, synonyms constitute correct responses. Of course, the fact that these children have quite different pronunciations for some of these words in their dialect was ignored. When children had particular difficulty in learning particular words, additional practice was given. Occasionally, when a child had consistent difficulty with a pair of symbols, we asked him to describe the differences between them or pointed out what we considered distinctive differences between them.

When a child seemed to have mastered the materials in one stage, one new symbol from the next stage was introduced, and a set of test sentences was constructed, each sentence containing the new symbol. This procedure guaranteed that the representation of the test sentences in Chinese orthography had not been seen before by the child. Tests were administered after each of the first five stages (8). Each of the tests included, at least once, every character taught up to that point. As a result of this constraint, plus the absence of articles and the use of the new symbol in each sentence,

Figures 1 and 2

Stage	Noun		Verb	Adjective	Other
I	母 Mother		見 See	大 Big	
	刀 Knife		有 Has	一 One	
II	書 Book	父 Father		二 Two	
	人 Man			小 Small	
III	家 House		買 Buy		跟 And
IV	你 You		說 Say	白 White	
				紅 Red	
V	車 Car		要 Want	好 Good	不 Not (don't)
	魚 Fish				
VI	他 He		用 Use	這 This	
	口 Mouth		給 Give		
Final Test	哥哥 Brother			黑 Black	

父買黑車

這人不見黑家跟二刀.

哥哥說母用白書.

你要一大魚跟黑家

他說"哥哥有小口".

好哥哥不給人紅車

Figure 1 (left). Order of presentation of Chinese symbols. **Figure 2** (above). Final test. Sentences including all symbols. The sentences read: "Father buys black car. This man doesn't (not) see black house and two knives. Brother says mother uses white book. You want one big fish and black house. He says 'brother has small mouth.' Good brother doesn't (not) give man red car." Eight subjects made a mean of three errors on this 40-item test. The four timed subjects took a mean of 1 minute and 40 seconds to complete this task.

some of the resultant sentences were not "well formed." We attempted to administer the tests at the beginning of a session, but, when that was not possible, the test was preceded by at least 10 minutes of non-Chinese material. No prompting was given, and the performance was recorded word for word. When we were convinced that a child had mastered a stage, by virtue of his performance on a test, material from the next stage was introduced.

For a final evaluation of performance, the children were presented with a set of sentences (Figure 2) that incorporated all of the 30 sym-bols taught. Each sentence included one of the two new symbols (Figure 1, bottom line) intro-duced after completion of stage VI. In addition, the children read aloud three short stories, which were made up from the 30 symbols but did not include all of them. In all cases, no cues or corrections were provided. The time required to complete the sentences and to complete each story was measured, and the experimenters made a written transcription of what the chil-dren said. Errors were then tabulated. After each story, the children were asked a few questions about the "plot" but were not allowed to refer back to the story to answer these questions (9). In three cases, the final readings were tape-recorded.

The basic results are presented in Table 1. Unfortunately, relatively little progress was made in reading the English alphabet. In no cases were there any major improvements in this area, although in most some improvement in letter-sound correspondences or word formation was obvious (Table 1). The improvement in reading level was probably due primarily to the regular classroom instruction.

In contrast, the tutoring with Chinese characters progressed rapidly and was quite successful. Children who had failed to master the English alphabet sounds in over 1½ years of schooling immediately understood the basic demands of the task and were able to read stage I sentences in the first 5 or 10 minutes of exposure to Chinese. As a measure of early progress, the performance on the stage II test (8) is presented in Table 1. In an average of 52 minutes of Chinese tutoring, the children were able to read the new material in the stage II test with few or no errors (Table 1). In an average of about 4 hours of Chinese tutoring, they were able to negotiate the final sentences and one story with relatively few errors and some comprehension (Table 1). Performance on two additional stories was comparable to that indicated for the mother-car story (9) (Table 1). On the total of three stories, there were 50 errors (137 characters in the three stories for eight children, or 1096 items). The comprehension score was 22.5 correct answers out of 48 questions.

Five children were retested on the mother-car story and the sentences in Figure 2 after 24 to 33 days had elapsed since the termination of the experiment (10). Two of the children seemed to have forgotten about half of the characters, but the remaining three made relatively few mistakes (a total of 36 out of 240 items).

In the early stages of tutoring, a number of children had difficulty in arranging the individually mounted characters to form sentences presented orally, even though they knew the correspondences of the appropriate symbols and words. This difficulty disappeared as tutoring progressed. After completion of the final tests, five children were asked to use the characters to form and rearrange sentences. Their performance on this test was excellent. In problems involving a single substitution, addition, or deletion, but no rearrangement (for instance, change "mother *sees* white car" to "mother *has* white car"), of which there were five examples, all of the five children tested averaged between 6 and 7 seconds to complete the task; they proceeded systematically and without error to find and insert a new element, or to remove or exchange an old element. The most complex task of this type involved two additional characters and some rearrangement (change "father sees mother" to "father and mother see car"). Four of the five children negotiated this problem in less than 1 minute.

The material in stage VI, with the notable exception of "mouth," seemed the most difficult. Some of the children began to get a little bored with the Chinese as they ran into some difficulty to stages V or VI. In a few cases, particular confusions ("see" and "say" in one case, for example) became partially "fixated." A certain amount of confusion resulting from visual similarity between certain symbols (for instance "say" and "and," or "give" and "red") was apparent.

In spite of these problems, all of the children read the Chinese materials adequately. Comprehension was clearly only partial, but it should be emphasized that we made little attempt in the tutoring to stress this aspect of the task.

In a total of about 4 hours we taught children to read English represented by Chinese characters that were in many ways more complex than normal English orthography. Yet these same children had failed to acquire the basics of English reading in almost 2 years of schooling. The private tutoring situation cannot account for the success with Chinese, since we also tutored these children privately in English orthography. Furthermore, in our experience of traditional tutoring with standard orthography and procedures, there is no marked improvement over equivalent time periods. We suggest that the main value of this demonstration is to highlight the factors that *cannot* be used to account for the reading backwardness of these children and the many like them in the Philadelphia and other school systems. There was clearly no problem with learning to associate more than 26 complicated and arbitrary visual symbols with certain sounds (words). Furthermore, there was no difficulty in ordering these sounds or symbols so that they could be read in a systematic pattern. Much of this ability, of course, such as the left-to-right reading habit, had already been acquired by the children in their minimum learning of English reading in school.

What, then, accounts for the large difference between the performance in Chinese and that in English? One factor may be increased motivation produced by the novelty of the Chinese material. Another factor is intrinsic to the nature of Chinese orthography, which does not map into the sound system altogether, in contrast to our alphabet, which maps (at least in large part) into the level of phonemes. What is the critical feature of the difference between the Chinese logographic and the English alphabetic system which leads to reading difficulty? It could be the complete absence of sound mapping in Chinese; it could be the particular properties of the phoneme, rather than sound mapping per se; or it could be the irregularities of the grapheme to phoneme mapping in English.

We suspect that the phonemic representation contributes most heavily to reading difficulty, We and many others have found that children with reading backwardness have difficulty in "constructing" words from these isolated sounds. There is further evidence both from speech output (articulation) and input (perception) that the alphabetic unit or phoneme is unnatural or at least highly abstract (11).

If our suspicions are correct, then some unit intermediate between the morpheme and the phoneme—for example, the syllable—might be more suitable as a vehicle for introducing reading. An efficient orthography must satisfy only two requirements. It must be easy to learn and it must be productive in the sense that, after mastery, new words can be read without learning new symbols. Hence, the ultimate unworkability of the whole word method (12).

The syllabary may meet these requirements (13). It has the advantage of pronounceableness (many phonemes cannot be pronounced in isolation) but still maintains its productivity or open-endedness. It may therefore be a good step on the road toward learning to read alphabetic writing (14).

REFERENCES AND NOTES

1. J. Money, *The Disabled Reader* (Johns Hopkins Press, Baltimore, 1966); A. J. Harris, *How to Increase Reading Ability* (McKay, New York, ed. 3, 1970).
2. P. Katz and M. Deutsch, in *The Disadvantaged Child*, M. Deutsch and associates, Eds. (Basic Books, New York, 1967), p. 233.
3. J. C. Baratz and R. W. Shuy, *Teaching Black Children to Read* (Center for Applied Linguistics, Washington, D.C., 1969).
4. Because homeroom classes were not graded by school performance, we can take the children selected to be representative of children with reading problems in the second grade of the school.
5. Levels 1 to 4 are intended to be completed in the first grade. Level 3 (Primer) includes learning of words by sight and "developing skill in 'attacking' new words through phonics." Level 4 (Book I) includes "developing additional skills in 'word attack' including compound words, contractions and possessives." Levels 5 and 6 are expected to be completed in the second year and involve completion of Books II-1 and II-2, respectively. The above descriptions are taken from the description of reading levels in "Progress Reports" of the Philadelphia public elementary schools. The books referred to in the description of levels are in the Scott-Foresman Reading Series.
6. Our familiarity with the Chinese language consists of a few hours spent reading elementary books on reading Chinese. We consulted with two fluent speakers of Chinese. Certain constructions that did not translate literally into English were avoided, and some minimal liberties were taken in creating correspondences between Chinese and English.
7. The lettering for the stories and sentences was done by a Chinese member of the staff of the Library of Oriental Studies at the University of Pennsylvania. Although the written symbols appeared to us to differ significantly in some cases from the Xerox copies of individual symbols, the children had little difficulty in generalizing from one to the other.
8. The second stage test was composed of the following sentences in Chinese orthography: "Man has house. Small mother has one house. House has two books. Big father sees one small house. House

has knife." The new element introduced for this test was the item "house."

9. One of the three stories was the mother-car story, which does not include all the symbols taught. It was: "Mother wants white car. Brother wants red car. Father gives mother white car. He doesn't (not) give brother red car. Brother says he wants red car. Father says, 'You use white car.' Brother doesn't (not) want white car; he doesn't (not) use car." The eight subjects made a mean of 3 errors (total of 23 errors) on this 40-item story. Seven timed subjects read it in a mean time of 1 minute and 43 seconds. The three comprehension questions were: (i) What did brother want? (ii) What will father let brother do? (iii) Who has the white car? A correct answer on each question is worth one point. Out of a possible total of 24 points, the eight subjects achieved 16.

10. Two of the children in the 24- to 33-day retest were tested without any practice or "warm-up." The remaining three were allowed to read one set of six sentences, with corrections, before proceeding to the retest. The practice set contained each character at least once.

11. A. Liberman, F. S. Cooper, D. P. Shankweiler, M. Studdert-Kennedy, *Psychol. Rev.* **74**, 431 (1967); H. Savin and T. Bever, *J. Verbal Learn. Verbal Behav.* **9**, 295 (1970).

12. J. S. Chall, *Learning to Read: The Great Debate* (McGraw-Hill, New York, 1967).

13. It is interesting to note that in Japan, where the written language consists of a syllabary (a much more "natural" transcription of the language), plus logographs, there is reported to be a very low rate of illiteracy [K. Makita, *Amer. J. Orthopsychiat.* **38**, 599 (1968)].

14. In a sense this experiment is simply a particularly clear demonstration of the fact that children with reading disability can learn many names of things in the visual world and can learn, to some extent, the connection between whole written words and their spoken equivalents ("look-say" method). The Chinese material may be easier because it is novel and because Chinese symbols are perhaps easier to discriminate visually than whole words written in English orthography. The point of the experiment is to highlight areas of competence and areas of specific difficulty in a type of reading disability commonly encountered in inner-city children, and to suggest new approaches to the problem.

15. Supported by NSF grant GB 8013 to one of us (P.R.). We thank the research office of the Philadelphia Board of Education and the staff of the Drew School for their cooperation; and H. Gleitman, L. Gleitman, E. Rozin, and H. Savin for their contribution to the formulation of the issues discussed and constructive comments on the manuscript.

30

National Research Council

Subliminal Self-Help

Building Self-Confidence is the title of an audio cassette tape manufactured and marketed by the Gateways Institute of Ojai, California. When the tape is played at a comfortable listening volume, all one hears is the rhythmic ebb and flow of a tropical ocean surf and the faint cry of gulls circling the shoreline.

At least, that is all one hears consciously. According to an accompanying brochure, the tape also contains dozens of positive suggestions or affirmations, such as: "I am a secure person. I believe in myself more and more every day, and my confidence naturally rises to the surface in every situation." Each of these statements is repeated hundreds of times in the course of the 1-hour program. Because the suggestions are masked by the ocean sounds, they cannot be perceived consciously. Nevertheless, according to the same brochure, these suggestions can be and are perceived subconsciously, and therein lies their purported power. The contention is that consciously imperceptible or subliminal messages

> reach the subconscious mind, which is the seat of all memories, knowledge and emotions. The unconscious mind has a powerful influence on conscious actions, thought, feelings, habits, and behaviors, and actually controls and guides your life. If you want to make real, lasting changes and improvements in any area of your life, you must reach the subconscious mind where the changes begin.

For a busy person who lacks self-confidence and lives on a tight budget, the *Building Self-Confidence* tape in question would seem to have strong appeal. It retails for $12.95 in the United States and, like several other Gateways Institute tapes, comes in a small carton carrying the advertisement: "Subliminal tapes work, so you don't have to. . . . Simply play the tapes while you work, play, drive, read, exercise, relax, watch TV, or even as you sleep. No concentration is required for the tapes to be effective. They work whether you pay attention to them or not." The brochure also notes:

A script is provided with each tape so you know the exact recorded subliminal message. It is not necessary to read the script while listening to the tape, although to enhance effectiveness, we suggest you use statements on the script as positive affirmations, repeating them to yourself from time to time. Many have found it very helpful to read the script aloud once each day just before going to bed at night.

To maximize results, play your subliminal tape at least once a day. The more often the tape is played, the faster and greater the effect. Because each person is unique, individual results will vary from person to person. Results are sometimes experienced within the first few playings, while in other cases it may take a few days or several weeks to see changes. Be assured that if you faithfully use the tape on a regular, daily basis, results will come.

Building Self-Confidence is but one of many subliminal self-help products sold by Gateways Institute, and Gateways is but one of many sources of such merchandise. According to one estimate (Oldenburg, 1990a), about 2,000 individuals or companies in America and Canada now produce subliminal self-help products for retail sale. That there is money to be made selling such products is suggested by a second estimate (Natale, 1988) that in 1987 American consumers purchased $50,000,000 worth of subliminal tapes intended for their personal improvement, a 10 percent increase over 1986 sales. Thus the subliminal industry is big and, by most accounts, getting bigger (see McGarvey, 1989; Moore, 1982; Natale, 1988; Oldenburg, 1990a).

It is easy to see why, for several reasons. First, the premise underlying subliminal suggestion—that a person can effortlessly accomplish in a matter of months or even weeks what others struggle but fail to do in a lifetime—is nearly irresistible (see Oldenburg, 1990a).

Second, as Oldenburg (1990a) has also pointed out, the promise of subliminal suggestion seems as inviting as its premise. To clarify, consider the catalog of products produced by Potentials Unlimited of Grand Rapids, Michi-

gan. This catalog cites more than 100 subliminal programs that are claimed to aid people lose weight, stop smoking, quit drinking, think creatively, make friends, reduce pain (whether due to arthritis, migraines, or premenstrual syndrome), improve vision, restore hearing (a particularly difficult goal to attain through subliminal *auditory* suggestions, or so it would seem), cure acne, conquer fears (of death, driving, or flying, among others), read faster, speak effectively, handle criticism, alleviate depression, assuage guilt, project astrally, heal psychically, mentally travel through space or time or both (e.g., imagine visiting Atlantis or searching for hidden treasure in the Sphinx), and become a better bowler. Though this partial listing provides a sense of the remarkably broad range of problems and issues that are allegedly amenable to hidden messages, it does not capture the subtle yet seemingly crucial differences that exist among the various subliminal programs. For example, Potentials Unlimited offers two programs, *Divorce—Yes* ("If you seek the divorce, this tape can free you from the other person.") and *Divorce—No* ("If you don't want a divorce, yet have no choice, quiet your fears and regain confidence to live and love again."): one can only hope that the company exercises as much care and caution in filling customer orders as they presumably do in producing their subliminal tapes, for the consequences of a mix-up might be catastrophic.

Yet a third reason for the rapid growth of the subliminal industry is tied to both the proliferation of new products and the development of new technologies. Though "pure" subliminal audiotapes—those containing virtually no audible messages—remain a fixture in the marketplace, "mixed" tapes, featuring subliminal messages on one side and supraliminal suggestions for guided relaxation and visualization on the other, are becoming increasingly popular. In both cases subliminality is achieved either by the traditional method of masking suggestions with the sound of music or waves or by the newer technique of speech compression, whereby the voice track bearing the suggestions (as many as 100,000 per hour) is accelerated until it becomes an unintelligible high-pitched whine. Although speech-compression technology is disavowed by some companies, including Gateways Institute, it is endorsed by others, including the Psychodynamics Research Institute in Zephyr Cove, Nevada, a firm that is also notable for being among the first to sell subliminal programs for children, including a potty-training tape for toddlers (see Oldenburg, 1990a).

To complement their line of subliminal audio programs, many companies now also offer an array of subliminal video tapes, in which suggestions are shown so briefly that they cannot be consciously seen. This procedure is part of the latest high-tech subliminal innovation, called MindVision, that was introduced in November 1989 by Gateways Institute. As described by Oldenburg (1990b:C5):

> ... this "inconspicuous box" hooks into the television and VCR to flash visual subliminal messages "hundreds of thousands of times each hour" on the TV screen while repeating auditory subliminal affirmations all during regular TV shows. "The lazy man's answer to a better life," Gateways boasts.

But is it really? More to the point, what evidence is there that mass-marketed subliminal self-help products are effective in practice? Even more fundamental, is there any scientific evidence that such products, in principle, could be effective?

SUBJECTIVELY PERCEPTIBLE VERSUS OBJECTIVELY DETECTABLE STIMULI

The question of effectiveness in principle has been addressed by Merikle (1988). In the introduction to his article, he remarks that, although the reality of subliminal perception continues to be a contentious issue in scientific circles, "recent research has led to a growing consensus that subliminal perception is a valid phenomenon that can be demonstrated under certain well-defined conditions" (Merikle, 1988:357).[1] The research to which Merikle refers has revealed two important observations that, taken together, provide strong support for subliminal perception. First, performance on a variety of psychological

tasks—for instance, deciding whether a string of letters forms a word (e.g., Marcel, 1983), whether a word has a good or bad meaning (Greenwald et al., 1989), whether an ambiguously described person is friendly or hostile (Bargh and Pietromonaco, 1982), or whether a geometric shape seems light or dark (Mandler et al., 1987) is influenced by information that people *claim* they did not consciously perceive. Second, information presented above and below the level of *claimed* awareness has qualitatively different effects on performance (e.g., Dixon, 1971; Cheesman and Merikle, 1986; Groeger, 1984; Jacoby and Whitehouse, 1989). The importance of the second observation lies in the fact that, given the demonstration of differential (possibly opposite) outcomes, "one can be certain that effects observed in the supposedly unaware condition were not actually due to the subjects' being aware of an item without the experimenter's detecting that awareness" (Jacoby and Whitehouse, 1989:127).

Why the emphasis on claimed awareness? The answer is suggested by the results of a study by Cheesman and Merikle (1984) in which subjects were asked to name, as quickly as possible, a "target" color (a patch of blue, for instance) that was preceded by either a congruent or an incongruent color-word "prime" (the word *blue* as opposed to, say, *green*). In previous studies using visible color words as primes (e.g., Dyer and Severance, 1973), it had been shown that a target color is named faster if it is preceded by a congruent than by an incongruent prime. Whether color words rendered invisible by backward masking also produce a reliable "priming effect" in the color-naming task was an issue of central concern in Cheesman and Merikle's study.

To investigate this issue, Cheesman and Merikle measured color-naming latencies under three threshold conditions: suprathreshold, objective, and subjective. Each of these conditions comprised many individual trials, and every trial conformed to the same sequence of events in rapid succession: (1) presentation of a congruent or an incongruent color word prime, (2) presentation of a central mask composed of random letters, (3) display of the to-be-named target color.

The critical difference among the conditions was the duration of the interval separating onset of the prime from onset of the mask: a constant 300 milliseconds (msec) in the suprathreshold condition, an average of 56 msec in the subjective-threshold condition and an average of 30 msec in the objective-threshold condition. Cheesman and Merikle settled on these intervals, or stimulus onset asynchronies (SOAs), by pretesting the subjects on the ability to detect which one of four color-word primes had been presented on a particular trial.

Results of this pretesting revealed that at the SOA corresponding to the suprathreshold condition, subjects stated that they could see the primes clearly, and they therefore estimated their performance on the test of four-alternative forced-choice target detectability would be perfect (100 percent)—which it was. At the SOA corresponding to the objective threshold, subjects indicated that they could not see the primes, and they therefore anticipated scoring at chance (25 percent)—which they did—on the test of target detectability. At the SOA corresponding to the subjective threshold, subjects again claimed that they could not consciously perceive the primes, and they therefore again anticipated scoring at chance as to which particular target color word had been presented on a particular trial. In actuality, however, their random "guesses" were, on average, 66 percent correct—a level of detection performance that plainly exceeds chance.

As the detectability of the primes varied across threshold conditions, so too did the size of the priming effect observed in the color-naming task. In the suprathreshold condition, a substantial priming effect was found (on average, target colors were named about 95 msec faster when primed by congruent than by incongruent color words); in the subjective-threshold condition, the effect was smaller but remained significant (mean difference of roughly 40 msec); and in the objective-threshold condition, the effect was virtually nonexistent (mean difference of less than 10 msec).[2] These results, in addition to those relating to tasks other than color naming (see Eriksen, 1960, 1986; Merikle, 1988), suggest that subjectively imperceptible but objectively detectable stimuli can affect certain actions. As such, these results are consistent with Merikle's (1988:360) conception of subliminal perception as "perception in the absence of subjective confidence."

There is one advantage of viewing subliminal perception this way (Merkile, 1988:360):

It eliminates much of the mysticism previously associated with the concept. No longer is it necessary to consider subliminal perception as implying the existence of some "supersensitive" unconscious perceptual system. Rather, the evidence simply suggests that we can sometimes discriminate among stimulus states, as indicated by our verbal responses, even when, based on our subjective phenomenal experiences, we have no confidence that sufficient stimulus information was perceived to guide response selection. Thus, according to this view, subliminal perception occurs whenever we can objectively discriminate among possible stimulus states but have no subjective confidence as to the correctness of our decisions.

A second advantage concerns the question, posed earlier, of whether it is possible in principle for mass-marketed subliminal self-help products to produce their intended effects. By Merikle's (1988:360) account:

When subliminal perception is viewed as a subjective state, there is a very clear specification of the minimum stimulus condition that must be satisfied before sufficient information is perceived, either consciously or unconsciously, to influence higher-level decision processes. Since, according to this view, subliminal perception reflects an absence of subjective confidence when responding discriminately to a stimulus, the minimum condition necessary for demonstrating subliminal perception is the presence of a detectable stimulus.

To determine whether subliminal self-help products, specifically, subliminal audio cassettes, meet this "minimum stimulus condition," Merikle (1988) performed two types of studies. First, if the cassettes actually contain covert messages, then frequency changes characteristic of spoken speech should be evident in spectrograms or "voice prints" derived from the tapes. Of the 40-odd spectrograms that Merikle culled from four subliminal audio cassettes (each produced by a different company), none showed any signs of hidden speech.

Though provocative, these null results are difficult to interpret because spectrographic analysis may not be capable of detecting very weak speech (e.g., at average signal-to-noise ratios of −10 to −20dB, see Borden and Harris, 1984). In addition, it is conceivable that in comparison with a sound spectrograph, the human auditory system is more sensitive to the detection and decoding of weak, degraded signals (i.e., embedded messages). In recognition of this possibility, Merikle (1988) performed a second type of study in which the human auditory system, rather than a sound spectrograph, served as the measuring instrument. In this psychophysical research, subjects were repeatedly tested for the ability to discriminate between two commercially produced cassettes that were identical except that, according to the manufacturer, one contained subliminal messages and the other did not. Merikle found that the subjects could not reliably distinguish between the "message" and the "no-message" cassettes, and he concluded (1988:370):

> Taken together, the empirical results lead to the inescapable conclusion that the widely marketed subliminal cassettes do not contain any embedded messages that could conceivably influence behavior. This conclusion is supported both by the results of the spectrographic analyses indicating that these cassettes do not contain any identifiable embedded speech and by the results of the psychophysical studies indicating that these cassettes do not contain any embedded signals whatsoever that can be detected under controlled conditions. Given that consistent empirical support for subliminal perception has only been found under conditions that allow stimulus detection, these subliminal audio cassettes do not satisfy the most minimal conditions for demonstrating subliminal perception.

An ardent advocate of subliminal self-help might challenge this conclusion on two grounds: (1) some, perhaps many, of the vast number of the audiotapes (or any or all video tapes) that Merikle did not test do meet his minimum condition for demonstrating subliminal perception and thus could conceivably affect behavior as advertised; (2) some, perhaps many, of the people who buy and use these tapes say that "silent treatments" do them good (see

McGarvey, 1989; VandenBoogert, 1984). We first consider in detail the second point and then discuss the implications of the first point.

MOBILIZATION, EFFORT JUSTIFICATION, AND EXPECTANCY EFFECTS

As noted by Oldenburg (1990a), many marketers of subliminal self-improvement products try to attract new customers by publicizing the ringing recommendations of past patrons. Oldenburg (1990a) cites several of these endorsements, and others may be found in *Discoveries Through Inner Quests*, a promotional magazine for the Gateways Institute. In the Winter-Spring 1990 issue of this magazine, a woman from Massachusetts writes: "Bless you! I'm listening to my tape on pain reduction. It is marvelous. I had almost instant relief from pain on first using it a few days ago. It's much cheaper than a doctor and much better than medication. Phenomenal is what it has done for my spirits." In the same issue, a California woman reports "dramatic results" in her eating habits after purchasing the subliminal tape titled Stop Eating Junk Food, and a man from Maine states that shortly after receiving the tape Wealth and Prosperity, he got a new job and tripled his old salary.

Though there is no reason to doubt the sincerity of these testimonials, there are several reasons to question the conviction that subliminal suggestions are in any way responsible for, or even play a part in, any self-perceived improvements in behavior. In the first place, by buying and using a subliminal self-help product, one demonstrates not only a desire for personal enhancement, but also a commitment to change one's ways. The very act of making such a commitment, of mobilizing oneself into action, may be therapeutic in its own right, in much the same way that some people realize marked improvements in behavior after they register for, but before they receive, individual psychotherapy (see Rachman and Wilson, 1980). Compared with undertaking psychotherapy, the commitment expressed through the purchase and use of a subliminal product is obviously much less. After all, such products are designed to work "so you don't have to," and its therapeutic potential is correspondingly much more modest in principle. Indeed, the commitment entailed in employing subliminal suggestions to, say, enhance one's popularity and make new friends seems comparable to the commitment involved in spending an hour every day for a month at the beach to accomplish these same goals. After visiting the beach on a regular basis, or following the steady use of a "be more popular" subliminal tape, one might in fact acquire some new friends. But surely this outcome is no more attributable to the properties of the beach than it is to the contents of the subliminal tape. Rather, responsibility rests with the person's decision to *do* something—go to the beach or play the subliminal tape—that might help him or her win friends. Consequently, the imaginary "beach therapy" might be every bit as effective, or ineffective, as the real "subliminal programs" that are purported to improve one's popularity.

A second, related reason that subliminal tapes, even those containing no detectable embedded messages, may seem salutary has to do with the social psychological phenomenon of effort justification: the finding that the harder we work at something, the more we like it (see Penrod, 1983). After buying a subliminal tape and using it daily for several weeks, as most manufacturers advise, many people would be reluctant to admit to themselves or others that they had wasted their time and money. Instead, they would be motivated to detect some sort of change in some aspect of their lives, in order to rationalize their investment (see Conway and Ross, 1984).

Yet a third reason for the possible effect of tapes without detectable messages, perhaps the most important, relates to expectancy effects. By way of background, most readers are familiar with the story of how, in 1957, an advertising expert named James Vicary subliminally presented the statements "Eat Popcorn and Drink Coke" to unsuspecting viewers of the film *Picnic*, resulting in an impulsive rush to the refreshment stand. Many readers may not know, however, that years later Vicary

admitted that his study was a hoax intended to increase revenues for his foundering advertising firm (see Weir, 1984). Vicary's "demonstration" sparked a storm of controversy (see Moore, 1982, 1988; Pratkanis and Greenwald, 1988) and stimulated many investigations of subliminal advertising. One of these was a study, brought to our attention by Pratkanis et al. (1990), that was conducted by the Canadian Broadcast Corporation in 1958. As described by Pratkanis et al. (1990:5):

> During a popular Sunday night television show viewers were told about the Vicary EAT POPCORN/DRINK COKE STUDY and were informed that the station would do a test of subliminal persuasion (although the content of the message was not revealed). The message "Phone Now" was then flashed subliminally on screen 352 times. Telephone company records indicated that phone usage did not increase nor did local television stations report an increase in calls. However, almost half of the nearly 500 letters sent in by viewers indicated that they felt compelled to "do something" and many felt an urge to eat or drink. It appears that expectations created by the Vicary study influenced what people believed had happened.

That subliminal methods of personal improvement, like those involved in public advertising, are susceptible to strong expectancy effects is a point made plain in a recent study by Pratkanis et al. (1990).[3] Through ads placed in local newspapers, these researchers recruited volunteers who were especially interested in the potential value of subliminal self-help tapes and who would probably be similar to those most likely to purchase such products.

On the first day of the study, the subjects completed a battery of tests to measure self-esteem and memory ability. Every participant was then given one or two commercially produced subliminal audiotapes: one claimed by the manufacturer to contain suggestions for improving self-esteem (e.g., "I radiate an inner sense of confidence"), the other claimed to contain suggestions for improving memory (e.g., "My ability to remember and recall is increasing daily"). On both tapes, the suggestions were recorded behind background classical music, so as to render them subliminal. The intriguing aspect of this study was that only a randomly selected one-half of the subjects actually got the tape they thought they were getting, one-quarter received the memory enhancement tape mislabeled as one to improve their self-esteem, and one-quarter received a self-esteem tape mislabeled "memory improvement."

The subjects took their tapes home and listened to them every day for 5 weeks, the period recommended by the manufacturer for achieving maximum benefit. After 5 weeks, the subjects were asked to indicate whether they believed the tapes had been effective, and they also completed a second battery of self-esteem and memory tests.

The tests showed that the tapes had no appreciable effect, positive or negative, on any measure of either self-esteem or memory, but many of the subjects believed otherwise. Approximately one-half of those who thought they had received the self-esteem tape—regardless of whether they had actually received it or the memory tape—stated that their self-esteem had risen; similarly, about one-half of those who presumed, correctly or not, that they had received the memory tape maintained that their memory had improved as a result of listening to the tape. In light of those results, the title selected by Pratkanis and his associates to describe their study—"What you expect is what you believe, but not necessarily what you get"—seems most appropriate.

CONCLUSIONS

There are some well-documented psychological reasons that subliminal self-help products may appear to work, even if they contain no detectable embedded messages and thus fail to satisfy the "minimum stimulus condition" set by Merikle (1988) for demonstrating subliminal perception. It is possible, of course, that products now available in the marketplace do meet the criterion of detectability (after all, Merikle tested no video displays and only a handful of audio cassettes) or that such products could be engineered in the future. Suppose, for the sake of argument, that one were to identify or in-

vent a subliminal self-help product that complies with the minimum prerequisite. What then?

Clearly, the mere presence of objectively detectable messages would by no means ensure the product's effectiveness. Recent research does suggest that subjectively imperceptible stimuli may have short-term effects on the performance of such relatively simple tasks as color naming or lexical decision under controlled laboratory conditions. But one cannot and should not infer from this research that long-term changes in complex actions, cognitions, or emotions—such as smoking, self-confidence, or depression—can be effected by exposure to subliminal suggestions under such varied real-life circumstances as reading, relaxing, or even sleeping. Such effects, if any, remain to be conclusively established and rigorously explored.

Rather, as Merikle (1988) has remarked, the presence of detectable messages would only imply that it may be worthwhile to carry out carefully controlled studies of the possible effects of such messages. Such studies would need to address a very long list of questions, some of which have been raised in prior research on subliminal perception. For instance, are there significant individual differences in peoples' sensitivity to the embedded but detectable messages (e.g., Sackeim et al., 1977)? Might one's receptivity to such messages be enhanced by the adoption of a passive attitude or frame of mind (e.g., Dixon, 1971)? Do subliminal messages serve only to amplify preexisting tendencies or can they induce novel ways of acting, feeling, or thinking (e.g., Kihlstrom, 1987)? Are there demonstrable qualitative differences between the effects of presenting one and the same message above as opposed to below the subjective threshold of awareness (e.g., Cheesman and Merikle, 1986; Dixon, 1986)? Finding answers to these and many related questions will doubtless prove to be a difficult and demanding task, but perhaps a rewarding one as well. At this time, however, on the basis of the committee's review of the available research literature, we conclude that there is neither theoretical foundation nor experimental evidence to support claims that subliminal self-help audiotapes enhance human performance.

NOTES

1. In the interests of brevity and in keeping with our current focus on subliminal perception as a commercial means of promoting self-improvement, neither the history nor the current status of subliminal perception as a scientific concept is discussed in detail here. Readers interested in these issues should consult Adams (1957), Cheesman and Merikle (1984, 1986), Dixon (1971, 1981), Eriksen (1960), Goldiamond (1958), Greenwald et al. (1989), Holender (1986), and accompanying peer commentaries, Marcel (1983), Merikle and Cheesman (1987), Reingold and Merikle (1988), and Swets et al. (1961).

2. In addition to manipulating the prime-mask SOA, Cheesman and Merikle (1984) varied the prime-target color SOA, either 50, 550, or 1,050 msec. Because this latter variable did not significantly influence the size of the observed priming effects, the results for each prime-target color SOA have been averaged to yield the above priming data.

3. This study is also described in Greenwald et al. (1990), together with two successful replications.

REFERENCES

Adams, J. K.
1957 Laboratory studies of behavior without awareness. *Psychological Bulletin* 54:383–405.

Bargh, J.A., and P. Pietromonaco
1982 Automatic information processing and social perception: the influence of trait information presented outside of conscious awareness on impression formation. *Journal of Personality and Social Psychology* 43:437–449.

Bordon, G., and K. S. Harris
1984 *Speech Science Primer: Physiology, Acoustics, and Perception of Speech,* 2nd ed. Baltimore, Md.: Williams & Wilkins.

Cheesman, J., and P. M. Merikle
1984 Priming with and without awareness. *Perception and Psychophysics* 36:387–395.

1986 Distinguishing conscious from unconscious perceptual processes. *Canadian Journal of Psychology* 40:343–367.

Conway, M., and M. Ross
1984 Getting what you want by revising what you had. *Journal of Personality and Social Psychology* 47:738–748.

Dixon, N. F.
1971 *Subliminal Perception: The Nature of a Controversy.* London, England: McGraw-Hill.

1981 *Preconscious Processing.* Chichester, England: John Wiley.

1986 On private events and brain events. *Behavioral and Brain Sciences* 9:29–30.

Dyer, F. N., and L. J. Severance
1973 Stroop interference with successive presentations of separate incongruent words and colors. *Journal of Experimental Psychology* 98:438–439.

Eriksen, C. W.
1960 Discrimination and learning without awareness: methodological survey and evaluation. *Psychological Review* 67:279–300.

Goldiamond, I.
1958 Indicators of perception: subliminal perception, subception, unconscious perception: an analysis in terms of psychophysical indicator methodology. *Psychological Bulletin* 55:373–411.

Greenwald, A. G., M. R. Klinger, and T. J. Lui
1989 Unconscious processing of dichotically masked words. *Memory and Cognition* 17:35–47.

Greenwald, A. G., E. R. Spangenberg, A. R. Pratkanis, and J. Eskenazi
1990 Double-Blind Tests of Subliminal Self-Help Tapes. Paper presented at the American Psychological Association Convention, Boston, August 1990. Unpublished manuscript, Department of Psychology, University of Washington, Seattle.

Groeger, J. A.
1984 Evidence of unconscious semantic processing from a forced error situation. *British Journal of Psychology* 75:305–314.

Holender, D.
1986 Semantic activation without conscious identification in dichotic listening, parafoveal vision, and visual masking: a survey and appraisal. *Behavioral and Brain Sciences* 9:1–66.

Jacoby, L. L., and K. Whitehouse
1989 An illusion of memory: false recognition influenced by unconscious perception. *Journal of Experimental Psychology: General* 118:126–135.

Kihlstrom, J. F.
1987 The cognitive unconscious. *Science* 237:1445–1452.

Mandler, G., Y. Nakamura, and B. J. S. Van Zandt
1987 Nonspecific effects of exposure to stimuli that cannot be recognized. *Journal of Experimental Psychology: Learning, Memory, and Cognition* 13:646–648.

Marcel, A. J.
1983 Conscious and unconscious perception: experiments on visual masking and word recognition. *Cognitive Psychology* 15:197–237.

McGarvey, R.
1989 Recording success. *USAir Magazine* February:94–102.

Merikle, P. M.
1988 Subliminal auditory messages: an evaluation. *Psychology and Marketing* 5:355–372.

Merikle, P. M., and J. Cheesman
1987 Current status of research on subliminal perception. Pp. 298–302 in M. Wallendorf and P. Anderson, eds., *Advances in Consumer Research*, Vol. 14. Provo, Utah: Association for Consumer Research.

Moore, T. E.
1982 Subliminal advertising: what you see is what you get. *Journal of Marketing* 46(2):38–47.

1988 The case against subliminal manipulation. *Psychology and Marketing* 5:297–316.

Natale, J. A.
1988 Are you open to suggestion? *Psychology Today* 22:28–30.

Oldenburg, D.
1990a Hidden messages. *The Washington Post.* April 3:C5.

1990b Silent treatments. *The Washington Post.* April 5:C5.

Penrod, S.
1983 *Social Psychology.* Englewood Cliffs, N.J.: Prentice-Hall.

Pratkanis, A. R., and A. G. Greenwald
1988 Recent perspectives on unconscious processing: still no marketing applications. *Psychology and Marketing* 5:337–353.

Pratkanis, A. R., J. Eskenazi, and A. G. Greenwald
1990 What You Expect Is What You Believe, But Not Necessarily What You Get: On the Effectiveness of Subliminal Self-Help Audiotapes. Paper presented at the annual convention of the Western Psychological Association, Los Angeles, California.

Rachman, S. J., and G. T. Wilson
1980 Using direct and indirect measures to study perception without awareness. *Perception and Psychophysics* 44:563–575.

Reingold, E. M., and P. M. Merikle
1988 Using direct and indirect measures to study perception without awareness. *Perception and Psychophysics* 44:563–575.

Sackeim, H. A., I. K. Packer, and R. C. Gur
1977 Hemisphericity, cognitive set, and susceptibility to subliminal perception. *Journal of Abnormal Psychology* 86:624–630.

Swets, J. A., W. Tanner, and T. G. Birdsall
1961 Decision processes in perception. *Psychological Review* 68:301–340.

VandenBoogert, C.
1984 A Study of Potential Unlimited, Inc. Subliminal Persuasion/Self-Hypnosis Tapes. Potentials, Inc., Grand Rapids, Michigan.

Weir, W.
1984 Another look at subliminal "facts." *Advertising Age* October:46.

31

Diane F. Halpern

Analogies as a Critical Thinking Skill

Abstract: *Evidence in support of the position that thinking skills can be enhanced with critical thinking courses is reviewed, and research on the effectiveness of analogies as a critical thinking skill is presented. Although analogies are a common component in many critical and creative thinking courses, there is little empirical evidence on the extent to which they can serve as an aid in comprehension, recall, and problem solving. Results suggest that well-chosen analogies can improve understanding and memory for events explicitly stated in scientific prose passages.*

Analogy is inevitable in human thought.
—*Oppenheimer (1956, p. 129)*

There has been a recent growing interest among colleges and universities across the United States and Canada, and in other countries around the world in the development of courses that are designed to help students improve their ability to think critically. These courses have been instituted in the belief that, far too often, instruction in traditional college classrooms has not encouraged the development of critical thought. Although there has been considerable debate over exactly what sorts of skills comprise critical thinking, the term is usually used to refer to systematic, goal-directed thinking that includes evaluation of the assumptions, processes, and outcome in making a decision, solving a problem, or formulating inferences from information given.

Traditionally, our schools have required students to learn, remember, make decisions, analyze arguments, and solve problems without ever teaching them how. There has been a tacit assumption that adult students already know "how to think." Recent research has shown, however, that this assumption is not warranted. Psychologists have found that only 25% of first-year college students scored at the Formal

Level of thought on Piagetian tests designed to assess the thinking skills needed for logical thought (McKinnon & Renner, 1971). Bertrand Russell summed up this situation well when he said, "Most people would rather die than think. In fact, they do."

Although virtually everyone agrees that critical thinking instruction is an idea whose time is long overdue, the mandate to teach college students how to think has raised numerous questions. The most important question is, "Can we teach college students how to think?" Or, more appropriately, "Can thinking skills be enhanced with proper instruction?"

Critical thinking and problem-solving courses are predicated on two basic assumptions: (1) that there are clearly identifiable and definable thinking skills that students can be taught to recognize and apply appropriately, and (2) that if these skills are recognized and applied, the students will be more effective thinkers. A list of such skills typically would include understanding how cause is determined, recognizing and criticizing assumptions, analyzing means-goals relationships, reducing complex problems to simpler ones, making appropriate inferences, and, one that I have chosen to focus on, using analogies as an aid to comprehension, memory, and problem solving.

As the number of critical thinking and problem-solving courses has proliferated, so has the number of skeptics claiming that it is not possible to produce long-lasting enhancement of students' ability to think effectively outside of domain-specific courses, that is, outside of courses that deal with a specific subject matter (Glaser, 1984; Resnick, 1983). I disagree. There is evidence to suggest that general thinking skills courses have positive effects that are transferable to a variety of content-specific domains (Block, 1985; Halpern, 1984).

Critical thinking instruction poses a unique assessment problem. Unlike other courses in which students are taught a specific content and then tested for their knowledge of that content, thinking and problem-solving courses aim to teach students how to improve their "ability to think"—a much more global and amorphous goal. In this chapter, I consider briefly some of the instruments that have been used as criterion measures to support claims that a course or other type of instruction has resulted in an improvement in the ability to think. I then present some research that I have conducted on the effectiveness of analogies as a critical thinking skill. Since the use of analogies is an important part of any critical thinking course, it is important to ascertain whether they are an effective aid to comprehension and problem solving.

EMPIRICAL STUDIES OF CRITICAL THINKING COURSES

At least six different forms of outcome evaluations for thinking and problem-solving programs have been conducted. I argue that since positive results have been obtained with each measure, it is reasonable to conclude that students have improved their ability to think critically. However, the data are still incomplete, and this remains an area in need of additional and improved research.

The most usual assessment instrument is the standard midterm and final exam written by the professor. Such exams have the benefit of being tailor-fit to the course content and objectives, but contain the obvious disadvantage of unknown reliability and validity. Most people view with skepticism any professor's claims that she or he has improved a student's ability for critical thought if such claims are supported solely on the basis of good grades earned on the professor's final exam.

A second approach to the assessment problem has been the evaluation of pre-course and post-course student self-reports regarding their thinking ability (Wheeler, 1979). There are obvious problems with using student self-reports to support the proposition that they have learned to think better. Self-reports may not reflect reality. Students may report that they can make decisions more intelligently when they cannot, or conversely, that they have not improved when they have. I would like my students to think more clearly and to know that they can, but I would not rely upon students' beliefs about their abilities as an index of those abilities.

A third way of measuring thinking improvement is with gains in IQ points on standardized intelligence tests. For example, Rubinstein (1980) reported on a midwestern study in which 82.4% of the students who participated in the problem-solving course he developed showed gains in IQ points. The reasoning behind this claim is that when people improve the way they think, they become more intelligent. It is difficult to know how to interpret claims like this one. (This particular study was flawed because the researcher failed to use a control group.) Hayes (1980) has said that he questions the data in support of this claim because he does not believe that the types of skills taught in these courses are the same ones that are tapped in intelligence tests. Experts have argued for years about the many bitterly disputed issues that surround the IQ controversies. There is always the lingering question of whether or not any gain in IQ points is merely the result of training in test taking or drill on the topics addressed in intelligence tests rather than a general enhancement of "intelligence." The students may not show similar gains when out of the classroom or away from testing situations. Whatever your point of view on the IQ issue, few would argue that IQ is a good way to measure the thinking skills that we hope to sharpen in our students.

One promising approach to the quantification of course-related improvement in the ability to think is the measurement of growth in cognitive development using Piagetian tasks. Such assessment will typically involve comparisons between students who have taken a thinking course and a control group of students who have not taken a thinking course on a variety of Piagetian tasks that measure an individual's level of cognitive development. Consider for example, Piaget's "mixing chemicals" task. In this task, students are given four colorless liquids and an activating agent. They are told to mix the chemicals and agent until they discover which combinations produce a yellow color. The correct answer requires a systematic approach, first mixing the chemicals with the activating agent one at a time, then two at a time, then three at a time, then all four together. A random or unsystematic approach is not a good strategy. There are many other tasks originally devised by Piaget that are used to determine the level of thought at which an individual is functioning. In one study that employed this method of assessment, the results generally supported the superiority of the students who had taken the thinking course (Fox, Marsh, & Crandall, 1983). Although this is a promising line of research, it requires that the Piagetian tasks used for assessment be novel to the students and that the professor eschew the temptation to teach tasks like the ones that appear on the test.

A fifth approach is the use of scores on standardized tests of critical thinking, such as the Watson-Glaser Critical Thinking Appraisal, the Ennis Weir Argumentation Test, and the Cornell Critical Thinking Test. Although such tests have a considerable literature attesting to their reliability and validity, they are designed to assess a narrow range of thinking skills, specifically understanding short prose passages, and thus do not match well with many course objectives. Most of these tests are concerned only with argument analysis including inductive and deductive reasoning.

One of the most recent and theoretically advanced means of exploring course-related changes in thinking ability is to examine the underlying structure of cognitive skills and knowledge. Much of the research in this area is based on comparisons between skilled and unskilled problem solvers. From these studies, we have learned that experts approach problems in ways that novices do not. Experts possess complex problem representations or schemata that allow them to make appropriate inferences from problem statements. Schemata are theoretical constructs that denote organized bodies of knowledge. According to cognitive theory, all of the information we possess about a topic is organized into a structural framework that represents the properties and relations that pertain to the topic. For example, a cognitive psychologist would have a complex schema or knowledge structure for "mental chronometry." It would contain information about the relationship between componential analysis and reaction time, and the underlying assumption that reaction times can be subtracted to isolate simpler thought processes. Information about mental chronometry can be encoded, utilized, and retrieved more efficiently by a cognitive psychologist (the "expert" in this example) than by someone who is less familiar with this topic. A novice's problem representation or schema is presumably less differentiated, contains fewer connections to other related schemata, and often may be faulty (c.f. Glaser, 1984; Kintsch & Greeno, 1985).

One excellent approach for measuring course-related cognitive growth is to demonstrate that novices who are given instruction in thinking and problem solving have underlying knowledge structures or schemata that are more similar to those of experts than a control group of novices who had some other educational experience. Following this line of reasoning, Schoenfeld and Herman (1982) had subjects categorize mathematical problems. The task for the subjects was to sort problems into different piles on the basis of their similarity. They found that novices tended to classify problems on the basis of *surface similarity* or topic. For example, problems about people working together might be perceived as being similar to problems about people traveling together because both types of problems involve group activities. However, both mathematics professors and students who had taken an 18-day course on problem-solving strategies classified problems according to problem-solving principles or what is sometimes called *deep structure*.

USE OF ANALOGIES

Although positive results supporting the hypothesis that it is possible to improve students' critical thinking ability with general thinking courses have been reported with each of the six assessment approaches discussed above, there are weaknesses and pitfalls inherent in each of these approaches. A better way to examine the efficacy of critical thinking instruction is to look at the components of a typical critical thinking course to ascertain whether they are effective aids to comprehension and problem

solving. To this end, I have begun research on the use of analogies. I chose to focus on analogies for several reasons. First, a national survey that I conducted with the help of a publisher (Lawrence Erlbaum Associates) revealed that virtually every college-level critical and creative thinking course, regardless of discipline, included instruction on the use of analogies.

A second reason for studying analogies is that they readily lend themselves to assessment by examining underlying knowledge structures, an assessment approach that I believe to be the most promising demonstration that general thinking skills courses can lead to improvements in domain-specific knowledge. I became intrigued with the possibility that an expert's representation of a problem space could be transferred to a naive subject or novice in a simple straightforward manner. One method to speed this transfer is to provide subjects with an analogy selected from a subject matter domain familiar to the novice. This method would be effective, however, only to the extent that the use of analogies is an effective cognitive tool.

Unlike some of the more artificial topics taught in many critical thinking courses, like drawing Venn diagrams or calculating Bayesian post hoc probabilities, analogies are used spontaneously by most adults. Sternberg (1977) has noted the ubiquitous nature of analogies in our everyday thinking: "Reasoning by analogy is pervasive in everyday experience. We reason analogically whenever we make a decision about something new in our experience by drawing a parallel to something old" (p. 353). Analogies are also frequently used in explaining scientific concepts. Analogies in cognitive psychology, for example, have always reflected the most advanced technology at the time, and include likening the human mind to a hydraulic system, indoor plumbing, a telephone switchboard, and, more recently, a computer and a hologram. Each of these analogies provides a framework for understanding the transfer or flow of information and its storage in the human memory system.

Consider, for example, that in learning about the structure of an atom, you are told that it is like a miniature solar system. Suppose further that you already have a great deal of knowledge about the solar system. If you don't, then there is no advantage in learning about the solar system. There is an important point because a working theory of analogies assumes that new information is efficiently acquired because of its parallel relationship to preexisting (i.e., already known) information. If the structural properties of the atom are highly similar to that of the solar system, then a new, but highly complex cognitive structure is quickly created. In the jargon of cognitive psychology, this is known as *structure mapping* because the structure of a base (or known) complex knowledge system is mapped onto a target (or unknown) domain (Gentner & Gentner, 1983). According to this view, analogies are much more than weak comparisons; they play a generative role in the formation of new schemata in which the relations between objects in the base domain are preserved in the target domain (D. Gentner, 1983).

A good analogy can facilitate comprehension and recall in several ways. It can function as an advanced organizer by providing a structural framework for interpreting new information (Mayer, 1979; Mayer & Bromage, 1980). The fact that recall is dependent on the organization of information that is to be learned is a well-known learning principle (Mandler, 1967). One of the functions of analogies is to provide logical interrelationship among ideas, which could serve as a means of organizing separate "facts" or initially disparate segments of information (Meyer & Mc Conkie, 1973). Kintsch and Greeno (1985) have argued that the ability to comprehend and solve problems depends on the nature of the internal representation. If analogies speed the formation of differentiated schemata, then comprehension and solution of the problem should be facilitated.

Analogies often make abstract concepts more concrete, usually by providing a memorial mental image. Concrete nouns are more easily remembered than abstract nouns, probably because they evoke clear mental images (Paivio, 1969). Thus, analogies to concrete objects should also function as a visual-imagery mnemonic aid in the retention of the new information presented. In addition to creating complex schemata and concrete images, analogies also evoke novel comparisons. All analogies suggest similarity between two disparate concepts. When the two concepts are very different, or in the jargon of cognitive psychology, the between-domain distance is great, the analogy becomes more striking, as in an analogy between love and a rose or between the mentally ill and weeds in a flower garden (Tourangeau & Sternberg, 1981). Early research in memory showed that people tend to remember the unusual or unexpected, a finding that is commonly called the von Restorff effect. The unexpected or surprise aspect of good analogies could also be a comprehension and retention aid.

The ability of analogies to function as a cognitive tool is important for both theoretical and practical reasons. Notwithstanding the widespread use of analogies in critical thinking courses, and the fact that there are several theoretical mechanisms by which they should serve as a thinking skill, very few studies have investigated the extent to which they improve comprehension, recall, and problem solving. The following research, which I conducted with the help of three students at California State University, San Bernardino (Cheryl Eberhardt, Joan Gonzales, & Carol Hansen) was designed to investigate this possibility.

Research Report

One hundred fifteen college students were presented with two different short prose passages about technical scientific topics. One passage described the purpose and the operation of the lymphatic system. The other passage described retrograde motion of the planets. Each of these passages was presented either with or without an analogy. The lymphatic analogy described it as being like "a wet sponge with spaces filled with water. If you squeeze it, you can force the water from one end of the sponge to another." The analogy for retrograde motion of the planets was that of "a car traveling westward in the fast lane of a freeway that overtakes another car. If you are a passenger in the faster moving car, it appears as though the car you passed is going in the opposite direction, that is, eastward."

One problem in conducting research of this sort is that highly motivated subjects are needed. Considerable effort is required if subjects are to learn about complex scientific topics. We tried various motivating tricks. First, we only used students in intact classrooms in which the instructors were willing to give extra credit for participation. In addition, the students in each classroom who answered the greatest number of questions correctly were awarded prizes.

Subjects were assigned at random to one of two testing groups. Group 1 subjects were tested for comprehension and recall immediately after reading each passage and again 2 days later. Subjects in Group 2 were tested for comprehension and recall only after a 2-day intervening period. Subjects were blind to the nature of these conditions and the purpose of the experiment. Filler activities were used immediately after reading the passages for subjects in Group 2 (delayed-recall-only group) to control for time variables and to disguise the nature of this manipulation.

All subjects read both the lymphatic and retrograde motion passages, with only one of the passages containing the analogy. Order of presentation was counterbalanced to control for order effects. Immediately after reading each passage, subjects were asked to rate how much they had learned from the passage. Subjects in Group 1 (the immediate and delayed-recall group) were then asked to list as many facts as they could remember about the passage they had just read. Following the free-recall task, they then responded to 10 multiple-choice questions, two of which required a thoughtful inference about information that was not explicitly stated. We believed that if analogies facilitate the establishment of differentiated knowledge structures, then subjects who read passages with analogies would be better able to make valid inferences about information that was not explicitly stated than subjects who read the same passages without an analogy. The ability to make correct inferences would result directly from the complex problem representation.

Two days later, all subjects were asked to list as many facts as they could recall from each passage. The same multiple-choice test that had been given to Group 1 immediately following each passage was given again, this time to all subjects in both groups. The test questions and possible alternative answers, however, were presented in a different order from that used earlier.

Overwhelmingly, the 115 students who participated in this experiment reported that they had learned a great deal about each topic (all p's < .001), with no significant differences with respect to the analogy/no analogy manipulation. We had expected to find a difference on this measure such that when subjects read passages with analogies they believed that they learned more than when they read passages without analogies; however, this didn't happen.

Figure 1 shows the results for subjects who were tested immediately after reading each passage. Results for free recall and multiple-choice questions for each passage were tested for statistical significance with separate analyses. Perusal of Figure 1 reveals that when the retrograde motion passage contained an analogy, subjects in a free-recall paradigm recalled an average of 1.2 more facts about it than when it did not. All analogy/no analogy comparisons with the retrograde motion passage either obtained statistical significance ($p < .05$) or approached statistical significance ($p < .06$ or .07). Results with the lymphatic system passage were less dramatic, with the analogy offering only a small advantage. For the most part, although the analogy/no analogy mean differences for the lymphatic system passage were in the predicted direction, they failed to obtain statistical significance.

Results from the multiple-choice test that immediately followed the free-recall test mirrored the free-recall results. Out of a possible 10 questions, the analogy improved comprehension of the retrograde motion passage an average of almost one question, with a smaller mean difference for the lymphatic system passage.

The analysis of the results from the delayed test that was administered 2 days later was

Figure 1 _____

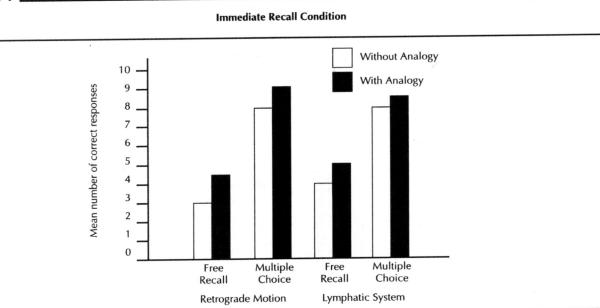

Mean number of free recall and multiple-choice responses for students who read scientific passages (retrograde motion or lymphatic system) either with or without an analogy.

more complex, as shown in Figure 2. Free-recall and multiple-choice data from the delayed recall test were analyzed separately for each passage. In general, subjects who were tested immediately following each passage tended to perform better than subjects who were tested only after a 2-day delay. This result was expected, although not directly relevant to the experimental question. Again the superiority of the analogy can be seen with seven out of eight comparisons favoring the analogy passage and more reliable results for the retrograde motion passage. However, the two questions written to require subjects to draw inferences about material not explicitly stated failed to differentiate between the analogy/no analogy conditions. I believe that this negative result was probably due to the relatively insensitive measure that was used. It is extremely difficult to get subjects to read highly technical material and then take a lengthy test on that material. For that reason, the number of test questions was kept small. I am currently conducting research to investigate the use of analogies for deducing information that has not been stated, using a more sensitive measure.

CONCLUSIONS

Experimental results support the position that analogies can be a useful tool in the comprehension and recall of scientific information. A logical follow-up question is whether college students can learn to generate their own analogies as a strategy to improve the comprehension and recall of technical material. The small amount of research that has addressed this question is mixed (e.g., Gick & Holyoak, 1980). It seems that this is not a spontaneous process, but one that can be learned. Many scientists and mathematicians report that their ideas or solutions to problems come to them by recognizing analogies drawn from different academic domains (Hadamard, 1945), and it seems likely that college students, our future scientists, mathematicians, and other professionals, would benefit from instruction on generating and utilizing analogies. There are, however, potential problems in teaching students to generate their own novel analogies when faced with new information that has to be acquired and assimilated into existing knowledge structures. Analogies are always imperfect because

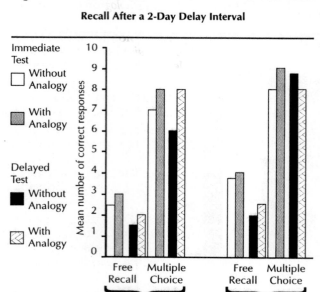

Mean number of free recall and multiple-choice correct responses for passages about a scientific topic (retrograde motion or lymphatic system) that either did not contain (left-most bar of each pair) or contained an analogy.

they suggest a similarity between objects and events that are not identical, and thus can be misleading. The strength of the analogy and the nature of the comparison also must be considered. Yet, despite any possible limitations on the use of analogies, they are one way of "making the unfamiliar known" (Halpern, 1984).

The present research provides a strong case for at least one of the types of skills taught in thinking and problem-solving courses. Much work must yet be done to determine the effects of the other types of skills taught in such courses. When this work is completed, we will be in a better position to ascertain the relative value of each of these skills. This will not only help us determine course content, but will help us determine the relative value of different approaches to critical and creative thinking courses.

Traditionally, instruction in how to think has been a neglected component in American education. Students were taught what to think more often than how to think. Education within most academic disciplines has primarily been concerned with presenting students with the "facts" on a variety of topics—the "knowing that"—while offering little on how to utilize this information or how to discover facts on their own—the "knowing how." Domerique (cited in Parnes, Noller, & Biondi, 1977) summarized this situation well when he said, "Some people study all their life, and at their death they have learned everything except to think" (p. 52). It is hoped that the introduction of critical thinking courses into college curricula will alter the perception that modern education is a mindless exercise and demonstrate that improvement in basic thinking skills can be an outcome of higher education.

ACKNOWLEDGMENTS

I thank Cheryl Eberhardt, Joan Gonzales, and Carol Hansen for their help with the research project described in this chapter.

REFERENCES

Block, R. A. (1985). Education and thinking skills reconsidered. *American Psychologist, 40,* 574–575.

Fox, L. S., Marsh, G., & Crandall, Jr., J. C. (1983, April) *The effect of college classroom experiences on formal operational thinking.* Paper presented at the 1983 Annual Convention of the Western Psychological Association, San Francisco, CA.

Gentner, D. (1983). Structure-mapping: A theoretical framework for analogy. *Cognitive Science, 7,* 155–170.

Gentner, D., & Gentner, D. R. (1983). Flowing water or teeming crowds: Mental models of electricity. In D. Gentner & A. L. Stevens (Eds.), *Mental models* (pp. 99–129). Hillsdale, NJ: Lawrence Erlbaum Associates.

Gick, M. L., & Holyoak, K. J. (1980). Analogical problem solving. *Cognitive Psychology, 12,* 306–355.

Glaser, R. (1984). Education and thinking: The role of knowledge. *American Psychologist, 39,* 93–104.

Hadamard, J. (1945). *The psychology of invention in the mathematical field.* Princeton, NJ: Princeton University Press.

Halpern, D. F. (1984). *Thought and knowledge: An introduction to critical thinking.* Hillsdale, NJ: Lawrence Erlbaum Associates.

Hayes, J. R. (1980). Teaching problem solving mechanisms. In D. T. Tuma & F. Reif (Eds.), *Problem* solving and education: Issues in teaching and research (pp. 141–147). Hillsdale, NJ: Lawrence Erlbaum Associates.

Kintsch, W., & Greeno, J. G. (1985). Understanding and solving word arithmetic problems. *Psychological Review, 92,* 109–129.

Mandler, G. (1967). Organization and memory. In K. W. Spence & J. T. Spence (Eds.), *The psychology of learning and motivation: Vol I. Advances in research and theory* (pp. 328–379). New York: Academic Press.

Mayer, R. E. (1979). Can advanced organizers influence meaningful learning? *Review of Educational Research, 49,* 371–383.

Mayer, R. E., & Bromage, B. K. (1980). Different recall protocols for technical texts due to advanced organizers. *Journal of Educational Psychology, 72,* 209–225.

McKinnon, J. W., & Renner, J. W. (1971). The college student and formal operations. In J. W. Renner, D. G. Stafford, A. E. Lawson, J. W. McKinnon, F. E. Friot, & D. H. Kellogg (Eds.), *Research, training, and learning with the Piaget model* (pp. 110–129). Norman: University of Oklahoma Press.

Meyer, B. J. F., & Mc Conkie, G. W. (1973). What is recalled after hearing a passage? *Journal of Educational Psychology, 65,* 109–117.

Oppenheimer, J. R. (1956). Analogy in science. *American Psychologist, 11,* 127–135.

Paivio, A. (1969). Mental imagery in associative learning and memory. *Psychological Review, 76,* 241–263.

Parnes, S. J., Noller, R. B., & Biondi, A. M. (1977). *Guide to creative action: Revised edition of creative behavior guidebook.* New York: Charles Scribner's Sons.

Resnick, L. B. (1983). Mathematics and science learning: A new conception. *Science, 220,* 477–478.

Rubinstein, M. F. (1980). A decade of experience in teaching an interdisciplinary problem-solving course. In D. T. Tuma & F. Reif (Eds.), *Problem solving and education: Issues in teaching and research* (pp. 25–38). Hillsdale, NJ: Lawrence Erlbaum Associates.

Schoenfeld, A. H., & Herman, D. J. (1982). Problem perception and knowledge structure in expert and novice mathematical problem solvers. *Journal of Experimental Psychology: Learning, Memory, and Cognition, 8,* 484–494.

Sternberg, R. J. (1977). Component processes in analogical reasoning. *Psychological Review, 84,* 353–373.

Tourangeau, R., & Sternberg, R. J. (1981). Aptness in metaphor. *Cognition, 13* 27–55.

Wheeler, D. D. (1979). A practicum in thinking. In D. D. Wheeler & W. N. Dember (Eds.), *A practicum in thinking* (pp. 6–18). Cincinnati, OH: Department of publications and printing services of the University of Cincinnati.

Index

abstract categories, expertise and, 150–151
acute disconnection syndrome, 56
affective discrimination of stimuli that cannot be recognized, 98–101
alcohol, influence of, on cognition, 228–240
amnesia, 63, 121
analogies, 30, 147, 148; as critical thinking skill, 287–295
analytical engine, Babbage's, 21–22
anthropomorphism, and use of language by apes, 201–206
apes, use of language by, 201–206
arrangement problems, 158
artificial intelligence (AI), 12, 15–24, 25–32, 83, 147, 238
associative chaining hypothesis, Chomsky's, 11
athletic performance, effect of adding cognitively demanding tasks on, 266–270
automatic generalization, in neural-network brain models, 38

Baker, Howard, 108, 109–110
Bartlett, Frederic, 7, 104, 113, 185
beauty, standards of, 242–251
behaviorism, 7, 12, 13, 14, 83, 164, 174, 191
Benton, A. L., 63, 64
Berscheid, E., 248–249
biofeedback learning, effect of cognitive interference on, 263–265
Blocks World expert AI system, 27
Bodamer, J., 60, 63
Bogen, Joseph, 50–51
Boltzmann architecture, 30, 37
Bower, G. H., 258, 261
brain: and developmental memory impairment, 59–69; effects of surgery to split, 48–58; memory and, 116–129; modeling the, 33–41
Bransford, J. D., 258, 260
Broadbent, D. A., 82, 175
Bruce, B., 62–63
Bruner, Jerome, 8, 136, 139
Burke, R. J., 161–162

categories: children's expectations concerning natural kind, 136–141; expertise and, 150–155
cause and effect, 288
Cheesman, J., 280–281
Chi, M. T. H., 152–153
chiasm, optic, 49, 53
children: expectations of, concerning natural kind categories, 136–141; joke-telling and, 214–219; with reading problems, teaching Chinese characters to, 271–277; understanding of thinking and consciousness by, 168–172
chimpanzees and gorillas, use of language by, 201–206

Chomsky, Noam, 10–12, 191, 193–194, 196, 201, 238
chunking: categorization and, 151; Miller's theory of, 8
Church-Turing thesis, 35
clairvoyance, 23–24
classical view, of categorization, 153–154
classification tasks, and children's expectations concerning natural kind categories, 136–141
Clever Hans phenomenon, 205
coexistence hypothesis, memory and, 125–128
cognitive behaviorism, 7
cognitive interference, effect of, on biofeedback learning, 263–265
cognitive interview technique, to enhance eyewitness memory, 252–256
coherence, categorization and, 151
commissurotomy, effects of, 48–58
communication, language and, 197–198
communications engineering, cognitive psychology and, 9–10
competitive learning, 36–37
compliant agents, infants' view of people as, 168–169
computers: artificial intelligence and, 15–24, 25–32, 34–36; cognitive psychology and, 11–12; problem solving and, 156–167
conative psychology, 239
concentration, 175–176
conceptual base view, of categorization, 154
conceptual blocks, 162
conceptual metaphor, 213
connectionism, in modeling the brain, 33–47
consciousness: argument from, and computers as thinking machines, 19–20; and thinking, children's understanding of, 168–172; will and, 173–185
constructive memory, 113
containing patterns, subjective contours and, 70–78
context effects, 147
continuity in the nervous system, argument from, and computers as thinking machines, 22–23
Cooper, Lynn, 92, 94
Coren, S., 76, 77
corpus callosum, effects of surgery to sever, 48–58
creativity: problem solving and, 159; visual imagery and, 86
crime detection: eyewitness memory and, 252–256; hypnosis and, 120
critical thinking skill, analogies as, 287–295
cross cuing, following split-brain surgery, 56
cross-talk, 39

Darwin, Charles, 32, 243
daydreaming, 157
Dean, John, memory of, and Watergate coverup, 102–115
deduction problems, 158
deep structure, of sentences, 11–12, 88, 290
Delgado, J. M. R., 122–123
designative meaning, 257
developmental psychology, and children's understanding of consciousness and thinking, 168–172
Didion, Joan, 86, 95
disabilities, arguments from, and computers as thinking machines, 20–21
distributed representations, in neural-network brain models, 37–38
dreams, 176, 177; following split-brain surgery, 55–56
Duncker, K., 162–163
dyslexia, 271

ecological validity, 229
education, and teaching Chinese characters to children with reading problems, 271–277
Einstein, Albert, 84–85, 86, 212, 213
electrical stimulation of the brain, as memory retrieval technique, 116–129
electromagnetic fields, visual imagery and, 84–85
embodied meaning, 257
engineering: communications, 9–10; human, 6–7, 8–9
Ennis Weir Argumentation Test, 289
epilepsy, effects of split-brain surgery to treat, 48–58
episodic memory, 102, 104, 114
epistemic correspondence, 208, 209, 210
Erdelyi, M. H., 123, 176
everyday life, cognitive psychology of, 228–241
exemplar view, of categorization, 152
experimental analysis of the mind, 6, 7
expert systems, computer medical, 25–34
expertise, and categorization, 150–155
expressive language, 218
extrasensory behavior, argument from, and computers as thinking machines, 23–24
eyewitness memory, 252–256

faces: beauty of, 242–251; difficulty with recognition of, 55, 59–69
Fechner, Gustav, 49
Feigenbaum, Edward, 27, 28
Feltovich, P. J., 152–153
Figure of Rey, 67
figures of speech, metaphors as, 207–213
Fisher, R. P., 252
fitting shapes, subjective contours and, 71–78
Fitts, P. M., 267